The Canadian House of Commons
Procedure and Reform

The Canadian House of Commons
Procedure and Reform

John B. Stewart

McGill-Queen's University Press
MONTREAL AND LONDON   1977

© McGill-Queen's University Press 1977

International Standard Book Number 0-7735-0256-4

Legal Deposit first quarter 1977
Bibliothèque nationale du Québec

Design by Naoto Kondo
Printed in Canada by Hignell Printing Ltd.

This book has been published with the help of a grant from the Social Science Research Council of Canada using funds provided by the Canada Council

Contents

Tables		vii
Preface		ix
ONE	The Functions of the House of Commons	1
TWO	The Basic Principles of Procedure	33
THREE	A Day in the House	51
FOUR	The Ordinary Legislative Process in the House of Commons	79
FIVE	Authorizing Taxes and Expenditure	97
SIX	The Standing Committees: The Pattern Established	131
SEVEN	The Standing Committees: The Pattern Varied	157
EIGHT	Doing the Government's Business	197
NINE	Closure and Time Allotment	237
TEN	New Remedies	259
Notes		291
A Note on Books and Articles		327
Index		333

Tables

1	A Week in the House	70
2	Use of the Time of the House	76
3	The Pattern of the Legislative Process	88
4	Annual Supply Business Timetable	122
5	Standing Committees, Sessions of 1867–68 and 1964–65	138
6	Size of the Standing Committees at Certain Sessions	146
7	Standing Committees, 11 June 1965	162
8	Standing Committees, 20 December 1968	165
9	The Legislative Record—1867–1974	198
10	Sittings in Years—1867–1975	204
11	Time Required for Sessional Business	218
12	Time Taken by Supply Business—1952–68	224
13	Use of Standing Order 26	232
14	Effect of Limits on Sessional Business	267
15	Time Taken at the Several Stages of Government Bills in the House	268
16	Time Taken by Government Bills at the Second-reading Stage	270
17	Standing Committee Meetings Per Month—1969–70	287

Preface

The reader has a right to know that on 18 June 1962 I was elected to the House of Commons as a Liberal. From January 1966 until 23 April 1968 I served as parliamentary secretary to the Hon. G. J. McIlraith, who throughout much of that period was the government house leader. During the 1966-67 and 1967-68 sessions I was the vice-chairman of the Special Committee on Procedure and Organization, which laid the foundations for the rules changes made on 20 December 1968 and on 24 July 1969. After the 1968 election, in which I was an unsuccessful candidate, I served for a year as legislative adviser to the Hon. D. S. Macdonald, the government house leader during the period when the 1968 and 1969 procedural reforms were made. I adduce this personal background both as a caution to the reader and in extenuation of any personal or partisan bias the reader may detect.

It would be disingenuous to say that the procedure experts in the House of Commons were excluded from the audience for which a book that concludes by recommending new remedies was written; yet they are not the readers whom I have had chiefly in mind. I have sought to address myself mainly to interested amateurs, those who know that the subject is important, but who have found it obscure. These are the readers whom I have had in mind while organizing the material and selecting the examples. Accordingly, the book is introductory. It is not a history. It is not a survey: only certain aspects of the subject are covered; for example, neither private bill legislation nor the relationship between the House and the Senate is examined. And it is not a parliamentarian's handbook, a source of magisterial quotations to be recited when arguing points of order.

Chapter 1 gives an interpretation of the place or role of the House of Commons in our system of government. The second chapter deals with certain fundamental principles of procedure. These are the kinds of chapters that a beginner might wish to pass over rapidly, reserving them for later study and criticism. In contrast, chapter 3 goes directly to the nuts and bolts: it presents many of the technical terms; it mentions some important topics—for example, the question period—which are not examined in separate chapters; and it provides the reader with a frame into which the rest of the material may be fitted. The next four chapters are on various related subjects. Since 20 December 1968, the House has used its standing committees in the process by which non-financial bills are passed and in the process by which it deals with supply business. I have dealt with the ordinary legislative process in chapter 4, and with taxing and spending in chapter 5, but in neither of those chapters have I dealt extensively with the background of the changes made in December 1968, nor with the controversies that followed. That material is dealt with in chapters 6 and 7. Chapter 9 supplements chapter 8. The latter shows how over the years the House has focused its attention more and more on the business put before it, not by the private members, but by the government, and examines the arrangements the House made from time to time to assure that recurring (or sessional) business is completed in reasonable time. However, much of the government's business is not sessional, and therefore lies outside the limits described in that chapter. Chapter 9 deals with the two main approaches—closure and time allotment—that have been used in the attempt to assure that the government can get its non-sessional business done by the House.

The House has a common-law mind. It has many rules which are conventional. However, the House, like the provincial legislatures before it, has found it desirable to make certain "standing orders." Indeed, it is mainly by changing old standing orders and by making new ones that the House changes its rules. (Although this is true, one ought not to overlook the innovative power of an able speaker supported by a solid body of opinion in the House and at the Table.)

The House adopted its first set of standing orders in 1867. These have been changed many times over the years, but chiefly in 1906, 1910, 1913, 1927, 1955, 1965, 1968, 1969, and 1975. I have not attempted to write a history of the standing orders, but inevitably I have had to refer again and again to those reforms. For example, I have had to deal with the reforms of June 1965, in chapter 7 (on the committee system); in chapter 8 (on the supply process); and in chapter 9 (on time allotment). An historical account of the 1965 reforms would present all that material as one inter-related package. Because of the nature of this book I have followed the main strands separately, even though this has made it necessary for me to traverse some of the ground two or three times, but for different purposes. This has made for some repetition, but the gain is that each of the chapters can be read separately.

On 24 March 1975, the House concurred in a report of the Standing Committee on Procedure and Organization. Therein the committee had recommended experimental changes—to be in effect until the end of the 1974-76 session—in (a) the program of daily business and (b) the supply process. These changes became effective on 7 April 1975. On 12 December 1975, the changes in the program of daily business were made permanent, while the changes in the supply process were continued into the next session. Chapter 3 is based on the new program of daily business. The experimental changes in the standing orders relating to supply business, which were made in response to the criticism discussed in chapter 8, are dealt with in chapter 10.

One of the advantages of having written a book is that it is in order to put some words of gratitude on the record; but so as not to detain the reader I shall indulge myself only a little. The unsung heroes of the House are the party house leaders. Each must have a dual loyalty: to his party and to the House. The root of many of their troubles is that their colleagues are either insouciant to the House or far too interested in it. At times they ignore the House. At other times it is all-important, so that every facilitating concession to the other side is seen as a disastrous surrender. Regardless of the conflict of ambition and opinions, the house leaders must make the system function. I count it a great privilege to have been able to observe at close hand the work of several house leaders: Mr. G. W. Baldwin, the Hon. Gordon Churchill, Mr. Stanley Knowles, the Hon. D. S. Macdonald, the Hon. A. J. MacEachen, and the Hon. G. J. McIlraith. Mr. Knowles read the first nine chapters of my manuscript with great care and made many helpful comments. I have enjoyed the full cooperation of the clerk of the House, Mr. Alistair Fraser, all the Table officers, and their staffs. I must single out the late Mr. Gordon Dubroy and Mr. Alex Small for constant help over the years. The information set forth in Tables 15 and 16 could not have been drawn together without the help of Mr. J. F. Cooke and hours of patient work by Mr. Roland Sabourin of the Parliamentary Returns Office. Mr. Jerry Yanover, the legislative adviser to the government house leader, read the first nine chapters carefully and made many valuable comments. I am especially grateful to Senator Eugene Forsey for his general observations on those chapters and for divers items of relevant information. Sister Isabel MacDougall, of the Angus L. MacDonald Library, was a constant source of materials and encouragement. Mr. Sean Riley, Mr. Ralph Kirk, and Mr. Patrick Sullivan assisted with the historical research. The manuscript was typed by Mrs. Beverly MacIsaac and Mr. D. Ross. Research money was provided by the Saint Francis Xavier University Council for Research and by the Canada Council. To all these and many others I am most grateful. Since at times I declined advice on substance and presentation I must accept full responsibility for any errors discovered by the reader.

ONE

The Functions of the House of Commons

I

The procedures by which our House of Commons does its work are in a sense a part of Canada's constitution. They are a part of the process by which we are governed. When the House of Commons makes a major change in the way it operates, the constitutional process, the governing of Canada, has been altered, perhaps not fundamentally, but certainly to some degree. There is a close causal relationship between how a body works and what that body does. Moreover, a body's procedures—how it works—are means; no matter how old and hallowed, they need reviewing and evaluation from time to time to ascertain that they are fostering, not deterring, the performance of the body's functions. Thus we come to our fundamental question. Assuming that we wish to retain the system known as Responsible Government, what are the proper functions of the House of Commons?

If we are to understand the functions of the House of Commons, we must begin by purging from our minds both every taint of congressionalism and the view that Parliament is "the legislature." This may not be easy. Over the years those ideas have put down deep roots.

The view that the House of Commons is a congress is incompatible with Responsible Government; yet this view is surprisingly common. Every constitution involves two elements: first, a formal or legal element; second, an informal or political element, which may or may not coincide with the first. By the early eighteenth century a reasonably satisfactory working relationship between the two elements had been achieved in Britain. The king was the governor, all who held governmental offices were his servants. They held offices under the Crown. To ascertain the formal or legal structure of the government one examined the duties and relationships of the bodies and offices under the Crown. Even statutes were made by the kings, as the enacting words in England and Canada still declare. But that was only half the story. For centuries kings had recognized the truth that the consent of those people who count—who they are has changed over the years—is highly desirable. Consequently, they held parliaments to which the Lords and, later, the representatives of the Commons were summoned. Those two houses were at the apex of the political element in the constitution. Very early—about the beginning of the fifteenth century—it was established that no new taxes could be imposed by the Crown without statutory authorization, and that a statute is an act of Parliament.[1] The two elements, the legal and the political, met in Parliament: no new statute could be made without the cooperation of the two. The obvious danger, demonstrated repeatedly throughout the seventeenth century, was that the Crown and one or both of the Houses might be in radical disagreement; but at the beginning of the eighteenth century a remedy was found by overlapping the two elements. Thereafter, not because of any legal requirement, but for practical reasons, the kings took as their chief advisers and administrators those men who brought with them the cooperation of the House of Commons. Soon it was discovered that cooperation was procured most easily when the advisers and administrators—the ministers—were present in each parliament as members of either the House of Lords or the House of Commons.

The leading argument of the American revolutionaries was that the British Parliament, which they saw as a domestic body with no authority outside the United Kingdom, had acted illegally by presuming to alter "the rights of Englishmen" in the colonies.[2] But behind that contention was the belief that the British Constitution had undergone "corruption": by various means, including the membership of the ministers in the Houses of Parliament, the balance between "the legislature" and "the executive" had been tipped disastrously in the latter's favour.[3] When the time came for them to create new constitutions of their own, they, of course, did not follow the British model. In any case, they had no king to take the role of head of state. The two elements, the legal and the political, could not be related, as in Britain, by having the legal head follow the advice of the political leaders; rather, those elected by the people would have to be the governors themselves. Here we have the essence of congressionalism: the body that represents the people is legally the government. But this idea, made ominous by the implication that the majority would have absolute power, did not stand alone. Concurrent with it were both the individualistic idea of inalienable rights and the elitist idea that the people, or at least those called "the multitude," ought not to be given direct access to power. It is not surprising, therefore, that the constitution produced at Philadelphia in 1787 was far from rigorously congressional. A second house, initially representing the several state governments, was included and given a part in legislation. Consequently, the Congress had a hybrid character.

Provision was made also for a chief executive, normally under the plan, it is true, to be selected by the House of Representatives from among those nominated by the electoral college, but with a far more active role in legislation than any British monarch had played since 1707.[4] To protect the rights of individuals the Congress was prohibited from making certain kinds of laws. Moreover, since 1789 the congressional quality of the functioning American constitution has been reduced even more. The President, the Senate, and the Supreme Court have grown in power, so that the House of Representatives at times seems the least of the partners, despite the implications of its name. Yet congressionalism persists in American thinking: the idea of "government by the people" is an integral part of the theory of government prevalent in the United States of America.

Although our constitution is similar in principle to that of Great Britain, many Canadians tend to think of the House of Commons in congressional terms. They mislead themselves. In shape the constitution somewhat resembles an hour-glass: one part, the upper part, is the Crown, made up of the queen and her servants; and the other is the people and their representatives.[5] The parts meet and overlap in the House of Commons: ministers are both servants of the Crown and members of Parliament. But the ordinary Canadian is far more keenly aware of the political element than of the legal element. Constantly he is aware of political activity and controversy; and it is in the political element that he participates personally as a voter. Besides, that element is indubitably Canadian, while "the Crown" sounds British. Accordingly, he tends to think of the House of Commons as a body elected by Canadians to govern Canada, and of the Cabinet as a kind of committee of the House.[6] The insistence that the ministers really are servants of the Crown to him seems a legalism, a shell dry of life, an intellectual toy for academics of antiquarian and colonial mind. It seems to imply that the ministers are agents of London; and that he does not believe. Yet in constitutional theory the queen is our governor, and the government is hers. Nor is this a mere myth, a relic not yet swept away because, although useless, it still retains some sentimental value. Rather it is a constitutional truth with very important practical implications. It is one of the main factors which determine how Canada is governed.

Inevitably a house that is a congress is different in its procedures from one that is not. In a congress all the members are expected to participate in improving the law by introducing bills and by helping to refine bills. All are eligible to participate in the preparation of the national expenditure programs. Because the distinction between government business and private members' business is irrelevant, a congress must be prepared to treat all items of business initially as equal. This means that it must make extensive use of committees (or some other mechanism) to separate out the important items, and to improve those items. Since the distinction between government business and private members' business cannot be made, efficient methods must be found by which to determine the priority of items of business on the floor of the House. In contrast, under our system we rely on the ministers of the Crown to bring in almost all the bills that become law, and to bring them in at a highly advanced stage of preparation. Where expenditure is concerned, although the House of Commons is free to criticize the purposes for which the Crown seeks money and the stinginess of the Crown, the House is restricted to approving or reducing the amounts proposed by the Crown. The committees, having far less important work to do, are far less prominent. Most of the time of the House is placed at the disposal of the government, and it decides in what order it wishes to advance its business. Clearly, how we think of the House of Commons—as a congress or otherwise—has procedural implications. Wittingly or unwittingly, by procedural changes we can give the House more and more of the congressional character. Congressionalism is appealing to many Canadians, including some members of Parliament. It seems simple, democratic, and Canadian. My submission has two branches: first, creeping congressionalism ought to be resisted; and second, salutary changes consistent with our system ought not to be rejected merely because superficially they seem congressional.

II

The second misleading idea from which we must make an escape, one with an even more pervasive sway, is that Parliament is "the legislature." Actually, it is *the* law-making body in only a very special and narrow sense, a sense which although of great constitutional significance, excludes the making of much of the law that is important to us in our everyday lives.

In the seventeenth and eighteenth centuries when the power of absolutist kings was under attack, the terms "legislature" and "executive" came to be used extensively as generic terms in the analysis of governance.[7] Depending on the local circumstances, the aim was either to strip the kings of some of their power or to prevent them from achieving absolute power. John Locke employs the distinction in his *Second Treatise*. Parliament, not the king, is the legislature; and the chief participants in Parliament are the representatives of the genuine members of society. Inside the country the king, aside from his part in Parliament, has only an executive role: through his courts he carries the general law to particular cases. (What Locke terms "the executive role" is what now is called "the judicial role.") In other words, ordinarily—we need not discuss the important exceptions he introduces in his discussion of "the prerogative"—the king is subordinate to Parliament in the internal government of England. Locke gave the king the "federative role" as well, but since this related to foreign affairs he did not depict it as a role to be performed under directions prescribed by Parliament. Locke states emphatically, but not as a novel discovery, the importance to good government of separating the legislative branch and the executive (i.e., the judicial) branch; but the main burden of his *Second Treatise* is to insist that a true king, the executive branch, functions under and within legal limits set by the representatives of the society.[8] Locke, we must remember, was writing in a country with a powerful House of Commons, and his work, although composed earlier, appeared as a defence of the strong and successful action that had been taken against James II in 1688.

It was Montesquieu, writing later but from a far weaker practical position, who did most to popularize the idea of three essentially different powers. His concern was not to subordinate the king to a representative assembly, but to show that there should be a law-making body distinct from the king, and also a truly independent judiciary. In order to be able to show that France needed these three bodies, he emphasized the essential difference of three "powers." In every state, he wrote, there are three powers: "that of enacting laws, that of executing the public resolutions, and of trying the causes of individuals."[9] Here then we have the now familiar triad: the legislative power, the executive power (effective in both domestic and foreign affairs), and the judicial power. Montesquieu follows this up by arguing that if there is to be liberty in a country each of these three powers must be vested in a different body. (This did not mean that the three bodies had to be totally separate in personnel; for example, the fact that the king was one of the three parts of a parliament did not disqualify England as a land of liberty.)

The American Revolution and after it the French Revolution created many opportunities for devising constitutions based on the doctrine of the separation of powers. Our interest, however, is not in the intricacies of that doctrine, but in the analysis of governance—the view that there are three essentially different powers—that the doctrine propagated. By the end of the eighteenth century that view had become a presupposition of much legal and constitutional thought in Europe, America, and Great Britain.[10] We find it expressed even in the British North America Act. The preamble to the act recites that "... it is expedient, not only that the Constitution of the Legislative Authority in the Dominion be provided for, but also that the Nature of the Executive Government therein be declared:..." Section 9 states that "The

Executive Government and authority of and over Canada is hereby declared to continue and be vested in the Queen." Provision is made in Part IV for the exercise of "the Legislative Power."

The truth, as most constitutional students would agree, is that the presupposition that there are three essentially different powers—the legislative, the executive, and the judicial—is invalid. In the case of Canada, for example, these terms imply that only statutes, acts of "the legislature," are law; that Parliament as "the legislature" should take the lead in governing the country; and that it is the House of Commons, the important part of Parliament, which is to originate the bills that become statutes. The terms imply that the proper function of the government is simply to carry out the directives given to it by successive parliaments. In addition, they conceal the vast legislative activity of judges. Or, to state the criticism in another way, because they focus on Parliament the terms imply that Parliament does both far more than it does, and far less than it does.

Let us look first at the overstatement. It is a fundamental principle of the British Constitution that Parliament is supreme, i.e., that a statute is superior to all other law whether that other law be the rules of the common lawyers, the orders made by the Queen in Council, or fiats issued by any other authority. A statute is superior to either an order or a resolution of either House, and to a joint resolution of both. The same is true of the Parliament of Canada within the areas assigned to it, and not to the provincial "legislatures," by the British North America Act. Therefore, it may be said that logically all law expresses the will of Parliament: either the law has been made by Parliament itself, or, although made by some other body, it has been found acceptable by Parliament, and so left undisturbed. In this ultimate sense, Parliament is the law-making body.[11] But to say this is to say far less than what seems to be implied when Parliament is described as "the legislative branch."

The doctrine of the Supremacy of Parliament does not imply that the senators and the members of the House of Commons, *qua* members, have the prime responsibility for improving the law. Because the ministers and the public servants who work under them administer the law, they are at the vantage point to detect defects in the law, and to devise suitable amendments. Moreover, in Canada, as in Britain, during the past eighty or ninety years the political parties regularly have sought mandates from the electorate to carry out party programs; and the political obligation to carry out a mandate rests mainly on the prime minister and his ministerial colleagues, not on the private members. Each session of Parliament begins with a Speech from the Throne, wherein the queen—in Canada almost always the governor general on her behalf—declares why the Parliament is being held.[12] The continuation of this practice, dating back to the first parliaments in the thirteenth and fourteenth centuries, is no mere antiquarianism. It shows that the relationship that prevailed in England in the past still prevails there, and now in Canada also; that is, that the members have been summoned, not so that they may introduce their bills, but so that they may consider the financial requests and any legislative proposals to be put before them by the queen's ministers. In Canada almost all the public bills that become law now are government bills, and few of them undergo much alteration in either the House of Commons or the Senate. The decisions as to what bills will go forward in a session and what the basic scheme and detail of each of those bills will be are made outside Parliament by the queen's permanent and political servants. They are made by "the Court." This does not mean that the knowledge that every bill has to pass the House of Commons and the Senate has no influence on particular bills or on the whole program for a session; rather, it means that under our constitution the onus for the initiation and the content of the bills that become law does not rest with the members of "the legislature." To a large extent it is only in a formal sense that Parliament is the statute-making body. A statute is an act of Parliament; but almost all the work has been done before Parliament begins to act.

And Parliament is not *the* law-making body even in only a formal sense. Statutes are only part of the law. It always has been true throughout the common-law world that much of the law is made by judges, who apply old principles to new situations; indeed, the prominence of Parliament as a source of general law in Britain is largely a feature of the years since 1832. In addition, the queen had, and still has, under the British and Canadian constitutions, the right to issue orders and to make proclamations of certain kinds based on the royal prerogatives, that is, based on the rights of the Crown at common law. And in recent times by acts of Parliament the right and duty to make "statutory instruments" —orders in council, regulations, minutes, and rules, all drawing their character as law from a parent statute—have been deluged on the Queen (or the Governor General) in Council, on particular ministers, on various boards, on tribunals, and on other authorities. For example, much of the governing related to Canada's war effort in 1914–18 and 1939–45 was done by statutory instruments. It is true, of course, that a statute over-rules law made by judges and administrators; but this does not alter the fact that the thick books of decisions in cases and the thick books of statutory and prerogative instruments are law until over-ruled.

According to Montesquieu's analysis the body known as "the legislature" is to make only general prescriptions: it is to focus on the general good and not to be distracted by particular persons or causes. On the other hand, both the executive and the judiciary are to deal with particular persons and cases, but always under, and restricted by, the overarching law. However, all that this insistence that the legislature is to make only general prescriptions amounts to in practice is that the executive and the judiciary are to be subordinate. They are to act within limits set by the legislature. Those limits may be narrow, leaving little power with the executive and the judiciary; or, as very often is the case, they may be very wide. As long as the acts of the executive and the judiciary are based on an act of the legislature, the theory that the legislature is the law-making body will not have been violated. As long as the legislature has provided an authorizing envelope, no matter how thin, either directly as in the case of statutory instruments, or indirectly as in the case of undisturbed common law, the requirements of the theory have been met.

To call Parliament "the legislature" is an overstatement because laws made by it are different only in status, not in essence, from the laws made by administrators and judges. The laws made by Parliament are superior. The theory serves to elevate Parliament—the Queen, the Senate, and the House of Commons—above the queen and her servants. But it does not determine either how little or how much power Parliament is to leave with the queen and her servants, or to thrust upon them. To say that Parliament alone makes the law is to hide the fact that a vast amount of law-making power always is left in the hands of administrators and judges.

The deceptiveness of the view that Parliament, as "the legislature," makes the law was shown dramatically in two notable Canadian cases. In 1918 in Gray's case the Governor in Council revoked certain exemptions from military service which had been established by Parliament itself in the Military Service Act, 1917.[13] The order in council revoking the exemptions was founded on the War Measures Act, 1914, which in very general language confers almost unlimited legislative capacity on the Governor in Council. The latter Act says: "The Governor in Council may do and authorize such acts and things, and make from time to time such orders and regulations, as he may by reason of the existence of real or apprehended war, invasion or insurrection deem necessary or advisable for the security, defence, peace, order and welfare of Canada; . . ." The Supreme Court held that on the basis of this authorization the Governor in Council could make an order over-ruling the will of Parliament as expressed in the Military Service Act.

The second case is the famous Drybones case, decided by the Supreme Court of Canada in 1969.[14] Therein the Court decided that Parliament by general and obscure language—sufficiently obscure that three of the nine judges dissented—has conferred on the courts the duty to strike down any or all the provisions of statutes that the courts find contrary to the Canadian Bill of Rights, 1960. The Court then proceeded to strike down just such a section of the Indian Act. In both these cases specific statutory provisions were put aside by servants of the Crown—in the first by ministers, in the second by judges—who found their authority in other statutes. These examples demonstrate how misleading is the idea that only "the legislature" makes the law. They are extraordinary only in that in each the will of Parliament as expressly stated in certain statutes was put aside. Law is made—less obviously than in these two instances, it is true—every day by administrators and judges.

The House of Commons passes bills for changes in the law, but it also passes bills simply to provide the money needed to cover expenses of the Crown approved by the House. Both these kinds of bills eventuate as statutes, but we must not let that formal similarity blind us to the material difference between them. The effect of the first kind of statute is to change the law by adding to it, by subtracting from it, or by altering the term during which it is to apply. The effect of the second is to support the Crown in its activities, and may involve no change whatsoever in the law other than the renewal of the right to withdraw money from the Consolidated Revenue Fund. Let us assume for a moment that in a period of great economic and social tranquility no need was felt for any changes in the law of the land. There then would be no need for legislation by Parliament. Government would be simply the execution of the existing prescriptions. The implication of the view that Parliament is "the legislature" is that in such a situation Parliament would have no work to do. However, under our constitution the House of Commons oversees the work of the Crown on an annual basis by examining the spending estimates. It concerns itself with administrative policies, with administrative acts, with the details of administrative performance, and with the conduct of the ministers and their subordinates. Even if it had nothing to do as a law-making body, it would have plenty to do annually as an inquest into the activities of the Crown. When we say that Parliament is "the legislature," we foster the view that legislation is the chief work, perhaps the only really important work of the House, and thus we may cause the supervision of administrative activities to be slighted.[15]

Let me conclude this section with a summary. Much of the law, I submit, is made, not by "the legislature," but by "the executive government" and the judiciary. Almost all the law, even the part that finds its way into the statute books is produced by "the executive." Moreover, the activities of the administrative servants of the Crown are so important a part of governing that the House of Commons ought to continue, or if necessary to renew, its historic concern to oversee and control that activity. We would, I contend, make discussion of our constitution easier to understand if we could jettison the terms "legislature" and "executive" as inapplicable in any strict sense to our system, and used instead the proper names, Parliament, the Queen, the Governor in Council, the House of Commons, the Supreme Court, etc.

III

We have rejected two relatively simple views of the functions of the House of Commons—the first that the House is a congress; the second that the House is "the legislature." Now, with the ground cleared, we can turn to the question, What functions does the House perform in our system of government? If at some moment in the past a plan of the British (or Canadian) constitution had been drawn up and accepted our task would be different. By analyzing that plan, as scholars have in the case of the American Constitution, we could try to discover the functions the House was intended to perform; and then we could go on to ascertain to what extent the House fulfils its appointed role. But there is no such plan. We are dealing with a constitution which is both conventional (or unprescribed) and historical (or susceptible to change). The functions of the British House of Commons today are quite different from what they were 200 years ago; yet nobody can say either that the true constitution is being abandoned, or that it is being achieved. For us, then, the functions of the House are not those assigned to it by the ideal constitution; rather, they are the functions that the House now performs, well or poorly, within the whole system. The value of those functions—and of the whole system—is, as David Hume would have said, a matter of moral judgement.

Canada's national government is similar in principle to that of Great Britain. In it two elements, one legal and the other political, meet and overlap in the House of Commons. At law the queen and her servants are the government, with duties and commensurate powers under both common law and statutes. The queen, we can say, owns the omnibus. Her title to it is unquestioned. However, because she lacks the fuel to operate it she seeks aid from the people. The power of the House springs ultimately, not from what it can do independently, but from what it can prevent. Without the consent of the House no money may be withdrawn from the Consolidated Revenue Fund for any new purpose. Without its consent no taxes may be imposed to recruit the Fund. And no new statute law, even law without financial implications, may be made unless it has been set forth in every detail in a bill that has passed the House of Commons. The power of the House to influence the policies of the queen's government is political, not legal. The House alone cannot give binding commands to the government; but its cooperation, made most tangible in the form of supplies of money, is so necessary that the will of the House must be respected. To make it easier—nay, possible—to secure the cooperation of the House no minister will continue long in office unless he is or becomes a member of either the House of Commons or the Senate. The ministers participate in the two elements, the legal and the political: they are servants of the Crown, and at the same time members of Parliament. This kind of system is known as "Responsible Government."[16]

At this point we must recognize that almost all the members of the House can be viewed in three different ways. Each member—the rare Independent is the exception—has three distinct standings. Accordingly, the House can be discussed at three different but compatible levels, with the second level superimposed on the first, and the third on the second. To understand how the House performs its functions we must understand the basis of these distinctions.

First, *legally* the House is simply a body composed of persons summoned from the constituencies in which they were elected. Legally each member is nothing more and nothing less than the free and independent representative of his constituency. In terms of the law each constituency simply elects a person to represent it in the House of Commons. The House is a body composed of those representatives. Legally it is a body of discrete members, each entirely free to vote as he wishes on every question put to the House; and the law seeks to guard each member's independence.[17]

But, secondly, because under Responsible Government the ministry is dependent on the support of a majority, the House *constitutionally* is not a simple aggregate of discrete members; rather, on each occasion when it deals with government business the House divides into two groups or sides, those who support and those who oppose the ministry. Although legally each member is free to vote as he wishes, free to vote on every question on its merits as he sees them, he must take cognizance of the ineluctable truth that on most questions how he votes bears directly on the fate of the government. Consequently, regardless of the substantive arguments, the supporters of the ministry normally vote with the ministers, and its opponents against them. That the House is divided in this way is recognized by the seating arrangements. The members are not assigned seats alphabetically by their names, nor by the names of their constituencies; instead, they are divided basically into "the government side," on the Speaker's right, and "the opposition side," on his left.

And, thirdly, the members are divided *politically* between (or among) political parties. Although the elementary theory of Responsible Government, which divides the House into two sides, remains basic to our system, over the years we have built upon it with the result that the bare theory seldom, if ever, now provides a full and accurate account of how the system really works. Most members have party loyalties and obligations. They act not as members free to vote as they wish, and not simply as supporters or opponents of the ministry, but as members of highly organized political teams. The business of the House is conducted mainly, not by individual players, and not simply by the government and the opposition, but by organized teams vying for power. These teams have their own internal structures and constitutions: by their own private methods and means they select their leaders, their policies, and their strategies and tactics. They are active not only in the House, but in the country at large.

If we are to understand how the House works we must bear constantly in mind the importance of the political parties. It is easy, indeed almost inevitable, to confuse the constitutional and the political levels when only two parties are on the field. Those two levels then fit and conform to each other perfectly. The result of the confusion is that Responsible Government is treated as the total political system, when it should be viewed as a constitutional system with important implications for party policies. This may lead to three mistakes. First, when the activities of the House are examined the fact may be overlooked, at least not given sufficient emphasis, that even when there are only two teams, the Ins and the Outs, both sides are made up of members of great organizations which reach far beyond the House of Commons, and which are almost entirely unknown to the law. (Being unincorporated, they are unknown to private law. The one major recognition in public law, the provision that a party's name may appear with a candidate's name on the ballot paper, has caused trouble—in Moncton in 1974—because it means that Parliament is intervening in party business.) In 1968, for example, the Liberal Party selected a new leader by its own private rules; immediately, without any prior action in the House of Commons, the governor general asked him to become the prime minister. Mr. Trudeau was a member of the House at that time; but the result would have been the same if the Liberal Party had selected as its leader a person who had never run for political office. Clearly, the rules of the parties are in effect a part of our system of government. Second, it fosters the assumption that the pendulum of electoral success will swing regularly, with each side having its turns at bat as in baseball; but the truth is that although the constitutional system may favour the regular alternation of the Ins and Outs, other factors, political factors, may override that tendency. One party may simply be stronger politically, and for years, even generations, its strength may prevent a regular alternation. In Canada, for example, the Conservatives were in power for twenty-five of the twenty-nine years after Confederation, but from 1896 to 1974 they were in power for less than twenty-one years. And, third, it may cause Responsible Government to be touted as a god-sent system which like the natural economy discovered by the laissez-faire philosophers automatically will produce the best possible results in all times and places. All other things being equal, Responsible Government will operate most smoothly when there are only two teams on the field, and when those teams are able and well-matched; and Responsible Government tends to foster that kind of participation. But the constitutional system does not operate in a vacuum. The society may be such that able men and women do not take part in politics. The diverse interests within the country—the economic, racial, religious, or regional interests—may be so complex that the field will be flooded by half a dozen teams. The parties, whether two or more in number, may be indolent and corrupt. In such situations Responsible Government will not work well. It may work so badly that the desirability of turning to some other constitutional arrangement, one less sensitive to political forces, may have to be canvassed. The dynamics of the game are not without their effects; but we must not pretend that they always will group the players into two teams regardless of the political realities, that they will keep out corruption, and that they will draw into political life enough of the able people in the society.

Although the House for constitutional reasons is divided into two sides, as we consider its functions and how they are performed we always must remember that nowadays the two sides are composed of two or more parties. At the same time we must keep in mind the fact that legally all members are independent and free.

Over the centuries since parliaments first were held in England the work of the House of Commons has grown greatly in volume and complexity; yet the basic purpose of summoning the representatives of the Commons to parliaments is the same in the twentieth century as it was in the fourteenth. The plain truth is that kings and queens, even those who trace their titles up to God, need the help of their people. They need the support and acquiescence called "consent." At law the constitution seems monarchical, but in its political element inevitably it is somewhat republican. The fundamental function of the House of Commons is to assure that the government and the important segments of the populace cooperate. At times in the past the House had to go a long way to meet the kings; and at other times kings had to bend to the will of the House. The House of Commons represents the important people—just who are deemed important at any period is revealed by the prevailing law on the franchise. The House brings their views and interests out into the open. It enables those people to make available to the Crown for ministerial appointment men and women whom they trust. At the same time, the House gives the government an opportunity to put its plans and proposals, and its requests for money, before the representatives, and thus before the people. The basic purpose of the House is *to promote government made acceptable by mutual adjustment.*

But this purpose—the achievement of what John Ruskin called "the deep consent of all great men"—although of cardinal importance, is very general. It is not sufficiently specific to provide us with criteria by which to judge the procedures of the House. Consequently, if we are to have a set of performance tests by which to evaluate the procedures of the House, we must ascertain what specific functions follow from this basic purpose.

Under Responsible Government there can be no government unless the House supports and cooperates with one. This means that the House has a constitutional function; not to govern, but *to support a government.*

This does not mean that the House elects or selects the government. Because the members are divided between (or among) parties the decision as to who will constitute the government is made outside the House. When the electorate has given one party a majority, it is the electorate, not the House, that has chosen the government. It has selected a party with a leader, and he has lieutenants. That leader becomes the prime minister, and is charged with the task of forming a government. Indeed the fate of the existing government is known without a meeting of the House. But it may appear that the House acts as a genuine electoral college when no party attains a majority. However, the truth is that in such a situation the task of selecting the government is shifted, not to the House, but to the third party, perhaps to the "third parties." Assuming that, as in Canada after the election of 30 October 1972, there are two major parties, and that they do not coalesce, the members in the third party make a choice. They decide, not who the ministers are to be, but which of the two major parties will form the government. Moreover, they make this decision not as independent members, but as members of a party. The decision is made by the leader and his followers. It is made in secret. It is carried out under party discipline. In short, even when the House appears to be acting as a ministerial electoral college, what it expresses is not the will of free and equal members, but the will of a political party, a party which chooses between two other parties.

Obviously, when we say that one function of the House is to support a government, we are not saying that the House never should defeat a government. Ordinarily if the government is in a minority position it will be defeated just as soon as the third party decides that, all things considered, including the public reaction, its own partisan commitments require it to bring the government down, and not before.

But the members always have an obligation to act primarily as good members of the House, that is, to put the maintenance of the constitutional system ahead of personal and party interests. This obligation is honoured every day in divers ways—by consultation over the order of business, by waiving the rules when to do so is desirable, by the use of "steering committees" of party representatives to plan the work of standing committees, etc. The obligation becomes most obvious and important when it has been demonstrated—two general elections in close proximity suffice—that no party can obtain a majority. In that situation, I suggest, all members are under an obligation to moderate their party loyalites, whether based on religion, race, region, class, or tradition, or all these mixed, to permit Responsible Government to work. Compromises by both the government and the opposition will be required. The government will have to accept minor defeats in the House without resigning, and without calling an election. The opposition will have to meet the government half way. A minority government is almost certain to be weaker than a majority government because decisions may have to be postponed or distorted to prevent the loss of vital support. But to say this is not to say either that all majority governments are good or that all minority governments are bad; and certainly except in the most extreme circumstances minority government is better than the collapse of the constitutional system.

But supporting a government is not simply a crisis function. While a government survives, the House ought to do that government's business as expeditiously as possible. Nowadays a government needs the cooperation of the House throughout much of the year. The government and the House are geared into each other: the corollary of the principle that the government is answerable to the House is that the House should deal with the business put before it by the government. Until a government is forced from office, the country has a right to expect the House to deal with that government's business decisively and without delays.

But why is this institutional function—supporting a government—genuinely important? Let us assume that the voters regularly give one or other of two parties a majority. In that simple situation, why should the House ever meet? The outcome of the election is ascertained. Then, following well-established practice, even without a preliminary vote in the House, the leaders of the successful party will either continue in office, or take office. If the House does meet the government's bills will be passed, its supply votes will be carried, and its policies will be extolled by its loyal backbenchers. Why should not the necessary constitutional alterations be made to let the government duly elected by the people govern without a parliamentary charade? Or, if such a change would be too traumatic for the public, why should not the charade be made just as brief, simple, and inexpensive as possible?

In meeting this challenge we must avoid the mistake of regarding elections as occasional, isolated encounters. The electoral process is a continuous contest between (or among) the parties for public support. A dissolution merely brings on a temporary climax: the contest then shifts to the hustings, and on polling day the voters record their judgement on the government (as compared with the available successors). The House of Commons is the ordinary scene of the battle. It is the great public stage at the centre of the national amphitheatre. The constitution assures that the ministers must appear on that stage. Because they need the regular cooperation of the House they must put their administrative and legislative activities before the public in the form of supply votes, substantive motions, and bills—all more or less specific—in the House of Commons. Thus, the House has opportunities to perform what we may call its democratic function. This involves four inter-related sub-functions. First, *the House can prevent the clandestine exercise of power by the government.* We may assume that the ministers will seek to sweep their measures across the stage with nothing unfavourable uttered against either themselves or the measures. But the House can examine both the measures and their sponsors. It can insist upon discoveries far broader than the minimal appearances required by the processes. The ministers may be required to provide information, explanations, and justifications; or if for any reason they decline to do so they must bear the suspicion their reticence will arouse. Second, *the House can serve as a proving ground for the administrative policies and legislative proposals of the government.* It can examine and assay their desirability, effectiveness, and costs. Third, *the House can constrain the government between elections.* Obviously it can bring down a government gone mad. But the constraint it exerts is effective far short of that extreme. The need to explain and justify has an effect upon ministers. They are likely to be more "responsible" in their administrative and legislative actions. Because it cannot act on its own year in and year out, but must meet the House regularly, a government tries to anticipate the criticisms of the private members; and it meets those criticisms as far as it thinks they are valid or would be politically damaging before it takes its votes, bills, and motions to the House. And, fourth, because it can explore and test in public, *the House can serve to inform and educate the electorate.* It can give the electorate the preparation without which elections would be largely meaningless. It can help to form the minds and the will of the people. We avoided a separation of powers along American lines; but never for a moment did we think of abandoning the idea that the government should be subject to regular examination and criticism in public. Indeed, disclosure, proving, restraining, and education are far more certain and effective because a separation of powers has been avoided. Under our system the government is required to bare its activities to scrutiny by two groups of private members, those who oppose the government and the backbenchers.

Functionally, the House is divided into three groups: first, those who hold offices of profit under the Crown, i.e., the ministers and parliamentary secretaries; second, those members who support the government; and third, those members who oppose the government. The term "backbenchers" often is used to refer to some members on both sides of the House. This usage suits the British House far better than the Canadian. Frequently we do not have a clearly defined "shadow cabinet." And we have "third parties"; their leaders hardly can be classed as backbenchers, a point that would be very obvious if a third party became strong enough to have a good prospect of winning a forthcoming election. But what is most important for our analysis is that the use of the term "backbenchers" to refer to some members on both sides tends to obscure the distinct role of the supporters of the government.[18]

The situation in the House is an adversary situation analogous to a tug-of-war. The government does its work on its financial requests and its legislative proposals before it brings them to the House. In the House it is confronted by institutionalized opposition. One team strains against the other; and the fact that the ministers and backbenchers together may be superior in numbers does not mean that the ministers and their measures will not be examined and tested, nor does the severity of the examining and testing depend on the size of the opposition. The effectiveness of an opposition is hard to gauge because much of its effect is anticipatory. An opposition, however able and effective, may never win an important vote in the House; indeed, it may not even score many debating points, for able ministers will strive to find the points open to attack, and by making improvements in advance leave the opposition with little to say.

At the same time the ministers neglect the backbenchers at their peril. The goal of the opposition is to supplant the government, not to improve its performance. Ordinarily the opposition will vote against the government if by doing so it can advance its own fortunes. In contrast, the backbenchers want the government to be re-elected, and therefore generally can obtain a patient hearing. The possibility that a backbencher will assert his right as a free and independent member to vote against the government always is there, but seldom is this seriously contemplated at Ottawa. The sense of party loyalty is very strong. Revolts and defections have been rare, and generally are attributable to disappointed personal ambitions. A deeply aggrieved member is more likely to let it be known that he does not plan to seek re-election. Much more important than threats is the influence that a good argument well and persistently presented by a backbencher can have on a minister. At Ottawa access to the better ministers is direct and easy. The numbers involved are small; the ministers and the private members have offices in the same buildings during the sessions; and often share tables in the parliamentary restaurants. There is no need to rely on the Whip as a medium as at Westminster. Generally a prime minister and his colleagues can carry the backbenchers along with them. The backbenchers may argue and protest; yet when the bells ring, they will be loyal. But winning votes in the House is not winning the next election. The candidate is the key man in most constituency campaigns; if a backbencher's heart is not in the battle because consciously or subconsciously he feels that the prime minister and the other ministers do not deserve re-election, his attitude will have an important impact on the outcome of the contest.

Because their roles are different the two groups of private members act very differently in the House. They share the gratifying notion that the people watch each ploy, and sedulously study the record of the debates and votes. But they have different parts to play. The proceedings of the House provide the opposition with its great opportunity. In a sense the House is the opposition's show. The ministers come to the House with their proposals and requests; but how they are received, aside from the voting, depends mainly on the opposition. Moreover, the sittings of the House afford the individual members in opposition a chance to challenge ministers publicly, and thus to advance themselves within their own party. Most members in opposition are eager for an opportunity to make trouble for ministers. In sharp contrast, the backbenchers attend the House chiefly as an audience. It is the ministers who must explain the votes and the bills. It is the ministers who must defend the administration. It is the ministers who must answer the questions and produce the papers. Day after day the backbenchers have to be content to observe and judge the contest between the government and the opposition; indeed, except during the sessional debates—notably the debate on the Address in Reply to the Speech from the Throne for which only limited time is available under the standing orders, normally the backbenchers will be assured by the government whip that silence is their finest contribution.[19] When they speak on government bills, it will be mainly to drive home to their own constituents, by repetition, perhaps embellished by local examples, the arguments already propounded by the ministers.

This difference in roles gives the party caucus a different significance for the two groups. When opposition members meet in caucus—if they are not distracted by internecine strife—they are chiefly concerned to conspire against the ministry. Their meetings are occasions to decide what ministerial requests and proposals are to be resisted and denounced, and by whom, and how. These caucus meetings are preparatory for the House. On the other hand, the backbenchers, who must do their own testing and exert their own influence outside the Chamber, and in private, use the caucus as a party court. The caucus meetings—held weekly during the sessions—give them an opportunity to discuss frankly, and in the presence of the entire parliamentary party, both the policies of the government and the conduct of ministers. Here it is that the ministers must justify their measures and methods in the presence of the prime minister and of party colleagues whose survival in the next election depends on their performance. Here it is that the ministers individually and collectively must create confidence, not merely the confidence that will carry a majority party to success in a division in the House, but the confidence that will send a keen, united, and confident party into the next general election.

Because the private members are divided into two groups, we do not depend on them as individuals to assure that the House performs its democratic function. We rely instead largely on the self-interest of the two groups. Naturally, the effectiveness of both the opposition and the backbenchers will vary from one Parliament to the next, and even from session to session. At times the opposition may lack talented men and women; or it may be racked by internal troubles. It may be slack and dispirited. At times the backbenchers may be lazy and incompetent. Many of them may be novices. Some of them may have remained backbenchers so long that they have become debilitated. Or the ministers may be so busy or so vain that they neither attempt to anticipate the opposition, nor pay attention to the backbenchers. To some extent, but by no means to the full extent, these defects may be caused by the system, for because most voters vote for the party, not for the man, able persons often are defeated while nonentities are elected. It is even possible that no members whatsoever will be elected in opposition. Yet, assuming that there is an opposition, the probability is higher that the two groups, each playing its role, will "govern" the government than if we were relying on the zeal, perceptiveness, and dutifulness of unorganized, individual members.

It is difficult to establish the degree to which the House is effective in making the government act responsibly. One might add up the number of government bills that die on the Order Paper, but which is evidence that the House is effective, a high or a low number of dead bills? One might add up the amendments to bills, the notable changes in policy, and the cuts in supply votes effected in the House, but a small total might mean simply that the government, fearing the criticism of the opposition and the backbenchers, had done its preparatory work with great care. A large and impressive total might mean that the government had acted recklessly in accepting unsound changes and amendments proposed either factitiously or simply to curry favour with special interest groups, or has accepted changes to draw fire away from more vital parts. Or a minister may have left flaws in his bill deliberately so as to be able to win applause from the opposition and gullible newsmen for his "flexibility." Besides, the notion that any change made by the House or a committee is an improvement is naive. In short, the public record provides no reliable evidence. What would be helpful is the detailed testimony of those who have participated in the preparation of the business of the House. In Canada such testimony is hard to come by.

The quality of the opposition is of the utmost importance to the system.[20] Understandably, ministers wish to remain in office. Understandably, they wish to have their measures approved by the House without the revelation of damaging information or contrary arguments. A wise minister will not delay his own measures or adduce evidence against them. Unless his tactic is to disarm the critics by candour, he will tend to emphasize the merits of his measures and to ignore their disadvantages. There is nothing sinister or even surprising about this. Long consideration or debate consumes scarce time. Besides, having decided individually, and also with his colleagues, for the vote, motion, or bill, perhaps after protracted negotiations in his department and the cabinet, and perhaps after intense discussion in the government caucus, it is unlikely that he will be eager to have the deliberation repeated in the House, especially if the measure is contrary to the interests or prejudices of any considerable group in the country. But rare indeed is the important item of business against which nothing can be said. Few measures entail no costs and disadvantages. Almost always there are arguments that can be made against a government's legislative proposals and administrative policies. And there may be reasons—some striking instances of misconduct, or even general incompetence—why a minister or the entire government should be driven from office. We rely on the opposition to ensure that the facts and the reasons are brought forth. Without an able opposition the opportunity to prevent the clandestine use of power may be unexploited, with the results that the people are not informed and that the government feels free to act irresponsibly. Not only does the opposition have its own role to perform, but in addition it serves to precipitate the reactions of the backbenchers. They are predisposed to favour the ministers and their measures; but the opposition by persuasive attack may sow doubt among them.

Let me again summarize my argument. The House of Commons, I submit, is not a body charged with the duty of governing the country;

neither is it "the legislature." When we think of the House as a congress or speak of it as "the legislature" we run the risk of misleading both ourselves and others. Rather, we should regard the House as the field and occasion for government by political parties. A general election is important because constitutionally the House has the power to make and unmake governments; consequently, in modern circumstances elections are contests between organized and cohesive parties. The successful party forms the government. But the government, once elected, cannot ignore the House. To perform their duties the ministers must meet the House and gain its cooperation. There they must display their legislative and administrative activities—their governing—and over the merits of those activities the parties joust in public. It is this public testing of governance, with the government and the opposition as institutionalized adversaries competing for the support of the voters, that is the hall-mark of contemporary Responsible Government. The great strength of the system is that it makes for acceptable government. On the one hand, the electorate selects a party to form a government; and by having to govern publicly that government is made to act "responsibly," i.e., in reasonably close accord with what is thought to be the will of the people. And, on the other hand, in the long run the views and will of the people are changed to suit the needs and possibilities of new times. Divine-right kings, unrestricted by public opinion, might provide wiser governing, but given the ethos of our times their governing would not be as good because it would not be accepted as readily by their subjects.

The implications of this analysis for parliamentary procedure are two-fold. First, the House ought to be prepared to deal with the government's business, for the government, which has the duty to govern under our constitution, must have the cooperation of the House. The procedures should assure that within a reasonable time the House takes decisions on the items of business put before it by the government. The main peril to be warded off here is that so much time may be lavished on a few items that other items, perhaps more important items, will either be slighted or seriously delayed. Second, the procedures should promote the thorough examination in public of the government's administrative and legislative activities. The peril here is that the House may permit its time to be squandered on superficial, repetitious speech-making.

The division of the time of the House between the government and the opposition, and then the apportionment of time among the various items of business, must be a central procedural question. It is a question that can be dealt with in rules of procedure. Equally important if the House is to perform its functions well is the intensity of attention given to the measures that come before it. This, however, is something that the rules can influence only indirectly. By its rules the House cannot command a good effort by the members: it can only try to make a good effort possible.

IV

Nowadays the complaint often is heard in Canada, as in Britain, that party discipline, especially when there are only two large parties, prevents the House of Commons from performing its proper functions. The argument is that given party discipline the majority party, whether right or wrong, always wins in the House, so that the debating and voting are mere hollow, vestigial rites retained from earlier, better days. Two solutions are advocated: (a) that the government should let more and more questions of important public policy be decided by "free votes" in the House, and (b) that the conventional emphasis on the value of majority government should be moderated so as to promote a multi-party House, one in which initially the members of the "third parties," and eventually all private members, would have decisive power. The cry is raised that, contrary to received opinion, minority governments do work well, even better than majority governments. Frequently resort is had to history to make this complaint persuasive: the pretense is that in the good, old days, if not in Canada then certainly in Britain, the members were free from front-bench control, so that the House really did govern. Sometimes the claim is less extreme: in the good, old days a healthy balance prevailed between "the legislative branch" and "the executive branch," whereas now the latter controls the former.

This argument is dangerous. Because it hints at an important truth it is hard to extirpate. Yet because it is false it tends to discredit proposals that the power of the private members should be increased in our own times. The more strongly the argument is made, the more it, like congressionalism, confirms the beliefs and the determination of defenders of the *status quo*.

The British House of Commons of the eighteenth century and the early nineteenth century—if that is the period of "the good, old days" —was far different from either the modern British House or the modern Canadian House. But what must be remembered is that in that era Britain was governed domestically in an entirely different way. The activities of the central government were limited mainly to foreign and colonial affairs, to defence, and to the collection of certain taxes, chiefly customs and excises. Otherwise, governing was in local hands: it was performed by justices of the peace, quarter sessions, and the other local authorities. That was an era when major bills for changes in the general law were few and far between. The time was yet to come when the central government would undertake to reshape and standardize important aspects of society—municipal government, education, sanitation, the poor law, housing, etc.—by means of great general statutes to be applied throughout the entire country by employees of the Crown. On the other hand, legislation by local and private acts was extensive; and it grew as the agricultural and industrial revolutions advanced. Before 1832, when the need to win the consent of a new class of "great men" was recognized by the enactment of the First Reform Act, innovation in economic and social affairs originated for the most part with local and private interests. This meant that it was local and private interests, not the queen's ministers, who came to Parliament seeking authorization to make changes—to enclose certain lands, to canalize specified stretches of rivers, to build turnpikes and railroads, to provide water and sewerage and docks to particular places. By its private bill procedure the House of Commons sought to reconcile the aims of the projectors and innovators with the rights of the vested interests and the local public. Consequently, much of the time of the House was given over to local and private business; and to the fate of that business the ministers were relatively indifferent. In that business the private members were left quite independent by the government. It is no accident that it was in that period, when most of the acts of Parliament had nothing directly to do with the central government, that Parliament came to be known as "the legislature."[21]

But we must not let the independence of the members in local and private business mislead us as to the practice of Responsible Government. For its own business—preeminently supply—the government needed the cooperation of the House; and where that business was concerned the government was far from willing to leave fortune untutored. From the time when the regular cooperation of the House first came to be regarded as necessary the Crown (the "Country" critics called it "the Court") took steps not only to woo the House, but to assure that the electorate produced a House inclined—if possible, certain—to cooperate. It was appreciated that the power to make and unmake ministries was far too precious to be left to the whim and judgement of free and equal members of Parliament. Ways were found to assure that many of those elected to the House, enough to produce ministerial stability, were not "loose fish." Because the peaks of political power were occupied by a few great landowners a ministry was an alliance of magnates, the heads of "connections." By combining their own control over various constituencies, especially pocket boroughs, with the effects of extensive bribery and Crown patronage the ministers could procure a reliable House. It can be said that between 1715 and 1832 the Crown never lost an election. In that period a prime minister's problems were (a) to maintain the alliance among the ministerial magnates, and (b) to retain the royal favour. Provided that those conditions were met, the election of a cooperative House was assured. At a session of Parliament the government's main concern was to defend its administration, mainly in foreign and colonial affairs, and to obtain supplies. But in such matters it was no less diligent in seeking a majority, albeit by different methods, than a modern government.

That the eighteenth century was not the period of "the good, old days" is shown by Bolingbroke's denunciations of "corruption" and "robinocracy." England's once-free legislature, he complained, had fallen under the sway of the Court; in turn, the Court was under the robinarch. Sir Robert Walpole was behaving as a "prime minister"! "The *Robinarch*, or chief ruler," wrote Bolingbroke, "is nominally a *minister* only and creature of the prince; but in reality he is a sovereign, as despotic, arbitrary a sovereign as this part of the world affords.... The *Robinarch* ... hath unjustly engrossed the whole power of a nation into his own hands ... [and] admits no person to any considerable post of trust and power under him who is not either a *relation*, a *creature*, or a *thorough-paced tool* whom he can lead at pleasure into any dirty work without being able to discover his designs or the consequences of them."[22] Those who in the twentieth century denounce the "presidential power" of prime ministers travel a well-blazed trail.

The First Reform Act, in 1832, made two important changes. First, it gave political power to a segment of the population that envisioned a new, reformed England, a new society to be achieved, not piecemeal by local and private interests, but by public bills introduced in Parliament by the government, and subsequently administered by departments and agencies of the Crown. The success of the reformers meant that increasingly thereafter the governing of England was centralized (or "nationalized"). Second, the Reform Act reduced drastically the dominance of the landowners and the Crown; all the pocket boroughs were abolished, and the efficacy of bribery and patronage was diminished by the enlargement of the electorate in many of the constituencies. Thereafter it was quite possible, as Queen Victoria learned between 1839 and 1841, for the queen's trusted advisers to go down to defeat at the polls, with results that even Her Majesty would have to accept.[23] There ensued a period when, with the old structure in decay, the House was divided among various groups, none a majority. During that period the government always was in a somewhat precarious position. But the House was still a creature of the electorate; consequently, after 1832, and especially after the great enlargement of the electorate by the Second Reform Act in 1867, it was inevitable that political leaders would seek new means and methods by which to have power in, if possible to control, the House of Commons. The result of their efforts was the nation-wide political party. The governing of the country had been nationalized; now electioneering was nationalized. The nation-wide party puts its leader and its lieutenants before the entire electorate; it seeks a national mandate for its program; and it aspires to nominate a candidate in many, if not all, the constituencies. Here was the new machine to shape, to evoke, and to express the will of the "great men."

Those who say that the British private members are less important now than they were 200 years ago are quite correct. At that time the House dealt with a wide stream of important business which did not originate with the ministers, and on which private members could vote according to their own lights. Where the critics go wrong is in asserting that the House controlled or "balanced" the government. The suggestion that the House should regain its former stature by becoming a congress —at the extreme a congress that would use the cabinet as its executive committee—is to reveal a deep misunderstanding of the historical development. For years the British House of Commons was a body of equal members, all free to make and unmake governments. But only at the legal level was this true. Throughout the eighteenth and the early nineteenth centuries politics in Britain was a game played by a few dominant figures and a larger number of somewhat smaller ones, each controlling his own followers. Once those men lost their followings, or once the followings had been rendered insignificant by the enlargement of the electorate, politics increasingly became a game to be played by disciplined teams.

The truly notable change has not been the emergence of disciplined parties; that was more effect than cause. Far more important was the nationalization of governance that came with the rise of modern industry and great cities. Once the domestic governing of Britain became the concern of the queen's servants at London, her ministers became responsible for what was done or left undone. Naturally, power and responsibility travelled hand in hand.

When we turn from Britain to Canada we find little evidence, certainly far less than in Britain, to support an argument that the House of Commons once was a highly independent body which dominated and directed governments. Here the social structure was quite different: there were no great men with entrenched local power comparable to the English magnates. Here, too, unlike Britain, there was no indigenous tradition, begotten in civil war and fed by Whig historians, of hostility to kings and courtiers, no tradition to make an elected assembly both jealous of its own dignity and suspicious of any member who went over to the Court by "kissing hands."[24] Something of the authentic Commons attitude emerged in the first half of the nineteenth century when the colonial assemblies squared off against the governors and their friends; but the achievement of Responsible Government wiped out suspicion of governments, perhaps not suspicion of British governors, as Mr. King was to demonstrate as late as 1926. Nor was there a fear of government activity within the country; on the contrary, the "war with the wilderness" was regarded as a great public enterprise. Public works, especially canals, roads, wharves, and bridges, as Lord Durham pointed out, were to governments in British North America what national defence was in Europe.[25] The introduction of Responsible Government meant that the popular men in the provinces became the ministers. Thus the provincial governments ceased to be forces to be regarded with hostility, and became instead trophies to be won in the political competition. The aspiration of the members of the assemblies was not to diminish the government, to make it a mere "executive body," but to win it, and then to use it. The introduction of Responsible Government in Britain, it must be remembered, was important mainly for one reason. The political relationship between the Crown and the House of Commons was changed. But in British North America it was also a key step towards colonial autonomy. It was this second aspect, the achievement of a high degree of self-government, that inspired the colonial advocates of Responsible Government. Once Responsible Government had been achieved the assemblies lost any strong sense of distinct corporate interest. They became links in the chains between the voters and the ministers. After the House of Commons was created in 1867 it too was viewed mainly as a link, not as an independent entity.

To a large extent Confederation was a product of the constitutional experiment conducted in the province of Canada after 1848. What that experiment showed—even more vividly than British experience—is the need for a stable majority to support the ministry if Responsible Government is to work well. Less than fifteen years after Responsible Government had been introduced it had become clear that the political interests—racial, religious, and regional—within the province were too diverse to produce a House in which a ministry could survive while doing its job.[26] It was seen that Responsible Government is well-nigh unworkable when the ministry is likely to be defeated again and again on the difficult questions. Consequently, to create circumstances in which Responsible Government could work, the province was divided into two parts, Quebec and Ontario, each with its own government and assembly, and to those provincial bodies were assigned the matters that regularly had separated the majority of the voters in Canada East from the majority of the voters in Canada West. Matters of a general nature were assigned to the government and Parliament of the new Dominion. In short, the very structure of the country was altered fundamentally to make stable majority government possible.

The bestowal of the historic name, "The House of Commons," by the British Parliament did imply a new status and importance for the representative body at Ottawa, a dignity no colonial body in North America had enjoyed previously. But the fact that under the British North America Act most matters of a local and private nature—the kind of business that had made membership in the British House highly desirable before 1832—were given to the provinces reduced the room for independent action by the private members at Ottawa. In the early years the House dealt with a considerable volume of local and private legislation, but this related mainly to two matters, the creation of companies to build and operate railways and the incorporation of companies proposing to do business inter-provincially. To that legislation the government, if not the individual ministers, seems to have been fairly indifferent.[27] Undoubtedly that business did enhance the stature of those private members who dominated the relevant committees; but that lasted for no more than twenty or thirty years. In any case, in public business the government was fully in charge from the beginning. The very fact that the new House of Commons was in session only two or three months out of the year—less even than the assembly of the late province of Canada—made it quite clear that the government, not the House, was the leading body. This the members understood from 1867. The government was expected to initiate the public business at the sessions. The private members from the first brought forward very little in the way of public business—that is, not until relatively recent times when scores and scores of private members' motions and bills are put down, but mainly for the sake of publicity. Even to this day far more private members' bills become law at Westminster than at Ottawa.[28]

During the first few years after 1867 party cohesion was fairly weak. The Macdonald government drew support from some members, not because they were party supporters of Sir John A. Macdonald, but because they were part of the coalition that had brought about Confederation. In the opposition were the Ontario Liberals, who had been most zealous for the new arrangement, but who had withdrawn from the coalition once Confederation was assured, and the *Rouges* and the Maritime Liberals, who had opposed Confederation. As a result sometimes some opposition members voted with the government, and sometimes the government lost votes in the House, but carried on.[29] But before long the House came to be divided distinctly between the supporters and the opponents of Macdonald, his party, and his policy.

The crucial event was the scandal election of 1874, when candidates stood either for or against the late Macdonald government. Then in 1874 the Mackenzie government introduced the secret ballot, which reduced intimidation at the polls, and simultaneous elections, which made it impossible for candidates to refrain from declaring their attitude to a government until after the trend of the voting had been revealed by the early results. In 1878, when the outcome of the election showed that the voters had decided that a new government should be formed by Sir John A. Macdonald and his party, Mackenzie submitted his resignation without meeting the House. Thereafter on public business the House divided quite regularly as the Ins and the Outs, with the former generally showing a somewhat higher cohesion and attendance record than the latter.[30]

In short, at Ottawa the private members never had, nor were they interested in having, a heyday of independence and dominance. The work of the House was conducted mainly by groups or by parties. From the very beginning the Canadian voter was keenly interested in political issues, political figures, and political platforms—in other words, the ingredients of party politics—not, as in England at times in the past, in the deferential privilege of sending his landlord or some other local notable to Parliament. This, of course, does not mean that there have been no members of independent mind. Such members always have been present in some numbers, and have made their presence felt in various ways. But to admit the obvious is not to say that "the legislature" was once free from "executive" control.

In our age of universal adult suffrage Responsible Government has developed into a system of government by cohesive political parties largely to prevent the House from acting as a congress or as a ministerial electoral college. Under party government each party selects its leader and its key players. It acquires its own style, character, and complexion. These are set before the voters at each election. By means of political parties with known leaders the electors are given a choice between (or among) potential prime ministers and ministerial teams, and by party cohesion they are assured that their members in the House of Commons will not frustrate their intentions after the election.[31] The people commit the conduct of the government to the ministerial team of a party, and to the general policies of that party.

It seems safe to say that, far from being incompatible with Responsible Government, our kind of political parties would not have appeared without Responsible Government. That system provides the playing field, with its ground rules, on which the parties compete. A different constitutional system would have produced a different kind of game, and teams of a different kind. To deplore the effects of party cohesion in Canada comes close to deploring Responsible Government.

But we can go further. We can assert that Responsible Government tends to produce not only cohesive parties, but a two-party system. In a congress the diversity of interests makes for shifting networks of alliances among congressmen. The survival of the government is not at stake. In contrast, under Responsible Government neither the government nor the House has a fixed term of office; accordingly, even in the absence of party loyalties, the members must make a choice between alternatives. They must decide either to support or to oppose the existing ministry. The precariousness of tenure tends to divide the House now, as it did in the eighteenth century, into two sides, the Ins, who want to remain in office, and the Outs, who want to supplant the Ins. This second level, what I have called "the constitutional level," does exert a powerful influence on the third or "political level." But at the same time we must recognize that the constitutional system does not operate in isolation from the political and social realities. As Canadian experience has shown, the interests within a country may be simply too diverse and intractable to be gathered into two parties, however loose and non-ideological.

Sometimes the complaints against modern party cohesion are unabashedly congressionalist: because it is the body to which the sovereign people delegate their power, the House should govern. On that view we need not pause. It has the merit of candour; but to sustain an argument for it on the basis of either British history or American practice would be difficult. More often what is implied is that once the government has been elected the private members ought to serve as a bench of unprejudiced judges, each diligently examining the activities and proposals of the government, and then pronouncing his own judgement of approval or disapproval. This is an appealing scheme; but it is naive. The aggregate of the judgements of the private members is either to count or not. If not, the scheme is pointless. If so, the result will be a system far more congressional than the American, for at Washington the president normally is not dependent for office on the Houses. The proposal would make governing largely accidental. The ship of state would be controlled in each successive instance by the aggregate of individual decisions, each attained separately and under whatever advice, pressure, or inspiration the member found compelling at that instant. A government cannot be conducted by taking opinion polls in the House of Commons, where most members do not occupy offices of "responsibility," and where scores of members are striving to embarrass and to defeat the government. Governing, like sailing, is a practical activity. The waves of the future always are unknown. Accordingly, our basic constitutional strategy is to focus on men and general policies, not on each and every measure. We emphasize primarily, not agreement or disagreement on each issue, but confidence

—or lack of it—in the men and women who constitute the ministry. We want a government with a high sense of responsibility. To cultivate such a sense of responsibility we concentrate power. We place the duty of using power, not in the hands of scores of private members, each elected in his own isolated constituency, but in the hands of the prime minister and his ministerial colleagues. By concentrating power we make responsibility difficult to evade. And then to assure that those who have power are held responsible we require them to submit their activities to hostile scrutiny in the House of Commons.

The specific functions of the House of Commons, I submit, are five in number: first, to support a government; second, to prevent clandestine governing; third, to test the government's administrative policies and legislative proposals; fourth, to constrain the ministers; and fifth, to educate the electorate. The vital tension within the system arises from the need to balance the first of these functions against the other four. On the one hand, we want a government that is stable and efficient. But, on the other, we want the chief governors to hold office precariously at the will of the House of Commons and the people, and at the same time to restrain and moderate the chief governors, we want their activities to be scrutinized in public.

V

Given its functions ought the House to sit throughout the year? Or is there a time limit beyond which an annual session ordinarily ought not to extend? Here is a question directly relevant to any discussion of the procedures of the House of Commons: the shorter the time available, the more rapidly and intensely the House must work to complete the business. My answer is that very long sessions are deplorable. The most general function of the House, as the body representative of the people, I have argued, is to promote acceptable government. The procedures of the House are important because they are related to specific functions, which we have discussed, but the proceedings of the House ought not to be allowed to crowd all the members' other public duties off the stage.

Those members who are ministers are charged individually with the running of their departments, and collectively with the coordination and planning of the public business. They are supposed to be the principal governors. They need time in which to perform their duties. Just how much time is a point on which the government and the opposition are almost certain to disagree. The House ought not to be the main scene of activity for ministers. The opposition, in contrast, is made up of assailants eager to gain the citadel of power; naturally, in an era of professionalized politics, they are reluctant to adjourn the assault for any long period.

They strive to wear the ministers down by attrition. In this attitude they are almost certain to be supported by the newsmen, who feel deprived when there are no parliamentary skirmishes to report.

The role of the private member, too, includes more than participation in the proceedings of the House. Because he sometimes gets results his constituents expect him to participate to a considerable degree in administration, regardless of the side of the House on which he sits. He is expected to use his knowledge in directing constituents to the proper offices when they want to apply for pensions, adult training, and passports; he is expected also to use his influence to assure that their applications are not dealt with carelessly or woodenly. If he comes from Toronto, Vancouver, or Montreal, he is likely to have a fair number of immigration cases and housing development projects to worry about. If he is from a rural area there are likely to be problems about rural mail routes, rail-line abandonment applications, or perhaps the prices of wheat or manufacturing milk. If he is from a seacoast area there will be a constant, urgent need for new navigation aids, for the repair of wharves and breakwaters, for dredging, and for the conservation of fish stocks. His flood of letters and telephone calls, each one dealing with a matter of some importance to a constituent, will serve to keep him busy from two to six hours on five days a week during sessions. Probably he will need to maintain an office in his constituency where he can be available to those who wish to talk with him, not about policies and legislation, but about items of administrative business. The work of this kind done by a member often is of greater value to the people of a constituency than that member's participation in the examination of estimates or in the passing of bills. If this work is to be done well, the members must be accessible.

There is an even more fundamental reason why a member—either a private member or a minister—ought to spend time in his constituency. The arch-purpose of representative government is the achievement of deep consent. A people and its government easily can become isolated from each other, with growing impatience and imperiousness on one side, and a sense of alienation on the other. The top public servants, because of their specialized education and their professionalism, are remote from ordinary society, and in any case many of them live in Ottawa, a city which, like Brazilia or Canberra, is separated from the normal flow of activity even in the central region of the country, let alone the West and the Atlantic provinces. The lower echelons are segregated and made to seem at least somewhat hostile because they act, not for themselves, but for an organization that is both highly bureaucratized and a monopoly. Notwithstanding the progress of radio and television broadcasting, in many constituencies the member is still the most direct link between the people and their government. He can serve to transmit attitudes and feelings and information both ways. He is an artery of personal communication through the paper and red tape. The decision-makers in Ottawa may resent bitterly the intrusion of political reality which the member effects; but he will continue to be valuable to them as long as governing requires some degree of consent. In turn, the electors may be displeased by what the government will not do, or by what it has decided to do; and they ought to be told the reasons. It is impossible for a member to serve well either his constituents or the country if he becomes a part of the Ottawa microcosm, sharing its special viewpoint, its concerns, and its beliefs, by reason of being immured there throughout most of the year. Hasty weekend excursions may suffice to take care of the most urgent casework; but this leaves most of a member's real work undone.

In short, the work done in the House and its committees is valuable, and ought to be done well; but its value ought not to be exaggerated at the expense of other important political tasks. Both the ministers and the private members, as key participants in the public life of the country, have other important duties, and these too require time. Obviously, the procedures of the House cannot make the members able and willing to do the work of the House thoroughly and efficiently, but the procedures ought not to hinder them. In addition, the procedures ought not to prevent them from performing their other public duties by prolonging the sessions.

TWO

The Basic Principles of Procedure

Behind the rules, practices, and standing orders followed by the House are certain principles so basic and essential that there rarely is any practical need for them to be stated. They are simply presupposed and applied. In this chapter we shall seek to discover those principles. As one would expect, they are closely inter-related.

The key principle is that, with the exception of a few elemental points dealt with in the British North America Act, *the House is master of its own proceedings.*[1] When a session shall begin and end is decided by the governor general as advised by the prime minister; but what the House does while in session, and how it does what it chooses to do, are matters to be decided by the House itself. Except when it has been summoned to his presence by the governor general to hear a Speech from the Throne at the beginning or end of a session or when the royal assent is being given, nobody who is not a member may lay claim to the time of the House, and members may do so only under the strict conditions laid down by the House.[2] The days and hours of sitting, the adjournments, how the time is to be divided between the private members and the ministers, the processes by which the various kinds of business are to be done, the rules of debate and conduct, the method by which votes are to be taken, and all other questions of order and procedure, with the exception of the points covered in the British North America Act, are within the power of the House alone. If, for example, the House were to decide that all public bills need to be read four times, or only twice, before they pass the House any criticism of that decision by, let us say, a senator or a judge would be a mere impertinence. This principle means that the House can change its established procedures freely to suit new needs and conditions. It means that the House is not bound by its own practices and rules: since those practices and rules are its own the House in particular cases can waive their requirements with the consent of those members who are present. This it often does, especially with regard to the notice requirement and the rule that bills ordinarily are not to move forward through more than one stage at a sitting.

The principle does not mean that ministers have no right to make motions relating to the procedure of the House, or to the conduct of members. Ministers are members; they have the full rights and duties of membership. It is true that the House by its rules distinguishes between ministers and private members; for example, ministers, unlike private members, may table documents without the leave of the House, and may make statements; but, unlike the private members, they may not ask questions during the Oral Question Period.[3] These rights and disabilities were created by the House itself. No special rights in the House, and no disabilities, follow consequentially from the status of some members as ministers of the Crown.

Another principle is that *there is to be no pointless discussion: all discussion is to be relevant to a motion (and to be directed to a decision by the House)*. To be effective the House, like any other body, must make up its mind. This it does by answering questions put to it by the speaker. (In committees of the whole House the questions are put by the chairman.) On many procedural questions the House has declared its will in advance by standing orders, so that if stated conditions are met there is no need to put a question to the House. For example, under the standing orders when a matter of privilege arises in the course of proceedings in the Chamber it is to be dealt with at once unless the speaker decides otherwise. Again, all items of business ordered for a sitting but not disposed of at that sitting are postponed until the next sitting day, and to the next and the next. Again, ordinarily at the end of a day the speaker adjourns the House without putting a question to the House. But most of the time of the House is spent in reaching decisions. In other words, the House spends most of its time dealing with motions (and the questions launched by them). What the principle means is that the House does not permit members to speak extensively, other than on a point of order, except when seeking to elicit a decision by the House, or in trying to influence the outcome of a debate. At one time at Westminster a topic might be discussed by members in an exploratory way for a time; then the speaker would bring the discussion into focus by proposing a question to be debated and ultimately to be answered; but early in the eighteenth century the procedure became stricter. The rule came to be that the member who introduced a topic was to frame a question himself and to move that it be the question. In short, no speech was to be made that did not include (or second) a motion, or that was not relevant to a question previously proposed to the House as the result of a motion duly moved and seconded. Similar prohibitions had prevailed for years in the process by which bills were passed.

The motion is the essential element of most modern procedure: it initiates the discussion and provides the question to be decided. Whether a member is introducing a bill, raising a point of privilege, making a statement about a misprint in *Hansard*, proposing the second reading of a bill, speaking on a substantive question, complaining at the time of adjournment about a ministerial reply to an oral question, or discussing "a specific and important matter requiring urgent consideration," he does so ostensibly or actually to make a motion, or to support or oppose a motion. Debate or consideration always entails a motion or a series of motions. The basic process of the House is: (a) the moving and seconding of a motion; (b) the statement of the question proposed in the motion to the House for debate; (c) the putting of the question; and (d) the answering of the question. Obviously, this process does not apply to routine proceedings other than motions moved under Motions; nor does it apply to either oral questions or order paper questions. These do not entail decisions by the House.

This rigorous adherence to motions as the basic mode of proceeding is relaxed considerably when the speaker is not in the Chair, i.e., when the members are working as a committee of the whole House. The requirement that there be a motion continues, but it is not kept as much to the fore. Indeed, in one such circumstance, the Committee of Supply, which no longer is used, motions were not moved explicitly. The reminder that there were motions—or proposed "votes"—before the committee came only when the chairman introduced the vote, saying, for example, "The estimates of the Department of Transport. Vote No. 1. Shall Vote No. 1 carry? Carried. Vote No. 5. Shall Vote No. 5 carry? Carried." But what is more important is that in committees of the whole House the members are allowed to speak more than once and are allowed to address questions to other members freely about the matter under consideration. The motion providing the question for the committee is there, perhaps only obscurely in the beginning, and at the end the chairman puts the question, but in the interval the members are permitted to range fairly freely. In contrast, when the speaker is in the Chair, each member is supposed to speak with strict relevance to the question, and only once. Queries may be directed to the member who is addressing the House, but only with his permission and out of his limited time; thus, the queries are enveloped by his speech.

When the time has come for a member to move a motion of which he has given notice, normally it is the speaker, not the member, who states the words of the motion. He simply reads out the text set forth in the notice, and then calls on the member. A motion moved when the speaker is in the Chair must have a seconder, but seconders seldom speak. If the notice has been given by a minister, the speaker will select one of the other ministers then present—probably the government house leader—to name as the seconder. When the notice has been given by a private member, unless the member indicates the seconder, the speaker will select some other member of the same party then present, perhaps the member's seat-mate, to name as the seconder; but since collective responsibility does not apply outside the government, the speaker sometimes has to use discretion in picking a seconder. Those chosen at random may decline the honour.

After the mover has spoken—or after the seconder in cases in which seconding is more than a formality, such as when an Address in Reply to the Speech from the Throne is moved—the speaker *proposes the question* to the House. The debate then begins. At the end of the debate, the speaker *puts the question* to the House. After the House has voted, he states how the question has been answered. The result of a decision by the House is either a *resolution* or an *order*. The House expresses its opinions by resolutions. It expresses its will by orders.

Taken alone resolutions bind nobody; but often they are sought by the government as evidence of support for government action. For example, in 1918, when the Borden government wished to put aside by order in council under the War Measures Act the exemptions provided by the Military Service Act, a motion was moved and carried in the House approving the terms that the government intended to include in its order in council.[4] Although the resolution of the House had no legal effect, when the validity of the order was tested in the Supreme Court of Canada some of the judges admitted that they found the resolution impressive as a support for the validity of the order. It is by resolutions that the House states its approval of treaties made by the Crown, if approval is sought. For example, in 1964, the House by resolution gave its approval to the Columbia River Treaty.[5] Again, in 1964, the House resolved to concur in the report of the Special Committee on the National Flag of Canada.[6] Subsequently, on 15 February 1965, the flag recommended by the committee became Canada's national flag, not by order of the House, and not by Act of Parliament, but by royal proclamation.

The orders of the House are narrowly limited in their immediate effect. They serve to guide the speaker and other members, and to direct the clerk, the sergeant at arms, and the other officers of the House. Some orders are particular; for example, an order that a specified bill be now read a second time, an order that the sergeant at arms take a specified person into custody, or an order made pursuant to Standing Order 33, the closure rule, that a debate is not to be adjourned to another sitting. Other orders are general. The latter continue in effect until revoked, and apply in all instances unless by special order an exemption is made.

Such general orders are known as *standing orders*. Orders made for the duration of a session, even although renewed regularly, are known as *sessional orders*.

It is by motions (and the consequent resolutions and orders) that various forms of messages are prepared and transmitted by the House. The contents of the Address in Reply are proposed in a motion, and that motion is debated. Motions to amend the proposed message may be moved. When the content of the message has been determined, another motion is moved directing that the Address be engrossed and presented to the governor general. (Before the 1968-69 session the motion provided that the Address was to be presented by "such Members of this House as are members of the Privy Council." Since 23 September 1968, the motion provides that the Address is to be presented by the speaker. This change, like his advancement in the order of protocol announced on 20 December 1968, was intended to elevate the speaker's status.) When an amendment by the British Parliament to the British North America Act is desired, a motion for "an humble Address" to the queen, specifying the terms of the amendment, is moved. If the House of Commons wishes to communicate with the Senate—in relation, for example, to the appointment of a special joint committee—a motion is moved that a message be sent (by the clerk) to the Senate. Unquestionably the most important form of message is the bill, a request by the House and the Senate to the Queen in Parliament asking that she state the law to be as set forth in the bill. The preparation of bills by the House takes place through a process of motions (and consequent orders).

The classification of motions is basic to the procedure of the House because some classes take precedence over others; some are debatable, while others are not; and some may be amended freely, while others may be amended only in specific ways, or not at all.

First, some motions are intrinsically procedural: they relate directly to the activities of the House itself, and only indirectly—but not necessarily insignificantly—to any business before the House. The most notable motions in this class are (a) the motion that the House do now adjourn, and (b) the motion that a debate be adjourned. In a committee of the whole House the motion comparable to the motion for the adjournment of the debate is the motion "that the committee rise, report progress, and ask leave to sit again." Each of these motions is standardized in form. Second, there are the motions ancillary to the legislative process. These are the motions by which a bill is moved forward stage after stage, e.g., "that Bill C-000 be now read a second time...." The ancillary motions, too, are invariable in form. Third, there are the motions by which the text of a bill is accepted in committee and at the report stage. A fourth kind is the substantive motion. Such motions stand alone. To have their intended meaning, they do not need to be related to some other resolution(s) or order(s) of the House. They are introduced to elicit an independent statement of the opinion or the will of the House. Fifth, there are motions to amend a question already under debate. In addition there are some special kinds of motions that can be moved only in special ways and circumstances, e.g., the motion to adjourn moved under Standing Order 26, the motion for the closure of debate in the House or consideration in a committee of the whole House under Standing Order 33, opposition motions on supply days under Standing Order 58, and time-allotment motions under Standing Orders 75A, 75B, and 75C. These will be explained in later chapters.

Since the House always must be in control of itself, the procedural motions for adjournment of the House or a debate always are in order, subject to restrictions imposed by the House; consequently, these motions can be used to disrupt debates. However, their effectiveness for dilatory purposes is limited. First, they are not debatable: they bring on only a division. Second, they may not be moved repetitiously: a new attempt to adjourn a debate or to adjourn the House may not be made unless there has been another proceeding subsequent to the previous attempt.

Mention must be made of the oft-misunderstood motion on "the previous question." This motion was originated at Westminster early in the seventeenth century as a means of terminating a debate without having to decide the question.[7] Those who for any reason wished to avoid a vote, and thus to avoid the results of voting against a popular motion, would have a member move a second motion, "That the question be now put." The House would continue to debate the previous question under the guise of this new question. (Since the previous question was not directly before the House, no amendments could be moved to it.) After all the members who wished to do so had spoken, the new question was put. At that point those who had promoted that question voted negatively. If they had the majority, the outcome was that the previous question was not put to the House; but if they were in the minority, the previous question was put immediately. In the British House of Commons the form of the previous-question motion has been changed—it now reads, "that the question be not now put"—to enable those who promote the motion to vote affirmatively.[8] In short, at Westminster the previous-question motion is still available, although it is used rarely, as a means of aborting a debate. In contrast, at Ottawa the motion has retained the earlier wording; and as a result the motion has come to be regarded as a closure motion. If the majority wishes to vote for a question, and can move "the previous question" before an amendment has been interposed, they can limit the debate to a single round. This form of closure is seldom used now because to avoid at least one amendment motion and one sub-amendment motion, and thus at least three rounds of debate—with each member eligible to speak once on the main motion, on the amendment, and on the sub-amendment—the previous question must be moved before even one opposition spokesman has had a chance to speak (and to move an amendment).

The most famous Canadian instance of the use of "the previous question" occurred on 9 April 1913. When Prime Minister Borden had concluded the speech in which he moved that a closure rule be added to the standing orders of the House, Sir Wilfrid Laurier attempted to gain the floor. He intended to move an amendment to the prime minister's motion, and thus to protract the debate. But Mr. W. B. Northrup was on his feet to move, "That the Minister of Marine and Fisheries, being the member for the City and County of St. John, be now heard." Amid cries of "Shame!" the House divided. Northrup's motion was carried. The minister, Mr. Hazen, then made a one-sentence speech: "I move, seconded by Mr. Cochrane, that this question be now put." Consequently, Sir Wilfrid Laurier had to speak, not on Mr. Borden's motion, which would have been amendable, but on Mr. Hazen's motion, which was not amendable; indeed, the entire debate on the 1913 rules changes took place on Hazen's motion for the previous question. The question on his motion was put to the House on 23 April 1913. After it had carried, Mr. Borden's motion was put to the House immediately.[9]

Once the House has begun a debate, or has resumed an adjourned debate on a motion, the debate continues—on the original question (and any proposed amendment and sub-amendment), or on the original question as amended, or on "the previous question"—until (a) it is interrupted by a decision to adjourn the debate or the House, (b) an appointed time that day—either the end of the private members' hour or the hour of daily adjournment—or (c) the question is either withdrawn or decided. If the appointed time ends, the question remains in suspense until the debate has been resumed at a later sitting. (This, of course, explains the fate of most private member's bills and motions: the session ends before the questions relating to them have been answered by the House.) If a motion or a bill has lost the favour of its supporters usually they will simply let it stand; but occasionally a member will seek the leave of the House to withdraw an item already under debate. Decisions are made by the House—it votes—when the members have nothing more to say, when the House has decided by special order that the question is to be put, or when the hour (if any) prescribed in the standing orders has been reached.

A maxim now followed so thoroughly that it ranks as a principle is that *if possible the House is not to be taken by surprise*. There is now almost no important proceeding that can be initiated without notice.

Until 1968 the standard period of notice was forty-eight hours; for most purposes it still is. If the motion to be moved will propose an Address to the queen, or a resolution of the House, or the appointment of a special committee, or that an order paper question be addressed to a minister, or that leave be given for the introduction of a bill, the member must give "forty-eight hours" notice. Such a notice is laid on the Table by the member—that is, it is handed to the clerk either at the Table or in his chambers—ordinarily before six o'clock p.m., but before five o'clock p.m. on Fridays. It then is deemed to be before the House, and may be examined by any member. A notice is effective from the day on which it is tabled. This means that a Member who has tabled a notice late on Monday afternoon will be in order insofar as the notice requirement is concerned if he moves his motion on the following Wednesday or any day thereafter. If he has given his notice on a Friday afternoon, insofar as the notice requirement is concerned he may move his motion on the following Monday or any day thereafter.[10]

For two kinds of motions that require written notice the period is only twenty-four hours. The first of these is "opposition motions" on supply days. Before the 1968 reforms the opposition could bring a question before the House without notice by moving an amendment to a government motion that the speaker leave the Chair (to enable the members to sit as the Committee of Supply). Often these amendments stated or implied no confidence. When an amendment might be moved was known because the government's motion was amendable and debatable on only certain occasions; but just what the amendment would say remained a guarded secret until it was moved—sometimes as the very last words of the mover's speech—with the result that the government might not be ready to debate the subject raised by the amendment. The minister under attack might even be in St. John's or Victoria. Under the new supply procedures adopted on 20 December 1968, the parties in opposition move their "supply day" motions as main motions, not as amendments; and do so after having given twenty-four hours notice. The second kind of motion that requires less than forty-eight hours notice are those proposing amendments to public bills at the report stage. Under the rules adopted on 20 December 1968, a member may propose an amendment to a public bill that has been considered by a standing committee (or a special committee) when the report of the committee is before the House. For each such motion a twenty-four hours notice is required.

Each member receives a copy of all written notices. Every morning during a session three papers, each in fascicle or pamphlet form, are distributed to all members. The best known of these is the *Debates of the House of Commons*, known to members and the public alike as *Hansard*. Each issue of *Hansard* contains a verbatim report of what was said at a sitting of the House. The other two papers are: (1) Votes and Proceedings, and (2) the Order Paper and Notices. The former, Votes and Proceedings, is compiled *after* a sitting. It contains, as its name implies, a terse or minute record of the decisions and transactions of the House at a sitting. At the end of each session a version of these minutes—excluding any items of only ephemeral importance—is published under the title, *Journals of the House of Commons*. The *Journals* are the official permanent record of the business done by the House at a session. The third paper, the Order Paper, is prepared and circulated *before* each sitting. In it are listed all the items of business in the various categories—Government Orders, Questions, Private Bills, etc.—that may be brought up, if reached, at the sitting for which the paper was prepared. In short, the Order Paper is the agenda paper.[11]

Until 1971 each notice given by a member was recorded in an appendix to the Votes and Proceedings of the sitting at which the notice was given. However, as already mentioned, when the standing orders were changed on 20 December 1968, provision was made for members to move amendments to public bills at the report stage after a twenty-four hours notice. So that the members could have the texts of these proposed amendments conveniently available whenever the report stage of a bill was undertaken by the House, which often is highly unpredictable, it was decided that these notices would be carried forward from day to day; as a result, they are now printed, not in the Votes and Proceedings of the day on which they were tabled, but in the daily Order Paper. At the same time it was decided that it would be more convenient for the members if the notices of opposition motions on supply days, too, appeared in the Order Paper. These two changes started a query: since the Order Paper for the next sitting and the Votes and Proceedings for the previous sitting are distributed to the members at the same time, why should not all notices be printed in the Order Paper? This practice was adopted on 27 October 1969. All twenty-four hours and forty-eight hours written notices now are printed in a Notice Paper which appears as the final part of the daily Order Paper. At the beginning of the 1974 session the Order Paper was re-titled Order Paper and Notices.

It is by examining the Notice Paper that a member first comes to know about the bills that the government and the private members intend to introduce, about government motions, about private members' substantive motions, about motions for the production of papers, about forthcoming order paper questions, and about motions for concurrence in the reports of standing and special committees. Here, too, the member first comes to know the content of opposition motions to be moved on supply days, and about report-stage amendments to bills. After the required period of notice has elapsed, each proposed motion or question is transferred by the clerk to the list under the appropriate handing on the Order Paper; for example, a notice of a motion for leave to introduce a bill given before six on a Monday will appear on Tuesday on the Notice Paper and on Wednesday on the Order Paper under the head, Introduction of Bills, one of the categories of routine business. Similarly, after standing for forty-eight hours as a notice an order paper question will be added to the list of such questions on the Order Paper.

In the case of a closure motion under Standing Order 33 or a time-apportionment motion under Standing Order 75C the notice is given orally "at a previous sitting" by a minister "from his place in the House." Since the debates to which these motions refer already are in progress the time of the notice is shorter than normal; however, the method is highly dramatic.

Since the House is the master of its own proceedings, the notice requirement often is waived to permit members to move non-contentious motions without delay, and sometimes even highly contentious motions are expedited "by leave" if all those present agree that some kind of action is needed just as soon as possible.[12]

But to say all this is not to say that no motions may be moved without either notice or leave; indeed, most motions require neither. First, every substantive motion—any motion that would eventuate in either an order or a resolution which would be fully meaningful without reference to any other decision of the House—requires a notice (or leave). But a motion to amend a substantive motion does not, for the members will have been alerted by the notice given for the substantive motion. Second, the motion for leave to introduce a bill requires notice, but all the subsequent motions in the legislative process, other than those for amendments at the report stage, require no notice. For example, no notice is required for a motion that a bill be now read a second time. These motions are moved at times which in theory are fixed by order of the House, and in completely standardized forms. Nobody can plead surprise. Third, certain motions directly related to the status of the House or the orderly conduct of business require no notice. If the speaker finds that the facts cited indicate prima facie that the privileges of the House have been breached, a motion to refer the complaint or charge to the Standing Committee on Privileges and Elections is in order without notice to the House. If two or more members rise to speak at the same time a motion may be moved that one of them "be now heard." If a member has been named by the speaker for disregarding the authority of the Chair a motion that the member be suspended from the service of the House for a stated period is in order. And, fourth, a simple motion to adjourn a debate, or to adjourn the House to the next sitting requires no notice.

When a bill is being considered in committee motions for changes in the text and for the approval of the clauses are moved without notice: that such motions may be moved has been made obvious by the decision of the House to send the bill to a committee. However, although no notice is required for the motion for concurrence by the House in the report of a standing (or special) committee on a bill, as mentioned before, any member who wishes to move an amendment to the text of the bill at that stage must, by notice, make the terms of his motion to amend available to the House at least twenty-four hours before the House begins the report stage.

At Westminster extensive use is made of the procedural motion, "That this House do now adjourn," to provide opportunities for debates on important substantive matters. Highly complex situations about which it would be virtually impossible to frame a satisfactory question often are debated on an adjournment motion put forward by a minister as the main item of business for the day. This is done only after consultation with the opposition through "the usual channels," and on a day announced by the leader of the House. In other words, in effect notice has been given. In contrast, the practice at Ottawa since 1906 has been that ordinary motions to adjourn are not debatable. The intention of the mover may be simply to terminate a sitting either before or after the fixed hour of daily adjournment, or it may be dilatory, but in either case the motion does not initiate a debate, and no notice is required. Since 1906 the only circumstance in which a motion to adjourn is debatable is when it has been moved under the terms of Standing Order 26; however, although under that rule no notice to the House is required, special leave is a prerequisite, and when leave has been given, the House is not asked to debate the motion immediately or to reach a decision at the end of the debate.[13]

The effect of the rules that there can be no debate without a motion and that a substantive motion must be preceded by a notice was demonstrated during the Munsinger incident. On Thursday, 10 March 1966, the Hon. Douglas Harkness, prompted by an answer given by the Hon. Lucien Cardin, the minister of justice, submitted that the minister's statement constituted a breach of privilege and then sought to move a motion. His proposed motion was, "That the Minister of Justice be required forthwith to substantiate the charges made inside and outside this Chamber which have reflected unfortunately and improperly upon members of Her Majesty's Privy Council, or alternatively that he be asked to submit his resignation and to atone by the forfeiture of his seat." Mr. Speaker Lamoureux ruled that while there was a prima facie case of privilege, the proposed motion was unacceptable because it did not specify the charge against the minister. The Hon. Gordon Churchill then said: "Mr. Speaker, you have allowed the question of privilege and it can be further discussed even though you suggest that the motion was not put in the proper form. Am I correct in that conclusion?" The speaker replied "No. There is nothing before the house. I know the hon. member realizes this. There was a question of privilege which was not followed by a proper motion. There is nothing before the house and we cannot debate a motion which has not been accepted." A minute or two later Mr. Eric Nielsen said: "Mr. Speaker, I should like to move, seconded by the member for Calgary North (Mr. Harkness), that the Minister of Justice do resign." Immediately the speaker responded: "I cannot accept this motion. I suggest to the hon. member that this is a substantive motion and would require notice." Somewhat later Mr. David Lewis sought to move, "That this house now stand adjourned until 6 p.m. this day." This motion, too, was out of order; because it was not a simple adjournment motion, it fell into the category of a substantive motion. Then when the minister of finance began to speak on the order of the day, the motion for the second reading of the bill to amend the Bank Act, Mr. Churchill moved, "That the hon. Member for Winnipeg North Center (Mr. Knowles) be now heard." That motion was defeated, 98 to 124, Later Mr. Knowles managed to get the floor, and moved, "That the House do now adjourn." This motion was defeated, 98 to 124. Despite the speaker's patient efforts to prevent discussion without a motion, the House wallowed for three days—Thursday, Friday, and Monday—but eventually demonstrated that he had been right from the beginning by abandoning as hopeless a situation in which the plaintiffs were not prepared to move an appropriate motion.

A majority of those voting, not a majority of the membership, is required to carry a motion. Standing Order 5 declares that: "Every Member is bound to attend the service of the House, unless leave of absence has been given him by the House." What we have here is an indicative statement disguised as an order. It is true, of course, as S.O. 6 implies—and this is what it was meant to imply—that membership in the House is not similar to membership in a club. Unfortunately the standing order, while valid with this meaning, is misleading: it seems to imply that attendance in the Chamber whenever the House is sitting is a member's most important obligation. Obviously this is not true for ministers; and, given the functions of the House and the range of public demands on their time, it is not true for private members either. Members will be away from the Chamber, and at times they will be away from Ottawa; therefore, means other than a standing order such as S.O. 5 are needed to assure that all the members are not away at once. Nowadays the parties, especially the ministerial party and the official opposition, undertake "to keep" a House.[14]

The fact that members will be absent from sittings for various reasons, legitimate and otherwise, raises the possibility that only a handful may be present at a sitting. That handful then would constitute the House. Since the House always is master of its own proceedings, it is quite conceivable that a small and unanimous clique, finding that it was the House, might allow substantive motions to be moved without notice and then to be carried, and might allow bills to be introduced without notice and to be advanced through all their stages at one sitting. Such sittings might not be calamitous in their immediate results, but at the very least they soon would destroy the authority of the House. The obvious means for preventing such a sitting, or anything resembling such a sitting, is a fixed quorum, However, a high quorum would make it possible for the House to be impeded by members who stayed away either unwittingly or deliberately. The higher the quorum the greater the power of uninterested members and of those opposed to parliamentary action. The conclusion must be that the quorum ought to be as low as possible, compatible with its purpose. In the case of the Canadian House of Commons the quorum as set by the B.N.A. Act is twenty members, in effect, the speaker and nineteen others. This means that decisions may be made by votes of ten to nine. It must be assumed that any member who absents himself is prepared to acquiesce in, and to accept as his own, the decision of the House, for the quorum requirement assures that business will not brought on surreptitiously.[15]

The House makes some decisions for which a simple majority is either insufficient or is not required under its standing orders. When a member proposes that the House continue to sit beyond the hour of daily adjournment the motion to sit late may not be put if ten members object. When a member asks for leave to move the adjournment under Standing Order 26, if the speaker decides that a discussion of the matter raised would be proper, the member needs the support of only twenty members to overcome any objection. But all such questions relate to proposed changes in the ordinary program of the House, and the special requirements are highly favourable to the private members.

Decision by simple majority is a method which has no procedural bias for or against change. When minority approval is sufficient to carry a motion, the procedure is loaded in favour of those who advocate change. When special majorities, e.g., two-thirds of those voting or a majority of the parties, are required, the procedure is loaded in favour of those who favour the status quo. From a procedural point of view the rationale of decision by simple majority is that it is the method that makes the least prejudgement.[16] The importance of this concept is best illustrated by reference to the tradition governing votes by the speaker. He is prohibited by the standing orders from participating in debates, and he is prohibited from voting ordinarily by the B.N.A. Act, but when the other members are equally divided on a question he is required by that Act to vote. The tradition, following Westminster, is that he is to vote in the way that will preserve the status quo, for thereby —by leaving the matter open—he is more likely to give the House an opportunity to deal with the question again later. Lord Campion makes the point as follows: "...it seems that the guiding principle is that a Speaker does not on his sole responsibility make a change in the *status quo*, and in particular that he takes the course which is best calculated to avoid change in the law, to uphold previous decisions of the House or a committee, or to maintain constitutional usage."[17]

How the House votes on a question is ascertained by the Chair by different methods involving different degrees of formality and accuracy. At one extreme are instances, as for example when a member moves for leave to introduce a bill, when the speaker knows what the almost unvaried decision of the House is in such instances, and accordingly simply puts the question and announces the decision, "Carried," in the same breath. A member or two, may cry out, "No," or "Never," but the speaker moves on to the next item unless he thinks that the objection is meant as a request that the vote be taken in a more accurate way, in which case he will ask for the "Yeas" and "Nays."

In committees of the whole House the chairman asks all those in favour of a motion to stand. After the members standing in a row have been counted by one of the clerks, beginning with the row nearest the centre aisle, they are asked to be seated to give the clerk an unobstructed view of the row immediately behind. Then all those opposed are asked to stand, and are counted in the same way. For votes in committees there is no bell to call in the members, a member need not be in his assigned place to be counted, and how each member has voted is not recorded.

Sometimes on minor questions or in reply to a series of related questions following a formal division of the House the members in the minority will call out, "On Division," to save the time and trouble of going through an actual count. In such cases these words appear in *Hansard* to indicate that the motion was opposed although no count was made.

On other occasions in the House the speaker gauges the relative strength of the sides by asking for the "Yeas" and "Nays" and then announces, "In my opinion the Yeas (Nays) have it." This method has the advantage of being fast; but it is uncertain, for sometimes the minority is in far better voice than the majority. Moreover, it measures only the views of those in the Chamber at the time. Accordingly, this method is used to attain final decisions on only minor questions. But it is used in a second way. It is always used as the preliminary to a formal division of the House. After the speaker has heard the Yeas and Nays and has announced his opinion, five members may bring on a division merely by rising. On seeing five or more members standing, the speaker orders, "Call in the members," and the Commons bells throughout the Centre Block, the West Block, and the Confederation Building begin to ring. (They have a harsh, importunate sound which distinguishes them from the tintinnabulation by which senators are called to their Chamber in the east end of the Centre Block.) How long the whips, one for the government and one for those in opposition, will keep the bells ringing is determined by various considerations. Naturally, the government whip will not let the division begin when he is short if by waiting he can remedy his plight; but for the opposition whip the number voting usually is of no great importance unless his party wants to make a very good showing for some special reason. Occasionally the bells ring long enough to let the prime minister, two or three ministers, or the leader of the opposition come bustling in from a dinner party somewhere in the city or its environs. Their advent in starched shirts causes merriment. Sometimes it is suspected that the whips conspire together to let the bells ring a few extra minutes on an amendment so as to leave just enough time for the vote on the main motion before the hour of adjournment, thus making it difficult for persistent members, who are often the most boring members, to take the floor once again.

When the whips have taken their seats, the bells are silenced. The speaker then rises to put the question. Thereafter, until the result has been announced, no member may enter or leave the Chamber, or move about within it. The speaker says: "All those *in favour* of the motion will please rise." If the motion is a party motion moved by the official opposition, the leader of the opposition will rise first, thus indicating that the party is to follow, and then each of the party faithful, starting at the speaker's left hand, row by row, rises and bows in the direction of the speaker, is recognized in a loud voice by name by the Table, and then seats himself. Each member's vote is recorded on a tally by the clerk (and subsequently in both Votes and Proceedings and in *Hansard*.) The larger (or largest) of the "third parties" votes next, and then the second (and third), if they are supporting the official opposition's motion. Finally, the speaker turns to the ranks of the government party to see if there are any dissidents. If the motion is a third-party motion the leader of the party and his followers vote first. When members no longer rise, the speaker says: "All those *opposed to* the motion will please rise." If the motion is a party motion moved by a member of the opposition, the prime minister always rises first. He is followed by the member seated at the speaker's right hand, and then, member by member, row by row, by all those voting with the prime minister. The other ministers vote in the sequence of their row, not as a group. Then the speaker always checks the other side of the House to see if there are those who wish to vote with the government. When all have voted, the clerk, in an audible voice, reports to the speaker the number of Yeas and the number of Nays, and then the speaker declares the motion lost or carried. Formal divisions often are referred to as "recorded votes." They are not "roll-calls," for the members vote by sides, Yeas and Nays, not alphabetically.

Some votes—notably those on the sub-amendments, amendments, and main motions relating to the Address in Reply and the Budget, no-confidence motions on supply days, and appropriations—come at times prescribed in the standing orders; for these the bells ring fifteen minutes, the time estimated as necessary to permit a disabled member to reach the Chamber from the upper floor of the West Block. (When the rule was adopted the Confederation Building, which is farther away, was not used as a members' office building.) The bell rings for fifteen minutes, too, when a recorded vote is to be taken at a time fixed in advance by a special order of the House. Other votes—for example, on dilatory motions, and, ordinarily, on second-reading and third-reading motions—take place at unpredictable times; for these the whips may keep the bells ringing at their own discretion.

A fifth principle is that *the session*, not the sitting, and not the life of a parliament, *is the basic time unit for procedural purposes.* It is the governor general who has the right to summon the members of the House and the senators to Parliament, and the right to terminate a session of Parliament; and only while it is in session is the House able to express an opinion or to have a will. Therefore on prorogation all the appointments made by the House expire. All the orders of the House die.[18] For this reason the House cannot appoint continuing executive, investigative, or legislative agencies. For example, no standing or special committee may sit between sessions.

The fact that the House is an active body only during a session is also of great importance in the conduct of parliamentary business. On the one hand it means that a new beginning must be made in each session: no bills and no motions carry over. The House may revive a bill from a previous session and give it an advanced standing.[19] It may send to a committee the evidence taken by that committee's predecessor in a previous session.[20] But this will not happen unless the House itself decides to order it in the new session. A prorogation wipes the slate clean. It frees the House from all the lumber which for one reason or another, including low priority, remains on the Order Paper at prorogation. On the other hand, the principle is the basis of two inter-related rules governing proceedings during a session. Once the House has declared its opinion or its will conclusively it cannot be asked to change its mind at that session. This means that defeated motions or hoisted bills cannot be brought forward again before the next session. Second, the House does not permit itself to be prevented from acting in the most effective way available at a session, e.g., one member by giving notice of a substantive motion cannot prevent another member from introducing a bill on the same topic at that session.

These five principles are basic. The most dynamic of the five is the principle that the House is master of its own proceedings. This is the one to watch. The House is limited by the constitutional fact that it cannot act except when in session, and by the requirement that decisions be made by majority vote, but beyond these points it is free to make its own arrangements and to change them. It can alter its notice requirements and even relax its emphasis on motions. Indeed, much of the procedure of the House is composed of rules and practices adopted by the House relative to the notices and motions required for the various kinds of business that come before it.

THREE

A Day in the House

Each sitting of the House of Commons normally takes place on a separate day of the week, but there is nothing to prevent the House from continuing to sit beyond midnight, or into a third or fourth day. For this reason the sessions are divided, not into days, but into "sitting days," or even more exactly, "sittings." There were 111 sittings in the 1912–13 session of Parliament, but two of those sittings lasted a total of twelve days. One sitting began at 3:00 p.m. on Monday, 3 March 1913, and continued until 12:00 p.m. (midnight) on Saturday, 8 March On the following Monday, 10 March the House met at 3:00 p.m., and continued until 11:32 p.m. on Saturday, 15 March. However, when there is no chance of misunderstanding "day" and "sitting" are used as interchangeable terms.

Visitors in the galleries often are bewildered by what they see and hear. Seldom do they have before them the Order Paper—the program for the day—but even if they did they still would have a great deal of trouble following the proceedings. The House does various kinds of business, each kind done in its own way. It moves from item to item. Some items move so slowly that a casual observer will detect no movement. Others go forward with astounding speed.

The basic distinction to be borne in mind when examining the procedures of the House is that between the horizontal and the vertical patterns of business. An ordinary bill normally takes at least three days (sittings) to pass the House. The bill will come before the House for at least a short time at three different, not necessarily consecutive, sittings. A budget debate requires slightly over six days: the minister of finance makes his budget statement in the evening, and then there are six days —not necessarily consecutive days—for the resumed debate. A total of twenty-five days in the House are provided for dealing with the Crown's annual requests for supplies of money. These are examples of movement across the calendar. But what is the structure of a day? What is the vertical pattern across which these horizontal patterns run? As we shall see, there is a program or structure of business which ordinarily is followed with great precision at every sitting. That program prevents members from asking questions, moving motions, and making speeches at will; but it does enable the House to work in an orderly way.

The program for a day in the House has been altered again and again over the years with two main aims. First, an effort has been made to apportion the available time among the various kinds of business according to their changing volume and importance. Some kinds that once figured prominently now require no more than an hour or two in an entire session. Second, an effort has been made to avoid wasting the members' time. On the one hand, a conscientious member has a great deal to do away from the Chamber. On the other hand, much that goes on in the Chamber requires the attention of only a few members, those who are interested in and informed about the business in progress. Nothing much is gained and much may be lost by arranging the daily program so that members have to sit in the Chamber or in the lobbies waiting. The most recent change—adopted experimentally on 24 March 1975, and made permanent on 12 December 1975—makes it possible for most of the ministers and private members to leave the Chamber shortly after 3:00 p.m.

We begin our analysis of the structure of a day with another distinction. The initial stages of the ordinary legislative process—the introduction of the bill and the first reading—are not debating stages. The later stages are. The motion for leave to introduce a bill and the subsequent motion for first reading are dealt with as routine proceedings. But once the first-reading stage has been completed the speaker asks, "When shall the said bill be read a second time?" The usual answer is, "At the next sitting of the House." In other words, the House makes an order specifying that the second-reading motion may be moved on a certain day. That motion—the standard second-reading motion—then is listed as one of the "orders of the day" for that day.

The distinction is between "routine proceedings" and "orders-of-the-day proceedings." It is not only the initial stages of legislation that are dealt with as routine proceedings. Various kinds of business—reports from committees, statements by ministers, etc.—are dealt with in that way. Nor are orders made only with regard to the later stages of bills. An order is made at each regular session—Government Order No. 1—for the business of supply. Orders are made specifying the day when the vote is to be taken on ways and means motions prior to the introduction of tax bills. What we have, then, is two phases of the daily sitting: one phase, Routine Proceedings, provides members with opportunities to bring certain business before the House, but usually without debate;

and the other, the Orders of the Day, is for dealing with items previously ordered for a day (or as many of those items as may be reached at that sitting).

The time during the orders-of-the-day phase is divided between the government and the private members. Under the standing orders made by the House in 1867 on three days of the week the balance of the sitting after the routine proceedings was available for business initiated by private members. On the other two days it was available for government business. Now, however, the basic provision for private members' business in one hour a day four times a week. All the rest of the time under Orders of the Day is at the disposal of the government.

Before 1913 it was fairly easy for private members to get the floor even on government days. Until 1906 the motion, "that the House do now adjourn" could be moved at any time by a member, and was debatable. This meant that a member who wished to bring up a matter had only to move the adjournment. Speaking to his motion he raised his grievance, question, or proposal. This put the government, indeed the House itself, very much at the mercy of individual private members. In 1906 the rules were changed so that thereafter an adjournment motion was not debatable except when moved under the strict conditions set forth in a new standing order—an order of which Standing Order 26 is the modern version. However, it still was possible for a member to raise any matter on any day when the government sought to have the members deal with either supply business or ways and means business. In 1913 that right was restricted. As their opportunities to take the floor were reduced the right of private members to address questions to the government "on the orders of the day" came to be of great importance.

From 1867 the House provided in its standing orders that members might address questions to ministers after written notice. To these the ministers made oral answer in the House. Because many of the answers were long and detailed, in 1910 the House changed its rules so that thereafter answers would be printed in the *Debates* unless a member had marked his question with an asterisk to indicate that he wanted the answer given orally. These questions—called "Order Paper Questions" because as soon as the notice time has expired they are printed in the Order Paper—lacked immediacy. Often they stood unanswered for days, even weeks. As a result, as the other ways in which private members could gain the floor were restricted, a new kind of questioning gained prominence. After the speaker has gone through the routine proceedings he announces, "Orders of the Day." This announcement came to be the signal for members to put oral questions to the ministers. "Mr. Speaker, before the Orders of the Day are called, may I ask the Prime Minister...." It was as if the private members could not bring themselves to settle down to the work appointed for the day until certain urgent and important questions about public affairs and national business had been answered. In this way a third phase, the Oral Question Period, was interposed between Routine Proceedings and the Orders of the Day. Although oral questions were not uncommon over the years, it was not until after World War II that they became a major part of almost every sitting. By 1964 so much time was being expended on oral questions that the appointed business of the day often was being reached very late. Accordingly, in that year the House by standing order placed a time limit on such questioning. At the same time, to compensate the private members for the restriction a period of short debates having their origins in members' dissatisfaction with the outcome of their interrogation of ministers was introduced at the end of the sitting on Monday, Tuesday, and Thursday. This proceeding—generally called "the late show"—is now another distinct phase of business on those days.

A sitting begins when the speaker takes the Chair at the hour fixed by the House in its standing orders (or in a special order made for a particular day) and sees a quorum. Once started, a sitting continues until the speaker adjourns the House by reason of the lack of a quorum, by reason of the arrival of the adjournment hour prescribed in the standing orders, or by reason of a special decision of the House to adjourn either earlier or later than usual. As a result of changes made in the standing orders on 20 December 1968, the sittings on Monday, Tuesday, and Thursday ordinarily begin at 2:00 p.m., and continue, with a two-hour suspension for dinner between 6:00 and 8:00 p.m., until 10:00 p.m., at which time the House turns away from the main business of the day. (If a vote is in progress at ten o'clock, it is not interrupted.) Then the House may spend up to thirty minutes on "the late show." On Wednesday the House ordinarily meets at 2:00 p.m., and adjourns at 6:00 p.m. On Friday it meets at 11:00 a.m., and continues until the hour of adjournment at 5:00 p.m., with a one-hour break between one and two o'clock.[1]

PRAYERS

Each day after the speaker has called the House to order, he reads the prayers. When he has concluded, he says, "Let the doors be opened." The various galleries then fill up with "strangers," and the members waiting in the lobbies enter the Chamber. Within two minutes he again calls the House to order.

STANDING ORDER 43

At almost every sitting the unanimous consent of the House is sought to make motions without notice. Standing Order 43 provides: "A motion may, in case of urgent and pressing necessity previously explained by the mover, be made by unanimous consent of the House without notice having been given under Standing Order 42." As we saw in chapter 2, it is a general requirement—under S.O. 42—that notice be given for all substantive motions. However, as we saw in that chapter also, the House is the master of its own proceedings: it can waive the notice requirement. The purpose of S.O. 43, which dates back to 1867, is to prevent the notice requirement from being waived too lightly: it can be waived only with the consent of all the members present. For over 100 years the rule caused no trouble; but in 1969, after the reforms of 1968 had been made, the possibilities for abusing the rule came to be appreciated and exploited. The rule allows a member to take the spotlight in prime time; it allows him to explain the urgent and pressing necessity for his motion; and then it allows him to read out the proposed motion.[2] Very rarely is consent given; but the real purpose of most of those who resort to S.O. 43 is to gain publicity for themselves or to draw attention to some cause or situation.

Again and again between 1969 and 1974 Mr. Speaker Lamoureux drew the abuse of the rule to the attention of the House; however, no way has been found to prevent abuse. Prior to 7 April 1975, when the new rules adopted on 24 March 1975 went into effect, members simply gave the speaker a private notice of their wish to be seen at the beginning of a sitting. But now requests for unanimous consent under S.O. 43 have been given a place in the daily program. They almost qualify as a routine proceeding. At the seventy-seven sittings from 7 April 1975, to 30 July 1975, when the summer adjournment began, there were 228 requests under S.O. 43. Only four were successful; none of these was of any great significance.

THE ORAL QUESTION PERIOD

Before 7 April 1975, the Oral Question Period came after Routine Proceedings and immediately before the main business of the day, and was limited to forty minutes. As already mentioned, it had developed from the early practice under which questions were asked occasionally just before the House turned to the orders of the day. In 1975 the Oral Question Period was cut free from the orders of the day, and moved forward. It now comes immediately after applications under S.O. 43 and any business for which there is time earlier, but never later than 2:15 p.m., and continues until 3:00 p.m. (On Friday the times are 11:15 a.m. and 12:00 noon.) The Oral Question Period is the high point of a sitting. Ordinarily it attracts more ministers, more private members, far more newsmen, and more spectators than any other part of a sitting. By moving it to a fixed hour the House has made it unnecessary for ministers and private members (and the press gallery) to sit through the routine proceedings, some of which are of unpredictable duration.

The Oral Question Period provides the most dramatic example of the operation of Responsible Government. The head of the government and many of his ministerial colleagues, as members of Parliament, are in their places in the House of Commons five times a week to deal with questions. The focus is not on legislation; rather, it is on the administrative policy and conduct of the ministers, both individually and collectively. The private members ask the questions; the ministers respond. The speaker sees first the leader of the opposition, then the leaders of the other opposition parties, and then other opposition members. Once in a while he glances to his right and sees a backbencher.

At Westminster the question period is based on what at Ottawa are called "Order Paper Questions." Each initial answer there is to a question of which a member has given notice, with the result that his question appears on the day's Order Paper. The minister then is the target of a small shower of oral "supplementaries" asked by the original questioner and by any other members who catch the speaker's eye. The minister has had notice of the initial question, but not of the supplementaries. Moreover, each minister answers questions on only specified days ascertained by a rota which brings up most ministers about once in every two or three weeks. This means that the question period on any day is a brief inquest into one department, or, if all the questions for the first minister(s) are dealt with quickly, into two or even three departments. If all the questions for the day have not been reached by the end of the time available, the answers are provided in writing, and, of course, in those cases there will be no supplementaries.

At Ottawa the question period is far more disorderly and exciting. There is no notice requirement; consequently, there is no danger, as at Westminster, that questions will have gone stale while waiting a minister's turn. Questions may be directed at any minister who is in the Chamber, including the prime minister. The result is that the period is a brief critical survey of the whole current operation of the Government of Canada based on news stories, on leaks by indiscreet or disaffected public servants, and on complaints from the public.

The basic requirement for an oral question is that it be sufficiently urgent and important to warrant the use of the time of the House. When the speaker thinks that a question does not meet these qualifications—urgency and importance—he may refuse to allow the minister to answer. This probably will annoy the minister more than the questioner, for the latter may have succeeded in putting a damaging suggestion before the public. Or the speaker may propose that the member put his question on the Order Paper. If the speaker thinks that a question is argumentative, frivolous, or hypothetical, he simply rules it out of order. For their part, ministers may deal with those questions allowed by the speaker as they think best. They may be painstakingly frank. They may be laconic. They may be verbose. They may "take the question as notice," and promise an answer later. Or they may say nothing. On 14 April 1975, Mr. Speaker Jerome commented that the basic principle to be followed during the question period "ought to be such that it will enable members to put questions with a minimum of interference. In examining the many precedents, I feel that the principle can best be stated as follows: a brief question seeking information about an important matter of some urgency which falls within the administrative responsibility of the government or of the specific minister to whom it is addressed is in order."[3]

Because of the gradual way in which the Oral Question Period emerged as a preliminary to the main business of the day, and the fact that no notice is required, the assumption was fostered that every minister in Ottawa was obliged to be present in the Chamber at every sitting. In the fall of 1968 in an effort to give the ministers more time for work in committees of the Cabinet or in their departments Prime Minister Trudeau made a small move towards the British system by announcing that only a certain number of ministers would be in the Chamber during the question period on each day or the week. This arrangement—known as "the roster system"—drew strong and constant denunciation as contrary to Responsible Government.[4] In January 1973, when the Liberals returned in a minority position after the election of 1972, the roster system was quietly abandoned.

ANNOUNCEMENTS, ETC.

Questions of privilege arising during the course of debate are to be taken up immediately, but the alleged breach may have taken place outside the House or during a member's absence. Immediately after the Oral Question Period a member who has given private notice to the speaker may raise a question of privilege. Although reminded again and again that "privilege" is a narrow term referring only to those special rights, those exemptions from the ordinary law of the land, that appertain to the House collectively and members individually to enable the House to function effectively as part of Parliament, members use the term very loosely to gain the floor to register complaints about ministerial announcements made outside the House, to correct newspapers, to give explanations, to mention birthdays, to mention the presence of sports stars in the galleries, and even to explain the presence of boxes of apples in the lobbies. On 9 July 1975, Prime Minister Trudeau raised "a special question of privilege" to congratulate Mr. Edward Broadbent on his elevation to the leadership of the New Democratic Party. That same point—immediately after oral questions—is used by the speaker, the prime minister, or the government house leader to make brief announcements. For example, on 14 April 1975, the prime minister drew attention to the death of the Hon. T. A. Crerar. Members who wish to correct mistakes in the *Hansard* report of their own words at the previous sitting may do so at this time.

Occasionally, when the number of applications under S.O. 43 is small announcements are made and minor points of privilege are raised before the beginning of the Oral Question Period at 2:15 p.m. On Thursday, 24 July 1975, the speaker was notified by Mr. J. M. Reid and two other members that they wished to raise questions of privilege as a result of an allegation in a Montreal newspaper, *The Gazette*, that Mr. Reid had leaked tax information. He proposed that Mr. Reid be heard before the Oral Question Period. This arrangement made it possible for Mr. Reid to bring up the matter before questions about the allegation were addressed to ministers. As a result the Oral Question Period began at 2:40 and continued until 3:25 p.m. Mr. Reid did not make his motion on Thursday because he wished to give the newspaper time in which to apologize. This it did not do. On Friday, 25 July the speaker recognized Mr. Reid under Motions, at which point he moved that the matter be referred to the Standing Committee on Privileges and Elections. The motion was debated for about one hour, and then was carried.

ROUTINE PROCEEDINGS

After the Oral Question Period has ended—ordinarily no later than 3:00 o'clock—the speaker reads through the list of all the categories of routine proceedings: (a) presenting reports from standing and special committees; (b) tabling of documents; (c) statements by ministers; (d) introduction of bills; (e) first reading of senate public bills; (f) government notices of motions; and (g) motions. Sometimes there will be no item in a category for days on end. Once in a while there will be at least one item under each head. Usually the speaker knows either from the notice paper or from private notices what reaction each head on the list of routine proceedings will evoke.

(a) Presenting Reports From Standing and Special Committees If one of these committees has a report ready for presentation to the House, the chairman of the committee rises and is recognized by the speaker, and then states that he has "the honour to present in both official languages

the Xth report of the Standing (or the Special) Committee on...." The report then will be printed in the Votes and Proceedings of that sitting. Long and substantively important reports may also be printed as separate documents so that they will be conveniently available to the public. Many reports are designed merely to inform the members; but some will contain recommendations to the House with the result that it may be thought desirable to follow the presentation of the report with a motion for concurrence. If the recommendations are important or controversial the chairman will wait for the notice period—forty-eight hours—to elapse; but if they relate only to the powers or sittings of the committee and he knows that no member of the committee is opposed, he may ask that the notice requirement be waived so that he may move concurrence at the sitting at which the report was presented. In that case, the chairman will pave the way for this alternative immediately after he has presented the report by adding words to the following effect: "I propose to move concurrence later this day, if the House gives its consent." When such advice is given a clerk at the Table will read out the report—these reports normally consist of no more than three or four sentences—so that the House will know to what its concurrence is about to be sought. Otherwise, as mentioned, the members will receive the text of the report in the Votes and Proceedings of that day.

(b) Tabling of Documents This is a new category of routine business. Until 1968 a minister who wished to make a paper, report, etc. available to the House (and the public) had to seek leave to lay the document on the Table unless the tabling was required either by a statute or by an order of the House. Normally he made a statement to justify his request, and that statement might evoke a flurry of opposition comments. On 20 December 1968, a new standing order was added. It allows a minister (or a parliamentary secretary on behalf of a minister) to state that he proposes to lay upon the Table any report or other paper dealing with a matter under the administrative responsibility of the government. Thereupon, the document "... shall be deemed for all purposes to have been laid before the House." Prior to 24 March 1975, there was no head under routine proceedings for the tabling of documents in this way. Usually they were tabled under Motions. Tabling, it will be noted, in the House of Commons means that a paper or notice is made available to the House for examination. It does not mean that a matter has been shelved.

(c) Statements by Ministers This, too, is a new head. Statements by ministers with regard to government policy, followed by comments by

opposition spokesmen, are far from new. The practice before 1964 was for a minister to make his statement about happenings or about changes in policy under Motions, which then was the second routine proceeding. Ostensibly he intended to conclude with a motion. In fact, at the end of his statement he simply resumed his seat. Out of fairness opposition spokesmen were allowed to comment on the statement. On 7 May 1964, in an effort to stop long, partisan ministerial statements and opposition comments, "statements on motions" were authorized by the standing orders, and limits on both the statement and the comments were prescribed. On 24 March 1975, these statements were removed from the old Motions grab-bag, and were given their own place in the daily program. Moreover, the procedure was changed so that it now is in order for members to ask the minister questions about the content of a statement.[5]

While Parliament is in session most important government announcements are made as statements in the House. For example, on 13 October 1970, the secretary of state for external affairs announced that diplomatic relations were to be established with the People's Republic of China. Occasionally, when Motions was the head under which statements were made, if the House had moved on to other business it would agree to revert to Motions. For example, on 22 October 1962, the House reverted to Motions so that Prime Minister Diefenbaker might make a statement about the Cuba crisis. Again, on 29 June 1965, the House reverted to Motions to permit Prime Minister Pearson to make a statement—in which he announced that the Hon. Guy Favreau had resigned as minister of justice—subsequent to the tabling earlier that day of the Dorion Report. On 24 February 1967, the House reverted to Motions to permit the minister of finance to table the report of the (Carter) Royal Commission on Taxation and to make a statement. It is to be assumed that under the new arrangement the House will revert to Statements by Ministers when to do so seems desirable.

(d) Introduction of Bills   After a member—either a minister or a private member—who wishes to place the draft of a public bill before the House has given the forty-eight-hours notice required by the standing orders, he will be recognized by the speaker under this head. The member merely bows to indicate his readiness to proceed. (If for any reason he does not wish to proceed that day he will say, "Stand.") The speaker then states the standard motion for leave: "(Mr. Macdonald), seconded by (Mr. Leblanc), moves for leave to introduce a bill entitled . . . ." It is unnecessary for either mover or seconder to utter as much as a single word.[6]

If the bill is being introduced by a minister the speaker assumes that the motion for leave carries, and at once proceeds to put the question on the next motion, the motion that the bill be read a first time. He assumes that this motion, too, carries. Next, he asks the House to make an order specifying when the motion for the second reading of the bill is to be moved. He suggests the answer to his own question by asking, "At the next sitting of the House?" If there is no objection—if there is, it will cause surprise—a second-reading motion will appear on the next day's Order Paper under the head, Government Orders.

If the bill is being introduced by a private member a little more time may be required. Since there is no other procedure by which a public bill may be introduced in the Canadian House of Commons by a private member after the beginning of a session, and since, as we shall see, the session probably will end before the member has had a chance to speak in support of the second reading of his bill, the practice is for a member's friends to cry out, "Explain" before the motion for leave to introduce the bill is carried. This gives the member an opportunity to state the purpose of his bill in two or three carefully prepared sentences, but no more. On 13 May 1975, for example, Mr. Leonard C. Jones, sought leave to introduce a bill—C-389 (1974–76)—to amend the Canada Elections Act. When invited to explain, he said: "Mr. Speaker, the purpose of this bill is to delete certain references in the Canada Elections Act to political party affiliation, and in particular the need for a certificate on a nomination paper by a party leader or his delegate, the reasons for which should be obvious to all members of this House and the public generally; that is, in order to preserve democracy and freedom of choice." Once the explanation has been given, the Speaker will assume, as he did in this instance, that the motion for leave has carried, and he will proceed to put the motion for the first reading. Normally this motion, too, carries without objection even when the bill treats of a highly controversial topic, for the members are reluctant to spend time in voting on a motion relating to a bill that they have not even had a chance to read.[7] Again, as in the case of a minister's bill, after the first-reading motion has been carried and a clerk at the Table has executed the order that the bill be read by announcing, "First reading of this bill," the speaker asks the House to make an order as to when the second-reading motion is to be moved. Normally again the decision is, "At the next sitting of the House." The standard second-reading motion then will be added to the next day's Order Paper under the head, Public Bills.[8]

Government bills and private members' bills are treated much the same when introduced and given first reading. Moreover, the legislative process is the same for the remaining stages. The great difference is that government bills are dealt with in government time while the others must wait their turn during private members' hours. It is when entered on the Order Paper for second reading that the wheat and chaff are separated. Only private members' bills are put down under the head, Public Bills. Government bills are put down under a special head, Government Orders. Before the 1974 session the obsolete idea that all bills are formally equal was retained in the numbering of bills: all were numbered in sequence as introduced. The new practice is to reserve a block of numbers—the first 99 in the 1974 session, the first 199 in the 1974-76 session—for government bills, so that the private member's bill first introduced in the fall of 1974 was numbered C-201. At the beginning of each session to show that the House may deal with items of business not initiated by the Crown a bill is introduced and given first reading before the House turns its attention to the contents of the Speech from the Throne. That bill is numbered C-1.

(e) First Reading of Senate Public Bills Once a bill introduced in the Senate has passed that House it is transmitted by the clerk of the Senate to the clerk of the House of Commons. No motion for leave to introduce is required, for the bill already is before Parliament. The motion for first reading carries without delay, and an order—again almost invariably, "At the next sitting of the House"—is made for the second-reading motion. If the bill is a government bill, the second-reading motion will be put down under Government Orders. If a private member moved for first reading the second-reading motion will be added to the list under Public Bills. Bills introduced in the Senate are numbered S-1, S-2, etc.

(f) Government Notices of Motions The standing orders require that the House be given forty-eight-hours notice of any substantive motion. Notice is given by having the proposed motion set forth, with the member's name, in the Notice Paper. After the required time has elapsed each new private member's notice is transferred by the clerk to the Order Paper at the bottom of the list under the head, Notices of Motions. (Although the notice time has elapsed, they are not motions until moved.) In contrast, since the government has the right to give a new motion priority over other items and may wish to do so, the speaker calls all government notices of motions as soon as the notice time has elapsed, and transfers them then and there to the Order Paper under the head, Government Orders. The government house leader then may have one or two of them dealt with by the House just as soon as the orders-of-the-day phase of that sitting has been reached.

(g) Motions Over the years various kinds of motions have been sorted out and assigned their own places in the daily program, e.g., private members' motions, motions for leave to introduce bills, and motions

to adjourn under S.O. 26. However, the general head, Motions, has survived to accommodate the residuum, which now consists chiefly of motions for concurrence in committee reports and motions intended to produce special orders relating to the sittings and proceedings of the House. For example, the chairman of a standing committee who, in the manner described above, has had a report read out at the Table will be recognized by the speaker after the head, Motions, has been reached; and the chairman then will seek leave to move concurrence. This he will do by saying: "By leave, I move that the Xth report of the Standing Committee on..., presented earlier this day, be now concurred in." If any member objects, i.e., refuses to agree that permission be granted to proceed without the forty-eight-hours notice, the motion will not be proposed by the speaker. On the other hand, if the chairman has opted for the usual method, i.e., if he allowed two days to elapse from the time the report was presented, the speaker will recognize him under Motions, and he then may move his motion for concurrence without leave. Motions for concurrence, as we shall see in chapter 8, may be moved by members other than committee chairmen.

When the government house leader wishes to make a motion of limited effect relating to the operation of the House—one that will not alter the standing orders—for example, the motion prescribing when a forthcoming Christmas, Easter, or summer adjournment is to begin and end, he will make it under Motions, either by leave or after notice.

The fact that the kind of motions admissible under Motions is strictly limited has important practical consequences. For example, in 1961 the Liberals were eager to have Mr. James Coyne, the governor of the Bank of Canada, appear before a committee of the House of Commons. Since private members' motions are dealt with during the private members' hour and in the order in which they appear on the list, there was nothing to be gained by putting down a motion of that kind. On 2 May 1961, the Hon. Paul Martin attempted to move under Motions that the annual report of the bank be referred to a standing committee. Mr. Speaker Michener ruled that such a motion could not be moved under Motions; in his ruling he outlined the kind of motions that may be moved under that head.[9]

One reason why motions under Motions are strictly limited is that they are debatable: if the head were interpreted broadly, the House seldom if ever would reach the orders of the day. But even with the limits now applied the fact that such motions are debatable may influence greatly the remainder of the day. Before the changes made on 24 March 1975, came into effect the first routine proceeding was Presenting Reports from Standing and Special Committees. Next came Motions. Until 1965 if a debate under Motions was not concluded at one sitting, it was resumed at the next, and perhaps the next and the next, just as soon as the head, Motions, was reached. This meant that on the first day and any subsequent day the House would reach neither any of the later routine proceedings nor the orders of the day. For example, on Monday, 30 November 1964, the chairman of the Special Committee on a Canadian Flag moved that the House concur in the recommendations of that committee. His motion was debated throughout that week and the next. The House finally reached a decision at the end of the sitting that began on the afternoon of Monday, 14 December and only after closure had been used. For over two weeks the House did not reach any head lower than Motions. On eleven days there was no Oral Question Period. Largely as a result of that experience the standing orders were changed so that the order for resuming a debate begun under Motions now is included under Government Orders. This means, of course, that the government decides if and when the debate will be resumed. But even a short debate, one lasting an hour or two, was somewhat disruptive. Neither the ministers nor the principal opposition spokesmen felt free to leave the Chamber because the debate might end suddenly, thus bringing on the Oral Question Period. By making Motions the last of the routine proceedings the way has been opened up for longer but less disruptive debates on Motions.

The head, Motions, formerly was used for two other purposes which have no direct relation to moving a motion. Ministers made statements at this time. This, as we have seen, is now a separate routine proceeding. Before 1964 a member who wished to correct an error in the *Hansard* report of his own words at the previous sitting might do so during the period between routine proceedings and the first order of the day. But once a time limit was imposed on oral questions that interval became the Oral Question Period; consequently, the speaker directed the members to make corrections under Motions. They make them now after the Oral Question Period.

The standing orders provide for three kinds of proceedings between Routine Proceedings and Orders of the Day. Two of these—Order Paper Questions and Notices of Motions for the Production of Papers—might be included as routine proceedings. The third, applications under S.O. 26, is *sui generis*.

QUESTIONS ON THE ORDER PAPER

Since urgent questions of national importance may be asked without notice during the Oral Question Period the central purpose of order paper questions is to bring forth precise, often detailed information or statistics generally about past transactions. A member may put as many of these questions as he wishes on the Notice Paper. When the forty-eight-hours notice time has elapsed, his questions are transferred by the clerk to the Order Paper under the head, Questions. These questions normally account for most of the bulk of the Order Paper, especially towards the end of a long session.

Before 1963 the speaker went through the entire list of questions on each Monday and Wednesday, with the ministers (or their parliamentary secretaries) interrupting occasionally to say, "Answered," when they wished to send an answer to the Table. Since all unanswered questions stand over until the next time, this became a very time-consuming operation. Under new arrangements inaugurated on 17 July 1963, when an answer to a question has been approved by the appropriate minister the answer is deposited with the Parliamentary Returns Office of the House. In the meantime the various departments tell the parliamentary secretary to the government house leader what questions they intend to answer that day, and a composite list of the numbers of all such questions is prepared. During the hour before the beginning of a sitting this list is checked against the answers actually deposited, for sometimes departments fail to fulfil their intentions. When the speaker calls Questions on the Order Paper the parliamentary secretary now merely reads out his verified list of question numbers. Each question and its answer are printed in the day's *Debates*. Under the rules adopted on 24 March 1975, Order Paper Questions are answered on all five days, not just on Monday and Wednesday.[10]

If a department cannot deal with a question adequately in a short reply suitable for inclusion in the *Debates*, or when a question elicits diverse information from various departments, information that cannot be drawn together into one answer, the parliamentary secretary to the government house leader has a file of the relevant papers prepared. When Order Paper Questions are being answered he proposes to the House that each such question be transformed into a motion for a return. When the motion for a return has been carried, i.e., when it has become an order for a return, he sends the file to the Parliamentary Returns Office. These returns are kept there, and may be examined (and copied) by members, newsmen, and others.

The standing orders permit a member to mark a question with a star (or asterisk), thus indicating that he wants the answer read out to the House, not merely printed in *Hansard*. Usually the purpose is to ensure that the House, but more especially the newsmen, will not remain oblivious to any horrendous information elicited about extravagance, patronage, or mismanagement. After the unstarred questions have been dealt with in the manner described above, the parliamentary secretary asks the speaker to call those starred questions for which answers are ready. The speaker repeats the number of each such question —using a list supplied in advance by the parliamentary secretary—and identifies the questioner. Then the appropriate minister (or parliamentary secretary) rises and reads out the answer.

NOTICES OF MOTIONS FOR THE PRODUCTION OF PAPERS

Ministers are required by statute to table various kinds of papers relating to the work of their departments. These they address to the clerk, but transmit to his assistants in the office where Votes and Proceedings is prepared. If a return is found to be as described, an entry is made in Votes and Proceedings of that day, and the return then is sent down the corridor to the Parliamentary Returns Office, where it is available for examination. From time to time, however, a member wants to see papers that are not required by law to be tabled. In such an instance the member has a notice of motion relating to the paper or papers entered on the Notice Paper. These notices are dealt with by the House once a week, on Wednesday immediately after order paper questions. The first such notice of motion for papers during the 1974–76 session was put down by Mr. Stanley Knowles. It read: "That an Order of the House do issue for a return showing, by electoral districts, the total amount of election expenses on behalf of each candidate in the General Election of 8 July 1974, as indicated in the return respecting election expenses submitted on behalf of each candidate, as required under the provisions of Section 63 of the Canada Elections Act; and showing also, by electoral district, the names of all candidates on whose behalf election expense returns have not been submitted." The return required by the order was tabled on 28 November 1974.

Here again the parliamentary secretary to the government house leader acts on behalf of the government. As soon as the speaker has called the head, Notices of Motions for the Production of Papers, the parliamentary secretary rises and states which of the proposed motions, if moved, would be acceptable to the government.[11] The speaker then asks the House if it wishes those notices of motions to be deemed to have been made orders for returns—by dealing with the notices in this way the formality of moving the motions is by-passed. Invariably the House concurs. The parliamentary secretary then goes on to mention, by number, those notices of motions that would be acceptable to the government if modified or qualified in some specified way. Frequently the member who has put down the notice is prepared to acquiesce in the change; and, if so, the notice, as altered, is deemed to have been made an order for a return.

Sometimes a notice of motion for papers is simply not acceptable to the government—perhaps because it would bring about the publication of papers prepared by servants of the Crown not responsible to the House, or perhaps because it would bring about the publication of information detrimental to the security of Canada. Or the notice may ask for the production of a paper that does not even exist. In such cases the parliamentary secretary will ask the speaker to call the notice. When this has been done, the appropriate minister (or a parliamentary secretary) will explain to the House either that there are no such papers or that the government thinks, for stated reasons, that in the public interest the proposed order should not be made. Usually the spokesman concludes by inviting the member to withdraw his notice. The member may agree.

If in either of the two situations described above the member is not willing to accept the suggestion made on behalf of the government, the member has two courses of action. He may ask to move his motion immediately so that—if the government does not object—a vote, without a debate, may take place at that time. Or if he wishes to have an opportunity to argue for his motion, he may ask that the motion be transferred to the list headed "Notices of Motions (Papers)," one of the categories of private members' business. If the government is reluctant, as it usually is, to see twenty or thirty minutes used for a division—Wednesday already is a short day—on an opposed motion for papers, the government house leader or the minister concerned, observing that the member does not intend either to withdraw his notice or to ask that it be transferred for debate, may ask that the notice of the motion be transferred for debate.

STANDING ORDER 26

Normally as soon as the order paper questions—on Wednesday, the notices of motions for papers—have been dealt with the House turns to the items of business previously ordered for the remainder of that sitting. However, occasionally it does not do so. In 1906 while tightening up its rules the House agreed that there are some occasions when it is desirable to turn away from the work planned for a day, and to take up some other matter. Accordingly, a special procedure was provided—in what now is Standing Order 26—by which such a shift may be made, conceivably over the objections of the government. Since most of the post-plenary time of the House at each sitting now is normally at the disposal of the government, this standing order almost always is used by the opposition; they do not regret seeing time allotted to the government pre-empted for the discussion of some emergency detected, not by the ministers, but by an opposition member, especially if the emergency can be attributed, as most can with a modicum of ingenuity, to ministerial sins of omission or commission. Since any private member may have resort to the rule, a motion to adjourn under Standing Order 26 is not a weapon reserved for the official opposition or for the leaders of the parties in opposition.

A successful application for leave to move the adjournment under Standing Order 26 brings on, not the introduction of a bill, and not even the statement of the opinion of the House, but simply a debate. Under the standing order, a member, if he can obtain the necessary leave, may move, "That this House do now adjourn." Normally, since 1906, an adjournment motion is not debatable; but when moved under the terms of Standing Order 26 it is debatable. Such a motion pushes aside the regular agenda, and serves as the procedural vehicle for discussing the matter to which the attention of the House has been drawn.

Prior to 20 December 1968, this standing order—or rather its predecessor, which bore the same number—was abused regularly. Under the order, as then worded and interpreted, a member, without notice, at the end of the plenary phase could apply to the House for leave to move the adjournment so as to be able to discuss "a definite matter of urgent public importance." If the speaker questioned the urgency of debating the matter specified—as he usually did—he would invite the House to advise him on the question of *the urgency of debate*. The result was that it became the practice for members to discuss the matter proposed for discussion if leave were given under the guise of discussing the urgency of discussing it. These encapsulated emergency debates usually ended, perhaps after twenty, thirty, or forty minutes, with the speaker ruling that his initial reaction had been confirmed, i.e., that there was no urgency of debate. In that case, under the standing order, the request for leave was denied. But if, either initially or after the preliminary skirmish, the speaker held that the discussion of the matter was urgent, and if there then was no objection to the member's application or if twenty members supported the application when there was an objection, the emergency debate began immediately. Since an objection could be overcome by such a small number of members governments usually saw nothing to be gained by raising an objection.

A new version of this important standing order adopted on 20 December 1968, permits members to apply for leave after notices of motions for the production of papers have been dealt with on Wednesday and after order paper questions on the other four days. The order requires the member to give a written notice to the speaker in advance. When called upon by the speaker the member simply reads out his notice without elaboration. Then the speaker is required to decide, without hearing arguments, whether or not the matter is eligible to be discussed in this way. If he decides negatively the application ends there. If he decides affirmatively and there is no objection to the member's application, or if twenty members support the application when there is an objection, the member may move the adjournment; but he may not do so immediately. Instead, he will be called upon to make his motion (and thus to start the debate) at eight o'clock p.m. on the first four days of the week and at three o'clock p.m. on Friday; but the speaker has the right to direct that the motion is to be moved at the next sitting.[12] These changes have eliminated debates on the urgency of debate; an application for leave to move the adjournment under Standing Order 26 now requires about three minutes, whether successful or not. The changes assure that some of the time of the sitting is preserved for the original agenda even when the motion is allowed. And they assure that the minister chiefly concerned with the matter to be discussed will have had an opportunity to prepare himself.

The House does not vote on a motion moved under Standing Order 26. The debate simply continues until the speaker decides that it has expired. If this happens before the normal hour of adjournment, the speaker declares that the motion has been withdrawn; then the House reverts to its scheduled business. If it happens after that hour, the Speaker declares the motion carried, and proceeds to adjourn the House to the next regular sitting.

ORDERS OF THE DAY

Even with the Oral Question Period strictly limited and prolonged wrangles over the urgency of debate under S.O. 26 eliminated, as they are now, the hour when the main business planned for a day is reached may vary considerably from one sitting to the next. A minor complaint that the privileges of the House have been breached may take up five or ten minutes. An important statement by a minister and the subsequent comments and questions may take up as much as twenty or thirty minutes. The government house leader will try to prevent more than one of his colleagues from making a statement on any one day, but sometimes it happens that two or three ministers feel obliged to give information to the House without delay, in which case upwards of an hour may be expended. Moreover, a motion, even a motion to authorize a standing committee to travel outside Ottawa or to engage counsel, may trigger a debate. But on an ordinary day all the initial business will have been completed by 3:15 or 3:20 p.m. Thereafter the House turns to the items planned for the day. Normally it continues on them

TABLE I
A Week in the House

HOUR	MONDAY	TUESDAY	WEDNESDAY	THURSDAY	FRIDAY
11:00 AM					S.O. 43
11:15 AM					Oral Questions
12:00 NOON					Routine ..... Orders of the Day
1:00 PM					suspension (lunch)
2:00 PM	S.O. 43	S.O. 43	S.O. 43	S.O. 43	Orders of the Day
2:15 PM	Oral Questions	Oral Questions	Oral Questions	Oral Questions	
3:00 PM	Routine ..... Orders of the Day	Routine ..... Orders of the Day	Routine ..... Orders of the Day	Routine ..... Orders of the Day	
4:00 PM					Private Members' Hour
5:00 PM	Private Members' Hour★	Private Members' Hour★		Private Members' Hour	
6:00 PM	suspension (dinner)	suspension (dinner)		suspension (dinner)	
8:00 PM	Orders of the Day	Orders of the Day		Orders of the Day	
10:00 PM 10:30 PM	Late Show	Late Show		Late Show	

★ After the private members' hour has been reached a total of 40 times on Monday and Tuesday in a session the provision for a private members' hour on those days lapses.

until the time for adjournment at the end of the day. Occasionally, as we have noted, the House will agree to revert to Statements by Ministers to permit ministers to give information to the House without delay.

The term "orders of the day," although now opaque, is still important. The British House found that once a bill had been introduced it was desirable to let the members know in advance when each of the main questions on the bill would be debated and decided, especially if the bill was important or controversial. To achieve this the House established the practice of making an order specifying the day, sometimes even the hour, for the next main motion in a bill's progress. If that motion carried, the House, again by order, specified the date for the next stage. The work of the Committee of Supply and the Committee of Ways and Means, too, was ordered for certain days. Initially this did not mean that members could not move substantive motions on "order days;" such motions were moved before and sometimes between ordered items. In 1811 a major move was made when Monday and Friday were set aside for dealing with ordered business, as distinct from motions of which members had given notice. This meant that thereafter there were "order days" and "notice days."

Since then the distinction between "order business" and "notice business" has been pushed into the background as a result of the segregation of government business from private members' business. Nevertheless, the basic idea of an agenda established by orders, although ordinarily submerged, still is retained for those kinds of business that normally require more than one day, e.g., the passing of bills, supply business, and ways and means business. As we saw, after the first reading of a public bill the speaker asks, "When shall the said bill be read a second time?" The usual answer is, "At the next sitting of the House." A second-reading motion then is added under either Government Orders or Public Bills, and that motion may be moved at the next sitting if reached. In the case of a government bill other items may be given priority over it by the government. In the case of a private member's bill other bills, far too many for the time available, may be listed above it. But the standing orders permit items not reached at a sitting to be taken up at subsequent sittings without restriction to the end of the session; consequently, the order that the second reading (or the third reading) is to be moved "at the next sitting of the House" does not become a nullity if the motion is not reached at that sitting. In short, the orders made by the House have become shells within which other factors determine when items of business are dealt with.

Occasionally, but only occasionally, the importance of these "orders" becomes obvious. If the House is prepared to have a bill move forward rapidly the answer to the speaker's question will be, "By leave, now" or "By leave, later this day." In that case the second-reading (or third-reading) motion may be moved either immediately or later that day. And, as we shall see in chapter 4, the main ancillary motions in the legislative process are motions for "orders."

On all five days of the week government orders are taken up first when the orders of the day have been reached. The list headed, Government Orders, includes all the orders made by the House at previous sittings relating to the items of government business then before the House. It is a heterogeneous list. In an annual session it will include (a) an order for resuming the debate on the motion for an Address in Reply to the Speech from the Throne, (b) an order relating to the business of supply, (c) orders relating to ways and means business, (d) orders relating to motions dealing with the government's non-financial bills, (e) orders relating to motions to refer business to standing or special committees, and (f) orders relating to motions moved under Motions but transferred to Government Orders after the adjournment of the debate. Possibly it will include (g) orders relating to motions intended to elicit a resolution of the House on some important topic, (h) orders relating to motions intended to produce an order of the House with regard to its own procedures, and (i) orders relating to motions intended to indicate the participation of the House in a Joint Address to Her Majesty. The government has been given its own time, and it is allowed to bring forward its items—to have the orders called—in whatever order it prefers. Almost invariably the order for resuming debate on the Address in Reply is discharged before other major items are introduced. The supply order must be called a specified number of days in each of the three supply terms. Otherwise, the government is quite free to manage its business as it sees fit.

Let us consider an example. On 3 March 1975, the House reached the orders-of-the-day phase about 3:20 p.m. The government brought forward first a motion for the appointment of a special joint committee of the Senate and House of Commons to consider the Green Paper on Immigration Policy tabled on 3 February 1975. After debate, the motion carried at 4:40 p.m. Next, after open consultation among the house leaders, the government called the order for moving concurrence in the report of the Standing Committee on Agriculture on a bill (C-10) to amend the Prairie Grain Advance Payments Act, then for concurrence in the report of the Standing Committee on Justice and Legal Affairs on a bill (C-43) to amend the Law Reform Commission Act, and then for concurrence in the report of the Standing Committee on Agriculture on a bill (S-6) to amend the Canadian Wheat Board Act. In each of these three instances the order of the House as to the time of the motion for third reading was, "By leave, later this day." After dinner the government called the order for moving the third reading of Bill C-43, which was carried out—the motion was moved and carried affirmatively—by 8:10 p.m. Next, it called the order for moving the third reading of Bill S-6, which was completed by 9:20 p.m. Finally, it called the order for moving the third reading of Bill C-10, which was completed just before ten o'clock. Those three orders for third-reading motions never reached the Order Paper: they were made and carried out on the same day.

The government house leader consults regularly and confidentially with the house leaders of the parties in opposition both in house leaders' meetings and individually to ascertain their preference as to the business to be done during a week, and on particular days. The government house leader will reveal the ministry's legislative needs and hopes for the next week or two, or even longer; the other house leaders indicate the order of business that would be most convenient for their party spokesmen; and efforts are made to work out a program. The usefulness of these consultations depends largely on the unity and harmony of each of the opposition parties. When the house leaders cannot commit all the members of their parties to terminate a debate after a specified number of speakers or at a specified hour the consultations tend to be exercises in frustration. Each Thursday, at the end of the Oral Question Period, the government house leader gives a forecast of the business for the next day and for the coming week; but given the inability of the other house leaders to make firm commitments—which varies from party to party, and from time to time—these forecasts always are highly hypothetical.

At five o'clock on Monday, Tuesday, and Thursday, and at four o'clock on Friday the House usually turns for one hour to private members' business. (There is no private members' hour on days when the Address in Reply is being debated, or during the budget debate, or on the twenty-five days allotted to the business of supply. Moreover, after a total of forty hours have been taken in a session by private members' business on Mondays and Tuesdays there is no private members' hour on those days for the balance of the session.) Despite the efforts made since 1972 to enhance its importance the private members' hour is essentially a relic from bygone days at Westminster. The decisive point is that nobody is in a position to decide what items of private members' business are important. Consequently those items, unlike government items, are dealt with (a) by categories and (b) in the order of their introduction. When each new item has been introduced it is added at the bottom of the appropriate list. The various lists are given priority on different days of the week. During private members' hour on Monday the House turns first to notices of motions. On Tuesday it turns first to public bills. On Thursday there is an alternation between private bills and notices of motions (papers) transferred for debate, so that on the first Thursday, the third Thursday, etc. private bills are dealt with first, and on the second Thursday, etc. notices of motions (papers) are dealt with first. On Friday, too, there is an alternation: on the first Friday, the third Friday, etc. notices of motions are taken first, and on the second Friday, etc. public bills are taken first.

If all the items listed in one of these categories are completed at a sitting the House is to turn to the category listed next for that day. In fact this happens only on Thursdays. Formerly there would be scores, even hundreds of divorce bills on behalf of residents of Quebec and Newfoundland; but now all divorce applications are dealt with by the courts. Moreover, by 1965 the number of bills relating to federally incorporated companies had dried to a trickle; since then Parliament by statute has provided for most of that business to be done by letters patent. In the 1970–72 session three private bills (out of six) were enacted; in 1972 one bill (out of one); in 1973–74 two (out of two); and in 1974 one (out of one). Since the second category on the first Thursday, etc. is notices of motions (papers), this has meant that the private members' hour on most Thursdays has been given over to debates on motions for the production of papers.

Formerly there was no prescribed limit on debate on motions for the production of papers. Therefore few of these motions ever came to a vote. (The practical effect of this situation was insignificant if the government had a reliable majority. The ministers and backbenchers always voted against such motions. If they had not intended to do so the motions would have been accepted by the government when called under Notices of Motions for the Production of Papers.) Now, under Standing Order 47(2), the debate is limited to one hour and forty minutes, i.e., two of the hours put aside for private members' business are needed to dispose of one such motion if the debate goes to the limit. The decision is made by a recorded vote. So many of these notices of motions (papers) are transferred for debate that only those members who put down their notices at the very beginning of a session have any chance of moving, and of speaking to, their motions.

On 15 March 1973, in response to the criticism that the government has become far too secretive, the government house leader tabled a set of guidelines for dealing with requests for the production of papers. These were referred to the Joint Committee on Statutory Instruments, but the committee was unable to study them at that time. On 19 December 1974, the guidelines were tabled again, and again they were referred to the committee for study.

Private members' motions—proposing that the House make an order or state its opinion on some topic—have even less chance of success, for there is no time limit on the debate. A motion can be "talked out" each time it comes up for debate. If the question has not been put to the House by the end of the hour in which debate began (or was resumed) the order for the resumption of the debate drops of course to the bottom of the list with the result that the debate will not be resumed (or resumed again) until all the items above it have had a turn. For example, on 10 October 1974, at the ninth sitting in the session Mr. Joe Clarke gave notice of the following motion: "That, in the opinion of this House, a Committee should be selected to consider the powers, prerogatives and privileges attached to the Office of Prime Minister and to report what safeguards are desirable or necessary to secure the constitutional principles of the sovereignty of Parliament and the supremacy of the Law." His notice was ninth on the list. On Monday, 9 December 1974, he moved the motion, and it was debated for an hour. The order for the resumption of the debate then was entered at the end of the list, in the forty-fifth place. By 30 July 1975, when the House adjourned for the summer, it had risen to the eighteenth place.

Much the same happens to private members' public bills. At the beginning of each session a ballot is held to fix the order in which the public bills ready at that time will be introduced. These bills and others introduced later, in the manner described above, are entered under the head, Public Bills. If the question on the motion that a bill be now read a second time has not been put to the House by the end of the hour in which it was moved an order for resuming the debate is placed at the bottom of the list under Public Bills. If the list is long—as it always is in a modern session—it is more than likely that the debate will not have been resumed before the end of the session. However, if a private member's public bill does get second reading, the government normally will provide time outside the private members' hour for the remaining stages.[13]

The remorseless slaughter of private members' motions and public bills reveals the modern constitution. It is the ministers, not the private members, who are held responsible for the governing of the country. They are expected to take the initiative.

DAILY ADJOURNMENT DEBATES

Ordinarily on Wednesday and Friday the speaker adjourns the House at the appointed hour without putting the question (on an adjournment motion) to the House. But there is provision for proceedings on the ordinary adjournment motion on Monday, Tuesday, and Thursday. When time limits on the Oral Question Period first were introduced

TABLE 2
Use of the Time of the House

1973–74 session
(in hours and minutes)

The heads are listed mainly in the order followed at the 1973–74 session, that is, in the order followed before 7 April 1975. Some heads have no fixed place in the program of a day, e.g., royal assents, points of order, and speaker's rulings.

1	Presenting committee reports		1:19
2	Motions under S. O. 43		
	548 proposed unsuccessfully	12:00	
	14 proposed successfully	:14	
		12:14	12:14
3	Motions for concurrence in committee reports		3:03
4	Statements on Motions—(90 statements)		30:43
5	Tabling of documents		2:41
6	Introduction of bills		3:07
7	Order paper questions		5:25
8	Notices of motions for the production of papers		2:08
9	Oral Question Period		156:07
10	Applications under S. O. 26		
	24 proposed unsuccessfully	1:04	
	4 proposed successfully	22:14	
		23:18	23:18
11	Government Orders		
	Address Debate	41:29	
	Supply (Allotted Days)	135:29	
	Ways and Means		
	Budget Debate	23:40	
	Ways and Means Motions	:46	
	Bills	429:46	

	Committees		
	Motions for the appointment of committees	13:41	
	Reference of business to committees	9:11	
	Debates on committee reports	10:42	
	Miscellaneous government business		
	Resolution re Viet-nam cease-fire	4:22	
	Resolution re official languages	17:01	
	Debate re Arab-Israeli war	2:23	
	Resolution re Middle East peace-keeping	4:21	
	Orders re adjournments at Easter, etc.	4:52	
	Other proposed resolutions	1:04	
		698:47	698:47
12	Private Members' Hour		81:31
13	Questions of privilege and points of order		20:48
14	Rulings from the Chair		3:46
15	Recorded divisions (including bells)		25:31
16	Adjournment Proceedings (the "late show")		41:49
17	Bells (calling quorum at hour of sitting and after dinner)		42:54
18	Royal assents		3:45
19	Miscellaneous		11:33
	TOTAL Hours and Minutes in Session		1170:29

Number of sitting days in session: 206

in 1964 a new order was made under which a member who is dissatisfied with a minister's answer or failure to answer, or whose question has been ruled out of order on the ground that it is not urgent may raise the subject of his question on the adjournment motion on one of those days. This arrangement, first introduced on 20 April 1964, was made permanent on 20 December 1968.

Some members will indicate their displeasure when their questions are ruled out of order or are not answered to their satisfaction by declaring, "Ten o'clock!" This is neither necessary nor sufficient. If a member is serious—some who call out, "Ten o'clock," soon lose interest—he must notify the speaker in writing. Ths speaker then will add his name (and a terse statement of the subject) to the list of members waiting for a chance to speak on an adjournment. At five o'clock on Monday, Tuesday, and Thursday the speaker tells the House the names of the members who will be recognized after ten o'clock that evening. Then, at ten o'clock, after the business ordered for the day has been interrupted—if it has not been concluded—the speaker will propose the motion, "That this House do now adjourn." He then recognizes the first member on his list. Each such member may speak for no more than seven minutes, and a minister or a parliamentary secretary may reply for no more than three minutes. No more than three members may be recognized in this way on any one evening. In other words, if the provision is used to its full extent, the "late show" will end at 10:30 p.m. However, it sometimes happens that only one or two members will wish to proceed on a particular evening. Obviously there is no "late show" when the House is debating the adjournment under S.O. 26. Sometimes when the hour of adjournment is unpredictable, as on budget night, or late because of a series of divisions the "late show" is suspended.

FOUR

The Ordinary Legislative Process in the House of Commons

At every annual session of Parliament—as distinct from special sessions called in extraordinary situations—there are certain kinds of recurring business: most notably the granting of supplies to the Crown and taxation. Each of these kinds of business is dealt with in its own established way. And at most sessions the House deals with scores of proposals for changes in the law of the land. These proposals, too, are dealt with in a standardized way; there are required stages, stages which ordinarily extend across three or more sittings. The process is repeated dozens of times at each session. It is used also when spending and taxing are authorized, but as only a part of the supply and the ways and means procedures. We may refer to the basic way in which the House deals with bills as the ordinary legislative process.

A bill that has passed both the Senate and the House of Commons is a request to the queen asking that she state the law of the land to be exactly as set forth in that document. When the royal assent is given to a bill, the bill becomes a new kind of document, a statute. The long process by which a proposed bill becomes first a bill and then a statute is an act of Parliament; consequently the products—statutes—often are referred to as "Acts of Parliament."

The term "bill," which seems devoid of meaning in an age when almost all the public bills that become statutes are initiated by the queen's own ministers, is redolent with constitutional history. The practice of submitting "petitions" or "bills" to the king—evidently the two terms were used interchangeably initially—asking that the law be declared to be as the petitioner believes it ought to be already was old when the representatives of the Commons of England first were summoned to Parliament in the thirteenth century. What those representatives, and others outside the parliaments, too, soon learned was that, given the Crown's need for supplies from the Commons, kings were inclined to be highly receptive to petitions from the House of Commons. This, of course, was only the beginning. Soon it became established that statutes, the highest statements of the law, could be made only in response to bills in Parliament. Gradually the next step followed: it came to be agreed that a statute must conform closely to the bill that had evoked it. By the sixteenth century this constitutional rule was so well recognized that the House of Commons began to present its own public bills to the king in the form and language of statutes, with only the royal assent required to make them statutes. This technique had been used from about the middle of the fifteenth century for private bills and for bills originating in the King's Council. Now it came to be used for private members' public bills. It gave the king a simple, stark choice: he could assent to a bill or he could withhold his assent.[1] Thus the possibility that the statute made by the king would be different in the slightest detail from the bill was excluded. At times, of course, bills that kings were more than eager to accept were put before the House by the kings' agents; but over the centuries the bulk of the bills were introduced by private members. Only within the last 150 years has the term "bill" lost its everyday meaning in Parliament. In our age, when the ministers of the Crown take the lead in initiating changes in the law, it would perhaps be more revealing to say that the Crown bills the House of Commons, and that the function of royal assent is mainly to mark the successful closing of the legislative circle.

At Westminster the legislative process is a matter of the rules and practices of the House. It is not laid down in standing orders. But in 1867 the new Canadian House thought it desirable to prescribe the basic process. The main order provides: "Every bill shall receive three several readings, on different days, previously to being passed. On urgent or extraordinary occasions, a bill may be read twice or thrice, or advanced two or more stages in one day." Since this is only a standing order, the House can set it aside either temporarily or permanently by another order.

For centuries in England public bills were read aloud to the House, sometimes many times, and each re-reading gave the members an opportunity to re-examine a bill once again before they were called upon finally to vote for or against it.[2] The "reading" is still the basic step in the legislative process in the House, both at Westminster and at Ottawa. Although no member nowadays would ask that the text of a bill be read aloud to the House even once, the form of reading is still retained: after the speaker has declared that the motion that a bill be read a first time has been carried, a clerk at the Table rises and proceeds to the reading. He simply announces the words, "First reading of this bill," thus signifying that the order of the House has been obeyed. The fiction is repeated after the House has ordered a second reading, and, again after it has ordered a third reading.

A bill is carried forward through the stages of the legislative process by a long chain of standardized motions. All these motions must be carried, but at Ottawa, as at Westminster, the number of them that is debatable has been reduced sharply in recent times.[3] In the Canadian House of Commons the crucial motions are to the effect: (a) that leave be granted to the member to introduce his proposed bill; (b) that the proposed bill be read a first time and be printed; (c) that the proposed bill be read a second time and be sent to a specified committee; (d) that the text of the bill reported by the committee, as changed by amendments made at the report stage, if any, be concurred in by the House; and (e) that the proposed bill be read a third time and pass the House. Immediately after each of these motions—known technically as "ancillary motions"—has been carried, the House makes provision by order that the next motion will have a place on the agenda of a specified sitting; consequently, after the first motion—for leave to introduce the bill—no notice is required.

On 17 March 1964, the House ordered that the motion for the second reading of Bill C-75, to establish the Canada Pension Plan, be taken up "at the next sitting of the House." As a result of tense negotiations with the provincial government at Quebec City the plan was modified extensively; and on 9 November 1964, a new bill, Bill C-136, was read a first time. To clear away the old bill the House discharged its order for the second reading of Bill C-75 and gave permission to the government to withdraw that bill. This example will be helpful to us in distinguishing between four terms. First, there is the bill itself. Unlike a substantive motion, a bill is treated as a physical object: it is introduced; it may be withdrawn; it may pass the House. Second, there are the ancillary motions by which the proponents of a bill seek to move it forward, e.g., "that the bill be now read a second time. . . ." These motions, not the bill itself, are what is debated, and perhaps amended, at the second and third-reading stages. Third, there are the "readings," now only formalities. And, fourth, there are the orders by which the House itself fixes the time at which the next ancillary motion may be moved.

The chain of ancillary motions is not a series of equal links. The House does not go over a bill again and again as in early times in England, as the repetition of the term "reading" implies. Rather, the motions now constitute a simple and logical process in which each stage transcends the one immediately before it, so that although the basic motions—that the bill be read a first (second, or third) time—ostensibly are the same, and seem repetitious, they have very different meanings. The key development that gave rise to the legislative process now followed in both the British and Canadian Houses was the full recognition of the truth that while the House is a suitable body to settle the goals of legislation, it is highly unsuitable for intensive consideration of either the details of clauses or the draftsmen's words. In the sixteenth century it became the practice of the British House to send to a committee every bill that it had decided to advance. As we shall see, "the committee stage" now is the main working stage in the preparation of a bill. It is the one stage at which the members examine the text of a bill word by word, and comma by comma.

The first reading of a bill serves only to put it before the House. (Once a bill has been "read" a first time at Ottawa, a copy is sent to every member's office.) Since a member may introduce as many bills as he or she pleases, scores, even hundreds of bills may be read a first time at a session. Obviously, not all these bills can be advanced. Historically one function of the second-reading motion, "That Bill C-ooo be now read a second time," was to let the House decide whether or not to go through that bill a second time. Thus the motion, or rather the decision on the motion, served as a screen. Nowadays, of course, the bills that are to be taken seriously (and advanced) are separated from the others in another way: the time of the House has been placed at the disposal of the government, so that almost all the government's bills are read a second time, and almost no private members' bills are. If the decision on the second-reading motion is affirmative, the bill is "read," and then sent to a committee. It is at this stage that the text of the proposed bill, as distinct from its end(s) or purpose(s), is examined by the members. When a committee has concluded its labours, it reports the bill with or without amendments. Then the House is asked to concur in that report. By concurring the House gives its approval to the committee's product, and thus establishes the text of the bill. This is not to say that the bill cannot be altered later. But the presumption is now in favour of the text. In committee the text had to be adopted clause by clause; but now the text stands unless a motion to amend it is carried. The question to be answered at the final stage, when the motion that the bill be read a third time is before the House, is the most complex of all: it is whether or not the House favours the end(s) of the bill together with the provisions made in the bill for the achievement of that end, and accordingly is prepared to have the bill leave (or pass from) the House.

The committee stage is the key phase of the legislative process. It is the only stage at which a bill is read in anything like the old sense. The important effect of an affirmative decision on the second-reading motion, is not that the bill will be read in the House, but that it will be sent to a committee. Afterwards, the votes on the report and the third-reading motion enunciate the reaction of the House to the work done by the committee.

The legislative process—the basic motions together with the amendments that may be moved to them—is the same for all public bills.[4] The

House recognizes the distinction between government bills and private members' public bills, not by a distinction of process, but in the orders it has made about the use of its time. However, since almost all the public bills that become law nowadays are government bills, we may think of this process, and evaluate it, as the process for dealing with government bills.

When the Special Committee on Procedure (1967–68) examined this process as performed by the Canadian House of Commons it concluded that the House was spending too much time on many bills, but that, despite this fact, most of the important bills were not being examined with sufficient care. This paradoxical conclusion arose from two observations. First, the members were treating the second-reading stage as the high and decisive point in the entire process, so that (a) long debates, often lasting two, three, or more days, were taking place at that stage on some fairly routine bills, (b) the members were taking stands for or against bills before they had had a chance to study them in depth, and (c) the interest of the House in many bills was being eroded by vain harangues. The second observation was that at Ottawa, unlike Westminster, the important task of considering the texts of bills was being undertaken in a forum which was highly unsuitable for meticulous legislative work—that is, in committees of the whole House—so that inefficiency and frustration almost inevitably went hand in hand at the committee stage. What the conclusion of the Committee amounted to was that behind the din of partisan warring, the House was treating government bills superficially, so that parliamentary pressure on the departments and the cabinet to bring forth soundly conceived, well-contrived bills was low. The debate on the second-reading motion often was long, trivial, and offensively partisan; and all the later stages were anti-climactic, for had not the House accepted the bill in principle?

The root cause why the emphasis given to the second-reading motion was, and is, excessive in the case of government bills is that the procedure of the House is anachronistic at this point. When the basic legislative process was evolving in England most public bills were what we today would call private members' public bills. The debate whether or not to have a bill read a second time came to serve as a final screen, after various coarser screens, such as the question on leave to introduce and the question on first reading, which then were debatable, to prevent weakly supported bills from advancing to the time-consuming committee stage. But the situation is very different now. It is assumed now that the government has the duty to take the lead in providing for the governance of the country according to the needs of the changing times; consequently, the House has put most of its time at the disposal of the government. And the House has ordered that the government may have its items of business dealt with in its own order of priority. In other words, the House has arranged to have the decisions as to which bills are to go forward made in an entirely different way. Yet the Canadian House of Commons continues to use the second-reading motion as if it were performing a genuine screening function. Indeed, it can be argued that the introduction, in 1927, of a fixed hour of daily adjournment, by fragmenting debates, has made the second-reading stage a greater obstacle in terms of days consumed than it had been previously. The legislative process worked out in England before the Crown became active as a source of bills is still being used in Canada, although only government bills now are advanced, and although very few government bills are screened out in a normal session.

This is not to suggest that the second-reading stage serves no purpose when the House is dealing with a government bill. First, the debate may publicize the bill. Second, the decision of the House to have a bill read sets limits on the work of the committee to which the bill is sent. The committee must confine itself to that bill. It may not bring back a bill irrelevant to or contrary to the end(s) of the bill sent to it by the House. Often it is said that on the second-reading question the House decides for or against "the principle" of a bill. That explanation emphasizes the truth that the committee is limited by the scheme or principle of the bill sent to it. However, otherwise the statement is incorrect and misleading. The second-reading motion is a procedural motion. It does not elicit an abstract expression of opinion. Presumably a member opposed to the ends of a bill will vote against second reading. But a member who favours the ends in the abstract also may vote against advancing the bill because he ranks higher other bills competing for the available time and money, or he may think that the circumstances are not right. He is not against the principle of the bill, but he is against moving the bill forward. Moreover, the explanation seems to imply that the House would be acting frivolously if it stopped at the third-reading stage a bill for which it had voted "in principle" at the second-reading stage. What must be remembered is that the legislative process is indeed a process. The House does not commit itself conclusively in favour of a bill at any stage before the final one, when it votes to let the bill pass from the House.

It was suggested by the Special Committee on Procedure (1967–68) that the question on the second-reading motion on a government bill in most instances should be put to the House at the same sitting at which the motion was moved. In short, the second-reading stage would be limited—as at Westminster—to a single sitting. The committee commented, also, that when dealing with a second-reading motion the House should not adjourn at the normal hour, but should continue to sit until the debate had been concluded, and the vote had been taken.[5] But nothing came of this approach. In the course of discussion between representatives of the Trudeau government and the official opposition late in the summer of 1968, prior to the first session of the 1968–72 Parliament, the Progressive Conservatives made it plain—and publicized their stand—that any such change would be totally unacceptable. Consequently, the Special Committee on Procedure (1968), which in the fall of that year originated the rules changes made on 20 December 1968, submitted no recommendations dealing directly with the problem of protracted second-reading debates.

The recommendations made by the Special Committee on Procedure (1967–68) for improvements at the committee stage were far more fruitful. Over the years since 1867, as we shall see in chapter 6, the House had sent many bills to standing or special committees after second reading, but those committees were not given the power to adopt the clauses of the bills. The "committee stage" always was taken later in committees of the whole House. The work of the standing committees or special committees was only investigative, not legislative. After a standing or a special committee had made its report, the proposed text of the bill had to be traversed again, clause by clause, by a committee of the whole House; and it was in its report that the House concurred at the "report stage." The Special Committee on Procedure (1967–68) recommended that almost all public bills not dealing with taxation or appropriation be sent to small standing or special committees after second reading, and that those committees should do the work of the "committee stage." Those recommendations were taken up and refined by the Special Committee on Procedure (1968). They were accepted by the House on 20 December 1968.

The two Special Committees on Procedure (1967–68 and 1968) anticipated that their proposal that the clause-by-clause consideration of most bills be undertaken by standing committees (or special committees) would arouse criticism. First, it would be said that a standing committee is composed of only a few members, while every member ought to have an opportunity to participate in the preparation of every bill to which the agreement of the House is sought. Second, it would be argued that even those members who were on a particular committee ought to have the right to have their proposed amendments dealt with, not only by the committee, but by the whole House. To meet those objections the Special Committee (1968) recommended that the stage at which the report on a bill from a standing (or special) committee is received by the House should be made an opportunity for members to move changes under special rules. Previously, the motion for concurrence had not been debatable because all members may participate in the work of committees of the whole House. This recommendation, too, was accepted by the House on 20 December 1968.

Under the new standing orders, then adopted, after a standing (or special) committee has reported a bill to the House no action is to be taken by the House for forty-eight hours. During that period any member may give notice of a motion to change the text of the bill as set forth in the report of the committee. This he does by giving the clerk a copy of his motion to change the bill. His proposed motion, together with any other motion(s), then is printed in the Notice Paper so that all members may examine it in advance and have it before them when the member moves it. This innovation prevents the House from being taken by surprise and obviates the need for it to deal with complex motions merely read out by the speaker. It also excludes the kind of meandering debate that formerly took place in committees of the whole House, for under the new standing orders debate at the report stage is to be relevant to a proposed amendment to the bill. If there is no motion to amend, there is no debate. On the other hand, the new procedure permits members to make a concerted attack on the text of a proposed bill at whatever point or points they find it defective.

At the same time the new procedure has the disadvantage of opening up the legislative process at the report stage to something like the kind of massive inflation that the House over the years had sought to avoid by stopping most private members' public bills after the first-reading stage. Different members may put down amendments that are the same in substance, although the wording may be different. Some amendments may be of little or no importance. Some may be merely dilatory. Indeed, some members who formerly would have been content to put two or three short speeches "on the record" in a committee of the whole House, now may feel required to offer amendments to bills so as to be eligible to talk; and each motion to amend starts a new debate. With this danger in mind, the Special Committee on Procedure (1968) recommended, and the House adopted, a standing order which permits the speaker, after he has examined all the notices of proposed amendments, to combine motions and to select those to be moved. This was intended to permit him to put aside proposed amendments that overlapped others, amendments that had been dealt with adequately in committee, and amendments that were insufficiently important to warrant debate. However, this power is one that a speaker is likely to use with great restraint as long as the time available for debating amendments at the report stage is unlimited.

Some bills still are sent to committees of the whole House; but these are not sent also to standing committees (or special committees). Such bills are of four kinds. First, there are bills that must be passed if grants of supply to the Crown are to be made good. From time to time—as we shall see in the next chapter—the government presents sets of spending estimates. These are studied by the members. When their approval has been given, an appropriation bill, founded on the approved estimates, is introduced. In this instance the work has been done on the estimates, and the passing of the bill making good the supply is only a necessary formality. At the committee stage on appropriation bills the House resolves itself into a committee of the whole, the clauses of the bill are approved in about one minute, and then the bill is reported back to the House. Second, there are the bills founded on ways and means resolutions, i.e., bills by which changes are made in the tax laws. The clause-by-clause consideration of these bills, unlike the consideration of appropriation bills, is a major undertaking; yet because the subject is taxation, and in view of the elimination in 1968 of a committee stage between the budget debate and the introduction of tax bills, the standing orders assign this task to a committee of the whole House.

The third and fourth kinds of bills that do not go to the standing committees are quite different. Standing Order 74(2) begins with the words, "Unless otherwise ordered, in giving a bill a second reading, the same shall be referred to a standing committee, but a bill may be referred to a special or a joint committee." The key words for our present purpose are, "Unless otherwise ordered, . . ." Here the House opened the way for two other kinds of bills to go to committees of the whole House. Some bills are so simple that painstaking analysis is unnecessary. This often is true of one-clause bills. Moreover, such simple bills often are moved forward, by leave of the House, through two or more stages at one sitting; this could not be done conveniently if they were sent outside the Chamber to standing committees. At the other extreme are bills, far fewer in number, which, although more complex, deal with matters of political importance and on which the members in general are well-informed. In the first five complete sessions after committal to a standing committee became the regular procedure—1969–70, 1970–72, 1972, 1973–74, and 1974—a total of 160 public bills, exclusive of both taxation and appropriation bills, were advanced to the third-reading stage in the House of Commons. Of these, twenty-four were sent to committees of the whole House. Most took very little time in committee. For example, Bill S-25 (1969–70) to make the Hudson's Bay Company a Canadian company took fifteen minutes; and Bill C-203 (1972) to amend the Representation Commissioner Act took four minutes. Only four of the twenty-four took much time. These were Bill C-215 (1969–70) to revise the Canada Elections Act, which took 20 hours, 51 minutes in committee; Bill C-181 (1970–72) the Public Order (Temporary Measures) Bill, which took 25 hours, 45 minutes in committee; Bill C-207 (1970–72), the Government Organization Bill, which took 46 hours, 16 minutes in committee; and C-217 (1973–74) to order the resumption of railway operations, which took 13 hours, 33 minutes.

TABLE 3
The Pattern of the Legislative Process

	C-181 (1970–72) Public Order (Temporary Measures)		C-176 (1973–74) Protection of Privacy	
	DATE	HOURS	DATE	HOURS
Introduction	2 Nov. 1970		13 April 1973	
First reading	2 Nov. 1970		13 April 1973	
Second reading moved and debated	4 Nov. 5 Nov. (Total)	2:59 5:23 8:22	7 May 8 May (Total)	3:56 3:48 7:44
Second reading and committal	5 Nov. (to a committee of the whole House)		8 May (to Standing Committee on Justice and Legal Affairs)	
In committee	6 Nov. 9 Nov. 10 Nov. 13 Nov. 16 Nov. 17 Nov. 23 Nov. (Total)	2:55 3:54 3:42 2:27 4:38 4:48 3:21 25:45	June — 5 meetings July — 4 meetings Sept. — 1 meeting Nov. — 3 meetings (Total)	 About 19:30

Reported back to the House by the committee	23 Nov. 1970			14 Nov. 1973	
Report considered by the House	23 Nov.	Nil		23 Nov.	2:18
				27 Nov.	4:45
				28 Nov.	2:37
				29 Nov.	3:40
				30 Nov.	:25
				(Total)	13:45
Third reading moved, debated, and carried	23 Nov.	:39		4 Dec.	2:40
	24 Nov.	4:01			
	25 Nov.	2:50			
	26 Nov.	2:37			
	30 Nov.	1:52			
	1 Dec.	:28			
	(Total)	12:27			
Senate amendments (if any) considered by the House				10 Jan.	:56
Royal Assent	3 Dec. 1970			14 Jan. 1974	

When a bill has gone to a committee of the whole House, where every member may participate in the consideration of the text, no motions to amend may be moved at the report stage; and, consequently, since no period of waiting for notices of amendments is required, concurrence in the report of the committee may be moved immediately, and is not debatable. The time pattern for two very important bills is shown in Table 3. One bill, which eventuated as the Public Order (Temporary Measures) Act, 1970, was sent to a committee of the whole House. The other, which eventuated as the Protection of Privacy Act, 1974, was sent to a standing committee.

Even when the report stage has been concluded the text of the proposed bill may not be in its final form. As we have seen, the next motion in the legislative process is that the bill now be read a third time. Unlike the second-reading motion, the third-reading motion has an obvious double meaning: it asks the House to give its approval to both the purpose of the bill and to the bill itself as the means for achieving that purpose. General argument for and against the whole proposal is permitted; but it is also in order for a member to seek to alter the text of the bill, not by moving an amendment to the bill, but by moving an amendment to the third-reading motion, an amendment that the bill be sent back to the committee, there to undergo the changes specified in the amending motion. For example, in the fall of 1970 when the Public Order (Temporary Measures) Bill was at the third-reading stage, Mr. T. C. Douglas moved that the third-reading motion be amended to read, "That Bill C-181 be not now read a third time but that it be referred back to the Committee of the Whole House for the purpose of reconsidering clause 12 with a view to the inclusion therein of a provision for the establishment of an independent body to review the administration under the said bill." The House divided, 78 Yeas to 113 Nays, against his amendment. Two other motions to recommit Bill C-181 were moved and defeated.

Procedurally, to vote for a second reading is to vote to have the bill go to a committee, but to vote for the third reading is to vote to have the bill go forward for royal assent. The former is exploratory, while the latter is conclusive. It would not be unreasonable for a member to vote for the second reading of a bill, and then to vote against a third reading. The difference between the meanings of the second-reading motion and the third-reading motion can be seen by examining the kinds of amendments that may be proposed to them.

First, there is "the hoist." In their basic form the second-reading and third-reading motions are identical: "That Bill C-000 be now read a second (third) time...." Therefore the same "hoisting" amendment may be moved against either of them; indeed, the reason why such an amendment may appeal to the opponents of a bill is exactly the same in both instances. If the opponents of a bill think they have a chance of winning the vote, they will not content themselves with simply voting against the second-reading (or the third-reading) motion, for all that would have been decided by a negative decision would be that the bill was not *now* to be read a second (third) time. Strictly speaking, the House decides on motions put to it; consequently, only motions, not bills, are accepted or rejected. A bill is a *projet de loi*, which once introduced may be withdrawn, allowed to pass the House, retained in the possession of the House, or rejected.[6] In this instance, the *motion* that the bill be now read a second (third) time would have been rejected. The House would have decided not to order that the bill be now read. The House would still be seized of the bill, but its forward progress would have been interrupted. Because of the negative vote the speaker would not have led the House—as he invariably does otherwise—to appoint by order a day for the next step. In short, the bill would have been side-tracked. Since no day had been appointed for the second (third) reading, the order for the second (third) reading would have been dropped from the Order Paper. But such side-tracking is not necessarily permanent. The supporters of the bill, if they can muster sufficient support, can bring the bill back into the program of the session by using either of two tactics. According to Beauchesne, they can have a member move without notice immediately after the defeat, "That the said Bill be read a second time on—next."[7] The second tactic is to move—without notice—for an order appointing a day for the resumption of the incomplete stage. May states: "To replace a dropped order of the day upon the notice paper, a motion is made before the commencement, or after the close, of public business, to appoint the order for a subsequent day. These motions, which are made without notice, are usually treated as purely formal motions."[8]

It is to block such attempts to bring a bill back onto the main track that its opponents, instead of simply voting negatively on the main motion, are likely to resort to "the hoist." They will move to amend the motion that the bill be now read a second (third) time by replacing the word "now" with the words "this day six months hence." By convention it is understood—from England in the days of shorter sessions— that this refers to a day on which the House will not be sitting. In other words, if this amendment carries an order of the House will have been made directing that the bill is to be read a second (third) time on a day when the House will not be sitting. Beauchesne, in words borrowed directly from May, comments: "The opponents of the Bill may vote against the question that the Bill 'be now read a second time'; but this course is rarely adopted as it still remains to be decided on what day it shall be read a second time, or whether it shall be read at all; and the Bill therefor is still before the House, and may afterwards be proceeded with."[9] The same is true for the third-reading motion. May says: "If the question 'That the bill be now read the third time' is negatived, such a vote is not necessarily fatal to the further progress of the bill."[10]

Hoisting attempts are quite common. On 13 May 1969, for example, after the motion that Bill C-150, to amend the Criminal Code, "be now read a third time and do pass" had been moved, Mr. René Matte one of the Créditiste members, moved, "That the word 'now' be left out and the words 'this day six months' be added at the end of the question." His proposed amendment was rejected, 53 Yeas to 151 Nays. Again, on 26 July 1973, after it had been moved, "That Bill C-196, An Act respecting the 1976 Summer Olympic Games, be now read a third time and do pass," Mr. Arnold Peters, of the New Democratic Party, moved that the motion be amended to read, "That Bill C-196 be not now read a third time but that it be read a third time this day six months hence." The House divided, 21 Yeas and 114 Nays.

One of the most controversial incidents in Canada's recent history centres around a third-reading motion. On Monday, 19 February 1968, the deputy speaker proceeded directly from the committee stage on Bill C-193, to amend the Income Tax Act, to the third-reading stage. He proposed the standard motion—that it had been moved by the minister of finance is questionable—that the said bill "be now read a third time and do pass." The hoist was not moved. Although the division bells rang for well over an hour the government whip could not find enough Liberals to carry the vote. The motion was defeated, 82 Yeas to 84 Nays. As soon as the House met the next day the government house leader took the floor. The following exchange took place.

>**Hon. Allan J. MacEachen** (Minister of National Health and Welfare):   *I move that this house do now adjourn.*
>**Mr. Stanfield:**   *Mr. Speaker—*
>**Some hon. Members:**   *Order.*
>**Mr. Speaker:**   *Is it the pleasure of the House to adopt the motion?*
>**Mr. Stanfield:**   *I think in the circumstances I might be permitted to say something.*
>**Some hon. Members:**   *No.*
>**Mr. Speaker:**   *Order, please. I am sure hon. members wish to proceed in an orderly fashion. I have to bring to the attention of the Leader of the Opposition that the motion is not debatable, though by consent he might be allowed—*
>**Some hon. Members:**   *No.*
>**Mr. Ricard:**   *It is a rotten Grit trick.*

Mr. MacEachen's motion carried without a division. The next day,

Wednesday, Prime Minister Pearson sought leave to move, "That this house does not regard its vote on February 19th in connection with third reading of Bill C-193 which had carried in all previous stages, as a vote of non-confidence in the government." Leave was refused. He then gave a forty-eight hours notice. On Friday, 23 February his notice was called and transferred to Government Orders. Immediately Mr. Pearson moved his motion. On 28 February it carried, 138 Yeas to 119 Nays.

The general view was that Bill C-193 had been defeated. The government did not accept this interpretation of the vote on 19 February; rather, they believed that, as stated by May and Beauchesne, the bill was still before the House, although side-tracked.[11] But they did not have a majority. Moreover, given the fact that strong action to arrest the withdrawal of foreign money from Canada was needed urgently, and the fact that no successor to Prime Minister Pearson, who had announced his retirement in December 1967, had been selected, the government was most anxious to avoid an election. In the circumstances the Liberals were not prepared to take the risk of failing to convince the other parties that Bill C-193 was still before the House. Instead they sought to evade that question by bringing in a new bill, C-207. As we saw in chapter 2, it is a rule that no question or bill is to be offered in the House that is substantially the same as one on which its judgement already has been expressed in the same session. The government argued that since the important clauses of C-207 were new the bill was not substantially the same as Bill C-193. However, after the order for second reading had been called the speaker ruled that Bill C-193 had been "defeated" and that Bill C-207 in parts was the same as Bill C-193. He said: "It will be seen, therefore, that while the substantive clauses of Bill C-207 are, in general, substantially new, clauses 2, 3, 4 and 8 of Bill C-207 are a repetition of the clauses in Bill C-193 which was defeated on third reading."[12] The House discharged the order for second reading, and the government withdrew the bill. The government then had to contrive a third bill, which being entirely new was found admissible.

The whole incident provides a miniature lesson in procedure. It showed that the same motion or bill may not be brought forward a second time in one session. It showed that an ordinary adjournment motion, which requires no notice, is not debatable. It showed that a substantive motion may not be moved without notice (or leave). It also left unanswered the question what would have happened if the Pearson government had had a majority and had moved for a new order for the third reading of Bill C-193.

A second type of amendment is "the reasoned amendment." Such amendments may be moved at both the second-reading and the third-reading stage. If a reasoned amendment carries, the House for a stated reason will have refused to advance the bill at that time. The House remains seized of the bill, although, as May comments, it probably will not be put back into the program of the session. According to May the technical effect of carrying a "reasoned amendment" is "to supersede the question for now reading the bill a second time; and the bill is left in the same position as if the question for now reading the bill a second time had been simply negatived or superseded by the previous question. The House refuses on that particular day to read the bill a second time, and gives its reasons for such refusal; but the bill is not otherwise disposed of."[13]

A reasoned amendment to the second-reading motion states why the bill—that is any version of the bill, for the clauses then in the draft may be changed in committee and consequently are irrelevant at this point—ought not to be advanced at that time. Beauchesne, following May, says: "It is also competent to a member who desires to place on record any special reasons for not agreeing to the second reading of a Bill, to move as an amendment to the question, a resolution declaratory of some principle adverse to, or differing from, the principles, policy, or provisions of the Bill, or expressing opinions as to any circumstances connected with its introduction, or prosecution; or otherwise opposed to its progress; or seeking further information in relation to the Bill by Committees, Commissioners, the production of papers or other evidence or the opinion of Judges."[14]

However, Beauchesne also states: "It [a reasoned amendment] must oppose the principle of the Bill."[15] This sentence—intended to mean that a reasoned amendment may not give the provisions of one or more of a bill's clauses, which can be changed, as the reason for not reading the bill—when read out of context seems to require that a reasoned amendment make a statement of principle with which the purposes of the bill are inconsistent.[16]

In contrast to the wide latitude at second reading suggested by Beauchesne, a reasoned amendment to the third-reading motion must state why the bill then before the House—the bill concurred in at the end of the report stage—should not be read a third time. Regardless of any reasons which were adduced or adduceable at the second-reading stage, the House did decide to have a bill prepared to achieve certain purposes. It is that bill, not the purposes in the context of the times, that may be attacked in the third-reading stage. Beauchesne says: "On the second reading of a bill, an amendment may be moved expressing opinions as to any circumstances connected with its introduction or prosecution, or seeking further information in relation to the bill by committees or commissioners, the production of papers or other evidence, or the opinion of judges. This cannot be done on the third reading because it is not directly connected with any provision of the bill."[17] A good example of a reasoned amendment at the third-reading stage was provided in 1970. On 17 December 1970, Mr. Waldo Monteith moved that the third-reading motion of Bill C-202, to amend the Old Age Security Act, be amended by striking out all the words after "That" and by adding new words, so that the motion would read, "That Bill C-202, An Act to amend the Old Age Security Act, be not now read a third time as this House is opposed to a Bill which fails to include any adequate cost of living provision in respect of the basic amount of the monthly pension." His amendment was defeated, 72 Yeas to 100 Nays.

Both "the hoist" and "the reasoned amendment" were brought into action in 1917 against the military service bill. On 18 June 1917, the second reading of the bill was moved by the prime minister, Sir Robert Borden. In amendment, Sir Wilfrid Laurier moved, "That all the words of the question after the word 'that' be struck out and the following be substituted therefor:—'The further consideration of this Bill be deferred until the principle thereof has, by means of a referendum, been submitted to and approved of by the electors of Canada.' " Two days later, Mr. J. A. Barrette moved a hoist. He moved to amend Sir Wilfrid Laurier's motion by striking out all the words after "That" and substituting "this Bill be not now read a second time, but that it be read a second time this day six months." Thus a hoist was piled upon a reasoned amendment.

On Friday, 29 June the speaker adjourned the House because there was no quorum. At the commencement of the next sitting, on Tuesday, 3 July, without notice Sir Robert Borden said:

> In consequence of the House having failed to maintain a quorum on Friday evening, it becomes necessary for me to move, seconded by hon. Mr. Cochrane, that the order of the day for "resuming the adjourned debate on the proposed motion of Sir Robert Borden for the second reading of Bill No. 75, an Act respecting Military Service, the amendment of Sir Wilfrid Laurier thereto, and the amendment to the amendment by Mr. Barrette," having lapsed by reason of the House being declared adjourned for want of a quorum on the 29th ultimo, when the said order was under consideration be revived and placed on the Order Paper for consideration this day.

An objection was raised against this motion. There was no question but that the dropped order could be revived, but the right of the prime minister to propose without notice the inclusion of the dropped order on the list of business for that day, 3 July, was challenged. The speaker ruled that there was no need to wait until a later day to resume the debate.

On 6 July, 1917, Barrette's hoist was defeated, 9 Yeas to 165 Nays. Then Laurier's reasoned amendment was defeated, 62 Yeas to 111 Nays.

At that point another reasoned amendment was moved; it was defeated, 56 Yeas to 115 Nays. Finally, Borden's motion was reached; it carried, 118 Yeas to 55 Nays.

A third kind of amendment calls for recommittal. At the second-reading stage the House is dealing with the question, should the ends (purposes) of this bill be sought at this time? The clauses of the draft bill may be altered drastically in committee provided only that the purposes to be achieved remain the same. Consequently, the House does not allow a member to seek by debate or amendment to anticipate the work of the committee. However, at the third-reading stage the House has the committee's product before it; therefore, it is in order to move to send the bill back to the committee so that a specified change may be made. Since all the members have had an opportunity to improve the draft at the report stage or in a committee of the whole House, such recommittal amendments are intended as a grand, final gesture of advocacy or resistance.

The Special Committee on Procedure (1968) recommended, and the House adopted, a change in the form of the second-reading motion that may prove troublesome in some instances. The decision that almost all bills are to go to standing committees made desirable some easy procedure by which the House could specify to which of the committees each bill was to go. The means adopted was the combining of two motions, the standard second-reading motion and a new motion: "That the bill be referred to the standing committee on...." The two-fold motion thus produced, reads: "That Bill C-000 be now read a second time and be referred to the standing committee on...." This means that the House is confronted with two distinct propositions in one question.[18] Since 1968 there have been some disagreements about which of the standing committees should deal with particular bills, but so far it has been possible to overcome them by consultation, and, consequently, to alter the motion—by naming a different committee —with the unanimous consent of the House. The desirability of relying on unanimous consent to overcome understandable differences of opinion is questionable.

The committee recommended, and the House adopted, a change in the first-reading motion, too. It now reads: "That the bill be now read a first time and be printed." This motion is unlikely to cause any procedural difficulty because the printing of the bill is a consequence, without alternative, of the first reading.

FIVE

Authorizing Taxes and Expenditure

The Crown may not tax the people or spend public money without statutory authorization; consequently, the procedures by which the House deals with tax proposals and expenditure proposals appear only as variants, albeit very special variants, of the ordinary legislative process. Formally it is accurate to say that they are only variants, for from the special taxing and spending procedures of the House emerge bills which must go through the normal first- and second-reading stages, the committee stage, and third-reading stage like all other bills. But taxing and spending are very special kinds of parliamentary business. To treat them as mere variants would be to bury a great deal of history of cardinal importance to an understanding of our modern constitution. For centuries what the kings of England needed most when parliaments were held, and hoped to extract from the common people after the acquiescence of their representatives in Parliament, was money. On the other hand, in the late Middle Ages generally it was the representatives of the Commons, not the kings, who wanted new statutes. They saw sessions of Parliament as opportunities to urge the kings to make clear pronouncements that the law of the land was as they believed it ought to be. In the early formative centuries money business was the king's business, while petitions for statutes—later, bills for statutes—were mainly the Commons' business. In addition, the kings' requests for money were addressed primarily to the House of Commons, not to the two Houses equally. As early as 1407, following precedents from even earlier times, it was established that such requests were to be dealt with first in the House of Commons, that the agreement of both Houses was necessary for a grant, and that any grant agreed upon was to be reported to the king by the speaker of the House of Commons. Given the very distinctive nature of money business—in which in fact, although not in form, the king billed the Commons—it was natural that the House of Commons should develop special procedures, procedures quite distinct from those used in the preparation of ordinary bills, for dealing with the Crown's requests for money. Those procedures became central to the constitution.

It was the aspiration of the Fathers of Confederation that the new Dominion of Canada should have a constitution similar in principle to that of the United Kingdom. Accordingly, the essentials of the financial relationship between the Crown and the Parliament in the United Kingdom were prescribed for Canada in the British North America Act. Indeed, it is not surprising that the Canadian House of Commons went beyond the bare essentials and undertook to model its procedures for ways and means business and for supply business as exactly as possible after the example of the British House. This means that if we are to understand how our House of Commons deals with taxation and expenditure proposals in the late twentieth century we must make our approach through the British House of the seventeenth and eighteenth centuries.

In that period the raising and the spending of public money by the Crown were connected closely. A request to the Commons that a sum of money be supplied for a particular purpose generally entailed a request for a new (or a renewed) tax. The statute that authorized the tax also authorized the expenditure of the yield—or the yield up to a specified amount—for a specified purpose.

It was understood clearly that the House never initiated expenditure by the Crown; that is—given the fact that spending and taxing went hand in hand—the House never initiated taxation. The established relationship was that the Crown, which had the duty to govern, requested money; then the House of Commons reacted to the Crown's requests. This relationship was so elementary that the House felt no need to prohibit private members from introducing bills to authorize taxing and spending. It simply was not done. However, early in the eighteenth century the tactic of authorizing the expenditure of a tax yield up to a specified amount produced a problem. Sometimes there were surpluses. Here then was loose money, money that could be spent on projects, persons, and purposes dear to private members, and on the initiative of private members, without violating the constitutional principle that the Commons never offered to authorize taxation. In 1713 the House made a standing order to cover this breach. In 1867, when the British North America Act was enacted, that standing order of the British House, as amended in 1852 and 1866, read: "This House will receive no petition for any sum relating to public service or proceed upon any motion for a grant or charge upon the public revenue whether payable out of the consolidated fund or out of money to be provided by parliament unless recommended from the Crown." In short, only the Crown could introduce measures to spend money.

By the seventeenth century a practice had evolved that the requests of the Crown for authority to tax and to spend were always discussed first in a committee of the whole House. It appears that in earlier times these discussions were undertaken in select committees to escape pressure and management by the speakers, acting on the kings' behalf; and that later, in an era when the Commons was bolder, committees of the whole House came to be used because select committees tended to fall under the sway of privy councillors and other prominent members. In 1667 the latter practice was elevated to a rule. The House then resolved that "if any motion be made in the House for any public aid or charge upon the people, the consideration and debate thereon ought not presently to be entered upon but adjourned to such further day as the House shall think fit to appoint; and then it ought to be referred to the Committee of the whole House and their opinion to be reported thereupon, before any resolution or vote of the House do pass therein."

The close coupling of taxing and spending to which we have referred continued until the Consolidated Fund was established in 1787. Before that date, pursuant to the rule made in 1667, the requests from the Crown for money, in estimated amounts for specified purposes, were considered by the members sitting as a committee of the whole House. Once they had concluded that phase of their work, the supply phase, the members, again sitting as a committee of the whole House, considered the ways and means that had been recommended for raising the money required to make good any supply that had been approved. In other words, the work of one committee, the Committee of Supply, led directly to the work of another, the Committee of Ways and Means. Only after the latter committee had come to its decision would a bill—one bill—be introduced to enable the Crown (a) to raise money in the way that had been approved by the Committee of Ways and Means, and (b) to spend that money, or part of it, for the purpose that had been approved by the Committee of Supply.

This direct connection between particular expenditures and particular revenues was broken by the establishment of the Consolidated Fund. Thereafter, ways and means business was divided into two separate parts. The Committee of Supply continued to perform the task of considering the proposals of the Crown that estimated sums be expended for specified purposes. When it had finished its work, the Committee of Ways and Means, as before, was confronted with the question: "Where is the money to be found to make good the approval just given to the expenditure proposed by the Crown?" Now, however, the Committee of Ways and Means had an easy answer: "In the Consolidated Fund." Once that answer had been given, a new kind of bill, a bill to appropriate from the Fund the specified sum for the specified purpose, would be introduced in the House. But the creation of the

Fund did not make all ways and means business a mere formality. Ultimately the grim inevitability of taxation had to be faced. Back beyond the Fund lurked the serious ways and means question: "How is the Consolidated Fund to be kept at a level adequate to meet the various demands upon it?" The answers proposed by the Crown from time to time to that question were considered by the Committee of Ways and Means; and after the committee had made its decision relative to any change in the tax laws, a suitable tax bill was introduced. In other words, two separate kinds of business had emerged: first the business of supply, which resulted in the passing of appropriation bills; and, second, the substantial ways and means business, from which emerged taxation bills. There still remained a ways and means phase between the business of supply and the introduction of the consequent bill appropriating money from the Fund, but that was a mere formality. When the Dominion of Canada was founded in 1867 this basic pattern for money business was carried over to Ottawa; indeed it already had been carried over into the provinces in preconfederation days. The British North America Act established a Consolidated Revenue Fund; and it provided that, except for certain payments authorized by the act itself, the Consolidated Revenue Fund "shall be appropriated by the Parliament of Canada, for the Public Service." That the elected representatives of the people have a greater interest in taxes and spending than the senators was recognized in s. 53, which reads as follows: "Bills for appropriating any Part of the Public Revenue, or for imposing any Tax or Impost, shall originate in the House of Commons." Next, the rule of the British House of Commons with regard to the initiation of expenditure was made constitutional for Canada by s. 54 of the Act: "It shall not be lawful for the House of Commons to adopt or pass any Vote, Resolution, Address, or Bill for the Appropriation of any Part of the Public Revenue, or of any Tax or Impost, to any Purpose that has not been first recommended to that House by Message of the Governor General in the Session in which such Vote, Resolution, Address, or Bill is proposed."

Among its own very first steps the new House of Commons adopted a standing order providing that tax measures and spending measures were to be dealt with first in committees of the whole House. This order, modelled after the British standing order then in force, read as follows: "If any Motion be made in the House for any public Aid or Charge upon the people, the consideration and debate thereof may not be presently entered upon, but shall be adjourned till such further day as The House shall think fit to appoint, and then it shall be referred to a Committee of the Whole House, before any Resolution or Vote of The House do pass thereupon." This standing order applied to both taxation and expenditure.

Against this background we can examine how the House of Commons now participates in (a) the authorization of taxation and (b) the authorization of expenditure.

TAXATION

The Consolidated Revenue Fund is replenished by moneys deposited to the credit of the receiver general for Canada from divers sources, but chiefly from the money collected by the Crown under the authority of the Income Tax Act, the Excise Tax Act, the Excise Act, and the Customs Tariff. In the United Kingdom a general Finance Act has to be enacted every year because certain taxes, most notably the income tax, are authorized for only one year at a time; but in Canada all the basic tax statutes continue in effect from year to year without renewal. This means that it is possible for one or more annual sessions of the Canadian Parliament to take place without the introduction of any tax bills. In the 1912–13 session, for example, the only change in the tax regime was an amendment to the Customs Tariff, 1907, prompted mainly by a trade agreement between Canada and certain of the West Indian colonies. In his budget statement of 12 March 1970, the minister of finance proposed no tax changes.

The procedure by which the House of Commons deals with tax measures was altered greatly on 20 December 1968. Prior to that reform the bills to amend the basic tax laws eventuated from resolutions adopted by the Committee of Ways and Means, and those resolutions in turn eventuated from a budget statement made to the House by the minister of finance. On budget night the minister of finance moved a procedural motion, "That the Speaker do now leave the Chair," so that the House might resolve itself into the Committee of Ways and Means. Speaking to that motion—that is with the speaker in the Chair—the minister delivered his budget statement. During the course of the statement, generally near the end, he laid on the Table notices of the motions—one for each basic tax statute which he wished to see changed—which he planned to move in the Committee of Ways and Means once that committee had begun its work. Prior to 1955 there was no time limit on the debate on the motion that the speaker leave the Chair, i.e., the budget debate was unlimited. In that year the standing orders were changed so that the resumed debate was limited to eight days. In 1962 the limit was reduced to six days; and there it has remained. Under the old procedure, after the budget debate had been completed, and the speaker had left the Chair, in committee the minister moved each of his ways and means motions. Each of those motions was considered separately by the committee, and, when carried, was reported to the House as a resolution of the committee. Subsequently, the minister introduced in the House a bill based on each of the resolutions adopted in the committee. Each of those bills—perhaps one, two, three, or four in number—then went through all the stages of the ordinary legislative process.

This complex procedure arose in Canada, as in England, from the insistence of the House that for taxation it would deal only with bills founded on resolutions adopted in a committee of the whole House. This insistence made necessary a decision by the House on a prior question, i.e., the question whether or not to sit as a committee; and this question came to be, formally, the topic of the budget debate. Since the main estimates of proposed expenditure are transmitted to the House some time prior to the beginning of the fiscal year on April first, the minister of finance normally made his budget statement, revealing how he proposed to meet the financial requirements of the new fiscal year, in April or May.

By 1968 it had become obvious that this procedure was highly unsuitable for modern conditions. First, because fiscal policy now is regarded as one of the main instruments by which a government can influence national economic activity, the need for changes in the tax laws no longer is tied directly to the main estimates. It may be desirable to increase or to decrease one or more of the taxes at other times during the course of a year, as new economic conditions emerge. But under the old procedures—at least as practiced—no move could be made by the minister to change a tax statute without a budget statement and a full six-day budget debate. Second, even when a budget debate was desirable, the procedure made for a great deal of repetition. Under it any tax changes proposed by the minister were discussed more or less fully during the six days of the debate. Then each change—each proposed resolution—was considered separately in the Committee of Ways and Means. And, finally, each was dealt with again, perhaps again and again, as the bills to amend the basic tax statutes were being passed.

The Special Committee on Procedure (1968) was concerned especially with the second of these criticisms. It decided that the middle step, the consideration of the minister's proposed resolutions in committee, should be eliminated. Whatever the advantage in England in the late Middle Ages of discussing the royal demands for money first in a committee, those advantages were not relevant in Canada in the second half of the twentieth century. However, there were two difficulties. The first was relatively minor. If the rule that a tax bill must eventuate from a resolution of the Committee of Ways and Means was to be expunged—thus eliminating not only the function of that committee, but the committee itself—a new motion would have to be devised to serve as the vehicle for the budget debate. The old motion,

"That the Speaker do now leave the Chair," would have been rendered meaningless. It would have to be supplanted by a motion that could be used by the speaker to keep the debate relevant to budget matters, but which at the same time would be sufficiently vague and innocuous to permit all supporters of the government to vote for it—and perhaps for those in opposition to let it carry "on division"—even if at that stage they had unresolved doubts about some of the minister's proposals. The budget motion suggested by the Special Committee (1968) and adopted by the House on 20 December 1968, reads: "That this House approves in general the budgetary policy of the Government."

The second difficulty was more serious. What the committee wished to eliminate was not the ways and means motions—i.e., the proposed resolutions—but the consideration of those motions which took place in the Committee of Ways and Means. The motions, or rather the notices of the motions, are very useful for four reasons. First, they help to maintain the government's monopoly of the power to initiate taxation. No private member can bring in a ways and means motion, and tax bills are founded on ways and means resolutions. Second, they serve as an exact statement to the House of the tax changes the minister is proposing. Third, since some tax changes become effective immediately to prevent profiteering and other forms of anticipation, the promulgation of a carefully drawn statement of the tax changes is necessary. Fourth, in some cases the minister wishes to publicize his scheme for tax changes so that those whose activities will be affected, and who therefore can be expected to know whether or not the scheme will be administratively feasible or will entail untoward effects, may examine the scheme, and subsequently make representations to him before he introduces his bill(s) in the House.

Under the procedure devised by the Special Committee (1968), when the minister of finance wishes to introduce a tax bill he tables a notice of a ways and means motion. Then, perhaps weeks or months later, after an order has been made appointing the day on which he will do so, the minister moves his motion in the House—not in a committee of the whole House—and the House, without debating it, or seeking to amend it, decides whether or not to accept his motion. If the decision of the House is favourable, the minister moves immediately that the consequent bill be read a first time.

But it is quite possible that as a result of representations from the public and of further work by his officials the minister may decide to modify his scheme before he introduces the bill. Under the old procedure this could be achieved quite easily. After the minister had moved his original motion in committee, he would prompt one of his ministerial colleagues to move an amendment to that motion. But under the new procedure a ways and means motion was not to be debatable or amendable. Consequently, the Special Committee decided to recommend that the minister should be permitted to supplant either an original notice or any subsequent notice(s) simply by tabling a new notice.

In short, the Special Committee (1968) decided to recommend two radical innovations: (a) that the minister of finance would be permitted to table new notices if he wished to change his tax proposals after budget night, and (b) that the House would vote on his motions without having had an opportunity to debate them or to amend them. At that point it was perceived that the other criticism—directed at the practice of having a full six-day budget debate every time a tax statute was to be changed—could be met easily. All that was necessary was to word the new standing order, the order that would enable the minister to table new notices of ways and means motions, in such a way that it would be clear that a notice did not have to supplant one that had been tabled in the course of a budget statement. Accordingly the Special Committee (1968) proposed the following wording: "A notice of a Ways and Means motion may be laid upon the Table of the House at any time during a sitting by a Minister of the Crown, but such a motion may not be proposed in the same sitting." The key words are, "at any time." On 20 December 1968, this recommendation was adopted by the House as Standing Order 60(1).

Once introduced, a tax bill still must pass through all the ordinary legislative stages like any other bill; however, after second reading a tax bill, unlike most public bills now, is not committed to a standing committee, but goes to a committee of the whole House.

The net effect of these changes has been to reduce the difference between the way the House deals with tax proposals and other legislation. A distinction still is maintained, but it is not nearly as great as formerly. The old link between tax bills and budget debates has been cut. As a result, it now seems reasonable to anticipate that ordinarily there will be only one budget debate in a session, coming about the beginning of the fiscal year, and that any changes in the tax laws to be made at other times will be initiated simply by tabling notices of ways and means motions.[1] Moreover, the elimination of the preliminary committee stage which sometimes dulled the interest of the members, means that tax bills are more likely to be given the same amount of attention as other government bills at the several stages of the legislative process.

Although the government began to make use of the new procedure at once, all its implications were not comprehended fully by some members until 1972 and 1973. In the 1968–69 session there were two budget debates, one begun on 31 October 1968, under the old rules, and one begun on 3 June 1969, under the new. The two ways and means motions of which the minister of finance gave notice on 3 June were adopted by the House, and the bills were read a first time before the House adjourned for the summer. On 22 October 1969, Parliament was prorogued. A new session began immediately. On the second day of that session, 23 October, the government revived its two tax proposals simply by tabling notices of ways and means motions under Standing Order 60(1). The two bills that eventuated from those notices were given royal assent on 19 December 1969. In addition, on 3 June 1969, the minister had forecast the introduction of a tax on air travel, but because he wished to discuss the details of the tax with the air carriers he did not table the notice of the ways and means motion in that session. Then on 14 November 1969, the notice was tabled. The consequent bill also became law on 19 December 1969. The new procedure was found acceptable to the House in those instances. At least, there were no objections.

During the fall of 1970 preparations were under way for the massive overhaul of the Income Tax Act started by the Carter Royal Commission, and a spring budget was planned to enable the government to present the scheme of its tax-reform bill. However, there were certain changes that the minister of finance wished to make at once. He considered initiating those changes without a budget debate, but finally decided to proceed in the old way so as not to startle the traditionalists. This meant that there were two budget debates, one in the fall of 1970, and one in the spring of 1971.

The first complaint against Standing Order 60(1) was not heard until the winter of 1972. On 14 October 1971, prompted by newly released unemployment statistics, the government house leader moved, "That this House do now adjourn," to permit the House to debate the state of the economy.[2] In the course of his speech on this motion the minister of finance tabled a notice of a ways and means motion to reduce corporation income taxes and to reduce personal income taxes for the period from 1 July 1971, to 31 December 1972. On 17 December 1971, two notices were tabled, supplanting the original notice. The first of these related to the period between 1 July and 31 December 1971, while the second dealt with the twelve-month period ending 31 December 1972. (Because the major revision of the Income Tax Act was to become effective on 1 January 1972, two tax reduction bills were needed, one for the old basic act, and one for the new one.) The first of the two motions was adopted by the House, and the reduction became law on 23 December 1971; however, the second motion had not been dealt with when Parliament was prorogued. On 22 February 1972, in the next session, the minister of finance, pursuant to Standing Order 60(1) tabled a notice of ways and means motion to apply the reduction to the 1972 tax year. When the consequent tax bill was under debate on 20 March 1972, the Hon. Marcel Lambert raised a point of order, not to challenge the right of the minister to proceed in this way, but to suggest that the standing order inadvertently had gone further than the Special Committee on Procedure (1968) had intended. He said:

> I would say that upon a straight-forward reading of Standing Order 60(1) the Minister of Finance may introduce any and every tax change he may wish to bring in, whether it is to the Income Tax Act, whether it is to the Excise Tax Act, whether it is to the Customs Tariff or otherwise, and whether it is an increase or decrease.
>
> Under Standing Order 60(3), it is not obligatory for the Minister of Finance at any time to bring in a budget presentation. It is only in Standing Order 60(3) that we get this reference to the budgetary presentation. Subject to political risk, there is no other provision in this House or in the statutes or regulations which binds the minister to bring in a budget. Yet resort now is being made to a Standing Order, or to a paragraph in the Standing Orders, which allows the minister to bring in any and every tax change he so desires. That is not what was in the contemplation of the committee and it is not what was contemplated by the House, I put it to you, Sir. I will agree there is a political danger in not bringing in a budget and not having, shall we say, a financial report to the House and to the nation. Actually, I believe there was a mix-up in the sequence of the paragraphs in Standing Order 60. There was obviously discussion at the time and I confess I was a member of that committee. This point did not occur to me at that time, however, nor to the others but it certainly does now and I want to raise it so that we might reconsider it.

Later, Mr. Lambert said: Let us consider what might happen if one interprets this rule in this way. Suppose this tax measure were not proceeded with at this time and that there should intervene an election— and God forbid the same administration would be elected, particularly this one—the first thing that the new parliament could be faced with, without notice, could be the notice of ways and means motion that had been presented by the previous administration, without any accounting whatsoever. I say this is wrong, Mr. Speaker.[3]

As Mr. Lambert had anticipated, Mr. Speaker Lamoureux ruled that the bill was properly before the House. In addition, he mentioned that there was nothing in the old rules either that prescribed a budget statement or debate. If the minister of finance had wished to put financial proposals before the Committee of Ways and Means, he would have to move that the speaker leave the Chair, but whether or not he would support that motion with a budget statement was not determined by the rules, and whether or not his motion would be debated was up to the members.[4]

By far the most dramatic episode so far involving the new tax procedure occurred in 1973. In his budget statement of 8 May 1972, the minister of finance, Mr. Turner, announced certain tax changes designed to prevent an increase in unemployment in Canada because of a new American program of assistance for manufacturers of export goods. As in the case of the budget of 1969 and the announcement of 1971, those changes were not dealt with before the end of the session. On 1 September 1972, the Parliament was dissolved. During the campaign leading up to the election of 30 October 1972, the minister's proposals were denounced vigourously by the New Democratic Party as a "corporate tax rip-off." After the election the Liberal government, headed by Mr. Trudeau, had only 109 members, while the Progressive Conservatives had 107, the New Democratic Party had 31, and the Social Credit Party had 15. In addition, there were two Independents, one of whom was the speaker, Mr. Lamoureux. Although Mr. Turner made known his determination to proceed with the controversial tax proposals, the New Democratic Party decided to support the Liberal government for a time. On 19 February 1973, the minister delivered a budget statement initiating certain other tax changes. Therein he stated that the measures to reduce the tax burden on manufacturers and processors would be brought forward, but he did not include the notice for those changes with the notices of ways and means motions tabled that day. As a result the New Democratic Party felt free to vote in favour of the budget motion, "That this House approves in general the budgetary policy of the Government," thus sustaining the government. Later, on 29 May 1973, the minister tabled the corporate tax reduction notice, and on 6 June he moved the motion. The consequent bill passed the House of Commons with Progressive Conservative support and over New Democratic Party opposition. Because the Trudeau government was able to bring forward that tax bill in isolation from the budget statement of 19 February 1973, it was able to carry both the budget motion (with New Democratic Party support) and the corporate tax reduction bill (with Progressive Conservative support), and thus to avoid a defeat in the House, a defeat which would have resulted in either the resignation of the government or the dissolution of Parliament. This instance demonstrated the constitutional importance of the procedures of the House. It is quite possible that if an election had taken place in 1973 the Liberals would have been defeated by the Progressive Conservatives; certainly, that was the general expectation at that time. However, the Liberal government was able to survive until 8 May 1974, when the budget motion was defeated. In the subsequent election on 8 July 1974, the Liberals succeeded in achieving a majority.

An important topic related to taxation that was not considered by the Special Committees on Procedure (1967–68 and 1968) is the provisional collection of taxes. In Canada there is no statutory authorization for the collection of new taxes between the time the minister of finance tables a notice of ways and means motion in the House and the time, perhaps many months later, when the consequent bill receives royal assent. Nevertheless, new or increased taxes often are collected from the day the notice is tabled. This illegal collection never has been challenged in the courts in Canada because nobody has thought worthwhile the hollow victory that might be achieved. The general assumption is that in each such instance the illegality will be remedied retroactively when the proposed law eventually is enacted by Parliament.[5] A similar lacuna in the British tax law was exposed in the courts in the United Kingdom in 1912 when a doughty Englishman resisted the tax collectors successfully. As a result in 1913 the Provisional Collection of Taxes Act was enacted. That statute, as amended in 1967, provides that taxes proposed by the chancellor of the exchequer on budget night are to be effective provisionally from the time stated by the chancellor if the House agrees that night to a motion showing continued support for the government. But, in addition, it provides that those taxes are to expire— in the United Kingdom, this would include the basic provisions of the income tax law—unless, *inter alia*, the bill to make the changes has received its second reading within twenty-five sitting days. In the case of the changes to be made by the main Finance Bill, which eventuates from a budget statement in the spring, those changes, in effect provisionally, are to expire unless the bill has received royal assent on or before August fifth. (In the British House, August fifth is the last day available under the standing orders for the business of supply before the summer adjournment. The comparable date in Canada is June thirtieth.)

The enactment in Canada of a statute similar to the Provisional Collection of Taxes Act, however desirable as a means of obviating the need for the Crown to act illegally, would have serious constitutional implications. Under the rules and practice of the British House the government can stop filibusters easily. It can bring on decisions on the Finance Bill before the deadlines prescribed in the Provisional Collection of Taxes Act. As long as the Canadian House lacks a fully satisfactory closure rule or time-allocation rule, the fixing of such deadlines would increase intolerably the power of the opposition.

APPROPRIATION

All the moneys received by the Crown in right of Canada, as taxes or otherwise, are credited to the Consolidated Revenue Fund; but no sum of money—other than what is required to make the payments prescribed in the British North America Act—may be withdrawn from the Fund without prior authorization by the Parliament of Canada. As we have noticed, under the B.N.A. Act all bills to authorize the withdrawal of money from the Fund must be introduced in the House of Commons, not the Senate, and the House may not deal at any stage of its procedure with any proposal that would entail such a withdrawal unless that proposal has been recommended to the House by the governor general. In short, the House may refuse to supply money for the purposes recommended by the Crown, but it cannot propose that the Crown be supplied with money for any purpose or in any amount beyond the Crown's own requests. The power and the responsibility to initiate expenditure are concentrated in the hands of the ministers.

The basic way in which Parliament authorizes the withdrawal of money from the Fund is by appropriation acts. The task of governing belongs to the Crown, but obviously the Crown cannot continue to provide its many services to the people unless some of the money accumulating in the Consolidated Revenue Fund is made available to it. At the same time the House of Commons is unwilling to permit the Crown to withdraw large sums from the Fund to be spent in unlimited amounts for unspecified purposes. The House insists that the Crown when requesting money must specify the particular purposes for which the money is needed, and must specify also the estimated amount required. After the House has agreed that the Crown may spend money up to stated limits for specified purposes the House passes an appropriation bill. Such bills, when enacted, set aside portions of the Fund for those purposes. They merely appropriate. They do not require the Crown to spend all or any part of the money. They merely authorize the Crown to withdraw those sums from the Fund. Moreover, this kind of appropriation always is made with a time limit: the authorization given by an appropriation act ordinarily expires at the end of the fiscal year.

To assure that its employees do not use money for any purpose for which it was not appropriated by Parliament the Crown employs various safeguards; and, in turn, the Crown is watched by the auditor general on behalf of the House of Commons. Regularly the public accounts for each fiscal year, once ready at the end of the year, together with the auditor general's report on them, are referred to the Standing Committee on Public Accounts.

By means of appropriation acts the Crown is provided with the money to pay all its civil and military employees—the public servants, the members of the Royal Canadian Mounted Police, the men and women in the armed forces, the crews of icebreakers operated by the Department of Transport, etc. In this way it is provided with money to pay for the construction of wharves, federal public buildings, ships, roads in national parks, and airports. In this way it is provided with the money to pay the suppliers of fuels, foodstuffs, uniforms, red tape, electricity, and telephones.

New items sometimes appear in the estimates without parallel legislation. The government already has the right to do what it proposes to do; and all that it needs from Parliament is the money. But more frequently nowadays new items, or enlarged items, result from the enactment of statutes that confer on the government the right to begin new undertakings or programs. This brings us to a second kind of appropriation. The expenditure of money may be either essential to a program or only incidental to it. For example, the Family Allowances Act authorizes the Crown to pay allowances on behalf of children under a certain age—the expenditure is essential to the program. But the costs of administering that statute are only incidental. In Canada the practice is that the money required to make expenditures that are incidental is appropriated in the appropriations acts, while the money required for transfer payments—payments to provincial governments, pensions, subsidies, *etc.*—is appropriated in the same statute that authorizes the program. For example, the money with which the Crown makes payments to the provinces under the Hospital Insurance and Diagnostic Services Act is appropriated in that act. And the money with which old age pensions are paid is appropriated in the statute that authorizes the Crown to pay those pensions.

Appropriations made in this second way differ from appropriations made by appropriation acts in two important particulars. First, the amount to be paid out in any year cannot be varied by the government; rather, it is determined by the provisions in the relevant statute and by independent factors such as the number of children born, the number of persons hospitalized, and the number of persons who attain the eligibility age. Second, these appropriations are made for the life of the program: they do not need to be renewed from year to year. However, because the amount that will be required by such programs bears directly on what will be left for other governmental activities, and also on taxation, before the beginning of each fiscal year the amount of money that will be required for each of these programs during that year is estimated. That amount is shown in the main estimates for the year, but each such item is marked, "statutory," to indicate that both the purpose and the amount required already have been approved by Parliament, and will not be dealt with in the appropriation act eventuating from those estimates.

Because of the number and extent of the transfer payment programs in which the Government of Canada has become involved the amount of money estimated to meet statutory obligations may equal or even exceed the amount requested in the annual main estimates. The main estimates for 1974-75, for example, included $11,544,507,219 as statutory, and $10,478,396,618 to be voted. For 1975-76 the total required to cover statutory obligations was estimated at $13,906,568,766, as against $14,335,293,269 to be voted.

In summary, we may say that ordinarily Parliament provides the Crown with money in two principal ways: first, by appropriation acts to maintain the machinery and activities of the Crown from year to year, and, second, by the statutes that establish certain programs of payments.[6] When we refer to the procedure by which the business of supply is done in the House of Commons we are referring to the first of these two kinds of appropriation.

A third kind of authorization for the withdrawal of money from the Consolidated Revenue Fund must be mentioned. At its first session the new Parliament of Canada enacted that, "If when Parliament is not in session, any accident happens to any public work or building which requires an immediate outlay for the repair thereof, or any other occasion arises when any expenditure not foreseen or provided for by Parliament is urgently and immediately required for the public good..." a special warrant authorizing the expenditure might be made by the governor general. That provision now appears in the Financial Administration Act in the following language: "Where a payment is urgently required for the public good when Parliament is not in session and there is no other appropriation pursuant to which the payment may be made, the Governor in Council, upon the report of the President of the Treasury Board that there is no appropriation for the payment and the report of the appropriate Minister that the payment is urgently required for the public good, may by order direct the preparation of a special warrant to be signed by the Governor General authorizing the payment to be made out of the Consolidated Revenue Fund." This provision makes it possible for prime ministers to have Parliament dissolved even although the annual supply business has not been completed. Special warrants are used to pay the Crown's bills from the time of dissolution until the new Parliament has met. This was done in 1896, 1911, 1926, 1940, 1957, 1958, 1962, 1963, 1965, 1968, 1972, and 1974. Clearly, special warrants have become an important part of the working constitution. Such criticism as there has been has focused on the instances when the new Parliament was not called into session as quickly as possible after the election. Every special warrant is to be published in the *Canada Gazette* within thirty days after it is issued; and within fifteen days after the commencement of the next ensuing session of Parliament the government must table in the House of Commons a statement showing what warrants were issued. Moreover, the amounts appropriated by special warrant are to be included in the next request for supply so that the payments made by warrant will come before the House.

APPROPRIATION: ANNUAL SUPPLY

At some point in the Speech from the Throne the governor general addresses himself to the Commons exclusively with words such as these: "Members of the House of Commons: During this Session, you will be asked to grant the necessary funds for the services and expenditures authorized by Parliament." Having been alerted, the loyal Commons make ready for the Crown's requests by entering on the Order Paper—under Government Orders—a continuing order for dealing with the business of supply. A few weeks before the start of the new fiscal year the governor general, by means of a minister, sends a message signed by his own hand transmitting to the House estimates showing what the government then calculates will be required by the Crown during the forthcoming fiscal year. This request—in the form of "the main estimates" or "the Blue Book"—is broken down into "votes," each specifying the purpose of an expenditure, and giving an estimate of the total amount of money that would be required for that purpose during the year.

Since the main estimates will have been prepared at least fifteen months before the end of the year in which they will apply, frequently it will be found that the amounts estimated for some purposes are too small or that expenditures for entirely new purposes should be made before the beginning of the next fiscal year. In short, the main estimates invariably now have to be supplemented by (a) votes to increase the sums provided in some of the original votes, (b) votes to allow money already granted for one purpose to be used for another purpose by the Crown, and (c) by entirely new votes. As a result, during a fiscal year one or more sets of supplementary estimates will be presented to the House. And, whether or not there already has been an earlier set of supplementary estimates, shortly before the end of the fiscal year the Crown regularly has to ask for moneys to supplement the amounts available under those votes where there will be shortfalls. Formerly these were referred to as "final supplementary estimates," but given the uncertainties of its requirements the Treasury Board now is reluctant to use that term other than retrospectively after the end of the fiscal year.[7]

If, as is now always the case, the money requested by the Crown in the main estimates has not been appropriated before the first payments in the new fiscal year are due, the Crown will ask for an advance—

known in Canada as "an interim supply"—against the votes in those estimates.

The main estimates, then, set forth the basic spending proposals for the fiscal year: to concur in them is to give approval to the government's spending plans for the year. Concurrence by the House in a request for interim supply, in contrast, does not constitute approval for the program. However, obviously it does express, although indirectly, a willingness to let the government begin its spending program. Supplementary estimates may or may not raise questions of policy. Some votes merely increase the money available for expenditures already approved in earlier estimates; other votes authorize new expenditures.

From the viewpoint of the Crown the important thing is the passing of the appropriation bills. However, the House of Commons, consistent with the tradition of the British House since 1667 and even earlier, insists that certain preliminary procedures be completed before an appropriation bill may be introduced. These preliminaries are what is known as "the supply process." Only when they have been completed successfully may the government introduce its appropriation bill. But once those preliminaries have been completed, since the bill is entirely consequential on decisions already made by the members, the House normally passes the bill without debate or amendments. The preliminaries may require months of work; but ordinarily an appropriation bill will pass through all the stages of the ordinary legislative process in less than five minutes.

The constitutional importance of the business of supply would be hard to over-state. Whether or not a government that cannot get other bills past the House can carry on in office is a matter to be decided by the prime minister and his ministerial colleagues. Basically, the same is true for tax bills, provided, of course, that the Consolidated Revenue Fund is not empty. In contrast, a government that cannot get its supply business past the House, has no alternative to resignation or dissolution. Ultimately the holding of regular sessions of Parliament and the co-operation of the House of Commons are indispensable to the Crown because unless money is appropriated from time to time to its requirements the Crown simply will not be able to pay the costs of its own maintenance.[8]

Moreover, while other government bills relate to changes in the law, and are dealt with one by one and on their several merits, the business of supply relates to the conduct and maintenance of the government itself. Therefore, this business gives the members an unrestricted opportunity to examine the performance by the ministers of all their duties under both the common law and statutes. Even if there was to be an annual session at which the ministers introduced no bills of any kind other than the appropriation bills, the members would have an important task to do, namely, to examine the conduct of the on-going business of the country at home and abroad, and, following that, to decide whether or not to vote the money without which the government could not carry on.

Finally, the business of supply now is increasingly important because it affords the members their best opportunity to examine the spending side of the government's fiscal policy.

The procedures by which the business of supply is done should conform to certain simple standards. First, they should enable the members to obtain an understanding of the operation of the various departments, branches, and agencies, and, also to obtain adequate explanations of the policies followed by them. Second, they should enable the members to criticize publicly both the operation and the policies of those bodies. Third, they should enable the members to discuss publicly from time to time the shortcomings of the ministers, both their sins of omission and of commission. Fourth, they should enable them to test from time to time whether or not despite the complaints and criticisms the government retains the confidence of the House. Fifth, the procedures should enable the members to see the entire panorama of public expenditure, both statutory and budgetary, as it increases from year to year. Finally, the business of supply should be done in an orderly way so that the Crown can have a sound basis for the conduct of its business, and so that the House itself does not remain in session too long or sit at unsuitable seasons of the year.

The time-table for the annual supply business and the timing of the annual sessions are related closely. If the sessions are started too late, the supply business cannot be completed early in the fiscal year. If the supply business is not dealt with in an orderly fashion, not only will it be finished late, but it will extend the session, thus delaying the beginning of the next session.

Until 1907 the Canadian fiscal year started on the first day of July. This, together with the fact that there was relatively little non-financial public business, helps explain why in the early days of the Dominion it was possible for the sessions to be started in January or February. All the work could be done in a few weeks; and the members could be back home before the fields and roads were dry. Later the sessions became longer; they began to run on into the late spring and the early summer. But that season, the members found, was neither convenient nor salubrious. The best time to be incarcerated at Ottawa, away from their constituencies and their private affairs, was the late fall and the winter. As a result in 1906 a plan was conceived that thereafter the annual sessions ordinarily would begin in the fall. To conform to the plan the beginning of the fiscal year—beginning with 1907-08—was moved back to the first day of April.

That plan did not succeed. Even though the sessions were started in the fall, they still dragged on into May, June, and July. Again and again the main appropriation acts were not enacted before the beginning of the new fiscal year, and the Crown had to ask for an interim supply. In this situation the early beginnings seemed pointless. After 1912 the sessions again were started regularly in mid-winter. This meant that no longer would there be any chance of having the main appropriation act through before the first of April. Consequently, requests for interim supply became a part of the normal annual supply business. Sometimes two, three, or even more interim supplies had to be sought when a session dragged on. This disorderly way of doing business continued until 20 December 1968.

Already we have noticed that in 1867 the Canadian House of Commons adopted a standing order under which the House would not deal with any request for supply or taxation until that request had been considered in a committee. Under the standing orders in effect before 20 December 1968, each request for supply—the main estimates, interim supply, and any supplementary estimates—was considered and then approved (or disapproved) by a particular committee of the whole House, namely, the Committee of Supply. (When that committee had recommended to the House that the supply requested be granted, and the House had concurred, the members went into the Committee of Ways and Means, where they resolved that the money should be appropriated from the Fund. Then, an appropriation bill based on that resolution was introduced.) Here, then, was one of the main supply proceedings: the consideration of the supply votes in the Committee of Supply.

The other main proceeding used in supply business before 20 December 1968, was "the supply motion." If the members, having met as the House, are to take up work of a kind that is done only in a committee of the whole House, they must cease to be the House and become a committee. What signals this metamorphosis is the departure of the speaker from the Chair. From 1867 until 1913 the motion, "That the Speaker do now leave the Chair," always was debatable, and amendments always could be moved. The result—especially after 1906—was that the members often got into the Committee of Supply only very late in the day, and sometimes not at all. In other words, the principle of "grievance before supply" was taken so seriously, and the members found that they had so much about which to grieve, that consideration of the estimates was pushed aside as secondary. Then at the very end of the sessions the estimates would be rushed through at a few long sittings. In 1913 the standing orders were changed so that on Thursday and Friday the speaker would leave the Chair without a motion if the business ordered for that sitting was supply business (or ways and means business); however, the Committee of Supply was not to consider any proposed vote unless it had been first seized of it on one of the other days of the week, i.e., every vote had to be entered into consideration on a day when the opposition or any private member could mount an attack on the government in relation to its conduct or policy in the field (or fields) to which the votes to be entered that day related. This new arrangement (a) retained the constitutional right of the members to state and publicize their grievances, great or small, before they dealt with the Crown's requests for money, but (b) assured that the Crown's requests for money would be considered on at least two days of the week.

These "supply motion debates"—dealing with the motion to change the House into the Committee of Supply—came to be of great importance. When the government sought to have the members turn to supply business by moving other than on a Thursday or a Friday, "That the Speaker do now leave the Chair," the House could react in four ways. The members could let the motion carry without debate. Second, they could debate the motion, with each member free to raise his own grievance or topic because of the procedural nature of the motion. Third, an amendment which did not raise the question of confidence could be moved. In that case the debate had to be relevant to the topic of the amendment until the amendment had been disposed of by the House. And, fourth, the amendment moved could be to the effect that for a stated reason the House did not have confidence in the government. In 1927 the standing orders were changed so that a relevant sub-amendment could be moved; thus it became possible for a third party to seek by moving a sub-amendment to put its own special edge on the amendment. The importance of supply motion debates was enhanced by the fact that after the motion for an Address in Reply had been dealt with supply motions provided the opposition with its chief opportunities to initiate debates on topics of its choice.

In 1955 another important change was made in the standing orders. Thereafter "supply motions" were to be moved only six times in each annual session, the group of proposed votes to be entered into the Committee of Supply on each of the six occasions was to be specified in advance, and the debate on each of the six motions was to be limited to two days. The main motion was to be moved as the first order of the day on a Monday, and the questions on any subamendment and any amendment were to be put to the House on Tuesday evening at 8:15 p.m. If such amending motions were defeated, the House would debate the main motion—with the members free to raise diverse grievances—until immediately before the hour of adjournment when the question was put on the main motion. If it carried the speaker left the Chair, the listed votes were taken up cursorily by the Committee of Supply, the committee then rose, the speaker resumed the Chair, and the House adjourned for the day. When next the Committee of Supply met it was free to deal extensively with the votes that had been entered in this way. Although the government almost always voted against any amendment, it was free to support an amendment. The first session after Mr. Pearson became prime minister affords an interesting example. On 12 November 1963, the minister of finance moved, "That Mr. Speaker do now leave the Chair." The Progressive Conservatives moved to replace all the words after "That" so that the amended motion would read: "That this House condemns the Government for its failure to carry out the spirit of co-operative federalism and for its neglect to consult with the Provinces before announcing or undertaking programmes which fall wholly or partly within Provincial jurisdiction." The N.D.P. proceeded to move that the amendment be amended by substituting the words "urges the Government to carry out more fully" for "condemns the Government for its failure to carry out," by deleting the words "for its neglect," and by substituting the words "to any extent" for "wholly or partly." The Pearson government decided to vote for the sub-amendment, which was carried by 128 Yeas to 60 Nays. Then the Progressive Conservative amendment, as amended, was carried by 187 Yeas to 0 Nays.[9]

The Diefenbaker government had not been so fortunate earlier in the year. On Monday, 4 February 1963, the Hon. George Nowlan, minister of finance, moved, "That Mr. Speaker do now leave the Chair for the House to resolve itself into Committee of Supply." The leader of the opposition, Mr. Pearson, moved that the motion be amended by deleting all the words after "That" and substituting other words so that the motion as amended would read, "That this government, because of lack of leadership, the breakdown of unity in the Cabinet, and confusion and indecision in dealing with national and international problems, does not have the confidence of the Canadian people." The leader of the Social Credit Party, Mr. Robert Thompson, then took advantage of the right to move a sub-amendment. He moved to delete all the words in Mr. Pearson's amendment after "government" and to substitute the following, "has failed up to this time to give a clear statement of policy respecting Canada's national defence, and has failed to organize the business of the House so that the 1963–64 Estimates and Budget could be introduced, and has failed to outline a positive programme of follow-up action respecting many things for which this Parliament and previous Parliaments have already given authority, and does not have the confidence of the Canadian people." Pursuant to the standing orders, at 8:15 p.m., on Tuesday, 5 February 1963, the speaker put the question on the sub-amendment. It carried by 142 to 111. Mr. Pearson's amendment, as amended, then carried by the same vote. The next day Parliament was dissolved. In the ensuing election, on 8 April 1963, the Diefenbaker government was defeated at the polls.

By 1965 both these supply proceedings were under strong criticism from all sides of the House. Let us begin with the "supply motion debates." First, one result of the change made in 1955 was that each of the six motions became the occasion for what generally amounted to a no-confidence amendment. The official opposition, regardless of its own wishes, felt obliged to move an amendment because if it did not one of the "third parties" would grasp the role of the opposition. Second, if the six debates came on in a period of a few weeks in the late winter and spring, as they would if the supply business was dealt with in an orderly way, the government was immune from no-confidence attacks throughout much of the rest of the year. Third, since no notice was given of the opposition's motion to amend the supply motion, the House did not know what the topic of the debate was going to be until the debate was underway. And, fourth, the crucial votes came on so early on Tuesday evening that the value of the debate on Tuesday was reduced sharply, especially if the routine proceedings had been long.

Criticism of the work of the Committee of Supply was even stronger. From about 1945 the view had grown that even when the committee was at its best, for various reasons its operations were an ineffectual exercise in tedium. It was too large a body to be effective. The Chamber was too large a setting. The meetings were dominated by the same small group of members who monopolized the time of the House. And, in addition, only ministers and parliamentary secretaries —not deputy ministers and other public servants—could answer questions about proposed expenditures. The inadequacy of the procedure was made manifest by the practice of allowing a minister to bring one or two department officials into the Chamber—they sat at a small table on the floor of the Chamber—to prompt him or to give him answers which he then relayed at second hand to the committee. The work, in short, was done poorly; and it was done in such a way that all members, save those few who saw themselves as the star performers, were bored. Moreover, since there was no limit on the time the committee could take for its work, since the House could not sit to do other business while the committee was at work, and since the committee met in the Chamber in the full glare of publicity, the committee had ceased to pay much if any attention to the spending proposals, and had become a cockpit in which the opposition parties waged a war of attrition against the government. From the ministerial viewpoint supply business had become a wearisome ordeal. It dragged on for months, but rarely had the government any reason to fear that the members would turn their attention to the policies behind the estimates.

The Special Committee on Procedure (1967-68) outlined all the major features of a fully reformed supply business procedure. In the fall of 1968 its successor, the Special Committee on Procedure (1968), drew up and recommended to the House the new standing orders required to bring in the reforms. On 20 December 1968, those standing orders were accepted unanimously by the House, but not before they had undergone harsh criticism from some members in the opposition. Indeed, it is doubtful that they would have been accepted—short of the use of closure—if the opposition had not concentrated its main attack elsewhere, on the proposed Standing Order 16-A, a time allocation rule that the Trudeau government was prepared to jettison.

The new procedure is designed to produce four effects: (a) to give the members an opportunity to examine the main estimates early and thoroughly; (b) to give the opposition opportunities less ponderous and more numerous than the old "supply motion debates" to elaborate a complaint or charge against the government, and perhaps subsequently to test the confidence of the House in the government; (c) to give the government some certainty as to when the House will decide whether or not to grant supply; and (d) to provide a reasonable structure for annual sessions of Parliament. The basis of the reform was the view that the examination of the policy and details of the government's program, on the one hand, and the highly institutionalized and publicized contention between the opposition and the government, on the other, are distinct operations, and that under the old procedure neither was successful because the two were badly confused. It was hoped that by separating the operations, each could be made more effective. This is not to say that under the new procedure the opposition cannot raise in the House matters first approached during the examination of the estimates; indeed, as we shall see, the new procedure was contrived to make it very easy for them to do so.

It is assumed that about the middle of February the Crown will present the main estimates for the fiscal year to begin on the first day of April. It is assumed also that supplementary estimates may be presented during the ensuing months, and that a set of final supplementary estimates will be presented shortly before the end of the fiscal year to enable the Crown to finish the year without unpaid bills. In addition, it is assumed that the main estimates will not have been dealt with before the end of the first pay period in April, so that the Crown will require an interim supply to cover expenditures during the first part of each new fiscal year.

The standing orders now provide that on or before March first all proposed votes in the main estimates are to be referred by the House to appropriate standing committees. These committees are to complete their examination of them before the first of June. Any supplementary estimates are to be referred to a standing committee immediately they have been presented to the House; and that committee is to report them to the House not later than three sitting days before the last sitting day for supply business in the current period. In this way provision has been made for the performance of the work formerly done by the Committee of Supply; consequently, that committee has vanished.

Instead of the old arrangement under which the opposition brought on debates in the House by moving amendments to supply motions, a a total of twenty-five days in the House has been put at the disposal of the opposition in each annual session. On those days—they are referred to variously as "allotted days," as "opposition days," and as "supply days"—the opposition, after having given twenty-four hours notice, may move motions relating to "any matter within the jurisdiction of the Parliament of Canada." The twenty-five days are divided into three groups: five days during the period ending on 10 December; seven days during the period ending on 26 March; and thirteen days during the period ending on 30 June. At the very end of the sitting on the final allotted day in each period, after the motions put forward during that period by the opposition have been dealt with, the House is asked to decide all questions relating to requests for supply (and, subsequently, for the appropriation of money) then before the House. In short, the House does not vote to grant (or to refuse) supply until the opposition has had opportunities to demonstrate to the House and the country why supply should be refused.

There was disagreement in 1968 as to whether the total of twenty-five days would be too few or too many for the purposes of the opposition. From the viewpoint of a government the number of days makes relatively little difference as long as the work of a session can be completed in seven or eight months. But some of the Liberals held that an opposition ought not to be expected to initiate too many debates under conditions requiring that those debates be well-planned, well-conducted, and noteworthy; otherwise, their efforts would appear trivial or ill-tempered, and supply days would lose their importance. In the fall of 1968 the Liberals suggested that fifteen days would be enough. This was met by a suggestion from the Progressive Conservatives that there should be thirty-five or forty days. Predictably, the figure finally agreed upon was twenty-five days.

The distribution of the days over the term of the annual session was not contentious. It was agreed that a normal annual session should begin in the fall and end about 1 July. If supply days in the fall were prescribed, it would be difficult for a government to revert to the old pattern of begining the sessions in January or February and ending them in mid-summer. Moreover, some provision was needed for dealing with any supplementary estimates presented during the fall. In addition, it was agreed that the fall supply period should not end so early as to require a very early meeting of Parliament. The deadline date finally selected was 10 December. It seemed obvious, too, that the second supply period should end on a date convenient for concluding the business relating to both the final supplementary estimates for the old fiscal year and the interim supply for the new fiscal year. The deadline date selected was 26 March. Finally, it seemed obvious that a fair number of days should be available to the opposition before the onset of summer for motions arising from the work on the main estimates done by the standing committees during March, April, and May. The deadline selected was 30 June.

How many of the twenty-five days would be allotted to each of these three periods was another question that aroused no argument. At the beginning of each session the opposition has an opportunity to denounce the government during the debate on the Address in Reply, and normally now an amendment and a sub-amendment are moved. Consequently, only five days were allotted for supply business in the fall. To enable the opposition to make an assault on the policies of the government, and to attack particular ministers, departments, and agencies on the basis of the main estimates by far the greatest number of days—thirteen—were allotted to the third period. The remaining seven days were allotted to the period that ends on 26 March. The annual supply business timetable is shown in Table 4.

Another point that had to be settled related to the number of supply days on which no-confidence motions might be moved. Although most amendments to supply motions between 1955 and 1968 did not mention confidence the government voted against almost all of them. In periods of high political tension it was understood that they entailed confidence (or no-confidence). But just how valuable those amendments were to the opposition was questionable. If those in opposition were strong enough to defeat the government, they did not lack opportunities. All they needed to do was to refuse to pass an appropriation bill. If not, the repeated defeats of their challenges probably were more advantageous to the government, for almost inevitably the official opposition was made to appear both power-hungry and ineffectual; yet if the official opposition refrained from moving an

TABLE 4
Annual Supply Business Timetable
Supply Business Completed (1 Jan. 1969 to 30 June 1970)

Session	Fiscal Year	Supply Periods		Appropriation Acts
12 Sept. 1968	1 April 1968		**1 January 1969**	
		26 March	Main Estimates, 1969–70, presented to House—4 Feb. Main Estimates, 1969–70, referred to the standing committees—20 Feb. Final Suppl. Estimates, 1968–69, approved by House—5 March Interim Supply for April–June approved by House—26 March last day in this period for supply business	No. 1 No. 2
1968–69 session	31 March 1 April		**New fiscal year begins**	
		31 May	final day for standing committees to report Main Estimates Main Estimates, 1969–70, approved by House—25 June	No. 3
		30 June	last day in this period for supply business	
22 Oct. 1969 23 Oct. 1969		10 Dec.	Suppl. Estimates, 1969–70, approved by House—9 Dec. last day in this period for supply business	No. 4
			1 January 1970	
		26 March	Main Estimates, 1970–71, presented to House—11 Feb. Main Estimates, 1970–71, referred to the standing committees—18 Feb. Final Suppl. Estimates, 1969–70, approved by House—24 March Interim Supply for April–June approved by House—24 March last day in this period for supply business	No. 1 No. 2
1969–70 session	31 March 1 April		**New fiscal year begins**	
		31 May	final day for standing committees to report Main Estimates Main Estimates, 1970–71, approved by House—18 June	No. 3
7 Oct. 1970		30 June	last day in this period for supply business	

amendment the first third-party spokesman was likely to do so. In 1968 a few members thought that formal no-confidence motions ought not to be allowed on supply days, but this view found little support. At the other extreme, the possibility of a vote with no-confidence implications on each of the twenty-five supply days also was found unacceptable. As a result the standing orders made on 20 December 1968, provide that six of the supply days may be used for motions entailing no confidence. They cannot be bunched together: only two no-confidence motions may be moved in each of the three periods. On the other nineteen days the proceedings on opposition motions simply expire without a vote at the end of the sitting. The standing orders do not confine the right to move no-confidence motions on supply days to the official opposition.[10]

Although the motions debated on the twenty-five supply days are opposition motions, supply business is government business. The government decides what days are to be supply days. It puts down motions for the granting of the supply then requested, but on every supply day any motion of which the opposition has given notice takes precedence over the government's motions for supply. Only at the very end of the last supply day in each of the periods—unless, of course, the opposition has decided not to move motions—does the House turn to the government's motions for concurrence. On those days, fifteen minutes before the hour of daily adjournment the speaker interrupts the proceedings. If the opposition motion is a no-confidence motion, he puts the question on that motion. If not, he simply cuts off the debate. Then, unless the government has been defeated, he proceeds to put the question on each government motion for concurrence in any supply request then before the House.

It still is possible for members to vote in the House against particular items (or votes) in a set of estimates. Formerly just before the Committee of Supply finished its work on the main estimates, often late on the last night before the summer adjournment (or before prorogation), the members had to deal separately with each vote not approved earlier. This meant that the chairman of the Committee of Supply regularly spent two or three hours calling off items, one by one—"Estimates of Department of Fisheries. Vote No. 1. Shall Vote No. 1 carry? Carried. Vote No. 5. Shall Vote No. 5 carry? Carried."—with occasional interruptions by loquacious or obdurate members who wished to ask questions about an item, to speak against granting the money, or to vote against the item. Under the new procedure, since it is in the standing committees that the members have their opportunity to deal with the items individually, it is possible that all the House itself may have to do is to adopt a single motion to grant the total supply. However, any member who wishes to challenge an item in the House may ask in advance that the item be treated separately. The speaker puts to the House a separate question on each item for which a separate decision by the House has been requested.[11] Then he puts to the House one question covering all the other items. Normally this saves a great deal of time. No debate and no amendment take place at this stage. The assumption is that the opposition will have made any item to which there is wide objection the subject of a debate on a supply day.[12]

Because of s. 54 of the British North America Act neither the House nor any of its committees can insert a new vote in the estimates; nor can they increase the amount requested in any vote. Similarly, the specific purpose for which an amount is requested by the Crown cannot be altered. On the other hand, a committee can recommend either that a vote be refused or that the amount requested be reduced; and the House, with or without such a recommendation, can refuse to pass the item or can reduce the amount.

If the House resolves to grant the amounts requested for the purposes specified—in the main estimates, in a set of supplementary estimates, or as interim supply—the supply business phase of the process has been concluded. But the House cannot stop there: to concur in the various votes in a set of estimates is not to authorize the withdrawal of the money from the Consolidated Revenue Fund. Formerly in Britain, as we saw, after the supply resolutions had been passed in the Committee of Supply, and concurred in by the House, the members went into the Committee of Ways and Means to consider how to find the money to make good the supply that had been voted. However, as we noted earlier, that step always was meaningless in Canada, for from the beginning it was clear that the money was to be taken from the Consolidated Revenue Fund; and the replenishment of that Fund was, and is, dealt with by a separate process, the taxation process. This old requirement—dating back to the days before the establishment of the Consolidated Fund in England—as an intermediate step between the supply resolution(s) and the introduction of the consequent appropriation bill was abolished on 20 December 1968. The appropriation bill to give effect to the supply resolution (or to supply resolutions when a separate vote has been taken on one or more opposed items) now is given its first reading immediately after the House has adopted that resolution. Since appropriation bills merely give statutory effect to decisions made during the supply business stage, those bills are moved forward immediately through all the stages of the ordinary legislative process without amendment and without debate. However, formal divisions on the stages of the bill may be requested. If no separate votes are requested on motions for concurrence, and if there are no divisions on the appropriation bill, the whole process may require less than fifteen minutes. Invariably this prompts news stories about billions of dollars being voted in a few minutes.

The fact that supply business is government business proved of great political importance in the spring of 1974. Early in April 1974, the Progressive Conservatives decided that there was a strong possibility that the New Democratic Party had grown tired of supporting the minority Trudeau government, and was ready to join the official opposition in a move to defeat the government before the minister of finance, Mr. Turner, had made his budget statement. On 8 April they began to make demands that the government bring on a supply day, which they intended to use to move a no-confidence motion. However, the government was not prepared to facilitate its own defeat. To increase the pressure on the government by extending the number of sittings at which no supply business was done the Progressive Conservatives indicated that they would debate the motion for an Easter adjournment; accordingly, the government house leader, Mr. MacEachen, did not move the adjournment motion of which he had given notice. No supply days were held in April. This meant that Mr. Turner was able to make his budget statement on 6 May 1974.

On that day he moved the budget motion, "That the House approves in general the budgetary policy of the Government." On the following day the Hon. Marcel Lambert, for the Progressive Conservatives, moved that Mr. Turner's motion be amended by replacing all the words after "That" with, "this House does not have confidence in the government by reason of its failure to propose effective budgetary measures to contain and reduce inflation." Then the leader of the New Democratic Party, Mr. David Lewis, moved that the amendment be amended by adding the words, "and its failure to propose any measures to assist pensioners and other Canadians on low and fixed incomes, to deal with the housing crisis, or to remove the glaring inequalities in the taxation system." On Wednesday, 8 May 1974, Mr. Lewis' motion was carried by a vote of 137 to 123. In the subsequent election campaign the contents of Mr. Turner's budget, which had been rejected by the Progressive Conservatives and the New Democratic Party, was of major importance. On 8 July 1974, the Liberal government was returned, and with a majority. The inevitable question is whether the outcome would have been different if the Progressive Conservatives had been able to defeat the government before the budget had been delivered.

It was foreseen that the supply timetable would not suit all situations: especially because of the length of time in Canada between a dissolution and the meeting of a new Parliament there would be times when the government could not wait for money until 10 December, 26 March, or

30 June. Accordingly, the House by Standing Order 58(18) provided: "In the event of urgency in relation to any estimate or estimates, the proceedings of the House on a motion to concur therein and on the subsequent bill are to be taken under Government Orders and not on days allotted in this Order." Two such instances occurred during the first six years, each brought on by an election. When the new Parliament met in January 1973, the Trudeau government presented a set of supplementary estimates in which was included the moneys appropriated by governor general's special warrants after the dissolution of Parliament. Given the government's minority position, the government house leader, Mr. MacEachen, was anxious to avoid a series of votes on isolated items, but he was even more anxious to prevent prolonged debate. Ordinarily items segregated for a separate vote are dealt with at the end of the last day on each supply term, when because of the time limit they were not debatable. Mr. MacEachen contended that the House should be asked to concur in the total supply, after which the bill would be introduced. Debate and consideration, he argued, would be in order on the appropriation bill. However, Mr. Speaker Lamoureux ruled that the opposition had the right to oppose each item if they wished. Since there was no guillotine this meant that they had the right to debate each item. Ten days were required for that set of supplementary estimates. The House began dealing with opposed items on 7 February. The bill was introduced, read twice, and sent to a committee of the whole House on 12 February. The committee reported on 20 February, when the bill was read a third time. In contrast, in the fall of 1974 the House followed the approach suggested in 1973 by Mr. MacEachen. Because of the dissolution on 9 May the proceedings in the House on the main estimates for 1974–75 had not been completed. In the fall the main estimates again were transmitted to the House. On 23 October 1974, the House concurred in all the votes without debate. Then the bill was introduced, and advanced without debate at the second-reading stage to the committee stage. As a result of an agreement among the house leaders three days, with extended hours, were taken on the bill in committee of the whole House with the time devoted to the estimates of six departments. At the end of the sitting of 25 October the bill was read a third time.

Pursuant to s. 53 of the B.N.A. Act all bills imposing taxes or authorizing expenditure either for the maintenance of the machinery of government or to pay for transfer payment programs are introduced in the House of Commons; but only appropriation bills are presented for royal assent separately. After an appropriation bill has passed the Senate, it is returned to the speaker of the House of Commons. When royal assent is being given to bills the speaker presents any appropriation bills that are ready. For example, on 26 June 1975, the speaker of the House, standing at the bar of the Senate, addressed the deputy to the governor general as follows: "May it please Your Honour: The Commons of Canada have voted supplies to enable the Government to defray certain expenses of the public service. In the name of the Commons, I present to Your Honour the following Bill: 'An Act for granting to Her Majesty certain sums of money for the public service for the financial year ending 31st March, 1976.' To which Bill I humbly request Your Honour's Assent." Then the clerk of the Senate, by command, replied: "In Her Majesty's name, the Honourable the Deputy of His Excellency the Governor General thanks her loyal subjects, accepts their benevolence and assents to this Bill." This reply is based on the Norman French used at Westminster: "*La reyne remercie ses bons sujets, accepte leur benevolence, et ainsi le veult.*"

APPROPRIATION: FOR CONTINUING PROGRAMS

As already mentioned, many statutes nowadays authorize payments to persons for welfare or social security purposes, to provincial governments for joint-cost programs, and to individuals and companies as incentive grants, supports, and subsidies. At the same time most new government activity, even when such transfers are not involved, entails costs. Section 54 of the British North America Act applies not only to the annual supply business but to all proposals involving payments or costs. It prohibits private members from taking the initiative in the kind of government activity that now is most prominent. Moreover, it prevents private members from moving to increase the government's proposals for payments or costs, or to change the purpose(s). The message of recommendation from the governor general prescribed by s. 54 defines both the purpose for which the House may provide money and the maximum amount.

As we noticed earlier, in 1867 the Canadian House of Commons made a standing order that all spending proposals, as well as all taxing proposals, were to be dealt with first in a committee of the whole House. Standing Order 61 provided: "If any motion be made in the House for any public aid or charge upon the people, the consideration and debate thereof may not be presently entered upon, but shall be adjourned till such further day as the House thinks fit to appoint; and then it shall be referred to a committee of the whole House, before any resolution or vote of the House do pass thereupon." This order was interpreted as meaning that no bill authorizing either payments or government activity entailing costs could be introduced unless a motion describing the expenditure in some detail and approving it first had been carried in a committee of the whole House. In other words, there was to be what came to be called "a financial resolution."

The procedure followed by the House before 20 December 1968, in dealing with such bills resulted from reading s. 54 of the B.N.A. Act and Standing Order 61 together. When the government wished to introduce such a bill, the governor general transmitted a Message of Recommendation in which all the major features and often many of the details of the proposed measure were set forth. The government then gave notice of a motion proposing, "That it is expedient to introduce a measure to...." These introductory words were followed by the text of the recommendation. This motion was moved in a committee of the whole House. In this way it was assured that the resolution of the committee was perfectly consistent with the recommendation. Only after the motion had been carried in committee and reported to the House was the government permitted to introduce its bill. In the 1963 session thirty of the thirty-eight bills introduced by the government, other than taxation and appropriation bills, were preceded by resolutions. In the 1964–65 session nineteen of forty such bills were preceded by resolutions. In the 1965 session fifteen of eighteen bills, in the 1966–67 session forty-nine of eighty-seven bills, and in the 1967–68 session fourteen of thirty-three bills were preceded by resolutions.

Before 9 October 1964, the consideration of proposed financial resolutions was unlimited as to time. On that date provisionally a time limit of one sitting day for each resolution was introduced; and in the case of an interruption a total of five hours was to be deemed the equivalent of a sitting day. That limit was still in effect in 1968.

The Special Committee on Procedure (1968) found that the requirement that bills authorizing payments or entailing costs be preceded by a financial resolution, however advisable in the sixteenth and seventeenth centuries, in Canada in the twentieth century produced undesirable results without any countervailing benefits. Not only did the requirement invite members to waste time on conjecture about the contents of forthcoming bills, but the debates on proposed financial resolutions, to the extent that they were meaningful, merely anticipated and rehearsed the second-reading debates.[13] Accordingly, the committee recommended simply that the requirement for a financial resolution, and thus for a preliminary committee stage, be stricken from the standing orders. On 20 December 1968, the House adopted that recommendation.

This change in the rules made itself felt at once. On the Order Paper for 20 December 1968, were various proposed financial resolutions. Since action on them no longer was required, six of the proposed resolutions were passed over, and immediately, one by one, the six bills were introduced and given first reading.[14] Under the old practice upwards of six days might have been required to move those measures forward to the first-reading stage.

The elimination of a financial resolution as a prerequisite of every bill appropriating money either expressly or incidentally has not modified the constitutional prohibition against appropriations that have not been recommended to the House by the governor general; indeed—to make it unnecessary for the speaker to try to decide constitutional questions—the substance of s. 54 of the B.N.A. Act now is set forth as S.O. 62(1) of the House of Commons.[15] The Crown retains control over the initiation of expenditure.

Formerly, to prevent variations between the appropriations recommended by the governor general and the financial resolutions of the House, the text of the message of recommendation was used as the text of the proposed resolution; but there remained the possibility that the bill would not be in perfect harmony with the resolution. The new standing order reads: "The message and recommendation of the Governor General in relation to any bill for the appropriation of any part of the public revenue or of any tax or impost shall be printed on the Notice Paper and in the *Votes and Proceedings* when any such measure is to be introduced and the text of such recommendation shall be printed with or annexed to every such bill." It is possible that divergence will creep in between the recommending message and the bill; but that danger is no greater now than it was under the old procedure. The speaker will rule inadmissible any bill that goes beyond the message of recommendation accompanying it; nor will he allow either a minister or a private member to move an amendment that goes beyond the original recommendation unless covered by a supplementary recommendation. On 23 April 1975, when the House was about to embark upon the report stage of Bill C-44, to increase parliamentary indemnities, Mr. Speaker Jerome directed that a clause added by the Standing Committee on Miscellaneous Estimates providing for the indexing of indemnities be struck from the bill because it would result in payments higher than those that had been recommended by the governor general. Then at the report stage, after a supplementary recommendation had been received, the president of the Privy Council moved successfully for a clause providing for indexing.[16]

CONCLUSION

Historically money business in the House of Commons at Westminster was quite distinct from the preparation of ordinary public bills. The decisions of the House on taxing and spending had to be set forth in bills if they were to become law, but for the most part that was only a necessary formality. The real work was done in committees of the whole House before the bills were introduced. For a very long time that procedure was sound. The ordinary legislative process at that time was mainly an exploratory process by which the House decided which of the bills the members had introduced should be presented to the king, and in what form. But money business was different: that business put the kings' demands before reluctant members. Understandably, they wished to discuss those demands freely and fully before any decision whatsoever was taken in the House. But since then the constitution has changed. The House no longer needs to haggle with the Crown over money: if the advisers of the Crown do not have the confidence of the House, they must go. Moreover, during the past 100 or 150 years the ordinary legislative process has lost almost all the exploratory character it once had. The House has come to rely on the government to introduce the bills that are to be taken seriously, it assumes that those bills will have been prepared carefully, and it puts most of its time at the disposal of the government. In short, the distinction between money business and ordinary legislation has been drastically reduced, and from both sides. What the Canadian House of Commons did in 1968 was to change its procedures to conform to this change of substance. Except that the need for recommendation by the governor general is retained, government bills which would authorize statutory payments are treated exactly like other government bills. Tax bills, too, are treated like ordinary bills, except that they are to be sent to committees of the whole House after second reading. In addition, the minister of finance still must table notices of motions setting forth his tax proposals; and he may initiate a budget debate. In the case of the annual supply business, provision has been made to enable the members to examine the estimates as thoroughly as they wish, and for the opposition to raise before the House and the public all its major complaints against the government.[17]

SIX

The Standing Committees: The Pattern Established

The advantages gained when a numerous body such as the House of Commons instructs groups selected among its members to deal with items of business and to report their findings are obvious: the business can be handled more thoroughly; the opinions, explanations, and evidence of persons who are not members can be heard conveniently; specific findings or proposals can be put before the parent body for acceptance or rejection; and when two or more committees operate concurrently without interfering with each other too much the volume of work that can be done is increased. At every regular session since Confederation the Canadian House of Commons has set up "standing committees" to facilitate its work; but prior to 20 December 1968, those committees ordinarily were of no great importance. During the first thirty years there was a considerable body of private legislation, and since all private bills were referred to one of three standing committees, at that time those committees were quite busy. But as the importance of private bill legislation other than to effect divorce dwindled, the share of the legislative work borne regularly by the committees declined. From the beginning in 1867 the House occasionally referred public bills to standing committees for examination; but even after the committees no longer were busy with private bills no attempt was made (a) to modernize the standing committee system, or (b) to change the main processes of the House by having public bills or the estimates considered in standing committees instead of in committees of the whole House. The dual result was that the committees came to seem somewhat quaint and peripheral, and that work that could have been done better in small committees continued to be done in committees of the whole House. Then, on 20 December 1968, the House gave the standing committees key roles in the processes by which two of its most important kinds of work—supply business, and public bill legislation[1]—are done; but it did so without reforming, or even examining the basic characteristics of a committee system that had changed relatively little in a hundred years. Understandably, serious technical, procedural, and constitutional problems resulted; and since 1968 the operation of the standing committees has caused a fair amount of tension and controversy among the members. Indeed, it seems safe to predict that the adaptation of the committee system to its new functions will be the most interesting aspect of the development of the House of Commons during the next ten or twenty years.

The British House of Commons uses three kinds of committees in addition to committees of the whole House and the committees appointed to deal with private bills. First, there are *select* committees, each of which is appointed by the House to inquire into a particular matter or to consider a particular bill, and expires when its task has been completed. These committees ordinarily are limited to fifteen members named by the House itself. Ordinarily a committee chooses its own chairman. Select committees usually are given the power "to send for persons, papers and records." On 28 January 1975, for example, a select committee on the Rt. Hon. Member for Walsall North (Mr. Stonehill), who disappeared in Florida in November 1974, but later was found in Australia, was appointed and nominated.[2]

Second, there are *sessional select committees*. These are set up at one session after another to do various kinds of recurring work or to examine certain important governmental activities. Some are appointed by standing order, so that all that has to be done each session is to nominate the members. Others are both appointed and nominated at each session. There has been a good deal of experimentation with the sessional committees since 1964.[3] New committees were originated; some of them survived, others were dropped. And some of the new committees now are appointed by standing order. Among those now (1974–75 session) appointed by standing order are the Chairmen's Panel, the Selection Committee, the Standing Orders Committee, the Public Accounts Committee, the Expenditure Committee, the Nationalized Industries Committee, the Overseas Development Committee, the Procedure Committee, the Race Relations and Immigration Committee, and the Science and Technology Committee. Among those appointed sessionally are the Committee on Privileges, on the Parliamentary Commissioner for Administration, on Statutory Instruments, on Unopposed Bills, on European Secondary Legislation, and the House of Commons (Services). The last of these oversees the food services of the House, the printing, broadcasting, the library, the publication of debates, etc. As the names indicate, each committee has its own unique task. The members of these committees are named by the House, and each selects its own chairman; but only some of them—Public Accounts, Expenditures, and Privileges—are given the investigatory power "to send for persons, papers and records."

The third kind of committee used at Westminster is the *standing committee*. Until 1883 the British House sent most public bills to committees of the whole House; and those few not treated in that way were sent to select committees for the committee stage. In that year an attempt was made to reduce the work done in the Chamber by establishing two select committees—one for legal affairs, and the other for commercial matters—to deal, not with particular bills but with whatever public bills in those categories the House wished to commit to them. These were specialized committees: each had its own field. They were given the investigatory power of select committees, i.e., they could send for persons, papers, and records. In 1888, after five sessions when they were not established, the two committees were prescribed in the standing orders. However, although the committees were nominated regularly thereafter, the bills committed to them, rather than to committees of the whole House or to select committees, were relatively few and uncontroversial. It was not until the session of 1906-07 that the modern British system of standing committees was revised to provide that all public bills other than those of specified kinds and those especially excepted by the House were to go to the standing committees for their committee stage. At the same time the number of standing committees was increased to four. It will be helpful to remember that at Westminster the term "standing committee" is reserved strictly for legislative committees, that the bills sent to those committees are public bills, and that a bill committed to a standing committee does not go also to a committee of the whole House.

These British committees began in the 1880s as standing select committees. They were modelled more after select committees than after the committees of the whole House. However, as a result of the changes made in 1906-07 their character was altered almost completely. First, they ceased to be specialized: since 1907 bills have been assigned to each of the committees—by the speaker, not the House—not on the basis of specialization, but on the basis of relative work-load. As a result the committees have no descriptive names; rather they are designated simply by letters: A, B, C, D, etc.[4] In 1933 the reference to specialization, inherited from the 1880s, finally was removed from the standing orders. Second, the committees changed their mode of operation. The original intention was that they would follow select committees in both their organization and procedures; but gradually they dropped the investigatory role, and came to model themselves after committees of the whole House. Because they were considering public bills after second reading, i.e., after the House had settled the principle of each bill, they allowed their investigatory power to atrophy. In 1947 the standing orders were changed so that the standing committees no longer have the power to send for persons, papers, and records. And, third, the basis on which the membership of the committees is composed was changed. Each standing committee is nominated by the Selection Committee; and changes in the membership are made by that committee after a standing committee has reported one bill and before it has begun to consider another. Because when first established in the 1880s the committees were to be specialized, it was provided that they were to be composed of two groups of members, a nucleus selected because of their special interest and knowledge in the field of the committee, and others with no claim to relevant expertise to be added to prevent the committee from becoming a functional chamber. Because the idea that each committee was to be specialized was abandoned in 1906–07, it was the specialists, not the generalists, who thereafter were added to the committees in preparation for particular bills. In 1960 all reference to the two groups—the nucleus and the added members—was dropped from the standing orders.

Because the British standing committees are not specialized the way is open for each committee to have a chairman whose chief qualifications are his impartiality and his concern for good order and procedure, not his interest or expertise in a field, or his support for the government. In this the chairmen resemble the chairman of the committees of the whole House, not the chairmen of select committees. The chairmen of the standing committees are named by the speaker from the Chairmen's Panel, which is composed of members who have demonstrated the suitable temperament and talents. Moreover, because the committees are not specialized, the way is open also for adversary contention between the parties, as distinct from collaboration across party lines for the benefit of particular interests.[5]

The standing committees at Westminster have nothing whatsoever to do with private bills. Those bills are dealt with, as they have been for centuries, by an entirely separate process. They are examined first by the Standing Orders Committee, which ascertains whether or not the promoters have given the required notice to interested parties and to the public, and also whether or not the bill itself conforms acceptably to the formal requirements of the House. After second reading each opposed private bill is sent to a very small private bill committee nominated especially for that bill by the Selection Committee.[6] Every private bill has a preamble wherein the promoters set forth the legal and factual conditions—the "whereas-es"—on the basis of which they have petitioned the House for action; and it is the task of the committee to decide whether or not the promoters of the bill have a true preamble, and, if so, what amendments, if any, are desirable in the clauses of their bill. The work of the committee is semi-judicial; its members sit *en banco* to hear the counsel for the promoters and opponents of the bill. If the committee finds the preamble true, it reports the bill favourably to the House, after having made necessary amendments to the clauses. If the clauses have been amended in committee, further amendments may be offered when the report of the committee is before the House. The final step is third reading. On the other hand, all unopposed private bills go to one small committee, the Committee on Unopposed Private Bills, which is concerned to protect the interest of the public at large. If they are reported favourably, they are ready for the report stage and third reading.

When we turn from Westminster to Ottawa we find that the Canadian House of Commons, too, since 1867, has used select committees, or "special committees," as they have come to be called at Ottawa. A special committee at Ottawa is similar to a select committee at Westminster in almost every way. But—and this is what concerns us— "standing committees" at Ottawa are radically different from "standing committees" at Westminster. As we have seen, the British standing committees were introduced in the 1880s for a specific purpose, namely, to consider public bills at the committee stage of the legislative process, and although initially they were quite similar to select committees, after 1907 they came to resemble committees of the whole House. In contrast, the committees now called "standing committees" at Ottawa began in 1867 as sessional select committees; and they have retained that character except that since 1906 they have been listed in the standing orders. They are not restricted to dealing with public bills; indeed, at Ottawa *consideration*—as distinct from *examination*—by a standing committee was not part of the legislative process for bills, either public or private, before 20 December 1968.

On 7 November 1867, the second day of the first session of the new Parliament of Canada, the House of Commons, following the pattern of the Legislative Assembly of the late province of Canada, resolved:

> That Select Standing Committees of this House, for the present Session, be appointed for the following purposes:—1. On Privileges and Elections. 2. On Expiring Laws. 3. On Railways, Canals and Telegraph Lines. 4. On Miscellaneous Private Bills. 5. On Standing Orders. 6. On Printing. 7. On Contingencies. 8. On Public Accounts. 9. On Banking and Commerce. 10. On Immigration and Colonization:—which said Committees shall severally be empowered to examine and enquire into all such matters and things as may be referred to them by the House, and

to report from time to time their observations and opinions thereon; with power to send for persons, papers and records.[7]

Two of the original committees were responsible for domestic management: the chief task of the Committee on Contingencies was to arrange for the employment of a sessional staff; and the Committee on Printing was to make arrangements for the printing of the papers of the House, and to decide what reports and returns should be included in the volumes of sessional papers.[8] A third committee, the Committee on Privileges and Elections, was to enquire into questions referred to it touching the status and integrity of the House. The Committee on Public Accounts had a very specific commission: with the assistance of the auditor general, to examine the expenditures of the Crown to ascertain that they had been made in accordance with the intentions of the House and in conformity with sound and honest business practices. Another committee, the one on Expiring Laws, had a special but temporary assignment, namely, to recommend what expiring statutes or parts of expiring statutes ought to be re-enacted by the Dominion Parliament. The work of the Standing Orders Committee was strictly formal: like its British counterpart, it was to examine each petition for a private act to ascertain that all the requirements laid down in the standing orders had been fulfilled before the House gave leave for a private bill to be presented. Three of the committees—those on (a) Banking and Commerce; (b) Railways, Canals and Telegraph Lines; and (c) Miscellaneous Private Bills—had as their primary task the examination of private bills. The last committee, on Immigration and Colonization, was left without any specific task in its field.

As shown by Table 5, almost one hundred years later this was still the basic list, although by 1964–65, after deductions, combinations, and additions, it had come to include sixteen committees. Before 1906 the committees were appointed at the beginning of each session; yet only two changes were made in the list throughout those forty years. At the first session provision was made by statute for a Committee on Internal Economy, composed of privy councillors named by the Governor in Council, to assist the speaker in securing a staff for the House. Consequently, in 1868 and thereafter no Committee on Contingencies was appointed. In 1887 the Committee on Immigration and Colonization, which in recent reports had treated of topics such as scientific butter-making and the grading of wheat, became the Committee on Agriculture and Colonization. Then in 1906 a new standing order was made appointing all the "select standing committees" to which members were to be nominated at each session. At that time the Committee on Expiring Laws, which had found relatively little to do since the early 1870s, and had not made a report since 1885, was dropped; and two committees—a committee on the Official Report of the Debates, previously appointed as a select committee at each session, and a committee on the Library of Parliament, previously a joint select committee of the Senate and the House of Commons—were added to the list. Between 1906 and 1964 a total of six new committees—on Marine and Fisheries; on Mines, Forests and Waters (created in 1924 by combining two committees which had been added in 1909); on Industrial Relations; on External Affairs; on Veterans Affairs; and on the Estimates—were added. In 1927 the Committees on Printing and on the Library of Parliament, which from the beginning had been joint committees of the Senate and the House of Commons, were segregated from the other committees in the standing orders, but both continued to be listed as "select standing committees." The changes in the list of standing committees from the time of the first Parliament until the session of 1964–65 are shown in Table 5.

From 1867 until 1964 the general powers of the committees were conferred on them, not by a standing order, but before 1906 by a sessional order made at the time the committees were appointed and after 1906 at the time their members were named. Over the years those general powers remained the same. Indeed, the words used by the Rt. Hon. L. B. Pearson on 11 March 1964, were almost identical with those used by the Hon. Sir John A. Macdonald on 7 November 1867. Mr. Pearson's motion was that the standing committees be empowered severally "to examine and enquire into all such matters and things as may be referred to them by the House, and to report from time to time their observations and opinions thereon, with power to send for persons, papers and records."[9] What these general powers show is that the Canadian standing committees originally were and continued to be modelled after select committees—the key power is the power "to send for persons, papers and records"—rather than after committees of the whole House. These powers are designed for investigative tasks, not for legislative work on public bills. Indeed, until 1936 the term "select standing committees" was used constantly in the formal records of the House, although as early as 1867–68 the committees were being alluded to in the debates as "standing committees." As a corollary, what now are called "special committees" were referred to formally after 1906 as "select special committees."

A quick survey of the original list of standing committees shows that each of six of them—like the comparable sessional select committees at Westminster—had a function unique to itself. Its function, whether it related to substantive business, as in the case of the Committee on Public Accounts, or domestic chores, as in the case of the Committee

TABLE 5
Standing Committees, Sessions of 1867–68 and 1964–65

1867	1964		Size and Quorum after 1927
1		Contingencies (supplanted by the statutory Committee on Internal Economy in 1868)	
2		Expiring Laws (dropped in 1906)	
3	1	Privileges and Elections	29 (10)
4	2	Public Accounts	50 (15)
5	3	Standing Orders	30 (8)
6	4	Banking and Commerce	50 (15)
7	5	Railways, Canals and Telegraph Lines	60 (20)
8	6	Miscellaneous Private Bills	50 (15)
9	7	Immigration and Colonization (renamed as Agriculture and Colonization in 1887)	60 (20)
	8	Marine and Fisheries (added in 1909)	35 (10)
	9	Mines, Forests and Waters (created in 1924 by combining the Committee on Mines and Minerals with the Committee on Forests, Waterways and Waterpower, both of which had been established in 1909)	35 (10)
	10	Industrial Relations (added in 1945)	35 (10)
	11	External Affairs (This committee and the preceding one were created in 1945, when the Committee on Industrial and International Relations, added in 1924, was divided.)	35 (10)
	12	Veterans Affairs (added in 1958)	35 (10)
	13	Estimates (added in 1959)	35 (10)
	14	Debates (1906)	35 (10)
10	15	Printing (a joint committee)	35 (10)
	16	Library of Parliament (a joint committee)	12 (7)

on Contingencies, was not shared with any other committee. It is only when we turn to the Committees on Miscellaneous Private Bills, Banking and Commerce; Railways, Canals and Telegraph Lines; and Immigration and Colonization that we find, not just a list of diverse committees, but the rudiments of a committee system. Of the six other committees on the list in 1964, one, the Committee on the Estimates, had a unique assignment, and the other five—Marine and Fisheries; Mines, Forests and Waters; Industrial Relations; External Affairs; and Veterans Affairs—had substantive fields. Our main concern as we examine the background of the modern problems is not with the unique committees, for the story of each of them is peculiar unto itself; and, indeed, only one of them, Public Accounts, has been of direct importance to the public.[10] Already we have noticed the fate of the Committee on Contingencies and the Committee on Expiring Laws. The Committee on Printing lost some of its early prominence when the Government Printing Bureau began to do the printing of Parliament in 1888, and more as the committees and departments came to present their reports and evidence to the House in printed form. In 1925 the publication of volumes of selected sessional papers—selected by the committee—was terminated. For some time thereafter the committee continued to meet, but increasingly only to decide that materials not already printed when presented or tabled ought not to be printed. Since 1948 the committee has been dormant. The Standing Orders Committee had only a formal role in relation to private bills; it lost much of the detailed part of that work when the post of examiner of petitions was created in 1906, so that thereafter the committee dealt mainly with those instances when a petition or a bill was found somewhat, but not necessarily fatally, defective on formal grounds. We shall have occasion to refer, but only briefly, to the Committees on Public Accounts, Privileges and Elections, and the Estimates.

At Westminster, as we have noticed, private bills are dealt with in a special and separate way. The chief function of three of the standing committees set up at Ottawa in 1867 was the examination of private bills. The Committees on Banking and Commerce; on Railways, Canals and Telegraph Lines; and on Miscellaneous Private Bills from the beginning in 1867 were the committees to which *all* private bills were referred. In 1876, in recognition of this fact, the House made the relevant standing order explicit by providing: "Every Private or Local Bill, when read a second time, is referred to the Standing Committee charged with the consideration of such Bill. Bills relating to Banks, Insurance, Trade and Commerce, to Committee on Banking and Commerce;—Bills relating to Railways, Canals, Telegraphs, Canal and

Railway Bridges, to the Committee on Railway;—The Bills not coming under these classes to the Committee on Private and Local Bills."[11] However, we must not let ourselves be misled: these committees were not to perform the functions of committees at the committee stage of the legislative process. Those functions—principally the adoption of the text of the bill—were reserved for committees of the whole House. Initially, from 1867 to 1873, private bills were sent to one of the three standing committees after *first* reading. Those committees, like the committees on opposed private bills at Westminster, were to test ("to prove") the preamble, and, if it was found true, to assure that the operative part of the bill was the proper consequence of the preamble; and this was to be done *before* the House was asked to give second reading to the bill. In 1873, to assure that the bills had been printed, and thus made available to interested persons before the standing committee began to examine them, the House changed the process so that each private bill went to a standing committee after second reading.[12] This meant that thereafter each private bill went to two committees successively. After second reading the bill was examined by a standing committee. If that body reported favourably, the bill was committed to a committee of the whole House where the text was considered. In short, the basic task of these three standing committees was to examine private bills in a preliminary way. These three committees had the investigative power of select committees; yet their main work was to examine private bills. In the early years this kept two of them quite busy. The third, the Committee on Miscellaneous Private Bills, led a relatively quiet existence.

The story, however, is even more complex and strange. From the very beginning the House sent some public bills to the Committee on Banking and Commerce and the Committee on Railways, Canals and Telegraph Lines; but from the beginning in the case of public bills the referral was made after second reading. Between 1867 and 1900 over seventy public bills were referred to the Committee on Banking and Commerce, and about forty to the Committee on Railways, Canals and Telegraph Lines. In the early days, before 1880, they examined some very important government bills. In 1871 the Committee on Banking and Commerce examined the bill that became the Bank Act. In 1873 it examined seven government bills, including those enacted as the Weights and Measures Act, the Wreck and Salvage Act, the Seamen's Act, and the Inspection and Sale Act. In 1877 it examined the government bill that became the Consolidated Insurance Act. The other committee—on Railways, Canals and Telegraph Lines—in 1868 examined the government bill that became the Railway Act, and in 1875 the government bill that became the act regulating the construction and maintenance of marine electric telegraphs. The purpose of sending a government bill to a standing committee seems to have been to let the members study the bill closely, and to enable interested persons to testify. However, between 1880 and 1898 no government bills, except three to make certain amendments to the Insurance Act, were referred. For example, the bills to amend the Bank Act were not referred in 1880 and 1890.

Government bills fared well in the committees: of the thirty-two referred between 1867 and 1900 only five were not enacted. On the other hand, private members' public bills fared poorly. Over two-thirds of the public bills sent to the two committees between 1867 and 1900 were private members' public bills, and only one-third of them were enacted. The fairly large total number of bills referred in this period is somewhat deceptive: after the first few years government bills were not referred; few private members' public bills became law; and none of the private members' public bills that did become law was of more than minor importance.[13]

The practice of referring public bills to committees that had been constituted primarily to deal with private bills inevitably caused procedural difficulties. A public bill may be introduced by an explanatory preamble, but such a preamble does not have to be proved; indeed, the purpose of a public bill is a matter for the House itself, not for any committee to which the House has sent the text of the bill. In contrast, the promoters of a private bill must begin by sustaining their preamble. On 1 June 1887, the Committee on Banking and Commerce, which had been examining a bill relating to insolvent debtors, recommended to the House that the rules be revised "to more clearly define the practice respecting Public Bills that may be referred to any of the Select Standing Committees charged with the consideration of Private Bills." Later that day a motion was made in the House to give effect to the recommendation. The following exchange took place.

Mr. McCarthy: *I would explain to the hon. First Minister (Sir John A. Macdonald) the object of the motion which my hon. friend (Mr. Hall) has made. We find that when public Bills are referred to the standing committees, which are really only, properly speaking, charged by the rules of the House to deal with private Bills, that we are in this position: that we go through the Bill first, step by step and clause by clause, before we deal with the preamble; and when we come to the preamble, we may find that the sense of the committee is against it, and the whole time spent on the Bill has been lost. If the standing committees are to deal with these Bills, there ought to be rules specially framed with reference to them. For instance, a Bill was before the Committee of Banking and Commerce this morning, relating to bankruptcy. The principle of the*

> Bill was not discussed, but when we came to consider the preamble, the committee voted that it was not proved; and as the preamble was that "Her Majesty, by and with the advice and consent of the Senate and House of Commons of Canada, enacts as follows," our proceedings seemed rather absurd. If the standing committees are to deal with Bills relating to public matters, there ought to be special rules for that purpose. I move the adjournment of the debate.
>
> **Sir John A. Macdonald:** *The motion is more important than it first appeared to be. I think the hon. gentleman had better leave it over for several days until we have an opportunity of considering the whole matter.*[14]

However, no provision was made in the rules either then or later to provide the standing committees with satisfactory guidance in dealing with public bills.

During the first two or three decades after 1867 the Committee on Banking and Commerce and the Committee on Railways, Canals and Telegraph Lines played a major part in the work of the House. During those years the House passed dozens and dozens of bills incorporating companies with interprovincial objects and dozens of bills for the creation of companies with rights to build and operate specified lines of railway. As a result, those two committees were then the great committees. Quite aside from their sporadic involvement in public business, both were busy and prominent throughout the short session. They dominated the scene except for the 1891–96 period when the Committee on Public Accounts stole the limelight with its investigations into scandals.[15] But after those early years the flood of important private bills subsided: the number of bills remained about the same, but more and more of them were for amendments or followed principles already established. This decline in private business placed the stature of the two key committees in jeopardy. Unless the volume of public business sent to them increased, their greatest days were over. The Committee on Railways, Canals and Telegraph Lines went into a long decline. It had become prominent in the era of railway construction. But it failed to move forward with the times in the period of railway consolidation during and after World War I. When it was decided, in 1924, that the operations of the nationalized transportation facilities should be observed by a committee, the House chose to originate a new committee, a sessional select committee on Railways and Shipping Lines owned by the Crown, even although the Standing Committee on Railways, Canals and Telegraph Lines was far from overworked. In most sessions between 1900 and 1945 the only grist sent to Railways, Canals and Telegraph Lines was a few relatively minor private bills and moribund private members' public bills. In contrast, the Committee on Banking and Commerce, which had received little public business after 1879, except for sudden flurries in 1899 and 1900, recovered and retained its status from about 1912–13. Various important bills were referred to it. Beginning in 1900 the bills effecting the decennial revision of the Bank Act were referred to it regularly. In 1914 the bills that became the Loan Companies Act and the Trust Companies Act were examined by it. In 1917 it examined the bill to consolidate and amend the Insurance Act. In 1930 it examined the bill to amend the Companies Act, and in 1931 the bill enacted as the Consolidated Revenue and Audit Act. In 1934 the bill to establish the Bank of Canada went to it, and in 1939 the bill to established the Central Mortgage Bank.

The Committee on Immigration and Colonization, unlike the Committees on Railways, Canals and Telegraph Lines and on Banking and Commerce, never was used as a private bills committee. During the years after 1867 it kept itself busy, without specific instructions from the House, by conducting investigations into the prospects and progress of farming in Canada, with special attention to the attractions of the West for colonists and to the great advantages of scientific farming; and year after its "report for the session" was given a prominent place as an appendix to the *Journals*. In 1875 it reported on the methods used in bringing "work-house and pauper children" to Canada from England. In 1878 it reported on the manufacture of peat and on navigation in Hudson's Bay. In 1901 it explained how chickens might be fattened for market. In 1914 it demonstrated the benefits to be gained by the use of hydro-electricity on farms. In 1915 it took up the merits of different manures and fertilizers. In 1916 it investigated Canada's standing with regard to livestock. The improvement of farm management quite soon had become the cynosure of its attention; yet, as shown by reports in 1915 and 1928, the close connection between Canadian agriculture and colonization was not forgotten. To a large extent, the committee's early aims were educational and promotional.[16] It elicited authoritative testimony, and this, often accompanied by pictures, was then made available for distribution to the people of rural Canada. In 1894, for example, the committee recommended that 150,000 copies of the Experimental Farms Report for 1893 be printed "for distribution to such Members of the House of Commons only as represent rural constituencies."[17] In the next year it recommended that 295,000 copies of the testimony of the Dominion dairy commissioner and agriculturalist be printed for distribution to farmers by senators and members.[18]

Evidently all the members were not equally enthusiastic about the work of the committee. In 1902 one member commented that, "If twice as many copies of this book [the Statistical Year-book] were sent out and fewer of the trash of question and answer and longwinded stuff of the Agricultural Committee, matter that is being sent out by the ton, but not half of it distributed—and nobody would read it if he got it—the country would be better served, and there would be less drain upon the treasury." However, another member explained that he had his own satisfactory system for dissemination of the reports. "For example," he said, "I get, let us say sixty copies of the evidence of Professor Robertson before the Agricultural Committee. I do these up in parcels containing eight or ten copies each and address them to postmasters at rural points where I am satisfied they will take considerable interest in handing them out to persons who call for their mail. . . . . I am satisfied that a great deal of information given in the way of question and answer is more readily grasped by the agriculturalists than if it were contained in a more closely written volume."[19]

From about 1900 bills concerning agricultural matters and the inspection and sale of farm produce began to appear in the House. The fact that the Committee on Agriculture and Colonization was not one of those to which private bills were sent did not hinder the House from using it occasionally for the examination of these public bills, which were designed to protect farmers and consumers. In 1898 two private members' bills, one on cruelty to animals, and one on speculation in butter and cheese were sent to it. Neither was enacted. In 1900 a bill to amend the Fertilizer Act was sent to it. That bill, too, did not pass. Two private members' bills were referred to it in 1906, one on the hay trade, which was not enacted, and one to regulate the size of milk cans, which was. In 1910–11 a private member's bill, which had been studied by the committee, was enacted as the Seed Control Act. In 1914 the committee examined and reported favourably two government bills, one prohibiting the sale of butter substitutes, and the other prohibiting the adulteration of certain foods. Both were enacted. During the second and third decades of the century, as the committee became more and more involved with public bills, the strong emphasis on edifying the rural population, which had been very evident earlier, slackened. The committee came to represent the farming interests, and ceased to be an instrument by which the farmers of Canada were to be enlightened and uplifted. During the 1920s and 1930s the Committee on Agriculture and Colonization and the Committee on Banking and Commerce were the most important committees.

Given the fact that most matters of "a local and private nature" were assigned exclusively to the provincial legislatures by the British North America Act, it is not surprising that the Committee on Miscellaneous Private Bills remained relatively quiet for years. Later, of course, that committee was inundated by wave after wave of applications for divorces, the first wave coming in 1920; but because divorce bills were private in the narrowest sense and were examined carefully by the Senate, they did not serve to push the committee to the front of the parliamentary stage.

None of the committees added in 1909 and 1924 ever achieved anything like major status. Private bills were not referred to them; and they attracted relatively few public bills. The Committee on Mines and Minerals and the Committee on Forests, Waterways and Waterpower, both established in 1909, and the Committee on Industrial and International Relations, established in 1924, seem to have been thought of as committees that would educate the public somewhat in the manner of the Committee on Agriculture and Colonization in its early years; but none of these had a large and distinct segment of Canadian society as its special audience.[20] The Committee on Marine and Fisheries, added in 1909, was to advance the interest of a particular interest group, but again, unlike Agriculture and Colonization, this was not an interest group that needed constant attention.[21] The Committee on Veterans Affairs, added in 1958, had a distinct clientele.

Of the new committees the Committee on Marine and Fisheries had the best record. It dealt with a fair number of government bills between 1909 and 1920, but thereafter its activity became sporadic. Between 1926, when the size of the standing committees was reduced to make them more useful, and 1945 it reported to the House in eight of the twenty sessions. The Committee on Industrial and International Relations, after an initial burst of action during its first sessions, when it investigated the desirability of family allowances, unemployment insurance, and peace scholarships, became dormant: it made no reports from 1936 until its demise in 1945. The Committees on Mines and Minerals and on Forests, Waterways and Waterpower were almost completely inactive throughout their entire existence. The same was true of the committee that succeeded them in 1924: between 1927 and 1945 the Committee on Mines, Forests and Waters had nothing whatsoever to report to the House.

From 1867 until after World War II the committee system was discussed very little in the House. Before 1909 and 1924 there was agitation for certain new committees; and they were added. The general feeling appears to have been that the system was reasonably well-adapted to the requirements of the House. Over the years the main complaint was that the committees had become too large. There was merit in that criticism. Before 1927 the initial size of each standing committee was determined at the beginning of each session by the small committee known as the Striking Committee, which had as its chief duty the preparation of the lists of members who would constitute the committees. At the beginning, in 1867, all were fairly small; but

TABLE 6
Size of the
Standing Committees at Certain Sessions

The membership of each of the standing committees at the beginning of certain sessions, and the size of the quorums, are shown here. When the quorum was reduced from half the membership by special order, the quorum is shown in [square] brackets. When it was set lower than half the membership by the Striking Committee, the quorum is shown in (round) parentheses.

	1867–68	1875	1885	1895	1910–11	1926	1928
Membership of the House	181	206	215	213	221	245	245
Privileges & Elections	21	23	35	41	45	29	29(10)
Expiring Laws	21[5]	35[7]	27[7]	30[7]			
Public Accounts	21[7]	64(9)	46(9)	65(9)	85(21)	62(21)	50(15)
Standing Orders	21[7]	35(7)	44(7)	46(7)	53(7)	33(7)	30(8)
Banking & Commerce	21[7]	65(9)	100(9)	119(9)	134(21)	89(21)	50(15)
Railways, Canals & Telegraph Lines	45	85	140	164[25]	202(25)	128(25)	60(20)
Miscellaneous Private Bills	21[7]	55(7)	71(7)	73(7)	87(10)	65(10)	50(15)
Agriculture & Colonization	21[7]	45(9)	84(9)	107(7)	134(12)	105(12)	60(20)
Marine & Fisheries					26(10)	37(10)	35(10)
Mines & Minerals					25(10)		
Forests, Waterways & Waterpower					26(10)		
Mines, Forests & Waters						36(10)	35(10)
Industrial & International Relations						35(10)	35(10)
Debates					15(5)	13(5)	12(7)
Printing	12[7]	15[7]	15[9]	22	25	23	23
Library					17	21	21

this happy condition did not long prevail. Over the first forty years all the standing committees grew in membership—including the Committee on Expiring Laws, even after it had become dormant. In the case of some committees it seems to have become accepted that no member who wished to have his name put down was refused by the Striking Committee. As shown by Table 6, at times the three committees to which public bills were sent before 1909—Banking and Commerce; Railways, Canals and Telegraph Lines; and Agriculture and Colonization—were virtually specialized committees of the whole House. After 1911, when the committees reached record sizes, the Striking Committee restricted the membership lists somewhat, but despite its efforts the committees still were too large. It is revealing that the chief point of the complaints about the size of the committees was not that they were too big to be efficient and manageable, but that they were too big to meet.[22] Since committee meetings generally were not scheduled on Monday and Friday, conflicts were common on the three available days. But even more important was the fact that most of the members on the very large committees felt no obligation to attend unless they were directly interested in an item of business to come up at a meeting. The basic rule was that the quorum for a committee was half its membership; but from the first, during the period from 1867 to 1874, the House showed no reluctance to agree to committee requests for quorum reductions. In 1875 and thereafter, instructed by the experience of those first few years, the Striking Committee took the initiative in proposing small quorums from the beginning of each session. But even the lowered quorums often proved too high. Evidently some committees frequently did business without having their quorums. In 1911, for example, the Committee on Banking and Commerce, with a membership of 134, asked the House twice—unsuccessfully—to reduce its quorum, the first time from twenty-one to fifteen, the second time from twenty-one to eleven, so that it could complete the work referred to it without continuing to hold meetings without a quorum.[23] Finally, in 1927 the total membership of each committee, at a much lower level in some cases, was specified in the standing orders, and, more significantly, the quorums were fixed, and at higher levels than had been required previously. The size of both the committees and their quorums remained unchanged from 1927 until 1965.

The depression and World War II altered drastically the work of the federal government of Canada. Not only was it using its old powers under s. 91 of the B.N.A. Act far more extensively, but it was deeply involved in federal-provincial programs and was intensely active in international affairs. This meant that at each annual session the government had bills to put before the House relating to various new matters

—treaties and conventions, housing, unemployment, health and welfare, loans and grants to promote economic growth, etc. At the same time the government was quite ready to have many of the more technical bills examined by the standing committees. Consequently they became more important than ever before in the transaction of public business in the House. On the other side, the House stopped using the committees as a means by which to disembarrass itself of private members' bills. Instead of giving such bills a second reading and sending them to a committee for burial, the House simply talked them out at the second-reading stage.

As earlier, the Committee on Banking and Commerce was the most active committee. It still examined private bills, but the major part of its work was with government bills. For example, in 1946 it examined the bill that became the Income Tax Act; in 1949 the bill that revised the Bankruptcy Act; in 1952-53 the bill to consolidate and amend the Public Service Superannuation Act; in 1953-54 the bill that became the National Housing Act, 1954, and the bill to revise the Bank Act. After 1949 the Committee on Railways, Canals and Telegraph Lines came back to life as government activities increased in the general fields of communications and transportation, as distinct from railways. In that year it studied the bills that became the Oil and Gas Pipe Lines Act and the Canadian Overseas Telecommunications Act. In 1950 it examined the bills to amend the Aeronautics Act and the Canada Shipping Act. Between 1950 and 1957 the bill to amend the National Harbours Board Act and the bill that became the Canadian National Railways Act, 1955, were referred to it, as were fourteen bills to amend earlier acts. It dealt also with a large number of private bills relating to pipe lines.

The Committee on Agriculture and Colonization now was somewhat less active than in its heyday in the 1920s. It examined bills to amend the Canada Grain Act, the Prairie Farm Assistance Act, and the Farm Improvement Loans Act. At times it studied the operations of the Wheat Board and the Board of Grain Commissioners. On the other hand, the Committee on Marine and Fisheries was more active than since its first years. For example, it examined bills to amend the Fish Inspection Act in 1945 and 1949, the Meat and Canned Foods Act in 1946, and the bill to amend the Fisheries Research Board Act in 1947. In 1952-53 it examined the bill to bring into effect the North Pacific Halibut Fisheries Convention and the bill that became the Coastal Fisheries Protection Act. In 1955 it examined the bill on the Great Lakes Fisheries Convention. In 1957 it examined the bill to give effect to the Pacific Salmon Fisheries Convention. However, like the Committee on Agriculture and Colonization, it made no reports to the House in about half the sessions.

The Committee on Industrial Relations and the Committee on External Affairs, both established in 1945, were kept fairly busy, but in quite different ways. The former examined two major bills, one respecting Industrial Disputes, and one enacted as the Unemployment Insurance Act, 1955. It also studied bills respecting vocational training, discrimination in employment, compensation for government employees, and compensation for merchant seamen. In contrast, the Committee on External Affairs attracted only five bills, all to give effect to international treaties or conventions. However, as we shall see, it studied the department's estimates for each fiscal year.

The only committee that was completely inactive throughout the post-war period was the Committee on Mines, Forests and Waters.

Although unhappiness with the procedures of the House of Commons was quite prevalent among the members during the last years of the war and throughout the post-war years, little of their criticism was aimed at the way the House dealt with public bills.[24] For the most part the complaints related to the maintenance of administrative responsibility. The heavy reliance on rule by delegated power during and after World War II, together with the vast increases in the amounts of money voted annually, aroused and sustained a gnawing dissatisfaction. The feeling was that the House had allowed itself to become only an observer, indeed at best merely a half-blind observer, of the activities of the government. The great criticism was that as long as the procedures by which the House approved the estimates remained obsolete, the government's administrative activity—its use of the power conferred on it by statutes and by common law—would remain largely concealed from the House. Almost inevitably the proposed solutions involved a greater use of the committees.

From 1908, even before the British House introduced its sessional committee on Estimates, complaints were voiced in Ottawa about the inefficiency of the Committee of Supply, and requests were made for the establishment of a small committee that would be able to examine selected sets of estimates efficiently and thoroughly. But the idea that it would be proper for the government's spending proposals to be dealt with anywhere but in the Committee of Supply was resisted staunchly by many members as a kind of heresy, a notion that could be flirted with at Westminster where the purity of the constitutional faith was beyond question, but to be eschewed at Ottawa where every innovation was feared as heretical. Yet over the years because of innovations made to meet special situations the idea lost its scandalizing novelty. A beginning was made in 1924 when the House appointed a sessional committee to examine the financial circumstances and requirements of the railways and shipping lines taken over by the Crown. Thereafter that committee

—for years referred to as the Committee on Railways and Shipping owned, operated and controlled by the government, but after 1958 as the Committee on Railways, Air Lines and Shipping owned and controlled by the government—was established annually.[25] To it were referred those items in the estimates relating to the corporations operating the services. Clearly, a foremost purpose of this innovation was to make the corporations assume some of the burden of justifying their demands on the public purse.

In 1950 the estimates of the C.B.C. relating to its international shortwave services were referred to a special committee on Radio Broadcasting. In 1952 the votes relating to Central Mortgage and Housing Corporation were referred to the Committee on Banking and Commerce. In both those instances, as in the case of the nationalized transportation companies, members were being put into direct contact with agencies not under the administrative responsibility of a minister. In each instance the motion referring the items made it clear that no derogation from the power of the Committee of Supply was intended: the smaller committees were to examine the estimates, but each vote would have to be carried later in the Committee of Supply.

More significantly, because an ordinary department of government was involved, the estimates of the Department of External Affairs were referred to the new Standing Committee on External Affairs in 1945 and in subsequent years. Here, again, there was a special reason. The Committee on Industrial and International Relations had been a dismal failure insofar as international relations were concerned; one reason for this was that the committee rarely had had anything related to external affairs before it. By referring the estimates of the Department to the committee annually the government sought to interest the members and the public in its bold initiatives in that field, and to recruit support for them. Again, the estimates had to go later to the Committee of Supply.

Yet another special reason for referring estimates to a small committee was exemplified in 1951 when a vote to provide assistance to unemployable pensioned veterans was referred to a special Committee on Veterans Affairs. Since that committee was composed of veterans and others keenly concerned for the well-being of that particular group, the reference at once gratified the committee, demonstrated the solicitude of the government for war veterans, and enlisted the support of the committee for the government's efforts. In this instance, too, the rights of the Committee of Supply were saved explicitly.

During World War II when the money to wage the war was appropriated without estimates, the House had appointed a special Committee on War Expenditures at each session. The work of that committee met with general approval. Against this background, after 1945 several leading Progressive Conservative spokesmen revived the early criticism of the Committee of Supply as a body highly unsuitable for detailed inquiry into administrative activity even in peacetime. The sound work of the Committee on External Affairs, they argued, was convincing evidence that a standing committee could do that kind of work better than a committee of the whole House. Satisfaction with the work of the Committee on External Affairs led some of them to propose the creation of a standing committee system parallelling the departmental structure of the government so that most of the estimates could be examined by specialized committees.[26] Later they shifted back to the idea of one new standing committee, a committee modelled after the British sessional committee on the Estimates, as recommended by Speaker Fauteux in a report on procedure in 1947.[27] Such a committee would have one and only one duty, namely to study in an intense way each year the estimates of two or three departments.[28]

By 1955 the Liberal government, which over the years had felt uneasy about the propriety of sending estimates to committees, at least committees operating as suggested by the official opposition, was ready to make a timid attempt to meet the constant complaint about the uselessness of the Committee of Supply.[29] It proposed the establishment of a sessional committee on the estimates.[30] The committee was appointed in 1955, 1956, and 1957. However, to the great annoyance of the opposition, the committee was not given the power "to send for persons, papers and records;" nor did the government allow it a free hand in deciding which departments it would study.[31]

The way in which the standing committees were employed after the Diefenbaker victories in 1957 and 1958 was predictable: the main emphasis was on parliamentary control of expenditures. The prime minister never had had much use for the committees: either the majority party would make the committees serve the government's purposes or alternatively the committees would come to challenge the government's right to make decisions and to lead. Yet Mr. Diefenbaker had denounced the Liberals unceasingly in the elections of 1957 and 1958 for arrogant contempt of Parliament, and had promised that under a Diefenbaker government the rights of Parliament would be revived. After winning 208 of the 265 seats he came to appreciate that the many new backbenchers very soon would grow bored and impatient unless directed to worthwhile work. And he had colleagues with high hopes for the committee system. "Naturally," said the government house leader, the Hon. Howard Green, "one way of making this house more efficient is to give every private member, no matter to which party he may belong, the greatest possible scope in taking part in the government of the country. This is something that should have been done by the former government and why they were not bright enough to see the need for it I never could understand."[32] About his own attitude the prime minister was candid: "As a matter of fact, [in defending the more extensive use being made of the committees] I speak as one who is not a very good committee man. Over the years I have more or less cast doubt on the efficacy of the committee system. However, others whose experience is wider as committee members than is my own were able to convince me that the committee system could indeed be incorporated into our system without borrowing anything from the constitutional position of the congress of the United States."[33]

Before 1958 the examination of the auditor general's report and of the public accounts by the Public Accounts Committee was not regarded as one of the regular sessional activities. Ordinarily over the years the opposition had had little interest in the committee unless there were accusations to be made against the government, or scandals to be revealed, while the backbenchers tended to see the committee as a forum in which they reacted as best they could in the government's defence to whatever the opposition had discovered. This attitude did not always prevail: there were sessions, e.g., those from 1950 through 1952, when the committee met even without the spur of opposition charges, and at which it settled down to do serious non-partisan work, work designed to encourage both better business practices and more careful expenditure of the money supplied to the Crown. In 1958, in the hope that a review of the public accounts and of the auditor general's commentaries could be made a part of the normal work of a parliamentary session as in Britain, the Diefenbaker government proposed that thereafter the committee's chairman should be drawn from the ranks of the opposition. The House adopted the proposal. Since then this had been the unvaried practice. Obviously, the temperament and skill of the chairman and of the other committee members, as well as the political circumstances, have a direct bearing on the work of the committee; however, the move seems to have been fairly successful as a means of assuring that the committee meets, and that it goes to work even when there is no immediate partisan motivation.[34]

Mr. Diefenbaker was interested also in improving parliamentary control of public money before it was granted. Before 1957 the Progressive Conservatives had expressed little discontent with the ordinary legislative process, but, as we have noted, constantly they had demanded a change in the supply process. Mr. Diefenbaker himself regarded the Committee of Supply as "almost totally ineffectual."[35] And the Special Committee on Estimates established by the Liberals in 1955 had lacked powers essential to its success. Now that he was prime minister, he perceived that a committee on estimates if elevated to the status of a standing committee—that is, if given the power to send for persons, papers and records—could serve as "a probing vanguard to the committee of supply."[36] As a result, in 1958 that committee was added to the list of standing committees. In addition, in each of those years, following the highly acclaimed example of External Affairs, the estimates of various departments were referred to the appropriate specialist committees. In 1958 estimates were referred to the Committees on Mines, Forests and Waters; on Marine and Fisheries; on Railways, Canals and Telegraph Lines; on Industrial Relations; and to the new Standing Committee on Veterans Affairs. In 1959 estimates were referred to the Standing Committees on Mines, Forests and Waters; Marine and Fisheries; and on Veterans Affairs. In 1960 estimates were referred to the Committee on Mines, Forests and Waters and to the Committee on Veterans Affairs. In addition, in 1960 the estimates of the Department of National Defence and of the Department of Defence Production were referred to a special committee. The reaction of the Liberals, who had won only forty-nine seats in 1958, to the practice of referring estimates to various committees was strongly adverse: they regarded the whole undertaking as an ill-conceived make-work program for the benefit of the bloated ranks of the Progressive Conservatives. For committees that were only "study groups," they felt neither need nor zeal.

In contrast, the government bills sent to the committees during the sessions of 1957–58, 1958, 1959 and 1960 were fewer in number and lesser in importance than in previous years—seven in 1958; five in 1959; and nine in 1960, in contrast with nine in 1952–53; eight in 1953–54; ten in 1955; and eight in 1956—but this fact may be attributable in part to a paucity of innovative legislation. Aside from the Public Accounts Committee, few committees received investigative references.

The deterioration in the parliamentary situation that set in during the session of 1960–61 led to a marked decline in committee activity. In that session only four government bills were referred, and three of these related to veterans; in 1962 only three, all dealing with C.N.R. branch lines; in 1962–63 only one, which was not enacted. At the same time, 1960–61, 1962 and 1962–63, the Standing Committees on Estimates fell into disuse. The only committee that studied estimates during those sessions—besides those two perennials, the Committee on External Affairs and the Committee on Railways, Air Lines and Shipping—was the Committee on Veterans Affairs.

Let us now describe summarily the main characteristics of the standing committees that had evolved by 1963. First, because the committees had originated as sessional committees their work was highly diverse. Some had unique tasks related to the status or the domestic management of the House, but others dealt with substantive business. Second, the committees were specialist committees both with regard to subject-matter and membership. Third, three of the committees dealt with private bills, but two of the three dealt with public bills also, as did certain other committees. Fourth, some of the committees had come to be used to examine the estimates of the departments and agencies parallel to their subject matter. Fifth, the committees were modelled originally, not after committees of the whole House, but after select committees; and they retained that character. All, except the Committee on the Restaurant, were given the power "to send for persons, papers and records," the essential power of an investigative, as distinct from a legislative, committee. Consistent with their character, the work of the standing committees on bills and on estimates formally was only investigative: all bills, both public and private, and all estimates had to go subsequently to a committee of the whole House. In short, the committee system, never having been reformed radically, was the product of its entire past. It was an extraordinary, even an amazing system.

That a system so unusual had developed can be attributed to the fact that the committees, aside from those with unique tasks, essentially were investigative. They were not integral parts of the machinery by which the basic processes of the House were performed. They did not supplant committees of the whole House. They merely studied bills and estimates. Undoubtedly the work that they did was valuable, especially with regard to private bills; but they were not used to reduce the number of stages to be done in the Chamber. Accordingly, often they were bypassed. Whether or not they reduced the work of the Chamber is debatable. Sometimes bills that had been studied in the standing committees subsequently moved forward very rapidly; but at other times the preliminary study seemed only to make the members more vociferous in the Chamber.

That no attempt was made to use the standing committees instead of committees of the whole House can be attributed to various causes. First, it was still possible to complete the work found necessary by the government without parcelling it out among smaller bodies. Second, it was considerably easier on the government to have its business done in the Chamber, where the ministers were present and in charge, than in scattered committees run by private members. Third, even after 1927 the committees were too large to be highly efficient; indeed it is quite possible that one of the reasons why the standing committees were valued by many members was that membership on three or four committees helped to create the illusion back home that the member, although silent in the House, was deeply involved behind the scenes in governing the country. A worthwhile reduction in the size of the committees would have made it difficult for many members to be included on the committees that their constituents regarded as important. And, fourth, the prevalent constitutional fetishism—the mistaken idea that the House was following faithfully in the footsteps of the British House—made highly suspect any hint that committees of the whole House, especially the Committee of Supply, might be supplanted by smaller committees without grave impropriety.

SEVEN

The Standing Committees: The Pattern Varied

When the move to reform the procedures of the House began after the election of 1963 the Special Committee on Procedure and Organization then appointed was convinced that a strong and modernized system of standing committees was one of the foremost means, probably the chief means, by which the House of Commons could be revitalized and restored to its proper constitutional place.[1] Consistent with this view, the committee's successor in the next session, 1964–65, studied the roles of committees in representative bodies long and carefully, and produced a major report—its fifteenth report, presented to the House on 14 December 1964—devoted to proposals for the reformation of the standing committee system.[2] The goal of at least some of the members of the committee was constitutional. Over the years, they believed, the balance between the government and the House had tipped badly: the government had become far too weighty. Now by reorganizing itself the House could redress the balance to a considerable degree. Strong and independent committees were the means by which the influence of party discipline on private members could be moderated. The need of "the executive" for great powers in modern circumstances, said Mr. G. W. Baldwin, one of the Progressive Conservative members of the committee, is obvious. "However, I suggest," he continued, "this makes it all the more essential to do what we can to repair the imbalance by strengthening the power of the legislative branch of government so it can continue to exercise proper control and scrutiny over the executive branch, rendered even more desirable by the strengthening of the powers of the cabinet which I have mentioned. To repair this omission, to bring the private member of parliament into a position where he can provide an adequate and intelligent means of controlling the executive, the committee system provides the answer."[3] Mr. Baldwin's statement drew strong approval from the prime minister. "I remember," said Mr. Pearson, "some years ago attending a luncheon in London, England, of some senior officials of the British government, departmental heads and some cabinet ministers. One of the ministers said to me as we sat down: 'Here is the government of the United Kingdom, with two or three ministers.' There is this problem—the growth of the executive, the new despotism, as Lord Hewart called it, and how to prevent it destroying the efficiency of the legislature. Could we strengthen the legislature by deepening and broadening the committees structure? There are some recommendations in this report which, I believe, when implemented may well have this effect. I hope so."[4]

The reaction of the leader of the opposition, Mr. Diefenbaker, to the report was unfavourable. When the Special Committee was established in 1963 he had expressed dissent from Mr. Pearson's high hopes for the committee system. "The Prime Minister," he said, "has mentioned the question of committees. I believe in committees, but experience has proven to me that if we endeavour to place controversial matters before committees they are not effective. Committees operate well in the field of external affairs. The public accounts committee has worked out very well.... But I have seen many other committees operate in which questions of a controversial nature were being discussed and which emasculated those committees and made them ineffective."[5] Mr. Diefenbaker now returned to this point. "Certainly my experience with committees," he commented, "has not led me to believe that, on any matter on which there is strong controversy or aroused partisan feeling, committees are divorced from the feelings of individual members, generally speaking, or the parties to which they belong. However, there is a place for the committees system."[6] The Progressive Conservative house leader, the Hon. Gordon Churchill, was even more critical of the Committee: "I think the committee on rules and procedure started off from the wrong premise. It started off with the idea that reform of parliament was necessary. I sometimes think it started off with the idea of change for the sake of change." Much that he had heard in the debate, he said, was tainted with congressionalism.[7]

The committees proposed by the Special Committee were to be genuine specialist committees; and to that end they were to be relatively small, and to be as permanent in membership as possible over the term, not of one session, but of a parliament. The list of committees was to be expanded to cover the full spectrum of governmental activity. In all there were to be fifteen committees: nine committees to be known as "Standing Committees on Legislation and Estimates" and six other standing committees with unique tasks, e.g., the Committee on Public Accounts. The standing committee system was not to be undermined by the appointment of special committees. The committees should not be dependent for their powers on the managers of the business of the

House; rather, they should have standing powers, which ordinarily would include "... the powers to send for persons, papers and records, to report from time to time, to adjourn from place to place within Canada, to appoint subcommittees and to refer to them such matters as may be deemed fit, to order the printing of any relevant documents, to sit while the House is sitting, and to sit during an adjournment of the House."[8] To enable the committees to function without having to compete with the House for time and attention, one week in five should be reserved for the meetings of the committees; and members should be required to attend the meeting of those committees to which they had been named.

Only with regard to supply business was the Special Committee prepared to make specific recommendations about how the standing committees were to be employed. It recommended that almost all the estimates—the exceptions were the estimates for the governor general, the speaker, and the Privy Council—were to be referred for study to the appropriate standing committees as soon as they had been presented to the House. Coupled with this went a portentous recommendation: "... that not more than 20 days be set aside for debating the main Estimates in Committee of Supply." In contrast, the Committee merely stated that the Standing Committees on Legislation and Estimates "would also consider such bills as the House might refer to them," and made no recommendation designed to eliminate or reduce repetition by the committees of the whole House of work done on public bills by the standing committees.

After the debate in the House, during which Mr. Diefenbaker and Mr. Churchill, as we have noticed, expressed their dissent from the Committee's confidence in committees, and government spokesmen indicated what they thought were the weaknesses in the recommendations, the Committee made two additional reports. One of these, its eighteenth report, set forth a new text for Standing Order 65, providing therein the structure and powers of a reformed standing committee system. The list of committees was somewhat different from the one given in the fifteenth report; and the powers to travel within Canada, to sit during adjournments, and to sit while the House was sitting were dropped. The other report, its nineteenth, dealt with supply business. It raised the proposed basic limit on the Committee of Supply to thirty days, but made provision for up to fifteen additional days. This recommendation—that the Committee of Supply work within a time limit —was based on the assumption that sets of estimates would be referred to the appropriate standing committees.

A brief and ugly, but revealing, exchange dealing with these two reports took place during the dying minutes of the 1964–65 session, while the House was waiting for the Senate to conclude the business of the session before royal assent and prorogation. Mr. Speaker Macnaughton pleaded with Mr. Churchill for concurrence, or at least agreement to discuss concurrence: "I would like to point out that very considerable inter-party work has gone into these two reports. In particular the 18th report dealing with committees is one which we think is a great step forward in committee work, and I believe was agreed to by all the members on the committee. Of course I am in the hands of the house and must take the decision of the house, but I do think it would be a great loss and we will not be making a forward step if we do not at least consider whether we should concur in these two reports tonight." But Mr. Churchill saw no prospect of progress. "I regret," said he, "very much that the committee failed to effect a compromise with those who did not agree with their suggestions, and this is the situation they have got themselves into now. Had they been prepared to compromise, then perhaps we might have made some progress, but when people take an attitude like that—and I do not care how long they worked or who the committee is—they cannot expect to force their will on other members of the house who have just as much right to deal with rules as people on these committees." A few minutes later, he said: "I explained my views to members of the committee the other day. They were rejected. I do not propose debating them at two o'clock in the morning. The compromise I have suggested is well known to the members of the committee. They did not accept it. I do not accept their suggestion. Consequently I propose calling it ten o'clock and bringing this session to a close."[9] After a short suspension, the House was summoned to the Senate Chamber, where the Parliament was prorogued.

In the meantime, throughout the sessions of 1963 and 1964–65 the Pearson government demonstrated its confidence in the standing committees by having a considerable number of public bills and some sets of estimates referred to them. As a result, there was a great deal of committee activity throughout the period when the Special Committees (1963 and 1964–65) were making their many studies and preparing their reports.[10]

All the members of the Special Committee had supported the fifteenth report.[11] The eighteenth and nineteenth reports—by increasing the number of days for supply business in the Committee of Supply—retreated somewhat in an effort to meet the objections that had been expressed by Mr. Diefenbaker and Mr. Churchill. The impasse reached early on the morning of 3 April 1965, demonstrated that the Committee could make no further progress, and that the involvement of the speaker no longer was desirable. Accordingly, at the next session, which began immediately after prorogation, the government took the initiative by placing its own plan for procedural change before the House. Its proposals, in the form of amendments to the standing orders, touched almost every aspect of procedure.[12] The plan was based on the work of the Special Committee, but went far beyond the Committee in some particulars, notably on supply business and time allocation, but drew back from its position in other particulars, most importantly with regard to the standing committees.

The government's plan was set forth in two motions. One of these proposed two major innovations: first, the introduction of a time limit on supply business in the Chamber, coupled with examination of the estimates by the standing committees; and, second, the introduction of a procedure—Standing Order 15-A—for the allocation of time to items of business. The other motion set forth the texts for various new and altered standing orders, and included a new version of Standing Order 65, on the committees. As expected, the first motion prompted a long and acrimonious debate. Eventually, on 8 June, the two parts of the motion were separated; and the first of the two innovations, dealing with supply business, was accepted, with amendments, on that day. The second part, on time allocation, was accepted on 11 June after a division. The members then turned their attention to the other motion. After very brief consideration, focussing mainly on the desirability of amending it to provide for a standing committee on statutory instruments, the motion was carried that same day, 11 June 1965. All the changes made on 8 and 11 June 1965, were temporary; they were to be in effect only until the end of the next ensuing session. In the event, this meant the end of the 1966–67 session. At the end of that session they were continued in effect with some modifications for another session, i.e., until the dissolution of the 1965–68 Parliament on 23 April 1968.

The list of standing committees set forth in the new Standing Order 65 provided a committee for each of the main groups into which the departments and agencies could be divided. Instead of the nine "Standing Committees on Estimates and Legislation"—that term was dropped—there now were fifteen, as shown in Table 7. Since the estimates of the departments and agencies were to be referred to the parallel standing committee, the Committee on Estimates, which had been added in 1958, disappeared; however, a Committee on Miscellaneous Estimates was added to deal with the estimates of those departments and agencies, such as the Privy Council, the Treasury Board, and the Public Service Commission, for which there was to be no specialist standing committee. As before, there was to be a Committee for Miscellaneous Private Bills; and, as before, two other committees also—now the Committee on Finance, Trade and Economic Affairs and the Committee on Transport and Communications—were to deal with private bills. To enable the

TABLE 7
Standing Committees
(as appointed on 11 June 1965)

		No. of Members	Quorum
1	Privileges and Elections	24	(12)
2	Public Accounts	24	(12)
3	Standing Orders	24	(12)
4	Miscellaneous Private Bills	24	(12)
5	Miscellaneous Estimates	24	(12)
6	Crown Corporations	24	(12)
7	Agriculture, Forestry and Rural Development	45	(23)
8	Broadcasting, Films and Assistance to the Arts	24	(12)
9	External Affairs	24	(12)
10	Finance, Trade and Economic Affairs	24	(12)
11	Fisheries	24	(12)
12	Health and Welfare	24	(12)
13	Housing, Urban Development and Public Works	24	(12)
14	Indian Affairs, Human Rights and Citizenship and Immigration	24	(12)
15	Industry, Research and Energy Development	24	(12)
16	Justice and Legal Affairs	24	(12)
17	Labour and Employment	24	(12)
18	National Defence	24	(12)
19	Northern Affairs and National Resources	24	(12)
20	Transport and Communications	24	(12)
21	Veterans Affairs	24	(12)
22	Printing (a joint committee)	unprescribed	
23	Library of Parliament (a joint committee)	unprescribed	

committees to handle the enlarged volume of business which was anticipated their size was reduced sharply, with half the membership as the quorum of each committee. As recommended by the Special Committee (1964–65), the powers of the committees were conferred in the standing orders. They were in conformity with the recommendation in the eighteenth report, except that the committees were not given the right to delegate their powers to sub-committees. The terms read: "The Standing Committees shall be severally empowered to examine and enquire into all such matters and things as may be referred to them by the House; to report from time to time their observations and opinions thereon; to send for persons, papers and records; and to print, from day-to-day, such papers and evidence as may be ordered by them, and Standing Order 66 [relating to the summoning and payment of witnesses] shall not apply in relation thereto."

These were by far the most important changes made to the standing committee system since its inception in 1867; yet they were not fundamental changes. The committees remained basically investigative; they could send for papers, persons, and records; they could examine and enquire; and they could report to the House "their observations and opinions." Even when they were examining bills and estimates, they were acting investigatively, as had all their predecessors since 1867. The main changes were (a) that the system was extended to cover the whole range of governmental activity; (b) that the committees were made more highly specialized by the reduction of their membership; and (c) that the committees were given a fixed role, albeit an investigative role, in the supply process. Subsequently, the committees became far more prominent and active; but to a large extent this was the result of the attitude of the members and of the decision of the government to have more reports, white papers, and subject matters, as well as more bills, referred to the standing committees.

During the two sessions—1966–67 and 1967–68—held between the restructuring of the committee system in 1965 and the end of the next Parliament, the committees were used extensively, and as intended. Never had they dealt with so much public business. The complaints most frequently heard related to the scheduling of meetings, the maintenance of quorums, and the facilities and accommodations available for the use of the committees: too many committees were holding too many meetings on too few days.

American discontent with the established political processes, with "participatory democracy" as the vaunted alternative, was at its crest in the late 1960s. As a result, some Canadian politicians, professors, and publicists were talking a good deal about participatory democracy. However, the next major change in the committee system, made on 20 December 1968, was prompted mainly by the desire to improve the processes of the House itself, not by a desire to involve the private members more deeply in governing the country, although it was anticipated that greater participation by private members would be a desirable side-effect of those changes. By the fall of 1968, as we saw in chapters 4 and 5, those most interested in procedural reform at that time had come to agree that committees of the whole House were unsuitable for considering the texts of most public bills and that the pretense that the estimates could be considered thoroughly in the Committee of Supply should be abandoned completely.

A question that followed logically was whether these tasks should simply be transferred to the existing standing committees, or whether an entirely new system composed perhaps of a set of unspecialized committees for public bills—committees A, B, C, etc., in the British manner—and a set of committees on estimates should be added. The latter alternative would entail the curtailment, perhaps the abolition, of the existing system. However, this question drew little, if any, attention in either of the Special Committees on Procedure (in the sessions of 1967–68 and 1968) which initiated the reforms made on 20 December 1968.[13] Public bills had been studied in specialist committees since 1867, and estimates had been referred to the Committee on External Affairs since 1945 and to other committees frequently after 1958, and all without untoward results. Alleged difficulties were merely conjectural. Unless the specialist committees were to be abolished altogether—a notion never discussed even in jest—it seemed natural that the estimates of the Department of Fisheries, for example, should be approved by the Standing Committee on Fisheries and Forestry, and that public bills relating to the fisheries should be considered by that committee. This was the committee on which, presumably, would be found those members most keenly interested in the problems of the fishing industry. Indeed, one of the criticisms of the old procedures was that reliance on committees of the whole House made it difficult for private members, including future ministers, to become knowledgeable about particular fields of public business, with the result that the public servants, already too powerful, were becoming increasingly dominant. It was hoped that under the new procedures the members of each standing committee during the course of a Parliament would acquire both knowledge and some authority in a field. In short, to be even considered, any proposals for procedural changes involving the standing committees had to be based on the assumption that the committee system would be the one that had grown up by accretion since 1867.

That no fundamental alteration in the character of the standing committee system was contemplated is shown by the sequence of events. The order of the House by which the list was modernized on 11 June 1965, was renewed for the 1967–68 session. It expired at the dissolution of Parliament on 23 April 1968. On 20 September 1968, to prevent reversion to the pre-1965 list, and in anticipation of the procedural reforms then under active discussion, the government house leader, the Hon. D. S. Macdonald, after a meeting of party house leaders, proposed that the 1965 list be reinstated with some modifications.[14] The House accepted his proposal. This assured that a modern list would be in effect whenever the new procedures for dealing with public bills and the estimates were adopted. When the reforms finally were made on 20 December 1968, the old standing committee system, as updated in 1965, and again in September 1968, was simply carried forward into the new procedural era. Certain changes were made in Standing Order 65 on 20 December, but none affected the essentials of the system. The committees were given (a) the right to sit while the House is sitting and during adjournments, (b) the right to delegate all their powers to sub-committees, except the right to report to the House, and (c) the right to receive evidence at non-quorante meetings. Provision was made for changes in committee membership by notice to the clerk of the House, rather than by order of the House as before. The maximum size of almost all the committees was reduced to "not

TABLE 8
Standing Committees
(as appointed on 20 December 1968)

1	Privileges and Elections	Not more than	20	members
2	Public Accounts	"	20	"
3	Miscellaneous Private Bills and Standing Orders	"	20	"
4	Miscellaneous Estimates	"	20	"
5	Procedure and Organization	"	12	"
6	Agriculture	"	30	"
7	Broadcasting, Films and Assistance to the Arts	"	20	"
8	External Affairs and National Defence	"	30	"
9	Finance, Trade and Economic Affairs	"	20	"
10	Fisheries and Forestry	"	20	"
11	Health, Welfare and Social Affairs	"	20	"
12	Indian Affairs and Northern Development	"	20	"
13	National Resources and Public Works	"	20	"
14	Justice and Legal Affairs	"	20	"
15	Labour, Manpower and Immigration	"	20	"
16	Regional Development	"	20	"
17	Transport and Communications	"	20	"
18	Veterans Affairs	"	20	"
19	Printing (a joint committee)	"	23	"
20	Library of Parliament (a joint committee)	"	21	"
[21	Regulations and other Statutory Instruments (a joint committee) added 7 September 1970]	"	12	"
[22	Management and Members' Services added 21 July 1975]	"	12	"

more than 20 members."[15] A new standing committee, on Procedure and Organization, was added.

As a consequence the committees to this day retain the specialized character given to them in 1867, when the main work, in many sessions the only work, of the two leading committees—the one on Banking and Commerce and the one on Railways, Canals and Telegraph Lines—was with private bills, and when the only work of the Committee on Immigration and Colonization was promotional. Indeed their specialization has been intensified greatly over the years by the reduction in the size of the committees. Yet the committees now play leading roles in both the supply process and the ordinary legislative process. The Committee on Agriculture, for example, now has (a) the ordinary power of a special (or select) committee to investigate any matter referred to it by the House, but it has also (b) in relation to some estimates the power formerly exercised by the Committee of Supply, and (c) in relation to some bills the power formerly exercised by committees of the whole House. Through this one committee normally will pass all the main work of the House relating to both administration and legislation in the field of agriculture. Clearly, at least formally, the House has given a great deal of power to specialized standing committees.

Initially the new close involvement of the standing committees in the main processes of the House caused a fair number of technical difficulties. This was the result of directing a heavy volume of urgent business into largely unprepared channels. Before 1963 the Committees Branch, which provides support services to the committees, had subsisted in a serene, almost stagnant nineteenth-century backwater. Modernization began as a result of the large amount of business sent to the committees in the 1963–65 Parliament. But after 1968 the committees were considering bills and estimates. This meant that sound procedure and rapid publication became very important. If it was to do its work the branch would have to be provided with additional meeting rooms, more clerks proficient in the basic rules of the House, more translators, and more electronic recording equipment. Formerly the evidence taken in standing committees often could be translated and printed at leisure during the summer months. Now in the case of bills it was needed by the House before the report stage had begun. The need for quick production in French and English of the evidence on estimates was not quite as great; yet the validity of the supply process, especially during May and June, depended considerably on the availability to the House of the record of what had been said in the committees. Once the standing orders had been changed on 20 December 1968, the speaker and the clerk, who could not properly have acted in anticipation of the decision of the House, tackled those difficulties vigorously.[16] Their more serious manifestations now have disappeared.

The constitutional change that could follow from the important work of the standing committees has proven far more persistent as a cause of concern. The fact that these committees are specialist committees heightens that concern. First, specialist committees, if powerful, tend to change the system of representation by introducing an element of functionalism. Members who have a special interest in common, e.g., agriculture, the fisheries, or veterans affairs, are given leading roles in the parliamentary processes that bear on those interests. Once this has been done the section of the public that shares the interest may seek to fortify the tendency of the committee to use its power on behalf of its particular industry, group, or region. Second, the existence of specialized committees provides individual ministers, departments, or agencies with a means of exerting special pressure on the prime minister and his ministerial colleagues when questions of policy are to be decided.[17] Third, committees whose members share strong, partial interests will have distinct or factious identities, so that quite apart from substantive considerations, the members on the committee, especially the chairman and perhaps the leading opposition spokesman, may become overly zealous for the perquisites, status, and convenience of their committee to the disadvantage of the rest of the House. And, fourth, the government may have so few supporters familiar with a major industry, e.g., agriculture or the fisheries, that the majority of the committee may be on the committee only to fill up the places.[18] Specialist committees can produce difficulties in a congressional system. If powerful, they may wreck a system based on Responsible Government. The opinion of Lord Campion is worth noting. He raises the question whether there is "... a place in a true parliamentary constitution for a system of permanent committees specializing in different branches of public service? The conclusion hitherto accepted by the [British] House of Commons on the basis of its earlier experience and that of some foreign Chambers seems to be that such bodies cannot be really important unless they are given control of policy, that to control policy they require to be able to initiate expenditure, and that, if they are given control of policy and the initiative in expenditure, they cannot fail more or less to duplicate the functions of ministerial departments, and thus produce an undesirable division of government responsibility."[19]

The law of our constitution, by which the Queen is the governor, is not grossly misleading, provided of course that when we refer to the Queen we mean, and are understood to mean, the principal political and civil servants of the Crown; the ministers, selected because of the success of their party at the last election, and the mandarins, selected on the basis of certain qualifications denominated "merit." The country is governed by a coalition of those qualified by popularity and those qualified by merit. The men and women who make up the coalition decide the content of the statute law, plan the programs that give rise to votes in the estimates, and make the subordinate decisions involved in administering the statutes. But this is not to say that they govern in isolation. Constantly they are under restraints, pressures, and influences from innumerable sources, in the case of ministers chiefly from the House of Commons. The House is divided between those who will support the government if possible, and those who will oppose it whenever to do so is expedient for themselves. We rely for good government, not on the wisdom and probity of the House, but on the adversary relationship between the government and the opposition. This, of course, is the standard relationship under Responsible Government. In an era when the government initiates most of the business dealt with by the House, that relationship becomes all-pervasive: in such an era very little discussion, debate, or voting takes place in the House that is not strongly influenced by it.

In the standing committees, however, the adversary relationship ordinarily is considerably less intense than in the Chamber. The party leaders are not present. The work of a committee is preparatory: the final decisions will be made in the Chamber. There is likely to be far less publicity and far more time; consequently, the members feel freer. But we must not plunge to the polar extreme: just as the adversary relationship is not absolute in the Chamber, neither the backbenchers nor the members in opposition are completely free from that relationship in the standing committees, especially with a minority government.

It seems reasonable that backbenchers should favour a strong and active committee system. There at least they can speak. They can interrogate ministers and public servants. They can make suggestions and put forward amendments to bills. In short, without embarrassing the ministers seriously and without delaying government business, they can participate in the work of the House. In contrast, the attitude of the opposition to the extensive use of small committees is likely to be ambivalent. Since the opposition ordinarily is in the weaker position, it may at times wish to play down the adversary relationship. Far more questions, members in opposition will contend at times, ought to be decided by "free votes." The ministers ought to let the backbenchers have, perhaps not complete independence, but certainly far greater independence. This line of thought sometimes will be applied to the House itself, but more frequently to the committees. The committees, after all, the argument runs, are agencies of the House of Commons; and the government ought not to meddle with them. They ought to be left free to reach their own recommendations on the investigative references, the bills, and the estimates sent to them. Consequently, to some extent each standing committee may be depicted by the opposition as a specialist cabinet for its own field—altering, perhaps even originating, bills; deciding policy questions; changing estimates; and dealing directly with the public servants in the departments and agencies under the committee—and all on the basis of the consensus of the committee. Since the idea behind the adversary system is fairly sophisticated, the opposition always can count on sympathetic support from some newsmen and intellectuals whenever it decries that system.

There are two special reasons why this congressionalist view is especially attractive to an opposition at Ottawa. First, since ministers no longer are appointed as members of the standing committees, while most members of the shadow cabinet are, the opposition may have the weight of ability and experience on its side in a committee. Second, unless the ministerial majority in the House is very great—about 165 to 97—by the time the ministers, the deputy speaker, and the assistant deputy speaker, as well as the parliamentary secretaries (most of whom serve on only one committee) and the chairmen of the committees have been subtracted, the opposition will enjoy also the advantage of having a relatively large number of members available to fill its places on the committees. At the same time it is the government, not the opposition, that cannot afford to lose votes on bills and estimates in the committees, and that must try to maintain the quorums so that the business will be done.

The alternative opposition view is one of hostility to the use of small committees. Assuming that the government does not relinquish or lose control in the committees, the opposition may conclude that committee activity is far more beneficial for the backbenchers, and thus for the government, than for the opposition. Since they cannot run the committees, and since they have nothing to gain in a partisan way from improving the government's administration and legislation, they may conclude that the business should be done, not in the standing committees, but in the Chamber, where the opposition's efforts at least will be publicized.

As we shall see, it was the government party, the Liberals, who became the champions of the use of the standing committees after 1968. The opposition, particularly the Progressive Conservatives—now under a new leader, the Hon. R. L. Stanfield, and with Mr. G. W. Baldwin, who had been an influential member of the Special Committees on Procedure in 1963, 1964–65, 1966–67, 1967–68, and 1968, as their new house leader—explored the extremes of both alternatives, as was predictable. Initially some of them demanded that the government give a great deal of power to the standing committees. Later, when it became clear that the government had no intention of going far enough to please them, they swung around to put their emphasis on doing business in the House and in committees of the whole House. This is not to say that either party took an extreme position. The Progressive Conservatives never denied that the standing committees, even with ministerial interference, were useful; and the Liberals never suggested that the House should be downgraded in importance. They differed considerably, however, over what was the proper balance.

The zeal for more "participatory democracy" voiced outside the House at the time was echoed by some members. The most notable speech along those lines was given by a Liberal member, Mr. Mark MacGuigan, on 24 September 1968. He put forward five recommendations designated to involve "the collectivity of members in real law making." His final suggestion was, "That bills should be referred to standing committees after first reading in the house." "This procedure," he said, "would give the committees the maximum opportunity to participate collectively in law making, and at the same time would provide the government, which up to that time would have had the advice of only a small circle of experts, with the maximum advantages of committee scrutiny." He commented that what he was recommending was "in large measure the structure of the United States congressional committee system." Later, in November 1969, Mr. MacGuigan repeated his call for "...increased participation in government, participation of the public as well as of members of parliament."[20] But the authors of the new standing orders did not contemplate anything so drastic when they recommended that more work be shifted to the standing committees. Their concern, as we have noticed, was to solve the procedural difficulties of the House. Indeed, they were far less involved with questions about participation than had been their predecessors in 1963 and 1964–65. Their intention was that the standing committees would exercise no more power than the committees of the whole House under the old rules; but they did hope that since the standing committees would examine the government's bills and estimates far more intensively, the government would have to take greater care in preparing them. In this way, indirectly, the private members would become more powerful. It was hoped, too, that the intensive examination of estimates and bills would make for better debates in the House at the later stages of both the supply process and the legislative process. And it was thought that the opportunities afforded by the use of the standing committees could not but produce a better-informed House, and that a better-informed House would be more powerful *vis à vis* the public servants. The aim, in short, was to strengthen, not to weaken, Responsible Government.

From 20 December 1968, until the dissolution of the 29th Parliament on 9 May 1974, the way the standing committees were operating was the object of constant criticism, and was a leading topic in several debates.[21] Never in the history of the Canadian Parliament have the committees attracted anything like so much attention. By the reforms of December 1968, the consideration of most public bills and the examination of all the estimates were given over to the committees. Many Progressive Conservatives, especially the Diefenbaker loyalists, were suspicious of both those changes, and would have resisted them *à outrance* if the government had not achieved consent by agreeing to have the proposed Standing Order 16-A—proposed as a successor to S.O. 15-A—to which they were adamantly opposed, reconsidered. It is understandable, therefore, that the Progressive Conservatives were quick to criticize the new procedures during the next few years. Moreover, their criticism of the new rules was harmonious with their general condemnation of Prime Minister Trudeau for downgrading the cabinet, and in turn the Parliament, by his presidential, even pontifical, attitude and conduct.

They had two basic criticisms which although quite different were not inconsistent with each other. The first, oft repeated during 1969, 1970, and 1971, was that the government was not allowing the private members to participate fully and freely in the governing of the country. It was their contention, sometimes stated, sometimes only implied, that the Liberals had led the House to believe that the procedural changes of 20 December 1968, would make the standing committees largely independent of ministerial guidance and control, and that the Liberal government now was subverting the will of the House. It was in the committees, they held, that the private members were supposed to be able to make their real contribution; yet the government was interfering with the committees. It was trying to assert party control over the backbenchers. It was rejecting the good advice and sound amendments of the private members in all the other parties. Moreover, when ministerial intervention failed to produce the results desired by the government, it had the committees' recommendations reversed in the House, or it simply ignored them.

During 1969 and 1970 the Trudeau government had almost constant trouble with certain committees. This was caused mainly by the failure of certain ministers to maintain liaison—to interfere—with committees to which had been given the right to make reports on topics of importance to the government, with the result that those reports, for one reason or another, could not be supported by the government. Inevitably, the government house leader, had to assume the unpopular burden of turning back or diverting those reports.

As early as December 1968, while the rules changes were still under debate, the chairman of the Standing Committee on Transport and Communications, Mr. Gustave Blouin, was accused by Mr. J. A. McGrath of having yielded to pressure from the government house leader, Mr. Macdonald, with the result that a resolution of the committee dealing with rail passenger service in Newfoundland had been omitted from the report of the committee. The Committee on Privileges and Elections, to which Mr. McGrath's accusation was referred, found his charge groundless.[22] Later the Committee on Transport and Communications, under a new chairman, recommended that "the Order of the Canadian Transport Commission, authorizing the Canadian National Railways to suspend rail passenger service in Newfoundland on 5 April 1969, be left in abeyance, until your Committee tables its complete report in respect to this question." This recommendation referred to the plan of the company to discontinue the operation of "the Newfie Bullet" between Port aux Basques and St. John's. To this report the government house leader objected on the ground that the procedure for dealing with rail service abandonment had been established by statute, and that the committee ought not to attempt to accomplish by a recommendation, to which the concurrence of the House was sought, what could be done properly only by a bill. At the end of a one-day debate the motion for concurrence was transferred to Government Orders in the usual way.[23] The government house leader did not have it called for debate again, thus evoking the charge that he had side-tracked the recommendation of the committee. Clearly, if a vote had been taken the government would have won; but presumably the Progressive Conservatives had no intention of allowing the debate, if resumed, to come to an early vote.

Another cause of embarrassment for the Trudeau Government was the report of the Standing Committee on External Affairs and National Defence on Canadian participation in NATO. During the winter of 1969 the Cabinet was engaged in a prolonged and contentious review of Canadian foreign policy. On 3 March 1969, the committee, which had been studying the same matter intensively, was authorized by the House to travel to Europe. After its return to Ottawa it presented a report to the House opposing a reduction in the level of Canadian participation. One week later, on 3 April 1969, the government announced its decision to reduce Canadian participation. Consequently, the government was denounced for having abused the committee: either its investigation ought not to have been encouraged by the government, or the government ought to have given more weight to the findings of the committee.[24]

The next major instance of committee trouble occurred in the following session. During September 1969, while the House stood adjourned, eleven members of the Standing Committee on Indian Affairs and Northern Development visited "... the Canadian Arctic to welcome the Humble Oil Company's ice breaking tanker, the S.S. *Manhattan*, to the waters of the Canadian Arctic Archipelago and to demonstrate the Canadian interest in its voyage through the Northwest Passage." Its report, presented on 16 December 1969, raised questions about pollution control in the Arctic and rejected "... the suggestion that an international waterway exists through the Canadian Arctic Archipelago."[25] The government, then engaged in negotiations over the status of the Arctic, did not wish either to reject or to support the report in the House. The committee did not instruct its chairman, Mr. Ian Watson, to move concurrence. On 19 January 1970, a Progressive Conservative, Mr. Paul Yewchuk, the vice-chairman, gave notice of a motion for concurrence. The government house leader, Mr. Macdonald, argued that Mr. Yewchuk could not make the motion because the committee had not instructed him or anybody else to seek the concurrence of the House. But the speaker, adhering to precedents, ruled that even a member who is not on a committee may move concurrence in a report.[26] On 22 January 1970, Mr. Yewchuk made his motion. After a one-day debate the motion was transferred to Government Orders.[27] That debate, too, was never resumed.

The complaint that the government was failing to heed the private members was not confined to the work of committees with investigative references. On 19 February 1969, the opposition house leader, Mr. G. W. Baldwin, read to the House a letter written by a Liberal member, Mr. Steven Otto, to his constituents. Therein Mr. Otto stated: "There have been some disappointments [in relation to the new rules], mostly in the composition and power of the committees, because although the committees have been given a great deal of work to do, the government members of the committee have been instructed to make no changes to the bills, coming before the committee and to vote exactly as they are told by the government."[28] Throughout the next year the Progressive Conservatives were delighted to quote this sentence as evidence supporting their complaint that the government was not allowing the private members to amend government bills freely.

The most revealing statements of this first criticism—that the government, in defiance of the spirit of the new procedures, was not allowing the private members to participate effectively in the government process—were made by Mr. W. B. Nesbitt and Mr. G. H. Aiken.[29]

On 10 July 1969, during the debate on Standing Orders 75A, 75B, and 75C, Mr. Nesbitt said: "When the new committee system was set up it was said that it was a great step forward. Members of parliament were going to become specialists in fields they were interested in—

agriculture, defence, transport, foreign affairs, health and welfare, and so on. All sorts of latitude was to be given to committees in calling evidence and witnesses. The committees were to be non-partisan and independent; they were to take over certain functions of the house with respect to the study of estimates and consideration of bills." After giving several examples of how the government had prevented the achievement of this ideal, Mr. Nesbitt continued: "The committees were to be non-partisan. They were to study matters carefully and make independent recommendations. Some of us who have been here a while and know how government parties operate had some misgivings whether that would be done. Despite the fact there was a new leader and many new members, some of us felt that the old tendencies would linger on, and they did." He continued: "All committee chairmen except one [Public Accounts] are government appointees and the government has control of all the committees so far as membership is concerned. That certainly has always been the custom. Under the old parliamentary scheme that was quite proper, but we were going to have a new sort of committee system, openly copied from the United States, with committees having some independence. It has not worked out this way at all."[30]

On 4 June 1970, speaking on the motion for a third reading of Bill C-144, which became the Canada Water Act, Mr. G. H. Aiken, who had been on the Procedure Committee in 1963, 1964–65, and 1968, moved an amendment: "That this bill be not now read a third time, but that it be referred back to the Standing Committee on National Resources and Public Works with instructions to amend it by providing for the continuing scrutiny of the management of Canada's water resources by a committee of the House, with a permanent staff of one or more persons to assist it, and that for the purpose of any additional expenditure, the committee request a further recommendation by His Excellency the Governor General." Speaking to his motion, which would have given a committee of the House the task of superintending resource administration, Mr. Aiken said: "The Parliamentary Assistant spoke of the searching inquiry that was made in the committee in respect of this bill. There was a full and searching inquiry. Yet I am sorry to say, except for the amendments the government itself proposed, no changes were made in the principle of the bill after it went to the committee. In fact, even amendments promoted by government supporters in committee, which were supported in the committee and passed, subsequently were reversed by the government when the bill was brought back to the House at the report stage. I believe that two opposition amendments were accepted. We are thankful for this, but I might point out they were so minor that they did not really affect the general direction of the bill. In spite of all the assurances we had that the bill would be carefully considered and would be altered in principle, and although it was altered extensively by the government, no opposition motions were accepted except two very small ones."[31] Mr. Aiken's motion was found inadmissible by the speaker on two grounds; first, an amendment which if adopted would require the House to establish a committee with such important duties went beyond the limits of what could be proposed at the third-reading stage; and, second, the proposal that the committee should request that the governor general recommend an expenditure was unconstitutional.

This first general criticism of the use being made of the committees, based on the presupposition that the House had intended to reduce the responsibility of the government while increasing the power of the private members, was repeated again and again by Progressive Conservative spokesmen. Some may have hoped, as did the Hon. W. G. Dinsdale in 1968, for an increase in the power of the committees as a means "... to slow down or reverse the drift to an all-powerful cabinet and the shift to authoritarianism, ... "[32] But many seem to have engaged in the criticism as a debating ploy, as a means to score off what they regarded as the prime minister's trendy rhetoric about "participatory democracy" before and during the 1968 election. Indeed, some of them, in the Diefenbaker faction, may have been twitting Mr. Baldwin and those other Progressive Conservatives who had been strong advocates of committee power in 1964–65.[33] To this criticism the government made the obvious response: under Responsible Government, it is the ministers, not the private members on either side of the House, who are responsibile for governing—and that includes legislation, as well as administration.

The second main criticism did not come to the fore until 1970; but thereafter it never lost pre-eminence. It related to the consideration of the estimates by the standing committees. Throughout the Pearson years the Diefenbaker loyalists had resented, and generally resisted the imposition of time limits on supply business. They were in eclipse in the fall of 1968, but there were other Progressive Conservatives who reacted with intense misgiving to the recommendation that the time-honoured Committee of Supply should be abolished. The difference between the two groups was one of emphasis: the Diefenbaker group put their stress on the perils of time limits, while the Stanfield group doubted that the consideration of the estimates—as distinct from examination—ought to be moved out of the Chamber. It was only the fact that the party was far more concerned by the proposed Standing Order 16-A—and perhaps the influence of Mr. Baldwin, who supported all the other changes—that kept it from uniting in intransigent opposition to the new supply procedure in December 1968.[34]

The first specific objection raised against the new supply procedure was that the task of reporting the activities of the various committees was too demanding for the Ottawa press gallery. On 18 June 1970 the Hon. Marcel Lambert said:

> *There is a mad rush, when the study of estimates is being undertaken, to have all possible committees sitting at one time so that even the government side, which has large numbers of members available, has to put on platoons or squads running from one committee to another merely to sit there and periodically provide quorums if there is to be a vote. Those members in most cases have not heard one iota of the evidence, nor have they been able to read one word of the evidence because no transcript has been available. Therefore, it has been merely an exercise of political muscle. The press is not in a position to cover all these meetings. The resources are not there and it would be unreasonable to believe they could be there. [Mr. Nesbitt: They were covering the Quebec election.] I recognize the mammoth difficulty in trying to get the transcripts of evidence before members so that the meetings become meaningful. We know that in the past when estimates were discussed in the House and a real problem arose, we could refer to the daily* Hansard *and to comments of all kinds by the press regarding major points of issue that were raised in the committees' studies of the estimates. Now that is all gone. It is almost government by default, government by snuffing out.*[35]

The second specific objection was that individual members had been deprived of their power to prevent the government from obtaining supply. The old argument that there ought to be no time limits on supply business was revived by Mr. J. A. McGrath on 14 October 1970. Consideration, he demanded, should be given "... to restoring just a part of our traditional rights and prerogatives. We can do this by making provision to bring back into Parliament certain predetermined departmental estimates, without any time limit on their passage. This would be done by agreement of the different house leaders. These estimates would come before Parliament, and would be examined by the committee of the whole house, without a time limit, so that members could give voice to their grievances, question government expenditures, and indeed withhold voting money for a department for that year unless they received a legitimate explanation with respect to their grievances."[36] During the next spring he returned to the argument. "We have lost," he said, "the main power that Parliament once had. We have lost the traditional and long fought for right of Members of Parliament to withhold supply until satisfactory answers have been received from the government. Under the old rules, any member of this House could withhold supply if he had a particular grievance and was not satisfied with the way the government was handling the matter. We have now lost that right."[37]

By the spring of 1970 the Progressive Conservatives had taken up again in a major way, as in the 1950s, the important question of the relationship between the Parliament and the government. By various portals Mr. Stanfield, Mr. Baldwin, and others approached this question again and again during the next four years. This gave them a theoretical frame into which their criticisms of the new supply procedure fitted neatly. It meant also that, as never before, the committee system was a leading topic of political controversy, entailing on three occasions the question of confidence in the government.[38] Their concern, unlike that of Mr. McGrath, was not that individual members could not raise grievances effectively, but that the House had lost its control of the purse-strings. On 5 March 1970, the leader of the opposition, Mr. Stanfield, moved a no-confidence motion: "That this House condemns the government for its arbitrary actions and destructive policies of secrecy and non-disclosure including its attitude towards parliament which deny the right of citizens in this country to be informed and to participate fully in the government of Canada, particularly through their elected representatives, and which endanger the balance between the two structures of government—the executive and the representative."[39] The real danger, the Progressive Conservatives now insisted was not that the prime minister would fail to live up to—or, alternatively, would live up to—his rhetoric about participatory democracy, but that he would become a presidential leader of the American type, and this without the various safeguards built into the American system. One important factor among several—including especially the use made by Mr. Trudeau of television—that opened the way for this dangerous development, they argued, was the loss by the House of Commons of true control over the appropriation of public money. Their foremost proof that parliamentary control had been eroded was the reports of the auditor general in 1970, 1971, 1972, and 1973.[40] By 1970 both Mr. Stanfield and Mr. Baldwin had concluded that the new supply procedures were a major cause of the loss of financial control by the House. The new procedures, under which the estimates were considered by the standing committees, they now insisted, made it virtually impossible for the private member to restrain the government from spending more and more money.

On 7 March 1972, Mr. Baldwin moved a no-confidence motion: "That this House condemns the government for its mismanagement and waste of taxpayers' money and urges that parliament take steps to exercise greater scrutiny and control over estimates and expenditures." In support of his motion, he said: "The parliamentary system of government should be like the two pans of a scale, evenly balanced between the executive branch on the one side, and the legislative branch on the other side. That is a principle that, I think, is acceptable to all people. But what has happened? There has been a grotesque distortion. There has been poured into the pan on the executive side of the scales more and more weight; on the other side, there has been a taking away from the legislative branch of many of the powers and authorities it requires. In the result, this distortion is very apparent in the limited way that this parliament can check expenditures and scrutinize the estimates of government."[41] In explaining how this unhappy state of affairs had come about, Mr. Baldwin stated: "In the first place, Mr. Speaker, the committee system has not worked as was expected and many of its original proponents now doubt its value. I have talked to hon. members opposite, who agree with me. Many of them, as I say, doubt its total value, particularly in so far as estimates are concerned. Mr. Speaker, there must be changes. All we have today is a minuet of committees. In many instances there is no opportunity and no means for hon. members to come to grips with the question of estimates, payments and expenditures. The basic principle governing supply, a principle that has come down to us through the ages, has been eliminated. This principle is that supply ought to be held up until basic grievances raised in this place by members of the House on behalf of the people of Canada have been answered. At present, Sir, there is no real opportunity for this to be done. At present, estimates must be passed by a calendar date. Even if there has not been adequate study with regard to some of the items, and in many instances that certainly has not, all the votes are automatically deemed to have been passed by a certain date [i.e., 31 May]. In committees, the intention was to provide government members with an opportunity to be objective and independent, and avoid the party whip. This has not been the case. Government members fall neatly into file and toe the party line when estimates are challenged." Turning to remedies, he said: "In addition to that [the provision of more information in the estimates], I suggest that the estimates of at least four or five departments must be brought to the House each session by way of Committee of Supply. These should be at the choice of the opposition. This would mean that, during the course of the average Parliament of four years, more than half the departments of government would have had their estimates discussed in the wider forum of the House of Commons. I am not suggesting at this time that we revert entirely to the old system. We may consider this, at least as a half-way house, but I think it is absolutely essential that commencing this session at least four or five departments should have their estimates considered in the House in Committee of Supply. Then, there should be a vote on every motion brought in by the opposition parties on the 25 opposition days, although only six of these would be construed as being non-confidence motions."[42]

In the following session, 1973-74, Mr. Baldwin returned twice to the same contention, but with considerably less feeling than before the the election of 30 October 1972, when the Trudeau government lost its majority. On 7 March 1973, during the debate on the motion by the government house leader, Mr. MacEachen, to have the Standing Committee on Procedure and Organization review the rules of the House. Mr. Baldwin said:

> I do not say that the committees cannot be used as an excellent means of providing an occasion for the examination of witnesses, of hearing evidence from ministers and from senior officials, of allowing the presentation of briefs by interested citizens throughout the country, because they are valuable means of obtaining the views of representatives of sectors of the public affected by issues which demand parliamentary attention. These things simply cannot be done in the House itself. Committees, used in the way I have described, are extremely effective in conjunction with the operation of the Commons.
>
> I have already suggested, however, that the right should be reserved to this House, either in committee of the whole or through the revival, in a limited way, of the committee of supply, to deal with several departments of governments, those departments to be selected by the opposition. The leader of the House has been good enough to indicate some acceptance of this view, subject, I agree, to certain safeguards as to the time to be taken and the manner of the proceedings. I should like to make a firm suggestion to the President of the Privy Council [Mr. MacEachen] right now. We would not be unwilling to agree, as an experiment, during this session, even while the standing committee on procedure is considering the matter, to allocate some of the opposition days during which the estimates of several departments might be examined. Hon. members to my left, as well as members of the Créditiste party, might agree to co-operate, and maybe one or two government days could be made available for this purpose.[43]

On 25 May 1973, Mr. Baldwin repeated this argument. At that time he went further in proposing that the proceedings of the revived Committee of Supply would be sufficiently important to be broadcast. "The proceedings in that Committee of Supply should be televised. They should be open to live radio and television."[44]

In summary, we may say that by 1972 the Progressive Conservative position on the use of the standing committees for the examination of the estimates was that the work of the committees went unpublicized, that neither the work of the committees nor the debates in the House on supply days served to restrain expenditure, and that the fixed supply deadlines had deprived the opposition of its power to control the government. The party had united in contending that what was required was the resurrection of the Committee of Supply, not for all the estimates, but for the consideration, *without time limits,* of the main estimates of a small number of departments selected by the opposition in each annual session.

As early as the fall of 1970 the New Democratic Party's spokesman on procedure, Mr. Stanley Knowles, was prepared to agree with the Progressive Conservatives that the standing committees were not serving to restrain government spending; however, at the same time he expressed doubt that the committees were any less effective than the Committee of Supply had been. He said:

> *I am not going to urge that we return to the old system under which every last estimate was dealt with in Committee of Supply. I think it became rather meaningless. That is the reason we agreed to send all estimates to the various separate standing committees. But I do not think anyone in this House can claim that in the standing committees the estimates are examined in any detail or that any parliamentary scrutiny is practised. I do not pretend to have the answer, but I would say that in our attempt to make improvements we have not gone very far with respect to the handling of estimates. Possibly the whole matter of estimates has become so huge in terms of the amounts of money that we have to deal with compared with what it was 100 years ago that we have to take a new look at this situation. Maybe we have to rely on the fact that we have a Treasury Board and a Treasury Board secretariat which does this type of scrutinizing before we ever see the estimates. Maybe we also have to rely on the fact that we have an Auditor General and his staff as well as a Public Accounts Committee to do the job afterwards and that in this whole picture there is not the need for what was thought to be necessary 100 years ago. Maybe Parliament has more important things to do.*[45]

Eighteen months later, on 7 March 1972, he proposed that three kinds of committees should be used to deal with the estimates: the standing committees, a committee of the whole House, and a standing committee on estimates. "I would like to see us arrange for the estimates to go to committees," he said, "and I want to make some suggestions about that, but I would like us to make it part of our rules that the opposition has the right every session to name three or four departments—and it does not have to name them until on in the session—that would also be dealt with on the floor of the House of Commons. Whether that would be done by a committee of the whole or a committee of supply does not matter. I would even go so far as to say that this should be without time limit. Lengthen the days if necessary. Have morning sittings then, instead of morning sittings in the debate on the Address in Reply to the Speech from the Throne. If there is anything to the supposition or myth that parliament controls the public purse, we ought to set it on a basis where we really will be doing this kind of thing." This put him very close to the Progressive Conservatives.

At the same time Mr. Knowles was quite prepared to say—as government spokesmen had been saying for years—that most members do not want to make specific reductions in spending. More money for their field of interest, not less, is their constant goal. This fact he did not deplore; indeed, he proposed that better services and facilities be provided for the specialized standing committees. But it led him on to another point; "... in my opinion there is a place for a committee on estimates made up of auditor types, public accounts types, members who will devote themselves to this and will scrutinize the estimates the way the Treasury Board is supposed to scrutinize them before they ever get into the book.... The job our committees do now on estimates is not an auditing job. It is not an inspection or scrutinizing job. It is a job that members do because they are interested in the subject of the committee to which the estimates have been referred."[46]

Before the election of 1972 the Liberals, with the Hon. C. M. Drury, the president of the Treasury Board; Mr. James Jerome, parliamentary secretary to the government house leader; and Mr. Grant Deachman, the coordinator of committees, as their chief spokesmen, defended the new supply procedures unyieldingly. Whatever purpose the Committee of Supply had served before 1968, it had not been the serious examination of estimates. Any suggestion that the committee had been used in recent times to curtail expenditure betrayed a very bad memory, and smacked of gothic romanticism. The new process, whatever its defects, was far better. It had not fulfilled all expectations, but that was because some members, especially Progressive Conservatives, had failed to meet the higher demands of the new process. They had failed to participate proficiently. Too many of the Progressive Conservatives were simply unable or unwilling to do the serious work on the estimates that the new procedures permitted; consequently, they had a very poor record of attendance at the committees. The support staff provided by Parliament for the leader of the opposition and the leaders of the other recognized groups were not being used efficiently to help opposition members. Moreover, they contended, if the Progressive Conservatives really were unhappy with the government's administration they could use their supply days in the House to focus public attention on the government's misconduct and errors; yet they were not doing so. Indeed, the opposition was having great difficulty in finding good topics for debates on the twenty-five supply days provided by the standing orders.

A general observation on the work of members in committees was made by a Liberal, John Reid, in 1971. The high hopes the government and some of the opposition had had for reform through the use of the committees had been disappointed. The reason was simple: the members had not taken their work seriously enough; they had not prepared. They had not realized that they could not get away with the loose talk that made them so impressive in the Chamber. Said he:

Whereas Members of Parliament had found it easier to speak in the House of Commons without preparation, since they could get away with statements that were not entirely accurate, they found in committee, for the first time, that their facts and interpretations could be challenged by experts. Consequently, their lack of preparation was not found compatible with the needs of committee work. The committee system brought parliamentarians, for the first time face to face with civil servants and ministers in a way which enabled meaningful dialogue to be undertaken.[47]

Mr. James Jerome, a future speaker, was far blunter and more partisan in his defence of the supply process against opposition denunciation. Speaking in the debate on 7 March 1972, he commented that the opposition critics might have cooperated, that the research staffs since 1968 provided to the opposition parties by the House might have been utilized, with the result that there would have been "a thorough and meaningful examination of the estimates." Said Mr. Jerome:

The truth is that this is not done, but that is not the fault of the system. The fact is that the research assistants are busy writing funny speeches for the Leader of the Opposition (Mr. Stanfield) or are campaigning for the New Democrats in by-elections. These are all areas to which these talents are being directed, and that is the choice of the opposition. If they want to be spendthrift and wasteful with these resources, fine —but why come here and say that the estimates are not being carefully examined? The truth is plain and clear—the facilities and opportunities exist but they are not being used to advantage. There are 25 opposition days in the three semesters in which the year is calendarised. Any opposition member who is truthful will admit that sometimes during the course of the parliamentary year it is difficult for the opposition to fill up those opposition days with a subject of criticism of the government.[48]

In the debate on 14 June 1972, Mr. Jerome again argued that the Progressive Conservatives had failed to use effectively the research assistance provided by Parliament, and repeated again an earlier charge that many Progressive Conservatives were neglecting their committee work.[49]

The first intimation from the Liberals that they were ready to concede anything to the opposition's demands for change came on 27 February 1973, at the beginning of the first session after the election of 30 October 1972. When the main estimates for 1973–74 were being referred to the committees, the government house leader, Mr. MacEachen, said: "There were certain controversial aspects of the rules changes but the House as a whole did accept the new supply procedures and the new committee structure with, I believe, a sincere hope that they would improve the situation. Having said that, Mr. Speaker, I am quite happy to co-operate with hon. members to bring estimates before the House of Commons provided there are certain safeguards."[50] A few days later, when his motion for a review of the procedures of the House was under debate, Mr. MacEachen said:

The hon. member for Peace River [Mr. Baldwin] mentioned the other day the possibility of bringing some estimates into a committee of the whole. I think that could be examined by the standing committee [on Procedure and Organization], because I believe it was beneficial to have had the supply bill for $1.3 billion before the House and before the committee of the whole [in February 1973]. I think it provided an excellent debate. It provided hand-to-hand fighting between the opposition and the government, and that is very healthy.

I have not discussed this with anybody else, and I speak only for myself, but I believe that is an aspect that should be considered, namely, whether we should not, with the proper safeguards and maintaining the predictability and the certainty that supply will be granted at certain intervals and the vote will be taken, be given some opportunity under carefully worked out safeguards to debate the estimates in a committee of the whole.[51]

Mr. MacEachen's motion was carried; however, the Standing Committee on Procedure and Organization gave most of its attention to questions concerning the House staff and had not made a report when the session ended on 14 January 1974. During the short 1974 session the committee was comparatively quiet because it was obvious that time was running out for the minority Trudeau government.

In addition to these two main criticisms, voiced chiefly by Progressive Conservatives—the first dealt with the effect of the Liberal government's insistence that the committees are part of the adversary system, and the second with the implication of the use of the committees for the consideration of the estimates—various specific questions and difficulties of a procedural and organizational nature related to the committees have prompted discussion, and at times have cause controversy. Some of these problems, but not all, derive from the threefold nature of the standing committees: the House, as we have seen, has not made adequate provision for their operation by establishing a suitable procedure for each of the three quite different kinds of work—investigative, legislative, and supply—now done by the committees. Of course, not all these problems are new; but the old ones have come to new prominence as a result of the enlargement of the committees' duties in 1968. Let us examine these problems one by one.

One area of trouble has to do with attendance. The fact that too many committees have been meeting on the same days has created what Mr. Baldwin called "a committee jungle."[52] Certainly, the committees have been active as never before. It is important to realize that the increase in committee activity has not been due entirely, or even mainly, to work on bills and estimates. Many members have been eager for parliamentary work; and since the committees have been their greatest opportunity, they have demanded that annual reports from departments, white papers, etc. be referred to the committees as bases for investigative studies. In the 1967–68 session a total of eighteen bills were referred to the standing committees, and these were studied at 104 meetings. In the 1969–70 session eighty-seven bills were committed, and these were considered at 254 meetings. In the former session, twenty-eight meetings were given over to the study of estimates; in the latter, 134 meetings. But the greatest increase was in investigatory work of various kinds—based on annual reports, the auditor general's reports, white papers, and subject-matters referred. This work took up 86 meetings in 1967–68, but 571 meetings in 1969–70. "There seems," lamented the government house leader, "to be no end to the appetite to send more things to the standing committees. Whether it be members or ministers, it seems that a standing committee is the outlet, forgetting all the while that the time of Members of Parliament is at a premium and that at present the committee system is overloaded." According to Mr. MacEachen there were 759 committee meetings during the 155-day 1969–70 session, as compared with 218 meetings during the 155-day 1967–68 session. "If we calculate these statistics in hours and relate them to the number of days on which the House sat," he commented, "the result is even more dramatic. In the two sessions of the twenty-seventh parliament [1965–68] the House sat for 405 days and committees sat for a total of 1,450 hours, approximately—an average of $3\frac{1}{2}$ hours of committee meetings for every day that the House sat. In the first two sessions of the twenty-eighth parliament the House sat for 353 days and committees sat for approximately 3,000 hours. This works out to an average of $8\frac{1}{2}$ hours of committee meetings for every day that the House sat. As a matter of interest, I might note that in the last two sessions of the previous parliament [1968–72] the House sat for 335 days and our committees logged 2,175 hours, for an average of $6\frac{1}{2}$ hours for every day the House sat."[53]

A study of committee attendance by each member was made covering the 1969–70 session and as a result a schedule was drawn up for the meetings of the various committees so as to accommodate as far as possible the 60 or 70 members who attended committee meetings regularly. However, this did not eliminate the complaints about conflicts. Almost all those complaints were made by Progressive Conservatives.

Closely related to scheduling difficulties are troubles about quorums and about changes in committee membership.[54] On these points the disputes have been symptomatic of the contrasting attitudes of most Progressive Conservatives and most Liberals to the extensive use of the committees. Some of the former have protested against committee meetings held without a quorum for the purpose of receiving evidence, a practice permitted since December 1968, under Standing Order 65(7). The Liberal retort has been that the attendance of Progressive Conservatives at the meetings has been low, with the result that the burden of manning committees has fallen largely on the Liberals. The New Democrats attended faithfully, but their representation on the committees was small. Again and again the Progressive Conservatives ridiculed and denounced as subversive of the specialized nature of the committees the Liberals' practice of replacing absent Liberals with available Liberals during meetings to provide quorums, and to assure that the party was adequately represented whenever a vote was to be taken. The Liberals replied that some Progressive Conservatives, instead of attending the committees regularly, played party games with them, that by machination they attacked the government in those committees in which they saw that the Liberals were poorly represented.[55]

Even more dangerous than conflicts among committee meetings, it was argued, is the fact that the surge of activity in the committees has drawn members away from the House and the committees of the whole House, especially on supply days when either there is no vote or the vote takes place at a fixed hour at the very end of the sitting. The lamentable, even intolerable result, it is contended, is that the importance of debate in the House has been diminished. The House has lost its dramatic tension. Predictably this complaint came chiefly from the Progressive Conservatives; yet it has drawn a sympathetic response from some Liberals and others.

The complaint did not go without rebuttal—or perhaps, what some might regard as confirmation. On 23 February 1973, Mr. Ian Watson, a Liberal, compared the value of debate in the House with work in the standing committees:

They [the electors] believe that by constructive criticism we can influence the direction of government policies and government initiatives, and that we can do all this right here in the House of Commons. This public belief is continually being reinforced by the traditionalists in this chamber, most of whom seem to be the really vocal members of the House, who keep insisting and pretending that the action on the floor of the House of Commons is all-important and that if you upgrade any other aspects of this institution, in particular the House of Commons committee system, you are somehow tampering with parliamentary democracy itself. Attach too much attention to committees, and the traditionalists hint darkly that we are moving toward congressionalism.

What are the facts, Mr. Speaker? I do not have to tell you that most of what goes on in this chamber is show business pure and simple. Most questions are not asked to obtain information. Nine times out of ten, questions are either asked to embarrass or the answer is already known. Few of the millions of words of speeches that flow across the pages of Hansard ever affect government bills or government policies. By the time these items reach the floor of the House of Commons the die has been cast and policy directions have already been decided upon. The sheer modern-day volume of legislation and programs makes it impossible to give any in-depth treatment to legislation or programs on the floor of the House of Commons. The traditionalists, by continuing to pretend, in the face of reality, that it is on the House of Commons floor that all the important action occurs, are minimizing the role of Members of Parliament as representatives of the people, and in the context of 1973 Canadian society they are doing a disservice both to parliament and to the Canadian people.[56]

One point on which all the house leaders seemed to agree emphatically is that if the committees were permitted to travel freely even in Canada, the work of the House and of the other committees must suffer; however, it would appear that on occasion committee members have bargained with their house leaders, with the expediting of business in the House being proffered in exchange for House concurrence in reports recommending travel.

One method of dealing with conflicts, both among the committees and between them and the House, favoured by some members is the adjournment of the House or the suspension of the sitting occasionally or, better, regularly, to permit the committees to do their work. The Special Committee on Procedure and Organization (1964–65), in its fifteenth report, recommended that the House adjourn regularly so that one week in every five would be fully available for the standing committees. During another week in every five the members were to be free to visit their constituencies. The government thought that this schedule would be too rigid: in the absence of a very effective time-allocation rule, it would be virtually impossible to fit government business into the three-week terms. Consequently, the recommendation was dropped. However, sittings have been suspended occasionally: this was done on 28 November 1968; 28 January 1969; 30 April 1970; and

27 May 1971. (When a sitting is suspended the day counts as a sitting-day, and members are under the same obligation to remain in Ottawa as if the House itself were at work.) The main objection to this method from the government's viewpoint is that while suspended sittings and adjournments cost time, they make no palpable contribution to the progress of the government's program for the session. The main objection from the opposition's viewpoint is that there is no Question Period on a day when the sitting has been suspended.

A second serious procedural or organizational difficulty relates to committee leadership. Before the twenty-first Parliament, elected in 1949, ministers served regularly as members of the committees. As the practice of nominating ministers ended each chairman came to perform two roles: he led or managed his committee, but now, in addition, he captained the ministerial side of the committee. All the chairmen, except the chairman of the Public Accounts Committee, are selected at the start of each Parliament from among the backbenchers, ostensibly by the members of the committees themselves, but ultimately by the prime minister, on the advice of the chief government whip and, perhaps, the minister(s) chiefly concerned with the fields of the committee. While this dual role and this method of selection may have been acceptable when the committees were dealing with relatively non-controversial investigative references, it is hardly tolerable now that the committees have been integrated into the basic operations of the House. What is required when a committee is examining estimates, and probably to an even higher degree when it is adopting the text of a public bill, is a neutral chairman, a chairman who, like the chairman of the committees of the whole House, merely presides over the contest. Since 1964 the desirability of having the speaker set up a panel of members from which the chairmen of the committees would be selected has been advocated again and again. But it is unlikely that fifteen able members willing to become strictly neutral committee chairmen can be found in the relatively small Canadian House.[57] Moreover, if the chairmen were to be neutralized, who would organize and lead the backbenchers? This has to be done to assure that government's business is moved forward. The obvious answer to that question—the one already given to some extent—is to give the parliamentary secretaries the key role on the ministerial side.[58] But for that approach to be fully successful the parliamentary secretaries would have to be taken into the government —not the cabinet—for as long as they are not in a position to acquire full information about the estimates and about the scheme of public bills, they will be regarded as little more than committee whips by the backbenchers. And who would lead the committees when they are engaged in investigative inquiries? Clearly, the chairmen could not if they were merely presiding officers. A parliamentary secretary could not because normally the activities of the government, probably the operation of his own department, would be touched by the investigation. An opposition member could not lead effectively because he would not have a majority to sustain him.

A third problem relates to the alleged desirability of providing the committees with permanent expert staff in addition to the committee clerks, whose main concern is procedural, not substantive. The basic argument, made most frequently by members of the New Democratic Party, is that to be effective the private members, like the ministers, need to be informed and advised by professionals.[59] But once the validity of this contention—which is challenged—has been tentatively accepted, certain specific questions emerge. Who would select the experts? Under whom, and for whom, would they work? These points are of great practical importance. Clearly, little would be gained by having the experts work for the leader of the majority in the committee. But if they were to work for the opposition, the backbenchers would be neglected. And would the official opposition, e.g., the Progressive Conservatives (or the Liberals), be content with experts who were acceptable to the New Democratic Party? The remaining possibility is that the experts work for the chairman; but, as we have noted, there are good reasons why the chairmen of the standing committees should take a neutral stance.

Occasionally in the past the committees have employed expert advisers when undertaking particular tasks; however, the experience thus acquired provides no easy solution to the problem. In 1969, during the debate on the motion to refer the white paper entitled, "Tax Reform Proposals," to the Standing Committee on Finance, Trade and Economic Affairs, the opposition house leader, Mr. Baldwin, commented: "I think it is fallacious nonsense to suggest that in all cases, or even in most cases, experts and staff hired by a committee function for the benefit of the committee and all the committee members. This is just not the case. I am not faulting anyone, but these are the facts of life. What happens in most cases is that the experts become an extension of the chairman and his supporting government members on the committee. I do not believe that should be the case. . . . I suggest that in a matter obviously as complex and as difficult as this, . . . it should be possible to ensure that all members of the House will have an opportunity to secure the expert assistance they may need in order that they may properly discharge their responsibilities. . . . The virtues of the adversary system must be maintained by permitting there to be engaged on behalf of the respective groups such experts, help and counsel as may reasonably be expected."[60] Obviously, to the extent that the experts are an extension of the chairman, they serve mainly as additional counsel and advocates for the government. It was hoped that the provision of research staff to each of the parties would meet the demand to some extent, although indirectly; however, it would appear that most of the efforts of the "researchers" are being used for partisan efforts outside the House and its committees.

There are those who do not concede the desirability of providing the committees with permanent staffs of experts. Some resent even the cost of experts hired for specific tasks. Others fear that the creation of committee bureaucracies would only increase and consolidate the power of the committees in relation to the House and the government. They fear that the committees would be used by the committee bureaucracy as a facade behind which to promote its own theories and its own approaches to policy questions. They are worried also that the members would feel relieved of all obligation to do basic work for themselves.

Yet another difficulty concerns the status of the public servants *vis à vis* the standing committees. Whereas only members may participate in the House and in committees of the whole House, public servants and other strangers may be called to testify in these smaller committees. The conventional constitutional position is that among the servants of the Crown only the ministers are identifiable as objects of blame and praise, that only the ministers are responsible; but even the general public no longer is satisfied by that doctrine. Perhaps because modern government requires that more decisions be made, and perhaps because public servants are making more of the decisions, or at least are giving technical and scientific advice in ways that amount to making the decisions, the ministers seem less willing than formerly to shield them, while the private members, especially off the political stage, have little zeal for pommelling ministers whom they often regard as mere fronts and scapegoats. Many private members prefer to get behind the ministers to those whom they regard as the real decision-makers; and this they can do in the standing committees. But the more they do this, the less important the ministers become, and consequently, the more indifferent the ministers can afford to be about what is done in their names.

Some anticipate that the ultimate outcome of strong committee staffs and of increased direct contact between the standing committees and the public servants would be a situation—comparable to that said to exist at Washington—in which the two bureaucracies dealt directly with each other behind the backs of the ministers and the private members alike.[61]

A fifth difficulty relates to uncertainty as to how the committees are to proceed. Since 1867 the chief power of the standing committees has been the general power "to examine and enquire into all such matters and things as may be referred to them by the House." This power was neither supplanted nor modified when the work of the Committee of Supply and of committees of the whole House on bills was transferred to them. Before 1968 the standing order conferring powers read: "The Standing Committees shall be severally empowered *to examine and enquire into all such matters and things as may be referred to them by the House: to report from time to time their observations and opinions thereon; to send for persons, papers and records;* and to print, from day-to-day, such papers and evidence as may be ordered by them, and Standing Order 66 shall not apply in relation thereto." On 20 December 1968, that section of Standing Order 65 was altered to read: "Standing Committees shall be severally empowered *to examine and enquire into all such matters as may be referred to them by the House, and to report from time to time, and, except when the House otherwise orders, to send for persons, papers and records*, to sit while the House is sitting, to sit during periods when the House stands adjourned, to print from day to day such papers and evidence as may be ordered by them, and to delegate to sub-committees all or any of their powers except the power to report direct to the House."[62] How this very wide power to investigate—the key clauses are "to examine and enquire" and "to send for persons, papers and records"—is to be brought to bear on estimates and on public bills is nowhere stated.

Of course, when a standing committee is dealing with a public bill the general provisions of Standing Order 75(1) apply. These are: "In proceedings in any committee of the House upon bills, the preamble is first postponed, and if the first clause contains only a short title it is also postponed; then every other clause is considered by the committee in its proper order; the first clause (if it contains only a short title), the preamble and the title are to be last considered." Aside from this, the standing orders give the committees no guidance. The problem now is to harmonize the basic power of the committees, their power "to examine and enquire," with their legislative function. Are they to act like select committees or like committees of the whole House? When, after its second reading, a bill goes to a standing committee, are outside witnesses—that is witnesses other than the minister, the parliamentary secretary, and officials—never to be heard, or always, or only sometimes? The standing orders are silent. Will outside witnesses be ready to confine their testimony to the details of a bill, which is all that is before the committee, rather than attacking or supporting the bill's basic purpose? And, assuming that outside witnesses are to be heard, at what point or points in the proceedings should they be brought in? The opposition will be likely to want to treat proceedings on a government bill as an investigation into the policy behind the bill, and to send for large numbers of hostile witnesses. On the other hand, the government will tend to prefer, unless it is thought that prestigious puffers would be helpful, that the proceedings be legislative in character, that is, that the example of a committee of the whole House be followed, with the one modification that public servants be permitted to reply to questions directly.

After 1968 those committees to which bills had been committed followed unquestioningly the pattern established when bills were only referred, i.e., the committees themselves decided whether or not to hear outside witnesses, how many, and whom. In 1971, after Bill C-180, dealing with packaging and labelling, had been sent to the Standing Committee on Health, Welfare and Social Affairs, the chairman, Mr. Steven Otto, instructed the committee clerk to write to a spokesman of the Grocery Products Manufacturers of Canada, who wished to testify, that the committee would hear only the minister and departmental officials, but that representations might be made in the form of briefs. In ruling on the propriety of this letter, Mr. Speaker Lamoureux followed the precedents from the years before 1968 in ruling that ". . . a committee proceeding is the responsibility of the members of a committee." Said the speaker: "The hon. member for Peace River [Mr. Baldwin] suggested that the chairman of the committee had no right to decide on his own which witnesses should be called by the committee of which he is the presiding officer. In that respect, the hon. member is on sound ground. Only the committee, by a majority, can make such a decision. . . . The Standing Committee on Health, Welfare and Social Affairs will meet in due course and will be free to adopt whatever procedure it may deem to be appropriate in the circumstances for the calling of witnesses including, if it so wishes, a procedure different from that suggested in the committee clerk's letter. All that is required is an appropriate motion carried by a majority of its members."[63]

On some bills only ministers and officials have been heard. In 1968–69 in the case of the omnibus bill, C-150, to amend the Criminal Code, a bill stubbornly opposed by the Ralliement des Créditistes, the Committee on Justice and Legal Affairs rationed the right to call witnesses: the Liberals and Progressive Conservatives each were permitted to bring forward two witnesses, and the New Democratic Party and the Ralliement des Créditistes only one each. In 1970–72 the Agriculture Committee was far more eager for outside advice when considering Bill C-176, the Farm Products Marketing Agencies bill. Indeed, the government house leader, Mr. MacEachen, was prompted to comment: "The bill, and it is an important one, has been before the committee and the House for more than a year. [Some hon. Members: Oh, Oh!] I believe that more than 140 meetings of the standing committee have been held, about 300 witnesses have been heard, and more than 3,000 printed pages of evidence have been taken."[64] In the 1972 session a dispute erupted over the calling of witnesses on Bill C-201, the Foreign Takeovers Review bill. Mr. J. H. Horner proposed in the House that witnesses should be heard on both "the philosophy" of preventing takeovers and the mechanics by which the review of takeover proposals would be made. He proposed that the committee on Finance, Trade and Economic Affairs "... should travel across the country to hear witnesses." The minister, the Hon. J.-L. Pepin objected that such a "road show" would delay the measure by at least two years.[65] In the event the committee decided by a vote of nine to seven to hear outside witnesses, by eleven to seven not to hear individuals, by twelve to six to hear the representatives of groups, and by eleven to seven not to hear the representatives of provincial governments.

Similarly, the standing orders give the committees no guidance as to how they should proceed when considering estimates. Is each vote to be called and decided, as in the Committee of Supply? Or is a committee free to pass over most of the votes and turn directly to those policy questions that concern the steering committee most? The fact that the committees are not required to report the estimates, and are deemed to have reported them if they do not, gives each committee a great deal of discretion as to how to proceed. And can a committee decide to hear outside witnesses? Obviously, the consideration of a department's estimates might easily be turned into a general inquisition —with outside witnesses—into the policy behind the votes; and in such an inquiry the committee would not be limited by a prior decision of the House, as it is by the second-reading decision on a bill. So far this possibility has been resisted: the committees have been satisfied to hear the ministers and parliamentary secretaries, and the departmental officials. But the query must be raised, if the committees may decide whether or not to call outside witnesses on public bills, why are they not free to decide to call outside witnesses on the policy implications of estimates?

And, finally, there are difficulties over the form and nature of some reports by standing committees, and over how the House should deal with those reports once they have been presented. When a committee is considering a bill, there is no problem about the report. It simply reports the bill with or without amendment(s); and the rules indicate clearly what is to be done next in the House. In the case of estimates, the matter is somewhat more complex. A standing committee, like the Committee of Supply when it existed, may make a report showing that it adopted, rejected, or reduced any or all the estimates committed to it, but may not increase the amount or alter the purpose of any proposed expenditure.⁶⁶ Again, the rules indicate the subsequent steps to be taken in the House after such a report has been received, or has been deemed to have been received. But the standing committees when dealing with estimates, although they do not hear outside witnesses, may report as investigative committees. They may, to borrow words formerly used in Standing Order 65, in the case of estimates report "their observations and opinions thereon." Motions for concurrence in such reports, Mr. Speaker Lamoureux ruled, may be moved and debated on supply days, but not under Motions.⁶⁷ The first such report was presented on 28 February 1969, when the Miscellaneous Estimates Committee expressed concern over the use of $1.00 items to effect changes in the law and to authorize the transfer of money from one vote to another. The opposition then initiated a debate on the topic by moving concurrence in that report on 3 March; however, although many of the reports made during the next four years expressed observations and opinions, none of them was debated.

Just as a committee may not increase the amount of an estimate or alter the terms of the vote, it may not include a recommendation for an expenditure among its observations and opinions. In fact, many reports did so between 1968 and 1973, but because concurrence was not moved, the speaker had no occasion to rule on their regularity. Then on 10 April 1973, Mrs. Grace MacInnis, of the New Democratic Party, sought to move concurrence in a report of the Special Committee on Trends in Food Prices. Following the speaker's ruling in the case of Mr. Yewchuk's motion in 1970, the fact that she was not the chairman of the committee was not an obstacle. However, the report included a recommendation: "That the Department of Consumer and Corporate Affairs make specific monies available to consumers groups to present briefs to various governmental boards where appropriate." Mr. MacEachen questioned the propriety of this part of the report. It was defended by both Mr. Baldwin and Mr. Knowles. In his ruling Mr. Speaker Lamoureux stated:

> Hon. members cannot convince me, however, that the Chair should disregard a practice which has existed over many years, probably for more than a hundred years. Hon. members may say that to recommend a course of action to the House is only a recommendation and that the government is not bound by it. My recollection is that just a few years ago, when the House adopted a report which recommended a certain course of action and when the government, in its wisdom, or lack of wisdom, depending on which side of the House hon. members sit, did not take action as recommended—and I insist on that word—by the committee, there were suggestions that the government was in contempt of the House and that the word 'recommend' could not be used in the sense

given to it by the hon. member for Peace River [Mr. Baldwin], but that the course of action in question had become an order of the House to which the government was required to adhere. That is, I suggest, the difficulty when we come to the expenditure of money.

It is fundamental to the parliamentary system that financial initiative belongs to the Crown and I think it is going around this well-established practice to suggest that after a committee has recommended an expenditure of money the House can approve a report from the committee and then consider that an order has been made, which the government must obey, that certain sums of money in respect of which there has been no [Crown] recommendation, should be expended.... It is a long-established practice of this House that recommendations coming from a committee and requiring expenditure of money include the traditional words that the government give consideration to the advisability of spending moneys, and hon. members should give serious thought to having these magic words included in their committee reports when such recommendations are made.[68]

However, the really serious difficulties relate to reports other than those on bills and estimates. Sometimes these reports are long, and contain argument as well as divers recommendations. The House expresses its opinion in the form of resolutions, and its will in the form of orders. What is the nature and status of a report in essay form once the House has concurred in it? Ought the House ever to be asked to concur in reports that in their operative parts are not in the form of proposed resolutions or proposed orders? Before 1968 this would have been a fair question. Since then, with more and more investigative reports coming from the committees, the question has taken on a new urgency.

Although many reports are concurred in by the House without debate—as was the report recommending important changes in the standing orders as of 7 April 1975—some reports bring on debates which if not cut short might continue for three or four days. Concurrence is moved under Motions. Before 7 April 1975, Motions was the second head under Routine Proceedings. At one time this meant that a long debate begun under Motions not concluded at one sitting was resumed just as soon as Motions was reached at the next sitting. However, the experience of the flag debate when the House reached neither oral questions, dear to the opposition, nor the orders of the day, dear to the government, for over two weeks, lead to a change. Since 1965 once a debate begun under Motions has been adjourned the order for the resumption of the debate is a government order. This means that the government house leader has the right to decide if and when the debate will be resumed. Clearly, this is an odious power. It gives the government the right to side-track a committee's report permanently. On the other hand, since 1970 it has been a power even more necessary than before to assure the orderly conduct of business. Before 1970 concurrence almost always was moved only by the committee chairmen, who were highly susceptible to guidance by the government house leader and, through him, to some extent by the other house leaders. However, because of the speaker's ruling on Mr. Yewchuk's motion in 1970, it now is clear that once a report has been presented any member may move concurrence, thus pre-empting the time of the House. Without a side-tracking power in somebody's hands, the time of the House might be consumed day after day by a series of resumed debates on motions for concurrence in committee reports. In his motion of 19 November 1971, Mr. Douglas Rowland proposed that the Standing Committee on Procedure and Organization should be authorized to devise rule changes "... (d) making it mandatory for a motion of concurrence to be moved in connection with all committee reports and discovering a means by which debate on such motions could be kept to a reasonable level, specifically the possibility of increasing the number of assigned days [allotted or supply days], the increase in number to be allocated to the discussion of committee reports, the reports to be considered to be determined by opposition parties;..."[69] Mr. Rowland's motion expressed the concern of many members to assure that committee reports be taken far more seriously by the House. It also suggested one way in which time could be provided for concurrence debates.

The fact that the heading Motions now—since 7 April 1975—comes after the Oral Question Period opens up the possibility of day-long debates on concurrence motions without disrupting the question period. This is highly advantageous to the opposition.

In conclusion, we can say that the standing committee system of the House of Commons acquired its two most notable characteristics—that it is made up of specialist committees, and that those committees are multifunctional—for the most part accidentally. The key committees in the early days—the Committee on Banking and Commerce; on Railways, Canals and Telegraph Lines; and on Agriculture and Colonization—in form were almost committees of the whole House for special fields; certainly, no member who felt that he ought to be included was denied a place. However, only those members who were interested attended regularly, so in fact the committees acquired a specialist character. The form and the fact were brought somewhat closer than hitherto when size limits were set in 1927. The Special Committee on Procedure and Organization in 1964-65 did propose highly specialized committees; but the House did not act directly on their reports. The changes made on 11 June 1965, did follow the committee's recommendations to some extent, but without attention to their implications. Operational efficiency, not higher specialization, was the main cause for the reduction of the size of the committees made at that time. Certainly, that was true for the reduction in size effected in 1968. Although the members of the committees now are named for the life of a Parliament, the ease with which membership changes can be made shows that even today specialization is not the prime consideration behind the small size of the committees. In any case, the committees are multifunctional; and that, too, is mainly a result of unplanned evolution. The practice of referring some public bills to committees which strictly speaking were private bills committees probably arose from the fact that insofar as the public interest was concerned the distinction between private and public bills in those fields was only formal—a bill initiated by a private company might be of greater importance to the public than one introduced by the government—and the fact that the committees included all those members who conceivably might be interested. When the decision was made, in 1958, to refer estimates to committees so that members could examine those areas of governmental activity in which they were interested, it was reasonable enough that the estimates should be parcelled out among the existing committees. And, on 20 December 1968, when the House decided to have both estimates and bills considered by the standing committees, the same idea was simply carried forward yet another step.

The House never has decided, with the implications clearly stated, whether or not it wishes to have strong multifunctional, specialized committees. Naturally, different attitudes prevail among the members. Some see the committee power as a clear danger to Responsible Government, while others, at the other extreme, see an increase in committee power as the most promising means for preserving representative government. The fact that the committees are multifunctional, as well as specialized, exacerbates the problem, for the kind of conduct by members that may be required by Responsible Government in relation to one committee function, e.g., the consideration of a government bill, may be quite unnecessary, even highly unsuitable, in relation to another function.

To propose that the House confront the main question—whether or not it wishes to have strong multifunctional, specialized committees—would be jejune, for the House prefers to grapple with particular cases, not with abstract questions. However, sooner or later, the House will deal with the troublesome procedural or organizational problems detailed above. Its solutions to those problems will presuppose an answer to the main question.

EIGHT

Doing the Government's Business

When the Canadian House of Commons on 20 December 1867 adopted with minor amendments the rules of the Legislative Assembly of the old province of Canada its assumption was that in short sessions, such as those to which many of the members had become accustomed in the assemblies of New Brunswick, Canada, and Nova Scotia, it could complete all its work—whether initiated by ministers or private members—without time limits on speeches, without prohibitions against debating routine motions, without limits on regular sessional debates (such as the debate on the Address in Reply to the Speech from the Throne), without a real closure rule, without timetabling for bills, and without using small committees to consider estimates and public bills. It was thought that the main riverbed was deep and wide enough to accommodate the full flow of business without extensive aids and restraints. The standing orders of 1867 were not intended primarily to focus the attention of the House on government business, or, beyond that, to ensure that the House reached decisions on that business; rather, their main purpose was to make the operations of the House orderly and predictable for the benefit of the members and to provide guidance for those members of the public who wished to petition for private acts. Moreover, during the early years the assumption proved quite valid. Indeed, the early sessions of the new Parliament were considerably shorter than had been those of the Legislature of the province of Canada. Since then, chiefly in two periods, 1906–13 and 1955–69, the rules have been altered fundamentally by the addition of new standing orders relating to public business. The main aim of almost all the reforms has been to ensure that the government can get its business dealt with by the House in sessions of acceptable length. Moreover, one change in the rules led to another. When the natural riverbed became inadequate because of the increased volume and because of delays and stoppages, the erection of one dike made yet another dike at the next most vulner-

TABLE 9
The Legislative Record
(1867–1974)

Acts initiated by private members to make changes in electoral constituencies are listed under the heading, "Constituency Acts." The common effect of these was no more than to make a change in the name of a constituency. The acts by which money was provided for defence purposes, including the suppression of the rebellion in the North West in 1885, are included with the acts for ordinary expenditures under the heading, "Appropriation Acts." Acts that received royal assent after having been reserved are included for the session at which they passed the House of Commons

Parliament and Session	Year	Sittings	Private Members' Acts	Con. Acts	App. Acts	Other Gov. Acts	Total Public Acts	Private Acts
1 (1)	1867–8	83	1	0	1	73	75	20
1 (2)	1869	49	0	1	1	46	48	27
1 (3)	1870	62	2	0	1	37	40	19
1 (4)	1871	43	4	0	1	30	35	23
1 (5)	1872	46	3	2	1	37	43	75
2 (1)	1873	59	5	1	1	53	60	68
2 (2)	1873	11	0	0	0	0	0	0
3 (1)	1874	42	3	1	1	46	51	67
3 (2)	1875	48	6	0	1	49	56	42
3 (3)	1876	46	2	1	1	35	39	36
3 (4)	1877	59	4	0	1	48	53	36
3 (5)	1878	67	3	0	1	18	22	26
4 (1)	1879	64	7	0	1	43	51	28
4 (2)	1880	57	3	0	1	39	43	33
4 (3)	1880–1	65	1	0	1	31	33	30
4 (4)	1882	68	4	0	1	50	55	72
5 (1)	1883	73	3	0	1	41	45	53
5 (2)	1884	67	2	0	1	42	45	62
5 (3)	1885	119	2	0	2	48	52	43
5 (4)	1886	65	5	0	1	49	55	59
6 (1)	1887	49	3	0	1	48	52	79
6 (2)	1888	61	3	0	1	43	47	64
6 (3)	1889	65	3	0	1	43	47	63
6 (4)	1890	80	2	0	1	35	38	71
7 (1)	1891	102	1	0	3	52	56	79
7 (2)	1892	87	2	0	2	25	29	53
7 (3)	1893	47	2	0	1	34	37	62
7 (4)	1894	89	3	0	1	56	60	74

Doing the Government's Business 199

Parliament and Session	Year	Sittings	Private Members' Acts	Con. Acts	App. Acts	Other Gov. Acts	Total Public Acts	Private Acts
7(5)	1895	68	1	0	2	41	44	53
7(6)	1896	70	3	0	1	10	14	39
8(1)	1896	34	0	0	3	2	5	11
8(2)	1897	78	2	0	2	30	34	63
8(3)	1898	98	0	0	1	53	54	69
8(4)	1899	102	4	0	2	43	49	86
8(5)	1900	115	0	0	5	43	48	81
9(1)	1901	73	1	0	2	40	43	75
9(2)	1902	63	1	0	1	35	37	78
9(3)	1903	155	3	0	4	67	74	132
9(4)	1904	103	4	0	2	36	42	100
10(1)	1905	129	2	0	2	45	49	127
10(2)	1906	88	3	0	3	46	52	133
10(3)	1906–7	95	1	0	3	50	54	88
10(4)	1907–8	148	1	0	4	72	77	96
11(1)	1909	84	0	0	2	35	37	117
11(2)	1909–10	102	5	0	3	54	62	115
11(3)	1910–11	117	2	0	3	23	28	122
12(1)	1911–12	75	2	0	2	53	57	113
12(2)	1912–13	111	1	0	3	53	57	152
12(3)	1914	103	0	0	2	57	59	128
12(4)	1914	5	0	0	1	7	8	0
12(5)	1915	51	1	0	2	21	24	74
12(6)	1916	88	1	0	3	25	29	65
12(7)	1917	135	0	0	5	36	41	64
13(1)	1918	47	0	0	3	49	52	44
13(2)	1919	93	0	0	5	71	76	78
13(3)	1919	50	2	0	1	28	31	5
13(4)	1920	86	0	0	4	69	73	130
13(5)	1921	79	1	0	2	51	54	144
14(1)	1922	75	0	0	3	50	53	128
14(2)	1923	98	2	0	3	68	73	152
14(3)	1924	95	1	0	3	71	75	159
14(4)	1925	98	2	0	3	51	56	158
15(1)	1926	111	0	0	4	13	17	131
16(1)	1926–7	54	0	0	6	70	76	232
16(2)	1928	93	0	0	3	51	54	268
16(3)	1929	83	1	0	4	59	64	272
16(4)	1930	62	2	0	3	45	50	276
17(1)	1930	13	0	0	1	2	3	0

200 The Canadian House of Commons

Parliament and Session	Year	Sittings	Private Members' Acts	Con. Acts	App. Acts	Other Gov. Acts	Total Public Acts	Private Acts
17(2)	1931	96	4	0	5	52	61	59
17(3)	1932	78	1	0	4	52	57	32
17(4)	1932–3	119	0	0	5	50	55	37
17(5)	1934	104	1	0	5	56	62	50
17(6)	1935	97	0	0	6	60	66	35
18(1)	1936	92	0	0	6	44	50	49
18(2)	1937	62	1	0	3	41	45	55
18(3)	1938	102	3	0	4	47	54	93
18(4)	1939	103	0	0	3	50	53	63
18(5)	1939	6	0	0	1	9	10	0
18(6)	1940	1	0	0	0	0	0	0
19(1)	1940	61	0	0	4	43	47	69
19(2)	1940–2	105	0	0	6	26	32	57
19(3)	1942–3	124	0	0	9	27	36	76
19(4)	1943–4	120	0	0	10	23	33	98
19(5)	1944–5	136	0	0	8	44	52	122
19(6)	1945	19	0	0	3	0	3	0
20(1)	1945	76	0	0	6	33	39	194
20(2)	1946	118	0	0	6	70	76	302
20(3)	1947	115	1	0	5	72	78	365
20(4)	1947–8	119	2	0	4	72	78	305
20(5)	1949	59	0	0	4	17	21	201
21(1)	1949	64	1	0	3	38	42	167
21(2)	1950	90	0	0	4	51	55	252
21(3)	1950–1	17	0	0	1	9	10	0
21(4)	1951	105	0	0	4	61	65	322
21(5)	1951	56	0	0	0	33	33	4
21(6)	1952	87	1	0	4	50	55	327
21(7)	1952–3	108	0	1	3	50	54	297
22(1)	1953–4	139	0	1	4	62	67	392
22(2)	1955	141	0	1	5	54	60	429
22(3)	1956	152	0	0	6	44	50	378
22(4)	1956–7	5	0	0	1	0	1	0
22(5)	1957	71	0	0	5	34	39	354
23(1)	1957–8	78	0	0	3	27	30	198
24(1)	1958	93	0	0	5	39	44	331
24(2)	1959	127	0	1	5	49	55	371
24(3)	1960	146	0	0	6	42	48	509
24(4)	1960–1	174	1	1	6	56	64	375
24(5)	1962	65	0	2	5	22	29	16

Parliament and Session	Year	Sittings	Private Members' Acts	Con. Acts	App. Acts	Other Gov. Acts	Total Public Acts	Private Acts
25 (1)	1962–3	72	0	0	3	14	17	7
26 (1)	1963	117	2	0	6	34	42	540
26 (2)	1964–5	248	2	0	12	40	54	26
26 (3)	1965	53	0	0	4	16	20	4
27 (1)	1966–7	250	0	0	14	83	97	24
27 (2)	1967–8	155	1	2	5	31	39	10
28 (1)	1968–9	198	0	0	5	51	56	13
28 (2)	1969–70	155	1	9	4	59	73	7
28 (3)	1970–2	244	1	5	5	54	65	3
28 (4)	1972	91	1	5	3	14	23	1
29 (1)	1973–4	206	0	5	5	43	53	2
29 (2)	1974	50	0	2	2	8	12	1

able point even more necessary. One feat of procedural engineering led to another.

The House of Commons was new in 1867, but many members had well-established views on the functions of the House, derived, like the rules they adopted, from their experience in the Legislative Assembly of the province of Canada.[1] It was accepted that the initiation of changes in the general laws was almost exclusively the task of the government. Although private members introduced a fair number of public bills, the standing orders gave priority on private members' days to notices of motions.[2] Moreover, in session after session, beginning with the very first one, the members were quite prepared to reduce private members' time—most frequently by giving up Thursday, the best day for their public bills—throughout the latter part of the session so as to expedite government business. In the early years private bills gave the House a degree of independence from the government—this business was not initiated by ministers; nor were the ministers prominently involved in its passage. At each session the private members sponsored scores of bills, especially for the incorporation of railway companies and insurance companies. But gradually, after the first twenty years, the time required to deal with private bills declined. By then the pioneer generation of inter-provincial companies had been launched, and the local railway lines in eastern Canada had been built, or at least authorized. Although the number of private bills remained fairly high, many of them now were only for minor amendments to the original acts. Insofar as the general laws were concerned, as shown by Table 9, the number of successful private members' public bills dropped after 1896, and again, sharply, after 1913. At the same time the government brought more business to the House. Its requests for larger and larger sums of money for increasingly diverse purposes made supply business more complex. And, as the country grew towards autonomy and maturity the government moved into new, often highly controversial fields.

This shift—the diminution of private bill legislation, and the increase in government business—had an effect on the character of the House. Because more and more of the time of the House was spent on business initiated by government, and therefore approached critically, at times antagonistically, by the opposition, the adversary relationship between the government and its supporters on the speaker's right and the opposition on his left became quite obvious. This change gave the ministers a special concern for any delays and stoppages; generally it was their business that was being retarded. In the first few decades after 1867 very loose rules had sufficed for public business, not only because the total volume of that business was small, but because the active members evinced a strong proprietary attitude towards the operations of the House. Another fact, perhaps the most important fact, was that the death of Macdonald in 1891 marked the end of a period of political history. Hitherto, the Conservatives, building on their pre-confederation strength, had been the dominant party. There had been occasional battles, sometimes sharp and bitter battles especially over constituency boundaries and the franchise, but little attrition warfare. But now, with Macdonald gone and with Laurier leading the Liberals, the question of long-term dominance was open for decision. Could the Conservatives, perhaps after a brief setback, re-establish themselves as the sun party, or was a long period of Liberal dominance beginning, a period during which the Conservatives would win in only extraordinary circumstances? Or was there to be an alternation, a swinging of the pendulum? This uncertainty set the stage for periods of prolonged wars of attrition. Yet it would be a mistake to put all the emphasis on the relationship between the government and the opposition. Naturally the dramatic crises in the party struggles attract attention; but as a cause of procedural reform we must not overlook the instances in which one member, or a few members, frustrated the House by exploiting vexatiously the looseness of procedures derived from more leisurely days.

Until recently the interest of the members in procedural reform was related closely to the length of time they had to spend in Ottawa each year. That was the final test of the rules as long as the indemnity was based on the assumption that members drew their principal incomes from other sources. When Parliament took relatively little of their time, the rules were regarded as at least tolerable. When it took a major part of the year, they were regarded as outmoded. Since almost all regular

Doing the Government's Business 203

sessions before 1952 began after Christmas a long session meant that discontent was fostered not only by the elapse of time, but by the fact that the House was sitting into the hot days of late June, July, and even August. What the record reveals is that the periods of long sessions have been the periods of procedural reform. As shown by Table 10, before 1878 the average number of sittings in a year was about 50.[3] During the next twenty-one years, 1878–98, the average was 75. Then from 1898 to 1915 the average went up to 104 a year. It dropped back to 90 during the period 1915–37. During the eight-year period, 1938–45, the average was 107. In the five years, 1946–50, immediately after World War II, the average number of sittings was 116. In the 1951–55 period, it was 127. During 1956–65 it was up to 139. In the three-year period, 1966–68, it was up again, to 158. During the first four years after 1968, i.e., after the reform of the standing orders on 20 December 1968, to the end of the twenty-eighth Parliament, the average was 155 sittings a year.

The relationship between intense political contention and procedural reform is notable. Undoubtedly one cause of the longer sessions has been the increasing volume and complexity of public business; however, the record of the years between 1914 and 1938 suggests that another cause was strongly effective before World War I and after World War II. In 1899 the Conservatives began their long climb back to the seats of power from which they had fallen in 1896. In 1911 they succeeded in dislodging the Liberals.[4] Thereafter until the outbreak of World War I the Liberals fought back stubbornly in the House. And, it was in the period after 1949 and especially after 1953 that the Progressive Conservatives were mounting the campaign that would give them victory in 1957. Once again the Liberals fought back; and this time their efforts were not cut short by war. By 1963 they had supplanted the Conservatives. Thereafter, from 1963 to 1968, one group of Conservatives, the Diefenbaker loyalists, assailed the minority Liberal Government obstinately.

The two periods of procedural change—1906–13 and 1955–69—were similar in another way. Although both were periods of keen political contention, the reforms made early in each were brought about by agreement among leading men from both sides of the House. But those reforms were hardly fundamental: they did not bear directly on the rights of the opposition. Rather, they eliminated practices with which most members had become impatient. They streamlined and made routine the methods by which certain kinds of business were done. They made it more difficult for mavericks to disrupt and frustrate the House. In short, their general purpose was to shorten the sessions. In contrast, the reforms adopted late in both periods—those of 1913, and

TABLE 10
Sittings in Years
(1867–1975)

Year	Sittings	Year	Sittings	Year	Sittings
1867	36	1904	103	1941	83
1868	47	1905	129	1942	124 (1+123)
1869	49	1906	107 (88+19)	1943	120 (1+119)
1870	62	1907	91 (76+15)	1944	136 (1+135)
1871	43	1908	133	1945	96 (1+19+76)
1872	46	1909	110 (84+26)	1946	118
1873	70	1910	96 (76+20)	1947	126 (115+11)
1874	42	1911	113 (97+16)	1948	108
1875	48	1912	78 (59+19)	1949	123 (59+64)
1876	46	1913	92	1950	106 (90+16)
1877	59	1914	108 (103+5)	1951	162 (1+105+56)
1878	67	1915	51	1952	107 (87+20)
1879	64	1916	88	1953	113 (88+25)
1880	68 (57+11)	1917	135	1954	114
1881	54	1918	47	1955	141
1882	68	1919	143	1956	156 (152+4)
1883	73	1920	86	1957	125 (1+71+53)
1884	67	1921	79	1958	118 (25+93)
1885	119	1922	75	1959	127
1886	65	1923	98	1960	171 (146+25)
1887	49	1924	95	1961	149
1888	61	1925	98	1962	125 (65+60)
1889	65	1926	116 (111+5)	1963	129 (12+117)
1890	80	1927	49	1964	214
1891	102	1928	93	1965	87 (34+53)
1892	87	1929	83	1966	180
1893	47	1930	75 (62+13)	1967	176 (70+106)
1894	89	1931	96	1968	118 (49+69)
1895	68	1932	113 (78+35)	1969	170 (129+41)
1896	104 (70+34)	1933	84	1970	164 (114+50)
1897	78	1934	104	1971	192
1898	98	1935	97	1972	93 (2+91)
1899	102	1936	92	1973	197
1900	115	1937	62	1974	117 (9+50+58)
1901	73	1938	102	1975	172
1902	63	1939	109 (103+6)		
1903	155	1940	83 (1+61+21)		

the new reforms of 1968 and 1969—were of fundamental importance, and were pushed through by the government against obdurate opposition resistance. To a large extent they were intended to enable the government to overcome deliberate obstruction.

The main line of action, the development that underlies and gives meaning to all the other changes, is the bestowal by the House of more and more of its time on the government. The rules adopted on 20 December 1867, gave precedence to private members' business on three days of the week, and to government business on only two days, Tuesday and Friday. But, even in 1867 it was understood that this division was unrealistic. Regularly after the first two weeks of a session the House gave the remaining Thursdays—and occasionally the remaining Wednesdays and Mondays also—to the government.[5] And it was customary that the government "by leave of the House" could use any time remaining after the completion of private members' business on Monday. In 1876 the rules were brought closer to the practice: thereafter, the time on Thursday previously allotted exclusively to private member's public bills—the time after dinner—belonged to the government, and "leave" no longer was required to turn to government business in any time remaining on a Monday or a Wednesday.[6]

During the next twenty-five years the government generally acquired Wednesdays and Thursday afternoons too either by leave or by special orders made fairly early in the session.[7] Occasionally a private member complained that private members' bills were being squeezed out; but since the opposition, like the government, interpreted the constitution as placing the responsibility for governing on the ministers, those members never received more than a perfunctory word of support, and seldom even that. Normally the motion to give more time to the government was carried without a word of dissent from anybody. On 10 February 1905, at the 22nd sitting in the session, when the prime minister moved that government business be given precedence on both Wednesdays and Thursdays, Mr. Frederick D. Monk protested. Sir Wilfrid Laurier replied: "My hon. friend will remember that every private member's day during this session has been in part taken up with government business. We have gone over the order paper day after day and exhausted all the business standing in the names of private members, and then have taken up government business. Under these circumstances I think it is fair that the government should have the time for its business."[8] The prime minister's motion was adopted.

In 1906 the weekly program as set forth in the standing orders was revised so that after the first four weeks of a session, the government was to have almost all Thursday as of right, as well as Tuesday and Friday. (At the same time, because of the decision then made to discontinue Wednesday evening sittings, the hour previously provided for private bills after dinner on Wednesday was shifted to Thursday.) In recommending the proposed changes to the House, Sir Wilfrid Laurier commented.

> *The observations of the leader of the opposition (Mr. R. L. Borden) answer fully the remarks of the hon. member for East Grey [Mr. Sproule]. In former years there was a great deal of private legislation and legislation introduced by private members, but of late years both here and in Great Britain the tendency has been to put on the government the responsibility of all legislation and my hon. friend [Mr. Sproule] as an old member knows that formerly the time on private members' days was fully occupied with private business but of late years again and again the paper has been exhausted and we have gone to government business.*[9]

Throughout the next fifty years the standing orders continued to give precedence to private members' business on Monday and Wednesday. But in practice the standing orders were observed during only the first few weeks of each session. Once the House got down to work the government would move for a sessional order giving it all the remaining Mondays and Wednesdays. Generally, its motions were approved without hesitation, although occasionally there would be a complaint that the government had made its move too soon. For example, when Prime Minister King, on 12 March 1925, moved that on and after Wednesday, 18 March government business was to take precedence, the leader of the opposition, Mr. Meighen, objected. The following exchange took place. The House divided on Mr. King's motion, which carried 117 to 74.

> **Mr. Mackenzie King:** *Mr. Speaker, I think my right hon. friend is the last person who ought to complain that a longer time has not been given for discussion of these [private members'] motions on Wednesdays. I have in my hand a statement of the dates at which Wednesdays were taken under his administration. I find that in 1920, twenty-three days were allowed to elapse from the opening of parliament before Wednesdays were taken, and in 1921, nineteen days were allowed to elapse before Wednesdays were taken.*
>
> **Mr. Ryckman:** *Is this not a different administration?*
>
> **Mr. Mackenzie King:** *Fortunately, yes. This administration has already allowed thirty-four days. I might also point out that, in the session of 1917, nineteen days were allowed to elapse and, in the session of 1918, twenty-two days were allowed to elapse before Wednesdays were taken.*
>
> **Mr. Jacobs:** *We did not have Progressive members in the House at that time.*

Mr. Mackenzie King: *I think the government of the day proceeded on the assumption that it was part of the government's duty to see that government business was expedited and that parliament was not kept unduly long in session.*[10]

The following examples show how little time was left for private members' business.[11]

> The government was given Mondays on and after
> the 64th sitting in 1925, after private members had had 6 Mondays,
> the 23rd sitting in 1935, after private members had had 3 Mondays,
> the 32nd sitting in 1945, after private members had had 2 Mondays,
> the 66th sitting in 1950, after private members had had 7 Mondays,
> the 25th sitting in 1951, after private members had had 2 Mondays,
> the 13th sitting in 1951 (2nd), after private members had had 0 Mondays,
> the 36th sitting in 1952, after private members had had 4 Mondays,
> the 35th sitting in 1953-54, after private members had had 3 Mondays, and
> the 37th sitting in 1955, after private members had had 3 Mondays.
>
> The government was given Wednesdays on and after
> the 34th sitting in 1925, after private members had had 5 Wednesdays,
> the 30th sitting in 1935, after private members had had 5 Wednesdays,
> the 39th sitting in 1945, after private members had had 4 Wednesdays,
> the 43rd sitting in 1950, after private members had had 2 Wednesdays,
> the 37th sitting in 1951, after private members had had 4 Wednesdays,
> the 15th sitting in 1951 (2nd), after private members had had 0 Wednesdays,
> the 25th sitting in 1952, after private members had had 2 Wednesdays,
> the 52nd sitting in 1953-54, after private members had had 6 Wednesdays, and
> the 49th sitting in 1955, after private members had had 3 Wednesdays.

It was not until 1955 that the standing orders were brought into conformity with the practice of the House. Private members' business then was limited, aside from an hour for private bills on Tuesdays and Fridays, to the first six Mondays and the first two Thursdays after the Address in Reply had been adopted. Finally, in 1962, private members' days were eliminated completely. Instead, the private members were given one hour each day immediately before the dinner recess. Under the standing orders adopted on 20 December 1968, the hour for private members' business on Wednesday was eliminated. In short, where in 1867 the time of the House after the daily opening proceedings belonged to the government on only Tuesday and Friday—and on one of those days there was an hour for private bills—now all the time between the opening proceedings and the adjournment proceedings is given to the government, with the exception of four hours a week, which exception is reduced to two hours a week after a total of forty private members' hours on Mondays and Tuesdays.[12] By changing its standing orders so as to put its time at the disposal of the government the House has given recognition to the fact that over the years legislation by statute has become increasingly important in governing; that it is the ministers, not the private members, who are expected to initiate such measures; and that the exploratory discussion of new policies and programs now takes place not in Parliament, but in the media, in party conferences, and various other extra-parliamentary forums.

In 1906, the year when the government acquired the greater part of the time of the House as of right, two other major changes were made to help the House accommodate the growing volume of business. Not only had the early rules given the government relatively little time, but its hold on that time was precarious. Before 1906 a motion that the House adjourn could be moved at any time and always was debatable. Consequently, by moving the adjournment either before or during a debate on a government measure a member could interpose a discussion of greater interest to himself. Only after the member had vented his ire or made his case to his own satisfaction, and any other member who felt called upon to speak had done so—prior to 1927 there was no time limit on speeches—could the House revert to the planned business. Obviously, any strong effort to maintain relevance in debate was pointless when any member could initiate his own debate.

During the 1904 session, for example, when the main government business before the House was a bill to amend the National Transcontinental Railway Act, motions to adjourn were debated frequently. On Monday, 9 May the seed grain shortage in part of the Northwest Territories took up a good part of the day. On Tuesday, 10 May a member moved the adjournment so as to be able to refute accusations made against him on Monday. On Wednesday, 11 May a member initiated a debate on railway freight rates in Ontario. The House did not sit on Thursday. When a member moved the adjournment on Friday, 13 May to call attention to the need to nationalize the telephone and telegraph systems in Canada, Prime Minister Laurier interjected testily: "A very urgent question."[13] To stop diversions—and threats of diversions intended to make the government submissive—in 1906 the House, following the British precedent of 1883, eliminated the right to debate a motion to adjourn except when the motion was moved under the terms of a special standing order then added. Ordinarily thereafter a motion to adjourn moved during the course of a sitting would be only dilatory: by moving the adjournment a member could bring on a division, not a debate. The new standing order—the ancestor of the present Standing Order 26—permitted debate on an adjournment motion, but only under strict conditions: leave to move the motion "for the purpose of discussing a definite matter of urgent public importance" had to be sought and obtained from the House; and this had to be done before the House had settled down to the work appointed for the day.

The other major change made in 1906 related to the timing of the annual sessions. As mentioned in chapter 5, since 1867 the beginning of the fiscal year had been July first. In the early years it was possible to finish the financial business well before that date in sessions started in January or February. For example, in 1875 the session opened on 4 February and was prorogued on 8 April. In 1883 it opened on 8 February and was prorogued on 25 May. In 1889 it opened on 31 January and was prorogued on 2 May. Prior to the session of 1891, which began late because of the general election on 5 March and was protracted because of the Langevin and McGreevy scandals, the members always had been out of Ottawa by the end of June, except in 1885 when prorogation was delayed until 20 July because of the Liberals' resistance to Macdonald's franchise bill. But after 1890 for various reasons the date of prorogation became more irregular. The session of 1903, the first very long one, began on 12 March and ended on 24 October. The next session began on 10 March 1904, and ended on 10 August. The following session began on 11 January 1905, but did not end until 20 July. This experience made many members, particularly those who could not visit their homes and businesses regularly, think (a) that the sessions had become unnecessarily long, and (b) that by reason of the late openings and the prolongation of the sessions, the House was being asked to sit at unsuitable seasons of the year.

It had become impossible to count on doing the annual financial business between January and the end of June. Prior to 1891 the House was able to deal with both the inevitable request for money to end the old fiscal year and the main estimates for the forthcoming fiscal year in a single annual appropriation bill. But in 1891 and each year thereafter two or more bills were needed to cover the supplementary estimates, to provide the government with an advance—"an interim supply"—with which to begin the new year, and to appropriate the money sought in the main estimates.[14]

On 13 July 1904, when the minister of finance asked the House for an interim supply, Mr. N. K. Boyd, the member for Macdonald (Manitoba) sought to express the annoyance of Western and Maritime members with the way the business of the House was being conducted.

> *I wish once more to enter my protest against the causes which have made it necessary to have this vote on account taken. That necessity is brought about by the late date at which parliament is called together, and I enter my protest most strongly against the present practice as I did last session; at that time, I procured from 'Hansard' that the premier when in opposition held views expressed by myself on this matter. Coming as I do from one of the outlaying portions of this country, coming here at a great sacrifice, at a session when every man who has any business to attend to should be at home looking after it, coming here in the spring and staying here away into the summer and fall as we have been doing for the past few years, and as we seem likely to continue to do. I once more protest on behalf of the people I represent, on behalf of those members who have to stay here Sunday after Sunday, week after week, month after month, when other members who happen to live in constituencies close to Ottawa, can come and go and attend to their business, spending three or four days out of each week in Ottawa, devoting the rest of their time to their business at home. Gentlemen representing constituencies in Nova Scotia, New Brunswick, Prince Edward Island, Manitoba and the Northwest Territories and British Columbia, have to stay here day in and day out, week after week, month after month, all to suit the convenience of the government of the day. This government is not the only offender; previous governments have been equally at fault in this respect. I say that this House should be called together not later than November and that members of the government should see that their officials have their reports ready so that the House may meet at some reasonable time and not have it sitting at such a late date to suit the whim of the government or of some official of the government as has been the case in the past.*[15]

In 1906 a plan to re-establish the synchronization of the fiscal year and the annual session was developed. First, the beginning of the fiscal year was to be advanced from July first to April first, thus setting a target calculated to discourage the continuation of the sessions into the summer. And, second, so as to make meeting of the new deadline feasible, the beginning of the annual session was to be advanced from mid-winter to the previous fall. In 1906 Parliament made the statutory change necessary to begin the 1907–08 fiscal year and all subsequent fiscal years on April first.[16] Laurier then had Parliament recalled for the 1906–07 session on 22 November 1906. During the remainder of his time in office he started all the sessions in the fall, except the post-election session of 1909. This scheme, it must be noted, was only partially successful. Some of the sessions did end earlier, but the financial business seldom was finished early enough to permit the House to deal with the annual requests for supply in one bill.[17]

The changes made in 1910 were more technical. They related directly to the conduct of business in the House. Taken together they went a long way towards the eradication of the early nineteenth-century style inherited from the Legislative Assembly of the province of Canada. First, following the example set at Westminster in 1867, the House sought to rein in the members by requiring that speeches in the committees be strictly relevant to the clause or item under discussion. Previously a good deal of latitude had been allowed because the speaker was not in the Chair. Second, the speaker and the chairman of the committees of the whole House were given the authority to direct a member to discontinue an irrelevant or tediously repetitive speech. Third, previously a member burdened with a petition to the House had to make the presentation from his place; the revised standing orders gave him the alternative of discharging his duty simply by handing the petition to the clerk. The petitions no longer were to be read to the House. Fourth, the method of dealing with order paper questions was changed. Previously, all answers to such questions had been read out by the ministers. Thereafter, although all answers were to be printed in the *Debates*, only the answers to questions that had been starred—"marked with an asterisk"—by the questioner were to be read to the House. Fifth, provision was made to permit questions to be turned into orders for returns if in the opinion of the responsible minister the information sought could be provided better in a return than in an answer. And, sixth, to discourage unnecessary debate, those notices of motions for papers that the government was prepared to accept, and on which the mover felt no need to speak, were to be carried without debate. Previously long debates sometimes had taken place on motions that eventually were carried without a dissenting voice.[18]

The reforms of 1906 and 1910 were made amicably, and were not in response to any immediate crisis. It was entirely otherwise with the three changes made at the sitting of 23 April 1913.[19] The occasion of those changes—the most important changes before 1968—was the Liberal filibuster against the naval aid bill; but the Borden government had in mind also the Conservative filibuster against reciprocity in 1911, and, more generally, the frustration sometimes felt in all quarters of the House when one, two, or a few members delayed, or perhaps even prevented, the work planned for a sitting, especially supply business. The first of the three changes had the effect of reducing sharply the number of motions that were debatable: a new standing order listed the debatable motions, and then provided that "... all other motions shall be decided without debate or amendment." In advocating the new standing order Prime Minister Robert L. Borden argued that in the past the House had been able to reach decisions only because the members had been in agreement that decisions had to be made. They had imposed what he called "closure by consent."[20] But a change had taken place so that "closure by consent" no longer was reliable. In the case of a bill preceded by a financial resolution there were eighteen points, exclusive of the committee stage, at which debate could taken place, and amendments could be moved. Mr. Borden commented:

> ... if hon. gentlemen will take the eighteen stages exclusive of the committee stage, and add to these all the amendments that are possible, they will readily see that there may be, when the Speaker is sitting in the Chair, fifty or sixty or seventy different motions which every hon. gentleman in this House is at liberty to debate to the fullest possible extent, and at such length as shall seem to him desirable. It is perfectly obvious, it seems to me, that such conditions cannot possibly result in the efficient or satisfactory transaction of public business, particularly if a certain number of hon. gentlemen—even though they may comprise a very small proportion of the members of the House—are disposed to oppose the transaction of that business. If you add to these stages the period during which the Bill is in committee, when every hon. gentleman in the House is at liberty not only to speak, but to do so as many times as may please him, it will, I think, be apparent to every hon. gentleman in this House, and to every intelligent and reflecting man in the country, that the transaction of public business in those cases becomes impossible, unless you have a convention—what one might call closure by consent—between the parties, so that, at a particular stage, the debate, however lengthy it may have been, shall at last come to a close, and the majority of the House shall be permitted to express their opinion by a vote upon the measure under consideration.[21]

The first of the Borden changes, limiting the number of points at which debate could take place and at which amendments could be proposed, applied not only in the legislative process, but in the work of the House generally.

The second change provided that when the work scheduled for a Thursday or a Friday was the resumed consideration in committee of either supply business or ways and means business, the speaker was to leave the Chair without a decision by the House. This meant that on those two days of the week the *resumed* consideration of the government's spending and taxing proposals—the motions had to have been put before the committee at an earlier sitting—could not be delayed or prevented by debating or seeking to amend the motion that the speaker leave the Chair.[22] Over the years the motion, "That the Speaker do now leave the Chair," which is moved to put the House into a committee of the whole House, often had been the occasion for clashes between the government and the opposition. For example, the minister of finance, Mr. Fielding, began the reciprocity controversy on 26 January 1911, when he moved that the speaker leave the Chair so that the members could consider his reciprocity resolution in the Committee of Ways and Means. The debate on his motion was resumed on 9 February and at the end of that sitting the motion carried. Fielding then moved the reciprocity resolution in the committee. That proposed resolution was still before the committee when Parliament was dissolved on 29 July 1911. On some days the motion that the speaker leave the Chair (to permit the committee to resume its work) carried without debate, but on other days it was debated throughout the entire day so that the committee did not sit. But situations such as that were not all that the Borden government had in mind when it proposed the new rule. It was seeking to provide a remedy for a far more common difficulty. Increasingly, the House was going into committee (of supply, or ways and means) to begin the main work planned for a day, only late in the day, and sometimes not at all, not because of deliberate efforts by the opposition, but because more and more the motion was being debated by individual members.[23] After 1906, when a motion to adjourn ceased to be debatable except under special circumstances, they had come to use this procedural motion as a recurring opportunity to raise grievances and to advocate special causes. What the Borden government wanted to assure was that on at least two days of the week the House would be able to get down to the details of the financial business of the session.

The third change made in the standing orders in 1913—the addition of the closure rule—was designed to enable the government to bring to an end either long debate in the House or prolonged consideration in a committee of the whole House. That change, for which the reduction in the number of debatable motions formed an indispensable basis, will be discussed in chapter 9.

For about thirty years after 1913 the standing orders were found adequate to enable successive governments to have their business dealt with by the House, and in sessions which generally were regarded as reasonable in length.[24] During those years, apart from the introduction of sub-amendments to supply motions, budget motions, and Address motions and the reduction in the size of the standing committees, only two important changes were made; and both were inspired by humanitarian motives, not government exigencies. In 1927, a limit was imposed on speeches.[25] And, in that year the hour of daily adjournment, a topic on which Prime Minister W. L. Mackenzie King felt strongly, was fixed for the first time—at eleven o'clock p.m.—by standing order.[26] Not until the government undertook to perform vast new tasks during and after World War II was the need felt for another major renovation.

The social crisis brought on in Canada and abroad by the great depression gave many Canadians a radically new concept of the proper role of the Government of Canada in the economic and social life of the nation. To what degree that concept could have been realized if World War II had not occurred cannot be said. The war made it constitutionally permissible and politically imperative for the national government to undertake the mobilization and management of all Canada's human and material resources. Both provincial rights and the ideal of a laissez-faire society were shelved for the duration of the war. But once highly centralized government had been achieved those politicians, bureaucrats, and other leaders who favoured an active national government were determined that there would be no return to the pre-war order. Moreover, it was thought necessary that the government should engage in a program of post-war reconstruction to avoid hardships and perils of the kind experienced in 1919 and 1920. And, as it happened, the period of reconstruction hardly was over when there occurred another centralizing episode, the Korean War. By 1953 it was evident that there was to be no return to pre depression "normalcy." Not only would the Government of Canada find new work to do in many of the fields assigned to the Parliament of Canada by s. 91 of the British North America Act, but it would be involved deeply in other fields, either directly as a result of constitutional amendments, or indirectly through shared-cost programs with the provinces. Moreover, the government had taken on the task of regulating the economy to prevent excessive booms and depressions by means of its fiscal and monetary policies. The volume of business brought to Parliament by the government would rise, not subside to pre-depression levels; and this would be increasingly true as the use of statutory instruments made under the War Measures Act and the successive post-war transitional powers acts tapered off in the 1950s. This transformation had important implications for the House of Commons. The kind of House that had suited an era when federal governance for the most part involved the establishment of general law for financial and commercial activities, the promotion and regulation of certain kinds of transportation and communication, and the prohibition of certain kinds of behaviour as criminal would be woefully outmoded in an era when the federal government had become an active manager of the economy. Not only the increased volume of business, but the size and complexity of many of the government's new undertakings and programs made it desirable that the House of Commons work with a new speed and thoroughness.

Throughout the period from 1940 to 1955 there was a constant undercurrent of uneasiness in the House about its procedures. Some of the members saw that the work of the government by necessity or choice was undergoing a transformation, and that in the emerging new order the House of Commons might play only a minor and ritualistic role unless it readied itself for the new times, and reasserted itself. They pressed for modernization.[27] Heavy emphasis was placed on the desirability of dealing with supply business far more thoroughly than was possible in the Committee of Supply. There was also a view that outmoded procedures were helping to prolong the sessions far beyond the term to which the indemnity was suited. In 1947 Mr. Speaker Fauteux in a careful and perspicuous report summarized the more notable criticisms that had been voiced, and analyzed the major areas where improvements might be made.[28] Special committees on procedure were established in 1940, 1944, 1945, 1946, in both sessions in 1951, in 1952, 1952–53, and 1953–54. But reformation came hard. The only changes achieved prior to 1955 were certain adjustments, made in 1952, in the hours of the sittings: the hour of sitting on Monday, Tuesday, Wednesday, and Thursday was advanced to 2:30 p.m. (from 3:00 p.m.); the hour of adjournment was advanced to 10:00 p.m. (from 11:00 p.m.) on Monday, Tuesday, and Thursday; and evening sittings on Friday were replaced by a morning sitting beginning at 11:00 a.m. Central to the problem of achieving reform was the fact that the task of recommending changes was given to the speaker and an assisting committee; but the speaker was not prepared to recommend any change that had not been supported unanimously in the committee.[29] As a result, the committees made no very important recommendations. At the same time the government was not prepared to initiate changes; its business was being done in sessions that the ministers did not find oppressively long.

Finally, after the election of 1953, the government took a more aggressive attitude. As we have noticed already, in 1955 a special committee on estimates was established. The question of the indemnity also was tackled. In 1945 a tax-free allowance of $2,000 a year in place of an expense account had been provided by Parliament. Now, in 1954, Prime Minister L. S. St. Laurent moved to have the indemnity changed from $4,000 a session to $8,000 a year.[30] In this thinking Mr. St. Laurent coupled this increase with the need to have something done to keep the sessions to a reasonable length. And in the new Special Committee on Procedure, appointed on 14 January 1955, the Liberals pressed for fundamental changes, but since that committee, too, was presided over by the speaker, they had to be content with the relatively minor improvements for which unanimous support could be gained in the committee. The major outcome was the introduction in 1955 of limits on all the general sessional debates.

The principal categories of sessional business for which provision must be made when an annual session is being planned are three in number: (a) the adoption of an Address in Reply to the Speech from the Throne, (b) supply, and (c) ways and means. Until 1955 the members were entirely free to take as long as they wished on each of these. There were no time limits.

After 1913, as we have noticed, the government could activate the Committee of Supply and the Committee of Ways and Means on any Thursday or Friday without a preliminary debate. But this did not mean that those committees would have work before them. As we noticed, to prevent the government from evading general attacks on its administration and its financial policies, the 1913 rule provided that no item of business—no vote in the estimates, and no tax proposal—could be dealt with in committee until it had been entered in the committee on a day when the motion that the speaker leave the Chair was debatable. This assured that the members would have opportunities—by debating that motion, and perhaps by seeking to amend it—to state general criticisms, and, if they wished, to bring on a vote in the House without being ruled out of order as irrelevant to a particular vote in the estimates or to the details of a particular tax proposal.

Insofar as ways and means business was concerned, if the minister of finance could restrict himself to one set of tax proposals, that is, to one budget statement in a session, he would need to move only once—other than on a Thursday or Friday—for the Committee of Ways and Means to sit; but the debate on that one motion could drag on for days unless the government resorted to closure. In 1955 a limit of eight days on the resumed debate—the sitting at which the minister makes his budget statement was not included—was prescribed by the House.

In the case of supply business the motion for the speaker to leave the Chair had to be moved repeatedly on days when it was debatable, i.e., until the estimates of all the departments had been entered into the Committee of Supply. Often the motion carried without debate, or after only a brief speech by one, two, or three members. But at other times an amendment, and perhaps a sub-amendment, was moved, thus launching a debate which, like the debate on the Address in Reply, might be protracted over several days. In 1955 the standing orders were altered so that thereafter all estimates could be entered by means of six motions: the motion that the speaker leave the Chair had to be moved only six times for the main estimates. And the proceedings on each of those motions (together with any amendment and any sub-amendment) was limited to two days, a Monday and the following Tuesday. This meant that only two days were required to put the estimates of any particular department before the committee, and that the time required to put all the main estimates before the committee amounted to twelve days.

These two changes did not restrict in any way the time that could be taken on tax proposals in the Committee of Ways and Means, or on the estimates in the Committee of Supply. What they did restrict was the amount of time that could be taken by the members on general debates in the House before they turned their attention in committee to the specifics of the government's taxing and spending proposals.

Little thought was given to limiting the debate on the Address in Reply until after World War II. Those debates, although often quite long, especially after 1909, seem rarely—the notable exception was in 1926 when the minority King government used the closure rule to terminate the debate at the end of twenty-six days—to have been employed to delay ministerial business in the regular sessions. Indeed, it seems probable that in many sessions the government was more than happy to have the private members air their grievances and dull their ardour by speech-making while the ministers continued in cabinet the disputatious preparation of the bills for which the diligent attention of the House had been solicited in the Speech from the Throne. As early as 1906 Henri Bourassa had given a shrewd explanation of the leisurely pace during the early part of a session and of the rush during the last weeks. He said: "The government keep us here for half a year when sometimes by a little activity, by the application of more business-like methods, by introducing their measures at an earlier period of the session and by knowing exactly what their policy is and sticking to it they could shorten the session by at least a month. That has been exemplified by all governments. . . . In England the budget is generally down the week after parliament is called, and all the government measures are brought in within the first month, while here we have been going on year after year since confederation deferring to the last of the session the most important measures, under the pretense that the government have to consult their friends, when the real reason is that the government prefers to have a tired parliament to discuss their policy rather than to bring their measures down at the beginning of the session when thorough and live discussion might be had."[31] Half a century later this analysis probably still was somewhat valid. The main complaint against the whole proceeding was that it did not qualify as a debate; instead, for the most part it was merely a long series of unrelated speeches, few of interest to anybody other than the members who delivered them, and perhaps a few ardent admirers back home. In 1955, at the same time when a limit was set for the budget debate and for the "supply motion" debates, a limit of ten days for the *resumed* debate on the Address in Reply—the day on which the mover and the seconder spoke was excluded from the count—was introduced.

The effect of limiting these three categories of business is shown by Table 11. It will be seen that the limits introduced in 1955 reduced drastically only the time taken by the Address debate. As for the budget debate and the "supply motion" debates, what was sought, or at least what was attained, was (a) greater predictability, and (b) the prevention of future increases. In the case of "supply motions" the change meant that the debates became more highly focused and intense: the first speaker for the official opposition almost invariably moved an amendment to the motion that the speaker leave the Chair, and a third-party spokesman followed up with a sub-amendment. Thus the possibility that the "debate" on a "supply motion" would be simply a series of unrelated grievances by individual members speaking on the main motion, as often as they had been before, was eliminated.[32]

In the field of parliamentary procedure the main emphasis of the

TABLE 11

Time Required for Sessional Business

Session	Days in Session	Address Debate	Budget Debate	"Supply Debates"	Total
1945	76	14 days	$1\frac{3}{4}$ days	$\frac{1}{4}$ day	16 days
1946	118	9 "	$9\frac{1}{2}$ "	$4\frac{1}{2}$ days	23 "
1947	115	12 "	11 "	$1\frac{3}{4}$ "	$24\frac{3}{4}$ "
1948	119	16 "	$4\frac{1}{4}$ "	12 "	$32\frac{1}{4}$ "
1949	59	21 "	$2\frac{1}{2}$ "	4 "	$27\frac{1}{2}$ "
1949 (2nd)	64	$5\frac{3}{4}$ "	$5\frac{3}{4}$ "	$1\frac{1}{2}$ "	13 "
1950	90	$12\frac{1}{4}$ "	$6\frac{1}{4}$ "	8 "	$26\frac{1}{2}$ "
1950–51	17	$2\frac{3}{4}$ "	$1\frac{3}{4}$ "	—	$4\frac{1}{2}$ "
1951	105	12 "	$8\frac{1}{2}$ "	7 "	$27\frac{1}{2}$ "
1951 (2nd)	56	$19\frac{1}{2}$ "	—	—	$19\frac{1}{2}$ "
1952	87	9 "	8 "	$12\frac{1}{2}$ "	$29\frac{1}{2}$ "
1952–53	108	18 "	$13\frac{3}{4}$ "	$8\frac{1}{2}$ "	$40\frac{1}{4}$ "
1953–54	139	14 "	$8\frac{1}{2}$ "	$11\frac{1}{2}$ "	34 "
1955	141	15 "	$11\frac{1}{2}$ "	$16\frac{1}{8}$ "	$42\frac{1}{8}$ "
1955 rule		10 "	8 "	12 "	30 "
1962 rule		8 "	6 "	12 "	26 "

Diefenbaker Government was on a more extensive use of the committee system in the examination of estimates. After the 1955 changes had been made, nothing was done to modernize the House itself further—aside from a reduction in the time for the Address debate to eight days, a reduction in the time for the budget debate to six days, and the replacement of private members' days with private members' hours, all these changes being made permanent in 1962 after a trial period—until after the climax of the political struggle of the Diefenbaker-Pearson era.

One valuable result of the intense struggle that began in 1960 as the Diefenbaker government began to crumble was a revival of interest in the working of the House among both the members and the public. Great battles that would affect Canada's future were being fought, and the main theatre of action was the House. In part those battles were shaped by the rules of the House; in turn the battles strained the rules to the breaking point again and again, thus revealing weaknesses. In addition, the clashes, the prolonged, angry confrontations, and the frequent elections aroused wide-spread criticism of politicians and Parliament. This, in turn, caused members to be embarrassed by the House's reputation as a pandemonium. The outcome was that after the sessions of 1962 and 1962–63, when the struggle reached its peak, members drawn from all parties insisted on reform with a zeal and determination far beyond anything known previously. The cardinal question was how the organization and procedures of the House could be altered so that the House could do its work more efficiently and without the adversary relationship between the government and the opposition breeding implacable hostility. However, parliamentary reform itself became a divisive topic. In the short run any change that permitted the House to work faster would be to the advantage of the government: its business would be completed, and the public would have been given the impression that affairs were being managed adroitly. It is not surprising therefore that the Liberals, who had taken office after the election of 1963, were solidly for reform. The Progressive Conservatives were divided. The Diefenbaker group, while not prepared to oppose all change, felt that the Liberals had exploited the rules to wreck the Diefenbaker government, and, having succeeded, now wanted to alter the rules radically, thus depriving Mr. Diefenbaker of a second chance; consequently, they were opposed to fundamental reform. Other Progressive Conservatives were more thorough-going. They were convinced that what was good for Parliament would not be disadvantageous to their party in the long run; therefore they favoured reform. Naturally, each of these two groups, especially the latter, had to defer somewhat to the wishes of the other. The New Democratic Party and the Social Credit Party favoured any reform not disadvantageous to third parties. The Ralliement des Créditistes, which came on the scene late in the summer of 1963 as a result of a split in the Social Credit Party, was far less interested in the whole topic, but was prepared to go along. For over six years, from 1963 until 1969, procedural reform was a leading topic of debate in the House; and during those years various alterations in the rules were made provisionally. The major changes made in December 1968, and in July 1969, were pushed through by a majority government; but it should be remembered that many of those changes were based on, or were developments from, the solutions to procedural difficulties adopted tentatively, by agreement among the parties, during the four or five preceding years.

By 1960 it had become clear that the two basic strategies on which successive governments ordinarily had been able to rely since 1867 to assure that their business was done had lost much of their efficacy. In the earlier days any obstruction, whether or not it was part of a deliberate scheme—unless very determined, in which case after 1913 the drastic remedy of closure might have to be applied—could be coped with by the simple expedient of letting the session run on a little longer. The ministers had to remain in Ottawa throughout most of the year anyway, so a few extra days or even weeks made little difference to them. But for those private members from the East or the West who made the journey to and from Ottawa by train only once or twice a year, who while there stayed in furnished rooms or hotels, who had law practices, businesses, or farms back home, and who received an indemnity commensurate with a session lasting no more than three or four months, every extra day in the early summer made for great impatience. In 1911 and 1912 Borden adhered to Laurier's plan for the timing of the sessions; but thereafter he abandoned it.[33] Not until 1968 was it revived. In the meantime a few sessions were started in the fall, but always for a special reason, most frequently the desire to have Parliament meet soon after a general election. Prime ministers had learned that the disadvantages —if any for them—of relying on interim supply during the first two or three months of the fiscal year were outweighed fully by the advantage of starting the session early in the new year, and then allowing it to run on until the heat of the summer brought it to a natural end. Closely related to the strategy of letting the House talk itself out was the strategy of leaving much of the work of the Committee of Supply on the main estimates to the last weeks before prorogation. In that way the situation was made obvious to the members: the work of approving the main estimates, acknowledged as necessary by all, would not be tackled in earnest until any government bills meeting resistance in the House had been passed. The result of these two strategies was that the heat and humidity of the Ottawa Valley in the early summer applied a kind of climactic closure to the government's bills, to the business of supply, and to the session.

These ministerial strategies presupposed that the private members were not professional politicians. By the middle of the 1950s, however, fewer and fewer members were part-time amateurs in the old sense. The various welfare and economic programs had created year-around casework for members. The demands on their time by the House itself had increased since 1937. The financial increases—the introduction of the expense allowance in 1945, followed in 1954 by the increase in the indemnity from $4,000 a session to $8,000 a year—made it possible for many members to give up the idea of gaining their main income from other employment. Travel by air had made the trip to Ottawa much less of an annual pilgrimage than it had been for the members from outside central Canada. As the attitude of the members changed, the old strategies became unreliable. Indeed, the time would come—in the 1970s—when the positions would be reversed. Although extra sittings in July still are an inconvenience to a private member who has planned to join his family shortly after the end of the school year—if he is in the opposition, he probably will leave Ottawa, and then return at public expense if his whip summons him for an important vote—they place extreme burdens on ministers who look forward to the summer as a time in which to spend a few uninterrupted days in their departmental offices, to conclude the preparatory cabinet work on the legislative program for the opening weeks of the next session, to make a foray or two into their constituencies, and to try for a brief holiday.

It would be easy to attribute the strife in the House in the mid-1950s and the 1960s to the prevailing political situation and to the behaviour of the leading politicians. The Liberals and the Progressive Conservatives were locked in fierce combat; and after the election of 18 June 1962, the turmoil in the House was compounded by the fact that minority governments were confronted by three, and then by four opposition parties, each eager to show that it was the true opposition. But we must recognize that a precondition of those severe crises was the change in the commitment of the average member, the change by which most had become full-time politicians prepared to stay on in Ottawa—or at least to travel to and from Ottawa at public expense—throughout most of the year if this was required by party strategy. That change would have had important results for the operation of the House even if there had been a majority government, and even if there had been only one party in opposition.

Symptomatic of the change was the fact that the work of the Committee of Supply, once a dull but necessary finale, almost certain to empty the Chamber before the end of the first week in July, now became the government's most persistent problem. The limits on the sessional debates introduced in 1955 had saved time insofar as the budget debate and the Address debate were concerned. In the case of the former, the members might have shifted their rhetorical endeavours to the consideration of the "budget resolutions" in the Committee of Ways and Means; but this did not happen. Most of those resolutions are narrow and technical in nature. Moreover, few ministers, let alone private members, understand the implications of many of them. In the case of the Address debate, there was no alternative occasion. But just as soon as a time limit had been set on the supply motion debates, the time taken by the Committee of Supply increased sharply, so that supply business often took more time after the reform of 1955 than before.

From 1907, when the beginning of the fiscal year was advanced to April first, to 1955 the annual supply pattern was quite regular. Late in March or early in April the House granted to the Crown the money needed to cover the shortfalls for the old fiscal year and an interim supply to begin the new year. Often a second interim supply was needed before the appropriation act based on the main estimates for the new year had been enacted. Normally the main appropriation act was law before 10 July. The exceptional years were 1917, 1924, 1931, 1946, and 1949; but in each of those years the session had been started late. In contrast, in 1955 and thereafter until 1969 the main appropriation act never was enacted prior to 10 July, and usually only much later.[34]

Before 1955 the Committee of Supply normally dealt with interim supply requests and with supplementary estimates with great dispatch. These items raised few policy questions. A request for interim supply ordinarily took less than an hour, and a set of supplementary estimates about a day. The committee moved slowly only when the main estimates were under consideration; but on even that business its pace became faster and faster as the prospect of escape from Ottawa approached. This pattern changed with the intensification of the political contention in 1953–54. Then and thereafter the members in opposition when required to do so by party strategy were prepared to spend extra days, even weeks, in the summer and fall on the main estimates to prevent the House from advancing controversial government measures, to vent their hostility to the ministers, and to create the impression among the electorate that under the government of the day all was chaos and inefficiency. In some years sets of supplementary estimates were treated in the same way. Moreover, once the main appropriation act had been delayed, the total number of days taken on supply business ceased to be the most important consideration. In that circumstance the government had to return to the House for additional interim supply—when the main appropriation act was very late, it had to return repeatedly—and since there was no time limit on the committee in dealing with such requests, each request could bring on a crisis. On the one hand, if the government was to carry on without an election, it had to get the requested supply before its deadline, generally the date on which mid-month or end-of-month pay cheques had to be available for the public servants. Just when the deadline would be passed—the date on which the Crown became insolvent—was kept a secret. Thus the tension in the committee was heightened by uncertainty. On the other hand, the opposition could argue that constitutionally it was obliged to use these occasions, unlike interim supply requests made at the beginning of a fiscal year, as opportunities to appraise the conduct of the government. The question of how long all the annual supply business—main estimates, supplementary estimates, and interim supply—would require always remained important, but frequently it was shaded by the far more dramatic question whether the opposition would permit the current request for interim supply to come to a vote, or whether it would talk beyond the deadline, thus plunging the country into an election.

During the period of procedural reform that began in 1955 the newspaper headlines were dominated by the battle over defence production powers (1955), the pipeline debate (1956), the Coyne affair (1961), the controversy over atomic weapons (1962–63), the flag debate (1964), the various scandals (1964–65 and 1966), and the unification of the armed services (1966–67); but as is inevitable under our constitution the basic question throughout was whether or not in the circumstances created by those divisive issues the government of the day, with or without a majority, could obtain from the House of Commons the money to meet the commitments of the Crown. This meant that the rules of the House governing supply business were crucial to the political developments. Year after year the question whether or not there would be an election at a time fatal to the government depended on those rules.

Table 12, covering the period from 1952, before the adoption of the rule that all the main estimates would be entered by six supply motions, to 20 December 1968, when the Committee of Supply was abolished, shows the number of days taken on supply business in the House and the committee during each session. What is notable is the close relationship between the intensity of political contention and the total time taken by supply business: the committee moved far more slowly when highly controversial measures, e.g., the pipeline bill in 1956, the flag motion in 1964, and the armed forces unification bill in 1966, were to the fore, and when the members—on both sides of the House—were making ready for an election.

The attack by the Progressive Conservatives and the C.C.F. on the

TABLE 12

Time Taken By Supply Business★ (1952–1968)

Session	House (Supply Motion Debates)	Committee of Supply: Supplementary Estimates (sets)	Committee of Supply: Main Estimates	Committee of Supply: Interim Supply (requests)	Total
1952–3	8½ days	(1) ½ day	20 days	(1) ⅛ day	29⅛ days
1953–4	11½ "	(1) ½ "	27¾ "	(2) ½ "	40½ "
1955	16⅛ "	(1) ½ "	30 "	(2) ¼ "	46⅞ "
1956	12½ "	(1) 1½ "	40¼ "	(3) 1 "	55¼ "
1956–7	—	(1) 1 "	—	(0) —	1 "
1957	2¾ "	(2) 4½ "	5¾ "	(2) 2¾ "	15½ "
1957–8	6¼ "	(0) —	15¾ "	(3) 2¼ "	24¼ "
1958	11¼ "	(1 special) 1 "	27⅛ "	(3) 1¼ "	41⅛ "
1959	9¾ "	(2) 7½ "	31¼ "	(2) 1¼ "	49¾ "
1960	10½ "	(3) 11¼ "	36¼ "	(2) 1¾ "	59¾ "
1960–1	10 "	(2) 4½ "	52¾ "	(3) 3 "	70¼ "
1962	2 "	(3) 27 "	—	(2) ½ "	29½ "
1962–3	4 "	(0) —	7 "	(3) 8½ "	19½ "
1963	10 "	(1 special) 1 "	20¼ "	(4) 7½ "	38¾ "
1964–5	6 "	(4) 15 "	36¾ "	(6) 23½ "	81¼ "
1965	2 "	(2) ½ "	¾ "	(2) 1¼ "	4½ "
1966–7	9¾ "	(4) 2 "	41¾ "	(7) 15 "	68½ "
1967–8	8 "	(1) 14 "	30 "	(1) ½ "	52½ "
1968	—	(0) —	16½ "	(1) 1½ "	18 "

★ The number of sittings given over to supply business in the Committee of Supply usually was determined by adding up the number of times the House went into committee; however, although formally correct this method was somewhat misleading, for on some occasions the committee did little or no work. The figures set forth in Table 12 are based on an estimate of the time spent on supply business in terms of "days" (or "sittings"); but it must be noted that no attempt has been made to standardize "days," i.e., a full sitting is a "day" regardless of whether it was on a Wednesday, a Friday, or another day of the week.

In 1956 an extra half day was provided by special order. In other years after 1955 the number of supply motions required to enter all the estimates was reduced by special orders. The figures for the 1966–67 session cover supply for the fiscal years 1965–66 and 1966–67. The 1968 figures refer only to supply business done before 20 December 1968.

St. Laurent government in 1955 was focused mainly on the defence production bill, and in 1956 on the pipeline bill, but in both years it found expression also in the prolongation of the work of the Committee of Supply. In the former year two requests for interim supply were dealt with in the usual expeditious way at the end of May and June, but the main appropriation act was not law until 28 July. In 1956 Parliament provided an interim supply for the months of April and May. The pipeline debate ended on Tuesday, 5 June and the main business for the rest of that week was the debate on the motion of the leader of the opposition, George Drew, to the effect that the House no longer had confidence in the speaker. On Friday, 8 June Prime Minister St. Laurent indicated that on Monday the government would seek an interim supply for June. It was clear that unless the House acceded quickly to this request the government would have to bring on an election (or to resign). Evidently it was the intention of Mr. Stanley Knowles of the C.C.F. and Mr. Davie Fulton of the Progressive Conservatives, who together had conducted the defence against the pipeline bill, that the two parties would continue their resistance to the St. Laurent government to the end by delaying supply beyond the date when the government would run out of money. But on Monday, 11 June the leader of the opposition informed the House that the official opposition would "... consent in the usual way to interim supply...." Mr. Knowles went along most reluctantly. The supply requested for June was granted immediately.[35] During the next few weeks two more one-month supplies were granted. The main appropriation act was enacted on 14 August. If Mr. Drew had not drawn back early in June—if the government had been forced to dissolve—and if the election outcome had been the same as it was to be in 1957, Mr. Drew, not Mr. Diefenbaker, would have been Mr. St. Laurent's successor as prime minister.

In 1960 the Liberals and the C.C.F., sensing that the popularity of the Diefenbaker government was waning rapidly, extended the work of the Committee of Supply so that the main appropriation act was not enacted until 10 August 1960. As a precaution, Prime Minister Diefenbaker started the next session in the fall of 1960, but by 13 July 1961, when James Coyne finally resigned as the governor of the Bank of Canada, the mood of the House was far from conducive to the dispatch of business; consequently, he had the House adjourned from 13 July until 7 September. The main appropriation act for 1961-62 was not enacted until 29 September 1961. In the following session, during the winter of 1962, the opposition, in preparation for the forthcoming election—the election of 18 June 1962—spent twenty-seven days on two sets of supplementary estimates.

The implication of prolonged deliberation over interim supply requests came to be appreciated fully during the session of 1962–63. Prior to the dissolution of Parliament on 18 April 1962, two interim supplies had been granted to cover the requirements of the first seven months—April through October—of the fiscal year 1962–63. The Diefenbaker government, a minority government after the election of 18 June, did not meet the new House until 27 September 1962, and then failed to press ahead with the main supply business. The House granted three interim supplies: one for the month of November, one for December, and one for January. Over the years, as we have noted, interim supply requests, coming at the beginning of the fiscal year as they did, ordinarily had been dealt with by the Committee of Supply and the consequent bill had been passed in less than an hour. The opposition saved its criticisms, questions, and condemnations until the votes in the main estimates were before the committee. The first interim supply request in the fall of 1962 was dealt with in less than two hours; the second in less than two days; but the third took seven days. However, the story does not end there. On 5 February 1963, for the first time in the history of Canada, a supply motion was amended to declare that the House had no confidence in the government. Parliament was dissolved the following day. From a constitutional viewpoint there was nothing remarkable about this: since 18 June 1962, the Diefenbaker government had been in a minority position. But if the defeat of 5 February had not occurred—a distinct possibility, as we now know— Mr. Diefenbaker probably would have been forced to the country by the Liberals. All that they would have had to do was to prevent the request for an interim supply for February—interim supply for the eleventh month of the fiscal year—which was then before the House, from coming to a vote. Moreover, either of the smaller opposition parties could have done the same thing at that time, or during the previous fall. As it was, the defeat on 5 February removed the need to obtain yet another interim supply: the Diefenbaker government was able to carry on through the election of 8 April 1963, by means of governor general's warrants. The main estimates of 1962–63 never were approved by the Committee of Supply, and the main appropriation act for that fiscal year never was enacted. There was only one precedent: the Parliament elected on 10 June 1957, was dissolved on 1 February 1958, before the 1957–58 estimates had been approved by the House. After the 1963 election the new government headed by Mr. Pearson removed any uncertainty as to the legality of the expenditures that had been made during 1962–63 by means of a special retroactive appropriation act. The vulnerability of a government to a long delay in the granting of interim supply had been demonstrated. By holding up interim supply, by simply refusing to let a vote be taken, an opposition group, not necessarily the official opposition, could have precipitated an election. The tactic would have been effective whether or not the government had a majority, unless closure was used successfully.

A more blatant example of the weakness of a government threatened with a stoppage of its interim supply business was provided in October 1963. As a result of the bifurcation of the Social Credit Party—into the Ralliement des Créditistes with thirteen members, and the Social Credit Party with ten members—a controversy arose as to the right of the Ralliement des Créditistes to be seated as a separate group. (Incidentally, if they were recognized as a separate group by the House the payment that had been provided earlier that year by statute for the leader of each group with twelve or more members, other than the prime minister and the leader of the opposition, would go to Mr. Réal Caouette, and not to Mr. Robert Thompson, who had led the party before the split.)[36] The question whether or not the House should take cognizance of the split, which had occurred after the election so that one or other of the two groups had not received electoral approval, was referred to the Standing Committee on Privileges and Elections.[37] The committee made slow progress. When the Pearson government sought an interim supply to carry it through October and November, Mr. Gilles Grégoire of the Ralliement announced that the House and the government were to be held to ransom. Unless the committee dealt urgently with the request of the Ralliement des Créditistes for recognition, the supply request then before the Committee of Supply would be delayed. On October Mr. Grégoire stated his position candidly: "Mr. Chairman, I must inform you that we do not intend to end the debate on interim supply either tonight, tomorrow or as long as the privileges and elections committee has not remedied the ridiculous and illogical situation which prevails in this corner of the house."[38] On 7 October the House arranged for the standing committee to deal with the matter immediately, whereupon Mr. Grégoire permitted the Committee of Supply to come to a decision on the request.

It was the session of 1964–65 that convinced most members that time limits would have to be placed on the Committee of Supply. That session showed that otherwise supply business was liable to be distorted grotesquely by political considerations, and that annual sessions of reasonable length were likely to be rare. The final supplementary estimates for 1963–64 took over thirteen and a half days in the committee. One set of supplementary estimates for 1964–65, dealt with in July 1964, took one and a half days. Although work on the main estimates for 1964–65 began fairly early, it was not finished until 27 November, and required thirty-one days. In the meantime the Pearson government requested interim supply on five occasions: the first request took one day; the second took two hours; the third took five and a half days; the fourth took nine and a half days; and the fifth took eight and a half days, for a total of twenty-five days. The normal supply business of the session—excluding the final supplementary estimates for 1964–65 and the first interim supply for 1965–66, both dealt with quickly in April 1965—had taken seventy-seven sittings. Although there was no summer adjournment in 1964 the session continued until 2 April 1965, for a record of 248 sittings, with the the flag debate and supply as the items that consumed most time.

Fresh from the experience of the summer and fall of 1964, the Special Committee on Procedure and Organization on 14 December 1964, the same day on which the government used closure to terminate the flag debate, recommended in its fifteenth report that in the future the main estimates should be referred for study to the standing committees and that the Committee of Supply should be limited to twenty days on the main estimates in one session.[39] Presumably, the special committee thought that this would enable the House to pass the main appropriation bill early in each fiscal year, thus reducing the government's dependence on interim supplies. In its nineteenth report, made on 26 March 1965, after a debate in the House had revealed how strongly the Diefenbaker group was opposed to time limits, the committee retreated from the bold stand taken in December.[40] In that report it recommended a far longer period—basically thirty days, but possibly up to forty-five days—for the work of the Committee of Supply. The Diefenbaker group objected to this limit also.[41]

On 8 June 1965, in the next session, after another angry debate, the House responded to the experience of the previous year by ordering that the number of "supply motion debates" was to be reduced from six to four, that the detailed examination of the estimates was to be assigned to the standing committees, and that not more than thirty days of the time of the House, including the time of the Committee of Supply, was to be allotted to the business of supply in each session.[42] This time limit applied to the main estimates, interim supply requests, and all supplementary estimates introduced before the committee had completed its consideration of the main estimates. Excluded from the limit were all supplementary estimates introduced after the main estimates had been passed and, of course, the final supplementary estimates. With this major innovation the House began a movement that was to terminate with the abolition of the Committee of Supply on 20 December 1968.

Before the House adjourned for the summer of 1965 it granted two additional interim supplies for 1965–66—one had been granted on 2 April, just before the end of the previous session. On 8 September, during the adjournment, Parliament was dissolved. The new House, elected on 8 November, 1965, met on 18 January, 1966. Since the main estimates for 1965-66 had not been dealt with—the government had used governor general's warrants after the interim supplies had been expended—the House on 21 January 1966, ordered that all the main and supplementary estimates for 1965-66 might be entered by one "supply motion," and that the time required for dealing with those estimates should not be included in the time prescribed for supply business in a session under the order of 8 June, 1965. In the event a total of twenty-six days—two days for a supply motion debate, and about twenty-four days in the Committee of Supply—were used to clear away that unfinished business. The main appropriation bill for 1965-66 passed the House on 9 March, 1966, only 22 days before the end of the fiscal year!

With the supply business for 1965-66 out of the way, the House was in a position to ascertain how satisfactory the thirty-day limit introduced on 8 June 1965, would be when applied to the supply business of a single fiscal year, i.e., 1966-67. Because supplementary estimates introduced after the main appropriation bill had been passed were outside the time limit, the government found it advantageous to move slowly on the main estimates. By the end of October 1966, the four supply motion debates had been held, but only fourteen days had been taken in the Committee of Supply. At that point—the contentious topic on the horizon at that time was the unification of the armed forces—the official opposition decided to precipitate an election by delaying the interim supply needed for November. That request was considered by the committee from 31 October until 15 November, and could have been held up for six more days, i.e., until the entire thirty-day period had been used. The prevalent assumption was that at some point about the middle of November the Crown would be unable to meet its pay rolls for the first half of the month. This intense crisis ended abruptly on 14 November, when the minister of finance spoiled the game by revealing that money had been found to meet the government's immediate requirements.[43]

When the new Special Committee on Procedure established on 25 January 1967, began its work, it found that the idea of time limits on the Committee of Supply was quite acceptable in most quarters of the House. Consequently, the committee focussed its attention on ways to use the time limits to assure that the supply business was done both efficiently and early in the fiscal year. Instead of making it advantageous for the government to delay the main supply business, the rules, the committee thought, should provide incentives to the government to return to the old practice of getting on with the main supply business in the spring. With this in mind the committee recommended that the thirty-day limit should not apply to interim supply requests introduced after the ninetieth day of a session; rather, the first request made after the ninetieth day was to be limited to three days, and there was to be no limit on the time that the Committee of Supply could take on any later request. On 26 April 1967, this recommendation was adopted by the House. The defect in this approach, under which the supply timetable was tied to the date of the first sitting in the session, rather than to the calendar, was demonstrated in the next session. That session began late, on 8 May 1967, and the main appropriation bill for 1967–68 did not pass the House until 2 November 1967, but that was only the seventy-first day of the session. As a consequence the Special Committee began to think in terms of a supply timetable with fixed calendar dates selected to assure that normally the government would have the sessions started early, thus making it possible for the House to conclude the main supply business before the summer.

The time limits on the Committee of Supply introduced on 8 June 1965, as modified on 26 April 1967, did not apply to the final supplementary estimates. The danger of leaving even this phase of the supply process undiked was demonstrated in the winter of 1968. On 19 February 1968, a motion for the third reading of a tax bill was defeated in the House, just a few weeks before the Liberal Party was to hold a leadership convention to select Mr. Pearson's successor. In the turmoil that followed the final supplementary estimates for 1967–68 were under consideration by the Committee of Supply for fourteen days.

By 1968, as a result of the almost constant trouble with supply business and of the experiments made to overcome that trouble, most members were ready to accept a radically new approach recommended by the Special Committee on Procedure (1967–68) in the winter of 1968.[44] The committee's recommendation was that the Committee of Supply be abolished, that the work of examining the estimates should be given over entirely to the standing committees, that a specified number of days in the House should be put at the disposal of the opposition, and that the House should decide on or before stated calendar dates selected to conform to the needs of the fiscal year whether or not to grant the supplies requested by the Crown. This approach opened up the possibility that the estimates would be examined thoroughly, that the opposition would wage war against the government by debate rather than attrition, and that a return could be made to orderly annual sessions. On 20 December 1968, the House adopted the new supply procedure recommended in outline by the Special Committee on Procedure (1967–68) and in detail by its successor, the Special Committee on Procedure (1968).[45]

The rules now provide—as we saw in chapter 5—that the most

essential annual business of the government, its supply business, is to occupy the House during three limited periods—one ending on 10 December, a second on 26 March, and the third on 30 June—totalling twenty-five days, and that the appropriation bill based on the main estimates is to be dealt with before the end of the third period, i.e., before the beginning of July. This means that the House will be in session during the fall, and that as far as supply business is concerned the House can adjourn late in June or early in July.[46] This arrangement, of course, does not guarantee either that the sessions will not be unduly long because of other reasons or that all the business regarded as essential by the government will have been completed in time for the House to adjourn at the end of June.

The exploitation of the government's highly vulnerable position in supply business was a major part of the opposition's parliamentary strategy in any crisis throughout the period from 1955 to 1968, but other weaknesses in the rules were used also. Fairly similar to the use of excessive time for supply business was the use of excessive time for the consideration of the resolutions then required before the introduction of bills authorizing or entailing expenditures. On 9 October 1964, by agreement among the parties, the House limited the time that might be taken on each such resolution to one sitting, or to a total of five hours if the consideration had been adjourned. On 20 December 1968, as we saw in chapter 5, the standing orders were changed so that such resolutions no longer are required.

Also, it was found that two of the preliminary proceedings—(a) oral questions and (b) applications for leave under Standing Order 26 to move the adjournment—tended to be prolonged so that the time available for government business later in the day was reduced.

The standing orders at that time made no provision for oral questions; however, the practice was that members were allowed to address questions orally, without notice, to the ministers immediately before the first order of the day had been called. Since there was no time limit on these oral question periods, it was not unusual for seventy or eighty minutes to be spent in this way day after day. The practice that developed under S.O. 26—the rule introduced in 1906 to keep the House from being diverted from its scheduled business—was that any member could seek leave from the House to move the adjournment, and in seeking leave could explain at length the urgency of having a debate on the specified matter. By the time he had finished all that he wanted to say, and the spokesman of each of the other parties in opposition had made his contribution, and a minister had replied, at least fifteen minutes, but perhaps as much as thirty or forty minutes, would have elapsed. In 1960–61, 1964–65, and 1966–67, as shown by Table 13, the number

TABLE 13
Use of Standing Order 26

Session	Sittings	Request Granted	Request Denied	Total
1957	71	1	4	5
1957–58	78	1	2	3
1958	93	0	1	1
1959	127	1	8	9
1960	146	2	5	7
1960–61	174	2	10	12
1962	65	0	3	3
1962–63	72	1	4	5
1963	117	0	6	6
1964–65	248	2	18	20
1965	53	1	5	6
1966–67	250	3	21	24
1967–68	155	2	10	12
1968–69 (to 20 Dec. 1968)	69	0	6	6
1968–69 (after 20 Dec.)	129	5	18	23
1969–70	155	8★	32	40
1970–72	243	3★	33	36
1972	91	1	10	11
1973–74	206	5★★	23	28
1974	50	1	5	6

★ There were two successful requests dealing with the same topic; only one debate resulted.
★★ As a result of a request a debate—but not under S. O. 26—was arranged on one occasion. That request is not included here.

of alleged emergencies was very high. Chiefly as a result of these two gambits—the first was more important than the second because it was used far more frequently—the initial proceedings sometimes took up as much as two or two and a half hours, so that after the hour for private members' business had been deducted from a long day—at that time the House met at 2:30 p.m. on Monday, Tuesday, and Thursday, and rose for dinner between 6:00 and 8:00 p.m.—only about two or two and a half hours remained for government business.

In 1964, by agreement, provision for oral questions was made in the sessional orders then adopted, and a time limit of 60 minutes on Monday and 30 minutes on each of the other four days was prescribed. In 1966 the Oral Question Period was extended to 40 minutes on

Tuesday, Thursday, and Friday. In the standing orders adopted on 20 December 1968, the question period was limited to 40 minutes on all five days. The rule adopted on 24 March 1975, provides for a daily question period no shorter than 45 minutes. In the case of applications for leave to move the adjournment, no change was made until 20 December 1968. Under the rules then adopted an applicant is limited to a brief statement. The speaker, who must be given a copy of that statement in advance, makes a ruling on the application without having heard any argument whatsoever from other members. Although the number of applications increased sharply immediately after the standing order was altered—perhaps because an applicant has only to read out a brief, prepared statement—the disruptive effect of such applications has been greatly reduced. It is notable also that although more applications were successful in the period immediately after 1968 than before, the record is somewhat misleading because eight of the thirteen successful requests in 1969 and 1970 brought on debates either on Wednesday evening or late on Friday afternoon. Evidently the speaker maintained a lower threshold for those times: the House ordinarily does not sit on Wednesday evening and turns to private members' business at 4:00 p.m. on Friday. In the sessions of 1970–72, 1972, 1973–74, and 1974 there were no emergencies on Wednesdays and Fridays.

The burden of this chapter is that as the nature of governance changed in Canada in the one hundred years after Confederation the procedures of the House of Commons were altered to enable the House to do the business brought to it by the government. In 1867 it was obvious that the government and the House of Commons were distinct entities with related but quite different tasks. The House met for a few weeks. While in session it dealt with proposals for changes in the general laws of the land, and it supplied the government with enough money to carry it through the forthcoming fiscal year. On the other hand, although even then most of the public business done by the House was initiated by them, the work of the ministers was chiefly administrative and extra-parliamentary. In contrast, the ministers now spend more of their time on work related directly to the House, and the House itself is an integral part of the year-round machinery of government. The government governs through the House. In the House the ministers constantly occupy the centre of the parliamentary stage, leading, explaining, and justifying, and being questioned and denounced. During the major adjournments the ministers spend much of their time making preparations for the House. As this change—which arose from the use of statute law, not as a set of permanent rules, but as instruments to be amended again and again as the government tries to manage the economy, indeed the whole society—took place, the House, while retaining some of the features of an annual convention, gave up the casual and spontaneous quality of such a gathering. The Speech from the Throne, to pick a glaring example, wherein the governor general explains to the assembled members why he has seen fit to have them summoned to a Parliament, and discloses the dread news that the queen will need aids from her loyal Commons, is still retained; but it would be hard for the members to give it their rapt attention or to strain to contrive a responsive Address in Reply when the previous session, prorogued the day before, dealt with much the same kind of business. As the House became a part of the year-round government machinery, it came to be assumed that only the motions and the bills put forward by the chief governors deserved attention; and, accordingly, the House reserved almost all its time for the ministers, and undertook to protect their business against diversions and delays. The House accepted the assumption that the people now want active government; that it is the government, not the House of Commons, to which the people look for active government; and that the people will not tolerate a House that impedes irresponsibly the efforts of the government. From this the House has drawn the conclusion that if it is to be relevant and valuable in this new situation, it must, eschewing almost all else, concentrate on doing the government's business.

As a result of the changes made over the years—especially those made in 1906, 1910, 1913, 1955, 1962, and 1968—it now is possible for the government house leader to predict fairly accurately, not only in days, but in hours, the time that will be available to the government during a session for its bills and motions. Either one or two days will be required to start the session, depending on whether the Address in Reply is moved on the same day on which the Speech from the Throne is delivered. Then provision must be made for the resumed debate on the Address, which if it goes to the limit will require eight days. The business of supply will take up twenty-five days in an ordinary session. The budget speech—there now is likely to be only one in a session—requires an evening for the minister of finance to deliver his statement, and then a total of six days on the resumed debate. In short, a total of forty or forty-one days must be provided for the regular sessional business. In a session started late in October and ended just before the st of July, after the prescribed holidays and reasonable adjournments at Christmas and Easter have been deducted, there will be about 152 sitting days. Out of that total about 111 or 112 days will be available for government business other than the Address, supply business, and the budget phase of ways and means business. What a government house leader cannot know is how long that other business will require. In the ten-year period, 1946–55, the average number of sittings a year was 122. In the period,

1956–65, the average number of sittings a year was 140. In the period, 1966–75, the average was 158.

There now are twenty-eight and a half hours in a full normal week, but from that total must be deducted four hours for private members' business, about five hours for the daily routine proceedings, and one and a half hours for proceedings on the adjournment motion on three days; in short, in a normal week, there are about eighteen hours for government business. (Given the fact that there is no hour for private members' business on a day when the main business is the Address debate, the budget debate, or supply business the forty hours, provided for private members' business on Mondays and Tuesdays will not be exhausted until about the end of a 152-day session.) The government house leader can estimate that, barring all interruptions, in such a model session the time available to the government for its tax bills, its other bills, and its motions will amount to about 396 hours. But he will have to be prepared to lose a day or two because of deaths. And he will have to be prepared to lose a few hours during the course of the session because of successful applications under Standing Order 26.[47]

NINE

Closure and Time Allotment

The constitution of the United States of America, with its structural checks and balances, is based on the presupposition that decisions (and consequent actions) should not be taken unless something like a consensus has been achieved. The assumption is that all will be well, or at least tolerable, even if one branch, the House of Representatives, for example, refuses to pass bills earnestly promoted by the Senate and the president. In such a situation, nobody breaks the stalemate by resigning. In contrast, under our constitution the queen's ministers have the duty to decide what they believe the good governance of the country requires, and to seek any necessary parliamentary action. Moreover, they have the right to resign—the duty to resign if the matters involved are important—when, either with or without an election, they cannot achieve that parliamentary action. Unfortunately the American view, which may be appropriate in the United States, has seeped into Canadian thinking. The effect has been to prevent a realistic approach to the use of closure and to the allotment of time in the House of Commons.

As has been argued in chapter 1, the paradigm that presents Parliament as "the legislature" and the government as "the executive branch" always was misleading, for it treats a difference of degree as a difference of kind. The truth is that all who engage in governing make law. The distinction to be made is not that Parliament enacts the laws, while "the executive" does something else, but that law made in Parliament is superior in status to law made by administrators and judges. The old paradigm was credible in eighteenth-century England chiefly because in a period when the central government did relatively little within the realm many of the statutes enacted by Parliament did not originate with the ministers. The activities of governments as socio-economic innovators and managers were not accommodated by the theory; but that could be overlooked because in the eighteenth century those roles generally were performed only extraordinarily—outside the realm, or in times of emergency. Now however in Canada, as throughout the Western World, the government is deeply involved in the shaping and management of the economy and the society. Much of the law is made and unmade again and again. In this new situation two quite different courses, together with the full range of intermediate possibilities, are open to Parliament. First, the members can set a few very general, relatively permanent principles of socio-economic development, authorize the ministers to provide the rest of the necessary law by making and unmaking orders, rules, and regulations from time to time, and try to keep the ministers under control by strict attention to the business of supply. Or, second, they can draw the line dividing parliamentary action from subordinate action far lower, and undertake to do by statute much of what on the first alternative would be done by statutory instruments. As one might have expected, what has happened in Canada since 1945 falls somewhere between the two extremes, and has varied from department to department. In short, the old distinction between legislation and administration, which always lacked an essential basis, has been ignored in practice. Not only has the volume of statutory instruments increased greatly, but the government now makes use of the Parliament constantly to adjust and readjust certain fields of the law—taxation (especially as an economic regulator), transportation, housing, immigration, economic expansion, etc.—in a way that would have been regarded as unthinkable only fifty years ago—for what, the old-time theorist protests, is "law" if it lacks permanence? A quick survey of the list of statutes enacted in almost any one of the past fifteen or twenty sessions will discover that Parliament has come to serve as the nation's chief practising economist. One result of this is that a ministry's legislative program for a session now is of vital and immediate importance to it, even when there are no great bills. Another result is that the House, now employed in the year-to-year, even month-to-month management of the polity, makes new demands on the members. No longer is it enough for them to concern themselves with very general ideas and principles on the one hand, and with particular local or private situations on the other. Nowadays many of the measures which come before them are designed to have a direct, managerial effect on economic and social activities and conditions.

The cumulative effect of the diminution of private members' business; of time limits on the debate on the Address in Reply, the budget debate, and supply business; and of the safeguards against frivolous pre-emption was to make more and more time available for the government's annual legislative program. But we must not rush to conclude that because more time is available it is easy for a ministry to get its bills through or even that it is easier now than it was fifty years ago. Formerly, the members could rely on the unlimited general debates and on the many opportunities to pre-empt the time of the House to query and, if they wished, to condemn or praise the ministry. Now, since most aspects of the nation's affairs are controlled or influenced, directly or indirectly, by federal statutes, and since most government bills are merely steps in the interminable process of amending and re-amending those statutes, the members have come to rely on the government's legislative program for their opportunities. There are few, if any, major topics which cannot be re-examined every two or three years during debate on government bills.

Consequently the struggle between the government and the opposition now centres mainly on the government's legislative program. Having relinquished or abandoned bogs and dunes such as the debates on the Address in Reply and on supply motions as fields of resolute resistance, the opposition now makes its great stands on the central ground, the annual legislative program. Time, we must remember, is a major dimension of contention: if an opposition takes up no time, it is not opposing. It may delay one or more contentious bills, and perhaps also the bills brought on before those bills, or even all the bills for the session. It is well to bear in mind the truth that to be successful the opposition does not have to win votes in the House, but has only to prevent votes. If the opposition's resistance is not overcome, it will have won, and the government will have lost.

The House knows, first, that even when ministers are very careful, they—and their advisers—make mistakes, and second, that ultimately, regardless of how assured an opposition may be in its criticisms, under our constitution it is the ministry, not the opposition, which bears the responsibility of office, and which therefore must have the power to decide what is to be done. This means that the key problem confronting the House is a time problem: the House must have rules which assure not only that ultimately the minority does not prevail over the majority, but that the minority has adequate time to put the ministers' measures to the test in public.

A ministry's legislative program for a session may be delayed in the House for various reasons. Partisan opposition sometimes expresses itself through a low degree of cooperation with the government throughout a session or part of a session. Business will be done, but it will drag. This many be caused by opposition strategy; or it simply may be the result of the inability of the leader of the opposition and his house leader to control their followers. At other times party opposition will take the form of a filibuster, when members of one (or more) of the parties in opposition decide to try to prevent—or perhaps, eager to win the favour of some interest group, decide to appear to try to prevent

—the House from coming to a decision on a particular motion, or from advancing a particular bill. In some instances the filibuster will be applied only against the offensive item; in others the items preceding it also will be delayed. In either case a filibuster almost inevitably slows the progress of bills other than the one against which it is aimed. This is the important point. Filibusters against government measures have had little success in the House since 1911 insofar as the bills or motion against which they were directed were concerned; but at times even quasi-filibusters have distorted seriously the business of the rest of the session, and by prolonging the session have made it difficult for ministers and private members alike to perform their various duties.

Filibusters and lack of cooperation by the opposition parties are not the only serious causes of delay. In every Parliament there are some members who retard business parasitically. Some feel that no debate is complete until they have spoken. Some want to put speeches "on the record" to elate supporters or to woo interest groups. Some who have been away for weeks want to register their return. Some adopt a "work-to-rule" attitude, speaking as often and as long as the rules permit, but insisting on the strict observance of the rules relating to the hour of daily adjournment, etc. The less disciplined a party is, the more likely its members are to feel free to speak irresponsibly. The ministers leave little new for the backbenchers to say. The official opposition, if it wishes to appear sufficiently responsible to govern, will try to control its ranks. But "third parties," whatever their members may do for personal reasons—many have shown a very high sense of responsibility—have little reason to refrain from taking advantage of the patience of the House.

Again, once the midway mark in the life of a parliament, even one in which the government has a strong majority, has passed, intimations of the next campaign appear. Members on both sides, wishing to impress their constituents, want to speak oftener. Besides, whatever the merits of a ministry's proposals, those in opposition have an understandable desire to prevent it from achieving too solid a record of success. In the case of recent minority governments in Canada, the slow-down set in about six or eight months after the post-election session began.

During the 1955–69 period the chronic ministerial problem, as we have seen, was the prolongation of the supply business. The next problem, one not nearly as obvious or crucial in the short run, but nowadays equally fundamental to the governing of the country, was how to get government bills, other than those patently attractive to the electorate, through the House, especially late in the life of a parliament. A stubborn minority or even a few talkative members could bedevil an entire legislative program regardless of the size of the ministry's support in the House. Many Liberals felt that this had been made all too obvious when the transitional powers bill was before the House in 1955, and the northern pipeline bill in 1956. Of course, to terminate a filibuster a ministry could resort to Standing Order 33—the closure rule—but to do so might merely compound its political troubles, as had been demonstrated in 1956–57.

Directly related to the problem of preventing delays and stoppages affecting the legislative program—and more important—was the problem of the superficial treatment of government bills by the House. Not only should the House try to deal with the program, but it should try to deal with each bill thoroughly. Politicians tend to spend more time on bills of immediate interest to newsmen and the voters than on duller but perhaps more significant bills. There is also a natural tendency for the bills brought forward early in a session to capture attention, at the expense of other bills advanced later. And there is a natural tendency for the members to thresh exhaustively the first parts of a bill, but to skim lightly over the later parts. The increasing importance of the annual legislative program has made it highly desirable that these tendencies be resisted.

In the nineteenth century the British House faced up to the need for both a sound closure rule and a rule for the allotment of time; but that happened late in the century, after the earlier British pattern had been received and enshrined at Ottawa. Ever since 1881 closure has been used at Westminster. Since 1887 the House has had a standing order which permits any member, with the leave of the speaker, to move "that the question be now put." If that motion, which is not debatable or amendable, is carried, the question on the motion under debate is put to the House immediately. That standing order, which sounds harsh to Canadian ears, is used, not once or twice, but dozens of times in most sessions. It is readily applicable in the House, a committee of the whole House, or a standing committee. The keys to its acceptability are two in number. The first is that the neutrality of the speaker and the other presiding officers has been fully established. If the speaker (or a chairman) thinks that a closure motion would be premature, he may refuse to let a member move it. The second key is far more basic. The British House operates on an unwritten rule that ordinarily it will vote on a motion at the same sitting at which the motion is moved. For this reason the House often sits late. The function of closure at Westminster is merely to decide at what hour a debate will end, not at what sitting.

At the committee stage and the report stage simple closure such as described above may be inadequate. There may be scores of clauses to be adopted in committee. There may be dozens of motions for amendments at the report stage. What is needed at those stages is a timetable—alloting time—to assure both that the whole stage is completed within a reasonable period and that the time available is distributed over the main parts of a bill with some regard for their relative importance, thus overcoming the tendency to lavish attention on the clauses or amendments taken first. A decision is needed—preferably a decision made not halfway through, but in advance—as to how the time is to be used; otherwise, with or without a filibuster, the parts or items taken last are likely to be dealt with in haste. The acceptance of a timetable for a bill's progress involves an element of closure, but its distinctive characteristic is that it allots time. Motions to establish timetables for bills—known as "guillotine motions" because the proceeding is cut off at fixed times—have been used in the British House since 1881. Unlike closure, their guillotine does not involve the speaker. The government simply moves for an order specifying when the decisions in committee on the various clauses, and on the amendments proposed at the report stage in the House, are to be taken. If a bill is unusually important, so that more than one sitting is thought desirable for the second-reading and third-reading debates, those stages, too, may be covered by the timetable; but this is relatively rare. Normally such debates are concluded at the same sitting at which they started, and can be ended easily by the use of closure.

The Canadian House of Commons was without a closure procedure of any kind—other than "the previous question"—until 1913. In that year the Borden government pushed through a closure rule as its third major procedural reform.[1] Although that rule has been excoriated again and again over the years, it still stands as it was adopted at the sitting of 23 April 1913, except that in 1952 the terminal hour was advanced from two o'clock to one o'clock. It reads as follows:

> Immediately before the order of the day for resuming an adjourned debate is called, or if the House be in committee of the whole, any Minister of the Crown who, standing in his place, shall have given notice at a previous sitting of his intention so to do may move that the debate shall not be further adjourned, or that the further consideration of any resolution or resolutions, clause or clauses, section or sections, preamble or preambles, title or titles, shall be the first business of the committee, and shall not further be postponed; and in either case such question shall be decided without debate or amendment; and if the same shall be resolved in the affirmative, no Member shall thereafter speak more than once, or longer than twenty minutes in any such adjourned debate; or, if in committee, on any such resolution, clause, section, preamble or title; and if such adjourned debate or postponed

consideration shall not have been resumed or concluded before one o'clock in the morning, no Member shall rise to speak after that hour, but all such questions as must be decided in order to conclude such adjourned debate or postponed consideration, shall be decided forthwith.

The flaws in this rule are fairly obvious. First, it may be applied in a committee of the whole House, as well as in the House, even although it is unsuitable at that stage except for the simplest bills. The immediate problem of the Borden government was that its naval aid bill had been under consideration in committee for fifteen days, and, given the fact that thirteen days had been required for concurrence in the resolution and seven days for the second-reading stage, a long debate on a third reading was predictable, that is, if the bill ever emerged from committee.[2] The bill was a simple measure, with five clauses, totalling twenty lines. As a result, the government took simple closure, not the guillotine, as its model. The difficulty is that while the termination of a protracted debate on a motion—for example, a second-reading motion or a motion that the House concur in the report of a committee—can be defended easily when it is obvious that all the arguments have been heard again and again, it always is hard to justify cutting off consideration of a complex bill at the committee stage, especially if the filibusterers have seen to it, as canny filibusterers will, that the committee has not got much beyond the first few clauses. And, secondly, even when employed to end a debate on a simple motion, the rule is unsatisfactory. When the Borden government examined the British closure rule, they saw that it could not be copied directly because at Ottawa the speaker was regarded as a party man. He could not be pressed into service as the custodian of the closure power. They realized that if the Canadian House was to have a closure rule, it would have to be one in which the government assumed full responsibility for deciding when it was to be used.

Arthur Meighen explained the Borden government's decision to write a rule with safeguards:

> *Following the great legislative bodies of the world, we must place the responsibility for choosing the time when closure shall be applied either on the Speaker or on the Government; under any rational rule of constitutional government it cannot be placed anywhere else. In England, for several years, the responsibility for the application of closure was placed on the Speaker. The result was that between 1882 and 1887 the closure was very seldom acted upon, because the Speaker was diffident about taking the initiative himself. Closure was in effect a failure....*
> *Consequently, I think about 1888 or perhaps a little later, the closure was changed so that the responsibility was lifted from the Speaker and*

placed upon a member of the House, which, of course, in the working out, means the majority. While the responsibility for moving the closure was placed upon any member of the House, the Speaker was left the discretion to say when it should be exercised. If we were to do that, it would be open . . . [to the objection that the Speaker is a creature of the Government]. They would have raised that objection and would have proclaimed it from every platform. The Government [under our proposal] take the responsibility, but under such conditions that they must give twenty-four hours' notice. After the discussion has proceeded for the length of time that in the judgment of the Government is sufficient, if any obstruction develops, all they can do is to move adjournment of the discussion and then the Opposition have the following day and until two o'clock the next morning to organize their attack and discuss the matter to their hearts' content.[3]

From the very first closure at Ottawa was far more momentous than at Westminster because at Ottawa debates often were (and are) adjourned from sitting to sitting. This fact—in addition to the non-involvement of the speaker—is why the rule provides for twenty-four hours notice and then a full day of debate after closure has been accepted. In 1927 a melodramatic touch was added inadvertently when the hour of ordinary adjournment was fixed at 11:00 p.m. Closure at Ottawa is a major rite. The entire operation—from the moment when a minister, standing in his place, gives notice to an excited House, through the moving of the closure motion at the next sitting and the immediate vote on that motion, through the tense day-long debate to the final vote before packed galleries well after midnight—resembles so much a death sentence and a public execution that ministers shrink from using it; and when they do, the opposition, regardless of their true sentiments, feels obliged to lament the end of a thousand years of freedom and democracy.

Given these defects it is hardly surprising that the rule has been used rarely. Prior to 1964 it had been used only fifteen times. In 1913 it was used to conclude the committee stage of the naval aid bill. In 1917 it was used twice, at the committee stage of the Canadian Northern Railway acquisition bill, and on the third-reading stage of that bill. Later that year it was used three times, to conclude the second-reading stage, the committee stage, and the third-reading stage of the wartime elections bill. In 1919 it was used to conclude the committee stage of the Canadian National Railways bill. All these were under the Borden government. It was used once in 1921, by the Meighen government to carry interim supply and an item in the estimates. In 1926 it was used by the King government to bring the Address debate to an end. In 1932 it was used twice by the Bennett government, first on the motion to go into committee for the resolution stage prior to the introduction of the Unemployment and Farm Relief Continuance bill, and later to conclude the committee stage of that bill.[4] Then in 1956 it was used four times on the pipeline bill by the St. Laurent government: to end the resolution stage, to conclude the second-reading stage, to conclude consideration in committee, and to end the debate at the third-reading stage.[5]

The fixing of the hour of daily adjournment highlighted the extraordinary character of closure. What is more important is the fact that it strengthened greatly the position of talkative and intransigent minorities. Before 1927 a sitting did not end—except on Wednesday after 1906—until an adjournment motion had been carried. This meant that the government could have the House and committees of the whole House continue to sit until an item of business had been concluded or until a convenient point for interruption had been reached. In 1913, to mention the extreme example, the House twice sat without interruption from Monday through Saturday. Even when there was no filibuster, the House often sat well after midnight. Then in 1927 the hour of adjournment for each of the four long days of the week—originally 11:00 p.m., but 10:00 p.m. after 1952—was specified by standing order. No provision was made for exceptions: by objecting a single member could prevent the House from sitting late. This made the Canadian House of Commons a forum for filibusterers even better than the Senate of the United States. This is not to say that filibusters were common. They were very rare. It was not until political contention became intense in 1955 and 1956 and again after 1960 that the automatic adjournment rule began to influence seriously the conduct of business. Finally, in 1965, driven to frustration by two or three members, the House altered the adjournment rule by sessional order so that it could not be prevented from sitting late by fewer than ten members. This order was renewed in 1966, 1967, and in the fall of 1968. With some changes as to when the special order to sit late may be sought it was incorporated into the standing orders on 20 December 1968, as Standing Order 6(5).

In the United Kingdom, in contrast, the House sits late frequently. The hour of daily adjournment is specified in the standing orders, but by winning a simple majority vote on a non-debatable motion the government may have the House continue to sit. In short, it sits late whenever to do so is regarded as desirable by the government, and it continues to sit until the government is prepared to have the sitting ended.

In chapters 7 and 8 we noticed that by 1963–64 it had been made very clear that under the existing rules there were various ways in which any group of members could prevent the House from working well, whether or not the government had a majority. Prompted by an appreciation of the constitutional perils inherent in that situation, and by the scathing public criticism, even contempt, provoked by the turmoil of the previous years, some of the members of the House undertook to devise remedies. Their efforts and those of some of the house leaders resulted in various changes made on 8 and 11 June 1965, on a sessional basis. Among the remedies was one—a sessional order, Standing Order 15-A—designed to make it easier for the House to deal efficiently with government bills.[6]

The furore brought on by the way the closure rule—Standing Order 33—was used in 1956 to put the pipeline bill through all its stages in the House in fifteen days, together with the defeat of the St. Laurent government in the next general election, made some members in all the parties think that the rule was dead. Never would a government dare to use it again. In 1957 Prime Minister Diefenbaker committed himself to the elimination of the rule, and even went so far as to give notice of a motion for its repeal. But his motion died on the order paper when Parliament was dissolved for the election of 1958. After the election nothing was done to prune the rule from the book. Then, in December 1964, the Pearson government with trepidation had resort to it to end the flag debate. The situation at that time was ideal for S.O. 33. What was before the House was a simple motion, a motion for concurrence in the report of the Special Committee on a Canadian Flag. All the arguments had been canvassed again and again. Moreover, the filibuster was unpopular even with many of those who did not want a new flag. But the favourable reaction to the use of S.O. 33 in that instance did not mean that the rule was any more suitable than before as a means to promote the thorough examination of a complex bill or to prevent the wrecking of the legislative program of a session. The new rule, S.O. 15-A, was designed for those purposes. It was adopted for the balance of the 1965 session and for the 1966–67 sessions. Subsequently it was renewed for the 1967–68 session.

Standing Order 15-A provided for a new committee, "the Business Committee," to plan the legislative timetable of the House. In a sense what it did was to give the house leaders' meetings an official status and important new powers. Each of the parties in the House was to have one representative on the committee. If the committee agreed unanimously on a timetable for a bill, that agreement was to be put before the House for acceptance (or rejection) without debate or amendment. But—and this was the key point—if such an agreement could not be attained, the government could propose to the House its own timetable for the bill, provided that any government timetable had to allow at least two sitting days for the second-reading stage, two sitting days for the committee stage, and one sitting day for the third-reading stage.

Closure and Time Allotment 247

The Business Committee was used three times, but in only one instance did a reference to the committee result in a time allotment order. The first reference was made on 25 April 1966, when the committee was charged with the task of arranging a fair schedule for the debate on the 33 objections lodged by members of Parliament against the constituency boundaries proposed by the first commissions under the Electoral Boundaries Readjustment Act; but an informal agreement was reached so that the committee was able to report that no recommendation by it was necessary. The third reference was made on 1 February 1968, when Bill C-163, relating to broadcasting, had been in committee of the whole House for eleven days. Once the reference had been made the committee began to move far more rapidly with the result that the bill was reported on 5 February, after having been in committee for fourteen days. The Business Committee made no report. The second instance in which S.O. 15-A was used was far more important immediately and far more influential for the future of time allotment in the House of Commons. In the fall of 1966 the subject of armed forces unification had been discussed for upwards of eleven days in the Committee of Supply (on the request for an interim supply for November). Then Bill C-243, the Canadian Forces Reorganization Act, was debated for five days (19 hours: 37 minutes) at the second reading stage before being referred to the Standing Committee on National Defence on 2 February 1967. The committee, which took twenty-six days, made its report on March 22. After the bill had been considered in a committee of the whole House for eight days the question of time allotment was referred to the Business Committee on 13 April 1967. On 18 April the committee reported that it had been unable to reach a unanimous agreement on a recommendation. Under S.O. 15-A the government then was free to move for the adoption of a timetable of its own. This it did on 20 April, proposing two additional days for the committee stage, and one day for the third-reading stage. After an angry debate which lasted throughout the day, the government's motion carried, 124 Yeas to 62 Nays, with Liberals, New Democrats, and Créditistes combining against the Progressive Conservatives.[7] Consequently, the bill was reported on 24 April, after having been considered in committee for fifteen days (or 62 hours: 53 minutes). The third-reading debate, which lasted only thirty-one minutes, took place on 25 April, 1967. This incident, involving as it did one of the most controversial measures of the entire Pearson era, served to convince the Progressive Conservatives that any standing order that permitted a time allotment motion to be moved when the parties were not unanimous was bad. In September 1968, when the various provisional rules, which had lapsed with the dissolution on 23 April 1968, were being revived pending a permanent reform of the standing orders, the one order that the Progressive Conservatives flatly refused to see revived was Standing Order 15-A.[8]

In contrast, by the fall of 1968 the Liberals were even more eager than before for some kind of time-allotment rule. They knew that the basic weakness of the government in the House had not been cured by the election of a majority government on 25 June 1968: the part they had played in bringing down the powerful Diefenbaker government and their own tribulations in 1963-68 had given them deep insight into the implications of that weakness. Besides, since the majority government elected in June, 1968, was a Liberal government, any change which overcame the weakness would be to their immediate advantage, especially in the last session or two of the new parliament. As the fall of 1968 wore on their eagerness became anxiety. They saw that the changes in the legislative process then being planned by the Special Committee on Procedure (1968) if adopted without a complementary time-allotment procedure would increase to an even higher degree the power of the opposition, the power of minor parties, the power of uncooperative members in all quarters to hold up particular bills and, consequently by cumulative effect, to prevent the House from dealing with a government's legislative program for a session, and, again cumulatively, for an entire parliament.

As we saw in chapter 4, the defects in the legislative process were to be overcome (a) by sending most bills to the appropriate standing committees after second reading, and (b) by permitting members to move for changes in such bills at the report stage. As the Special Committee on Procedure (1968) worked out the details of these proposals, the Liberals on the committee came to the conclusion that these reforms, although highly attractive, entailed serious dangers, and could not be accepted unless those dangers were exorcised. They saw that if most bills were to be sent to standing committees, the chairmen of the committees, their members, and perhaps even their staffs would acquire a considerable degree of control over the work of the House. Their power would be less than at Washington where bills go to the committees before the House (or the Senate) has given them a second reading; nevertheless, unless the House of Commons was to specify when each bill was to be reported, or, alternatively, adopted a procedure by which bills could be retrieved easily, the standing committees would be in a strong position to bargain with the government over the content of bills. In addition, there was the possibility that different committees inadvertently and independently would fail to report bills before the closing days of a session. In that event, the later stages might be rushed in the House, which would be to the disadvantage of members not on the committee. Then the bills would go over to the Senate too late for more than cursory examination. If the avalanche of late bills was heavy, the summer adjournment might have to be postponed, with serious consequences for the preparation by the cabinet of the business for the next session.

The proposed new procedure for the report stage, too, entailed difficulties. At the second-reading stage and the third-reading stage the House has under debate a single main motion: "That Bill C-000 be now read a second (third) time...." Consequently, no matter how profound or wide-ranging the debate, the procedural situation is simple: there is only one debate, and no member may speak more than once on the main motion and on each motion to amend it. In contrast, if motions to change the text of bills were to be moved and debated at the report stage, each such motion would be an independent main motion, and would initiate a new debate. This stage, therefore, would be ideal for the orators, whether or not they were filibustering, for by putting down notices of motions to amend they could guarantee that they would be seen by the speaker; alternatively, they could speak on each such motion moved by any other member.

Standing Order 33 met neither of these dangers. It could be used readily to terminate debate on a second-reading motion or a third-reading motion. It could even be used—very awkwardly, as in 1956—in a committee of the whole House; but it could not be used to prescribe when a standing committee was to report a bill. Moreover, since each motion to change a bill at the report stage would be a new main motion, the closure rule might have to be used to bring to a vote each such motion on a highly controversial bill. If, for example, fifteen motions to change such a bill were moved, and S.O. 33 was used to bring each of those motions (and all the amendments to each one) to a vote, the time required on the report stage of that bill would be at least thirty days.

These considerations together with the powerful arguments for the better use of the time of the House derived from the experience of the previous decade, led the Liberals to propose in the Special Committee on Procedure (1968) that a rule based on the practice at Westminster be recommended to the House. The proposal was unacceptable to the Progressive Conservatives. They were prepared to agree to a rule that would authorize a business committee on which each of the parties would be represented equally to propose a timetable for a bill going to a committee of the whole House if all the parties were in agreement —quite reasonably they feared that anything short of unanimity would allow the Liberals, the New Democratic Party, and the Social Credit Party to combine against them. The minor parties were prepared to go further: the New Democratic Party position—and perhaps that of the Social Credit Party—was that a rule based, not on unanimity, but on agreement of the majority of the party representatives would be acceptable; but both the Liberals and the Progressive Conservatives saw this approach as a method to gain a decisive role for minor parties. When it became obvious that negotiations directed towards a solution of what they regarded as the genuine problem would be impossible in the Committee on Procedure (1968) the Liberals voted that their own draft, prepared as a basis for negotiation, be incorporated—as S.O. 16-A —in the proposed rules to be submitted to the House by the committee.[9] Thereby they put the Trudeau government in a position to agree to the new rules relating to the legislative process, but only on condition that the House make some provision for the eventual solution of the time-allotment problem.

The debate in the House on concurrence in the proposed set of new rules lasted for eight days. By 20 December 1968, the parties in opposition were ready to accept all the new rules as recommended by the Special Committee if the Liberals would agree to the deletion of S.O. 16-A. For their part, the Liberals were prepared to accept all the new rules as recommended, including the two important changes in the legislative process, and to agree to the deletion of S.O. 16-A, but only on condition that the House would order the Standing Committee on Procedure and Organization, a new committee to be established under the new standing orders, to recommend a time-allocation rule to the House. The outcome was that the standing orders recommended by the Special Committee (1968), with S.O. 16-A omitted, were adopted unanimously by the House. At the same time the House, by a unanimous decision, ordered its new standing committee to recommend a time-allotment procedure.[10]

Six months later, on 20 June 1969, the Standing Committee on Procedure and Organization fulfilled the order of the House by recommending three new standing orders: 75A, 75B, and 75C. These were adopted, without alteration, by the House at the sitting of 24 July 1969, but only after closure had been used to terminate a filibuster by all the opposition parties.

The three new standing orders are as follows:

> 75A. When a Minister of the Crown, from his place in the House, states that there is agreement among the representatives of all parties to allot a specified number of days or hours to the proceedings at one or more stages of any public bill, he may propose a motion, without notice, setting forth the terms of such agreed allocation; and every such motion shall be decided forthwith, without debate or amendment.
>
> 75B. When a Minister of the Crown, from his place in the House, states that a majority of the representatives of the several parties

have come to an agreement in respect of a proposed allotment of days or hours for the proceedings at any stage of the passing of a public bill, he may propose a motion, without notice, setting forth the terms of the said proposed allocation; provided that for the purposes of this Standing Order an allocation may be proposed in one motion to cover the proceedings at both the report and the third reading stages of a bill if that motion is consistent with the provisions of Standing Order 75(13). During the consideration of any such motion no Member may speak more than once or longer than ten minutes. Not more than two hours after the commencement of proceedings thereon, Mr. Speaker shall put every question necessary to dispose of the said motion.

75C. A Minister of the Crown who from his place in the House at a previous sitting has stated that an agreement could not be reached under the provisions of Standing Order 75A or 75B in respect of proceedings at the stage at which a public bill was then under consideration either in the House or in any committee and has given notice of his intention so to do may propose a motion for the purpose of allotting a specified number of days or hours for the consideration and disposal of proceedings at that stage; provided that the time allotted for any stage is not to be less than one sitting day and provided that for the purposes of this Standing Order an allocation may be proposed in one motion to cover the proceedings at both the report and the third reading stages on a bill if that motion is consistent with the provisions of Standing Order 75(13). During the consideration of any such motion no Member may speak more than once or longer than ten minutes. Not more than two hours after the commencement of proceedings thereon, Mr. Speaker shall put every question necessary to dispose of the said motion.

Standing Order 75(13) provides that when there has been debate at the report stage, which can happen only when a bill has been committed to a standing or special committee, the third-reading stage is not to begin until the following day.

The fact that the Liberals supported the recommendation of the committee, while the Progressive Conservatives, the N.D.P., and the Social Credit Party opposed it should not be interpreted as meaning that the parties in opposition were in full agreement among themselves. Actually the Liberals found themselves involved in a two-front war in December 1968, and in June and July 1969. Their argument with the Progressive Conservatives was basically constitutional. The Progressive Conservatives, instructed by the many occasions when the Liberals, the New Democrats, and the Social Credit had combined against them during the previous six years—most notably on 5 February 1963, 14 December 1964, and 20 April 1967—were prepared to have the parties agree to time allotments that would be binding on individual members of Parliament; but they could not bring themselves to accept a rule under which the other parties could impose time limits on the official opposition. Their argument was based, as was Laurier's in 1913, on a theory of decision by parliamentary consensus or alternatively by plebiscitary elections. The House, they held, ought not to deprive the official opposition of the power to prevent questions from coming to a vote; otherwise, the official opposition would be unable to precipitate an election when it though that the government was wrong on a vital question. The leader of the opposition, the Hon. R. L. Stanfield, contended in an amendment moved on 10 December 1968, that the rule should be that "a motion to accept the decision of the proceedings committee shall only be made following the unanimous decision of the proceedings committee arrived at during a meeting properly convened upon adequate written notice."[11] The Progressive Conservatives were as strongly opposed to the proposal that eventually became S.O. 75B as they were to the idea behind S.O. 75C. At least the latter did not lump the official opposition with the minor parties. The Liberals, forgetting Laurier, countered with the argument that the principles of Responsible Government require that a government should not be deprived of opportunities to have its proposals accepted or rejected by the House after examination. They contended that the Progressive Conservative theory of government by consensus or by plebiscite inevitably would lead to weak government.

The N.D.P., with the Social Credit Party going along, had even less patience for the Progressive Conservative position than had the Liberals. Time allotment was a matter for the parties, with each party being counted as equal to every other party, regardless of size or constitutional position. Moreover, a minority of the parties ought not to be able to prevent time allotment. On 8 July 1969, Mr. Stanley Knowles revealed the provenance of the standing orders:

> The government house leader and others who will take part in this debate may say that 75A and 75B represent suggestions I made before the committee. That is correct. The minutes of the committee will show that I proposed them almost in the wording in which they can be found now. But I proposed 75A and 75B as a total package. If you remove 75C I will still buy 75A and 75B and be proud to have had something to do with suggesting them, but I cannot buy 75A and 75B in a package with 75C which completely nullifies any possibility of the kind of bargaining that should be possible under 75A or 75B. It is like collective

bargaining with compulsory arbitration hanging over people's heads or the threat of government action.[12]

It was precisely because of the bargaining power that 75B would confer on minor parties that the Liberals regarded the N.D.P. package as worse than no rule. Indeed, they saw the proposal as simply a power grab. Meetings of house leaders, with each party represented by one person, were fine, but to give formal authority to a body in which all the parties would be represented equally was to slight the rights of both the government and the official opposition. It would be contrary to the principles of both democracy and the constitution. The parties simply were not equal in either size or constitutional status; and the effect would be to give minor parties political power far out of proportion to their strength in the House. Said the government house leader, the Hon. D.S. Macdonald:

> *Rule 75C has a deadlock provision, Mr. Speaker. It is to apply in a situation where, as I have said, there is a united opposition against the government or where even two of the opposition parties, perhaps two of the minor opposition parties, are united in opposing the timetable which may be agreeable to the other two parties in the house.*
>
> *I think it is only fair to point out the particular aspect of 75B which makes this safeguard proposal necessary, and that is that 75B really declares those things equal which in effect are not equal. For example, 75B declares that the 153 Liberals in the house are equal in weight and quantity to the 14 Creditistes. It declares that the 22 members of the N.D.P. are equivalent in size to the 72 members of the Progressive Conservative party....*
>
> *[There is] the possibility of two opposition parties using the leverage which 75B would give them to hold the house up to ransom, or even the possibility of one of the minor parties—where the other has indicated it was unalterably opposed to the legislation—trying to squeeze concessions in terms of time or of amendments to the legislation or other particular concessions which in the opinion of the majority might be neither wise nor just. It is because of this leverage that we feel there should be some safeguard....*
>
> *.... The hon. member for Winnipeg North Centre (Mr. Knowles) was prepared to claim fatherhood for 75B, and I am prepared to accord him the responsibility or, if he prefers it, the credit for having produced this particular proposal. But I just point out that in trying to get minority control of this house under 75B, and 75B only, he is really reaching for that which the electors of Canada refused to him and his party, namely, control of the House of Commons.*[13]

Ultimately the Liberal position prevailed, not because they succeeded in convincing the other parties, but by closure. The Liberals were prepared to see S.O. 75B included, but only because S.O. 75C provides a government with the means by which to assume its responsibilities without yielding to third-party demands and threats.

The three standing orders set forth three situations in which the government house leader can apply to the House for a time-allotment order. The prime aim of the scheme of the orders is to promote all-party agreements, or, failing that, agreements between the government party and at least half the parties in opposition. But if the leader of the house can attain neither full agreement among the parties nor agreement by a majority of them, he may make his own proposal to the House. Under this scheme it is advantageous to both the government and the opposition to try to come to an agreement. By acquiescing in an agreement under S.O. 75A or 75B the government can avoid having to go to the House under the narrower terms of S.O. 75C. On the other hand, if the opposition parties will not enter into an agreement with the government, they may have to live with the government's timetable. Without these mutual advantages neither the government nor the opposition would have anything to gain by coming to an agreement.

The intention was that the government might resort to S.O. 75C after ascertaining that an agreement acceptable to itself is attainable under neither of the other two orders. However, S.O. 75B refers to "a majority of the representatives of the several parties," without spelling out that the majority is to include the representative of the government party. Consequently, an argument can be made that S.O. 75B means that if all or most of the opposition parties come to an agreement unacceptable to the government, the government may not resort to S.O. 75C.[14] This interpretation is attractive, but only if S.O. 75B is read out of its context. First, the House would not have provided for an order to eventuate from a motion that could not be moved. Only a minister may propose a motion under S.O. 75B. The rule presupposes that the minister is part of the majority. Second, this interpretation would give a minority—a very small minority if the "third" party (or parties) had only a few members—a veto power over the majority of the House, possibly over the combined government party and the official opposition. After the Standing Committee on Procedure and Organization had made its report on 20 June 1969, the Liberals recognized that the meaning of S.O. 75B as set forth in that report was not explicit. Since the report of a committee may not be amended in the House, the Hon. Donald S. Macdonald, the government house leader, in an attempt to obviate the need for the speaker to decide sooner or later between the two interpretations, put forward a government motion embodying the texts of the three standing orders as proposed by the committee but with the words, "a majority of the representatives of the several parties, including that of the government," instead of the words, "a majority of the representatives of the several parties."[15] This motion, unlike the report, would have been subject to amendment in the House, and therefore could have been advantageous to the opposition if they had wished to alter the proposed standing orders; however, they raised objection on the strong ground that a government motion was to supersede a motion to concur in a committee report. As a result Mr. Macdonald announced that he would not move his motion. This meant that the debate took place on a motion for concurrence in the report of the committee, and that it was the texts recommended by the committee that finally were adopted by the House on 24 July 1969.

Under the basic British guillotine rule the government may move in advance for a timetable for all the stages of a bill, and the time at the committee and the report stages can be divided among the clauses according to their importance. There is no stated minimum time for the stages. In short, the government is free to propose any timetable that it is prepared to defend as reasonable. This approach has two great advantages. First, the rule can be used for genuine time allocation. Second, the impossible task of prescribing a minimum time suitable for vastly different bills is avoided. However, when in the fall of 1968 the Liberals proposed that the British approach be followed, they found that this was absolutely unacceptable. It was denounced as dictatorial both inside the House and outside. Consequently, the standing orders produced by the Standing Committee on Procedure and Organization take a different approach. Like Borden's closure rule, they place a strong emphasis on safeguards. Under Standing Orders 75B and 75C both the second-reading stage and the committee stage require a distinct motion; and when a bill had been committed to a standing committee (so that the report stage is more than a formality), the third-reading stage cannot be started on the day on which the report stage is concluded. A motion under these orders may not be proposed unless the stage to which the time allotment is to apply already is underway. And the minimum time to be allotted under Standing Order 75C to a stage is prescribed.

The minimum time that may be allotted under S.O. 75C is one sitting day. The rule also provides for two hours of debate on the motion to adopt the time limit; and that motion requires a notice given on a previous day when proceedings at that stage already were in progress. This means that if a second-reading motion was under debate on a Tuesday the notice of a motion could be given on that day. On Wednesday the motion could be moved and debated. If it carried, the earliest hour at which the second-reading debate could be terminated would be at the end of the sitting on Thursday. Taking into account the provision that both the report stage and third-reading stage may be dealt with in the same proposal, but that one separate sitting day for each of those stages is the minimum when the report stage is debatable, the total elapsed time for the passing of a standing-committee bill to which S.O. 75C was applied without any delays whatsoever would be ten sitting days counted from the beginning of the second-reading debate. (In the case of a committee-of-the-whole bill the time would be nine sitting days.) This does not mean, of course, that the bill would have to be under debate constantly during the ten-day period.

Although the procedure established by the three standing orders is applicable to all the main stages of the legislative process, it is most important for the reformed committee stage and the activated report stage. The closure rule is still available for the other two stages. That rule—Standing Order 33—remains unchanged. When it was used in 1964 to end the flag debate there was no outcry in either the House or the country. Evidently the rule, if once discredited, had been rehabilitated by the conduct of the House during the intervening years. Even declared abolitionists, e.g., Mr. Diefenbaker, Mr. Knowles, and Mr. Pickersgill, fell silent. Indeed, during the procedure debates of the 1960s the closure rule seldom was mentioned. The unspoken consensus seems to have been that, despite its flaws, until something better has been devised, it should be retained.[16] It must be noted that Standing Orders 75A, 75B, and 75C do not parallel S.O. 33 completely. The former rules apply only to public bills. For example, they could not have been used to end the flag debate where the motion was for concurrence in a committee's recommendation.

The government resorted to time allocation under the new standing orders on only two bills during the course of the twenty-eighth Parliament. On Thursday, 2 December 1971, pursuant to notice given on Wednesday, the government house leader, the Hon. A. J. MacEachen, made a motion under Standing Order 75C in relation to Bill C-259, the bill derived from the report of the Carter Royal Commission, to amend the Income Tax Act. The second-reading motion had carried on 12 October 1971, after twelve days of debate. Then the bill had been before a committee of the whole House for twenty-seven days, and as a result of informal agreements among the house leaders and the financial critic of the official opposition, all the major provisions of the bill had been considered. The possibility of an agreement under Standing Order 75A had been explored, but the house leader of the Progressive Conservative Party had had to report that he could not commit his party. Nor could an agreement be attained under Standing Order 75B. Having explained the situation to the House, Mr. MacEachen moved that four days be allotted for the completion of the committee stage.[17]

(This meant that a total of thirty-two days would have been spent on the committee stage.) His motion carried; accordingly, the committee stage was completed on Wednesday, 8 December. Since the bill had gone to a committee of the whole House, no amendments could be offered at the report stage. On Friday, 10 December, the third reading was moved. On Tuesday, 14 December, after notice on Monday, Mr. MacEachen moved under Standing Order 75C that three days be allotted for the completion of the third-reading stage.[18] (This made a total of six days at that stage.) His motion carried; and the bill passed the House on Friday, 17 December 1971.

The second bill was Bill C-176, to establish a National Farm Products Marketing Council, which had been dealt with extensively in both that session and the previous one. Most, if not all the major objections had been met—or would be met—by ministerial amendments; yet, since some members still were somewhat unhappy with the basic policy of the bill there was a strong possibility, not of a filibuster, but that time would be frittered away in petulant argument, with the result that the bill, then at the report stage, would not have passed the House by the end of the session, then imminent. Therefore, the house leaders came to an agreement; and the leader of the house, on 30 December 1971, made a motion under Standing Order 75A.[19] After an objection to the procedure by one member on the ground that the parties were ignoring the rights of individual members, the motion carried.[20] It provided that the sitting on that day might be extended, that the report and third-reading stages were to be completed at that sitting, that speeches were to be limited, and that time was to be allotted to specified proposed amendments. The bill finally passed at 6:40 a.m. on 31 December 1971.

Standing Order 75A was used twice in 1975 prior to the summer adjournment. On 13 June an order was made to conclude the report and third-reading stages of Bill C-8, to establish a national petroleum company, in two sittings. At that time it was thought that the House might be able to adjourn early in July, shortly after the end of the budget debate. Six weeks later, on 25 July, renewed hope for adjournment—and a promise of an amendment to the bill—led the parties in opposition to agree to conclude the report stage and to complete the third-reading stage of Bill C-2, the competition bill, in two sittings in the fall. In both these instances the rule was used to achieve closure by party agreement rather than to make a time allotment. Moreover, adjournment, not orderly debate, seems to have been the motivating goal.

Standing Orders 75A, 75B, and 75C do not constitute a satisfactory time-allotment procedure. The efforts made by the Liberals in 1969 to win agreement among the parties by including elaborate safeguards had the effect of making the rules too complex and cumbersome for that purpose. What happened was that, paradoxically, the emphasis on safeguards produced rules—the important one is S.O. 75C—that have far more the character of closure rules than time-allotment rules. The safeguards, as we have noted, for the most part take the form of prescribed minimum times. Now, while it is possible to allot more than the minimum time (to a complex bill), it is impossible to allot less than the minimum (to a simple bill). Given the fact that the same rule was to apply to both simple and complex bills, this logical point made it almost certain that the minimum time specified in S.O. 75C would be quite low. As a result the rules appear as only an elaborate form of closure. This is how S.O. 75A was used in each of the three instances mentioned above. This is how S.O. 75C was used in the case of Bill C-259. It would seem that if a genuine time-allotment procedure is to be achieved the British approach, which gives both the power and the responsibility to the government, is far better than a legalistic scheme such as the one now embodied in Standing Orders 75A, 75B, and 75C.[21]

The real importance of these rules—although so far there has been no occasion to use them in these ways—is that they do provide a method by which to retrieve bills from standing or special committees and a method by which to set a time limit for debate at the activated report stage. For this reason, and not because of any prospect that these rules will be used to improve the legislative process, it is desirable that the meaning of S.O. 75B should be settled, and not by the speaker, but by an amendment made by the House.

TEN

New Remedies

I

Sweeping denunciations of the House of Commons—its members, its procedures, and its general performance—should be heard sceptically whatever the source. It is to be expected that some ministers, baffled by the unwillingness of the House to do their bidding with alacrity, will complain about its inefficiency. Understandably some members in opposition will conclude that since their party did poorly in the last election the rules must be wrong. For private members and newsmen grown world-weary the House, perhaps once thrilling, may be a bore. Political scientists, exhilarated by the last faculty meeting, could run the whole show far better, just as their colleagues in economics could in the case of the Bank of Canada or the Department of Finance.

But this is not a chapter in praise of the House. Since we are here to recommend remedies we must dwell on ills. Although the House did improve its procedures greatly in the period from 1955 to 1969, there still are grounds for valid criticism. Obviously, procedural changes will not transfigure the House: other factors are involved. It is easy to imagine an ideal House, one composed of public-spirited men and women, all fully knowledgeable on every major matter of concern to the country, and able to devote all their time and energy to public affairs. Under Responsible Government such an ideal House would be divided into two sides—the government and the opposition, each composed of a single political party—with the swing of the political pendulum allowing each party regularly to enjoy periods of responsibility and periods of revival. The debates would be well-organized, brilliant, and never too long, with the key issues tackled directly in pithy speeches, each meeting head on the arguments advanced from the other side. The work would be done quickly, but above all thoroughly. While we may want to move toward such a House, we must remind ourselves that our House of Commons has certain characteristics, characteristics which now seem constant.

First, a very high percentage of the most active members are lawyers.[1] Given our lack of a genuine leisure class, and given the fact that participation in politics usually has been, and is, easier and far more profitable for lawyers than for physicians, farmers, businessmen, labourers, etc., this is not likely to change. We seem destined to be represented mainly by lawyers. They are as close as we in North America are likely to come to Plato's philosopher-kings. They have a basic familiarity with the terminology; they are practised in the arts of advocacy; they are skilled in appeasement and compromise; they understand the adversary system. Unless they mistook their calling, temperamentally they are suited to the politician's role. They have the office facilities, and they can find the time for politics. By participating as party activists and candidates they gain prestige among their fellows, and also palpable benefits of many kinds; and for the afternoon there is the bench.

Next, we must remind ourselves that the turnover in the Canadian House of Commons is very high, and tends to be especially high among the abler members, who often come from the more competitive constituencies, where winning a party nomination and then an election are real tests.[2] Given the fact that safe seats ordinarily go to local candidates—there have been notable exceptions, e.g., Mr. Pearson in Algoma East, Mr. Pickersgill in Bonavista-Twillingate, and Mr. Douglas in Nanaimo-Cowichan-The Islands—the party managers in Canada, unlike their British counterparts, can do little to build their teams by maintaining a "protected list."

These two points—the large number of lawyers and the rapid turnover of members—have taken on new significance since 1939. Prior to World War II the government of Canada and the Parliament were not involved in direct economic and social management to a very high degree. They made trade treaties and fixed tariff thresholds. They promoted and regulated the construction and operation of the canal and railway infrastructures. They provided navigation aids and shipping regulations. They governed banking, weights and measures, currency, interest rates, and bankruptcy. But in "normal times" beyond such things they were not expected to go very far. When they did attempt to deal with crises, as in 1919 and 1935, they soon were put back in their place by the Judicial Committee. In short, the government and Parliament of Canada were confined largely to the establishment of codes of individual and corporate conduct. With that world of legal standards and regulation the lawyers already were familiar. The major areas in which the government undertook to do things itself were railroading, the army, public works, and territorial land management.

Now, however, the government and therefore the Parliament are deeply involved in the production of goods and services, and in economic and social management. By its immigration and housing policies it attempts to influence employment levels. It operates a vast railway company, a major airline, airports, and radio and television networks. It is deeply involved in medical and physical research, in both technical and academic education, and in the promotion of the arts. It has assumed responsibilities in the field of regional economic growth, in the management of oil, gas, uranium, and other natural resources, in the conservation of fish stocks, and in the preservation of the air and water environments. All these, and others like them, are fields in which engineers, scientists, and economists are far more at home than lawyers. Unfortunately, given the rapid turnover of the membership of the House, not many have an opportunity to acquire even a basic understanding. Consequently, sometimes the blind question the blind. The experts brief their minister; then he is questioned by other lawyers. This is not to say that any other group—chemists, agriculturalists, physicians, bankers—either alone or in combination with others, would make a better House. Every professional tends to see the world from his own viewpoint. The lawyer, now as in the sixteenth century, is unusually useful because essentially he is an amateur equipped with special clerical skills.

Third, we must take into account the "sun-moon" nature of Canadian federal politics. Pendulum factors—for example, the fact that a party in office often becomes tired, lazy, and corrupt after about two terms—are far from unimportant in Canadian politics; but the truth is that in Canada the sun-moon paradigm is more apt than the pendulum paradigm. From 1867 to 1896 the Conservatives were the sun party, with the Liberals winning only once, in the unusual circumstances of 1874. Since 1896, largely because the Conservatives turned away from Quebec, their former bastion, the Liberals have been dominant, going into eclipse only in 1911–21, 1926, 1930–35, and 1957–63. This has had three important results. First, more and more the Liberal ministers are selected from men and women who never served in opposition, and who consequently tend to regard the House as an unfortunate restraint and obstacle. They fail to see that the House basically, now as in the late Middle Ages, is a means by which the government may win the consent of the people. They fail to see that the constitution does not pit the government against the House, but that it provides for government through the House. Second, at the other extreme the Conservatives tend to become opposed, not simply to the ministers, but to the system. They denounce the Liberals, not only for governing badly, but for having corrupted the constitution. And, third, many Conservatives believe that any change in the rules that makes the House work better almost by definition is beneficial to the Liberals.

Fourth, despite the two-party implication of our simple sun-moon history we will continue to have a multi-party system. This is important for various reasons. First, it makes for minority government, albeit in the past for Liberal minority government. Minority government makes for frequent elections. Frequent elections make for delays and disruptions in the conduct of parliamentary business. Second, the presence of "third" parties makes the conduct of business far more complex. Finally, what is most obvious, as a review of the *Debates* since 1962 will reveal, "third" parties consume time far out of proportion to their numbers. They are not just more players; they are additional teams. Much of the frustration during the Oral Question Period over the past ten years has sprung from the fact that the speaker has felt obliged to see the leading men in each of three or four opposition parties. Some of the disjointedness of debate arises from the fact that various distinct party views are being expressed, with each party having its turn. This is painfully obvious when a Social Credit spokesman takes the floor during almost any debate on economic matters.

Fifth, the House is and will remain bilingual. The Parliament of Canada is the world's only major French-English parliament. Since 1885 the standing orders have provided that the deputy speaker must possess the official language other than the one spoken by the speaker, but the increasing use of French has made it highly desirable that the speaker be fluent in both languages. This restricts the eligibility of members, especially members from outside Quebec, to serve as speaker. The requirements of bilingualism complicate the appointment of Table officers and staff. What is said in the House and its committees is translated simultaneously; yet the use of the two languages often weakens the unity of debates. The record of all proceedings is provided in both English and French. From a procedural viewpoint this last requirement is perhaps the most important, for it means not only that accurate translations of highly technical material must be made rapidly, but that copy must be edited and printed quickly, not in just one, but two languages; otherwise, items of business may be delayed.

Let us now turn to the criticisms. That the debates are dull and disjointed, that supply business is treated too lightly, that committees are overworked—these and similar criticisms are important, and we must deal with them. But they are less than fundamental. What must be constantly borne in mind are two major criticisms, which taken together embrace all the others. Neither, we must notice, is a flat condemnation. Both assert that to some degree, to some extent, the House falls short of a realistic ideal. Some critics would say that it falls very far short; others that it does quite well; and still others that at some times it does better (or worse) than at other times. Clearly, we are not seeking complete and final remedies. We are prepared to settle for moves in the right direction.

The first major criticism is that the House, and therefore, the individual member, is not of much value any more. The House, it is contended, now is of only tertiary importance. Many members of the public, many private members, and even some privy councillors share the view that given the government's deep involvement in economic and scientific matters since 1939 only a very few men, almost all of them in the public service, can pretend to know the basic aims and policies of the government, so that most ministers are only spokesmen and public relations officers, while the private members make by far their greatest contribution, perhaps their only important contribution, by faithful attention to administrative casework about pensions, wharves, and grants.

As we noted in chapter 1, in the eighteenth century the British House did a great deal of vital work related to domestic affairs, but the nationalization of governing shifted the locus of power away from local interests and authorities to great, new central departments headed by ministers. Domestic governing came under ministers, who in turn were held responsible by the House. Thus the direct involvement of the House in domestic governing ended. The House thereafter derived relatively little in the way of stature from local and private legislation.

Given Canada's federal constitution, the Canadian House of Commons never was involved extensively in local and private affairs except for railways and company incorporations, fields which soon lost their early prominence. From its beginning our House primarily was a body that met to do the business put before it by the government. Its importance derives from its relationship with the government. Both the institutional function and the democratic function of the House refer to the relationship between the House and the government. To perform its democratic function, the House, or at least some of the private members, must know what the government is doing, and must understand the implications of the measures brought to the House by the government. To the extent that the House passes the ministers' bills, motions, and votes after superficial, although perhaps tediously long debate, while doubting that the ministers themselves really know what their measures are all about, the House performs its democratic function poorly. The first criticism, stated in other words, is that the House sometimes, perhaps often, performs its democratic function poorly.

The theory of Responsible Government rests on the assumption that the ministers are the principal servants of the Crown, not only in title, but in fact. By holding the chief advisers and administrators of the Crown answerable to the House, the theory runs, men and women in whom the people lack confidence will not gain office or will be ousted from office. Even in the nineteenth century nobody contended that all the important officers of the Crown had been made directly responsible. Certainly nowadays in an era when governing requires a great deal of professional knowledge nobody would ask that all ministers, or even most, be meritorious. The ministers, who achieve office because of popularity, all would concede readily, must be complemented in the service of the Crown by men and women who attain office by reason of those qualities labelled "merit." Popularity and merit are not mutually exclusive; yet ordinarily they are brought to the required degree by quite different kinds of efforts and experience. Under Responsible Government the country is governed through the cooperation of those who are temporarily popular and those who are permanently meritorious.

There is a view—certainly it is not a new view—which insists that the balance between the two groups, between the ministers and the mandarins, has shifted, that more and more power has slipped away from the ministers to their managers. The view is that the ministers are joining the governor general as ornamental figures in the façade atop the constitutional edifice. The real legislator-administrators, i.e., the real governors, are not the ministers, but their advisers; and the result is that the theory of Responsible Government now functions as a myth to shield the mandarins from popular ire and clamour. It is quite possible to hold this view in whole or in part without believing that there is a mandarin conspiracy, or that all mandarins are knaves, or that all the ministers are slack and indolent.

Another view, also directly relevant to the status of the House of Commons, is that in recent times for various reasons, perhaps chiefly the influence of television, the prime minister has become a presidential figure. Two points are made. First, success in an election now depends more on the prime minister's own appeal and effort than on the strength of his party. Second, as a consequence a prime minister tends to act as a "prince" rather than as *primus inter pares*. He surrounds himself with courtiers—his White House cabinet—that is, with persons qualified by neither of the established processes, neither that of merit nor that of popular support. The result, the argument runs, is not only that the ministers have become even less important than before, but that the mandarins themselves have lost something from their power.[3]

Such shifts of power among the governors cannot be measured exactly. What may be quite true of one prime minister may barely be true of another. What may be true of some ministers—all the dull ones, some new ones, and the drones—in their relations with the public servants and with the prime minister and his staff will be far from true of others. The question for us is not if and how the government should be reformed, but how the House of Commons, by modifying its own conduct and procedures can foster Responsible Government in the highest possible degree.

The second criticism is that considering the amount of work to be done the sessions are far too long. As compared with both Great Britain and the United States of America, Canada is a relatively small country. It has no far-flung foreign political involvements and no great imperial ties. Almost all the local and private business is done by the provinces, and, as a result of the decisions of the Judicial Committee, so is much that the Fathers intended to be federal. Yet since 1937 the sessions have grown longer and longer. It would be a mistake to assume that the length of the sessions is determined mainly by the amount of work to be done. At times the shoe has been enlarged to accommodate the foot, but to an even greater extent the foot has grown to fill the shoe. The removal of those practical considerations—chiefly the need to earn a livelihood by gainful employment elsewhere—that in earlier years made many members, especially those from the extremities of the country, impatient with long sessions, gave loose rein to other practical considerations that tend to foster long sessions—for example, the desire of some members to reside in Ottawa rather than in their constituencies, and the desire of the opposition to allow the government no respite. It is true that the volume of work has increased, but it is true also that it has been stretched to fill longer and longer sessions. The weekly hours of sitting were shortened, most notably by the elimination of sittings on Wednesday and Friday evenings, and by the reduction of the time for public business after dinner on the other days to a total of six hours a week. At the same time, during the years between 1890 and 1957, when the standing and special committees were relatively unimportant, the practice became established that a committee week was a two-day week: meetings on Monday and Friday would be inconvenient for members who spent those days in their offices in Montreal or Toronto; and Wednesday, a short day after 1906, is caucus day. Moreover, as the sessions became longer (and the working days and the working weeks became shorter) the newsmen propagated the notion that unless Parliament is in session nothing is being done—for Parliament is "the legislature"—about the ever-present crisis: the inflation, the unemployment, the recession, the run-away boom, the high interest rates, the strikes, the low number of housing starts, etc.

Unnecessarily long sessions are deplorable for two reasons. First, the ministers spend too much of their time away from their departments, and are kept busy throughout the year on activities related to the House. Physically, both individually and collectively, they now are based in the Centre and West Blocks, near the Chamber. The more time they spend away from their departments, the more their deputies run the departments. Responsible Government focuses on the relationship between the ministers and the House of Commons, but it presupposes that the ministers genuinely are in charge in their departments. To the extent that they are not in charge, Responsible Government is a delusion. To the extent that the House by demanding the attendance of ministers promotes their divorce from their departments the House itself erodes Responsible Government. In the second place, prolonged sessions may have one of two bad effects on private members. Some, like students and professors at a university, tend to lose contact with the outside world. They become intent on parliamentary ploys, questions, privileges, debating points, and press gallery opinions, most of which count as nothing with the people. Others, obliged to be in Ottawa throughout most of the year, yet unengaged by the House, come to devote themselves to perpetual reelection campaigns conducted from their Ottawa offices. The work of Parliament has been allowed to overflow too much of the year. The result is that both the operation of the government and the role of the member have been distorted. We must eschew the easy assumption that Responsible Government works best when Parliament is in session. Long, unbroken sessions are counter-productive. They cost far more than they are worth.

The new remedies should have two main goals. First, they should enable the House to perform its democratic function better. Second, they should promote shorter sessions.

II

THE LEGISLATIVE PROCESS

During the past twenty years the House took two major steps limiting the time for various kinds of business. In 1955, as we saw in chapter 8, limits were placed on the general sessional debates: the resumed Address debate was limited to ten days, the resumed budget debate was limited to eight days, and the "supply motion" debates were limited to twelve days, for a total of thirty days. In 1962 the total was reduced to twenty-six days by cutting back both the Address debate and the budget debate by two days. Then in 1968 a second major step was taken when the House set a limit of twenty-five days on all supply business in the House.

The sessions since 1955 have varied greatly in length; the legislative programs have differed; and political circumstances have been far from constant. Accordingly, it is impossible to state precisely the effect on other business of those two steps; yet certain conclusions, accurate

TABLE 14
Effect of Limits on Sessional Business

Session	Address Debate	Budget Debate	Supply Debates	Total	Committee of Supply	Total	Sittings
1955	15 days	$11\frac{1}{2}$ days	$16\frac{1}{8}$ days	$42\frac{5}{8}$ days	$30\frac{3}{4}$ days	$73\frac{3}{8}$ days	141
1956	10 "	8 "	$12\frac{1}{2}$ "	$30\frac{1}{2}$ "	$42\frac{3}{4}$ "	$73\frac{1}{4}$ "	152
1967–68	8 "	6 "	8 "	22 "	$44\frac{1}{2}$ "	$66\frac{1}{2}$ "	155
1969–70	8 "	6 "	—	14+25 supply days		39 "	155

enough for our purposes, can be drawn. Table 14 shows the time taken by sessional business in four sessions, one before and one after each of the two steps.

What is evident from the fact that the sessions did not decrease in length is that when the general debates were limited the members redirected their attention to government bills and to the Committee of Supply, and that when supply business in the House was limited to twenty-five days they shifted their efforts even more to government bills. Since the rules change of 20 December 1968, by far the greatest part of the orders-of-the-day time of the House has been spent on government bills.

The following table, Table 15, covering the five sessions immediately after the 1968 rules change, shows the time expended in the Chamber on all government bills other than appropriation bills. (Appropriation bills are dealt with on supply days.)

Speaking generally, so as to exclude bills that meet strong resistance, we can say that the second-reading stage serves to acquaint the members who are interested—often only a very small part of the House, as attendance shows—with the purposes of a bill, and that it gives those members an opportunity to deliver general speeches on the subject-matter of the bill. An examination of Table 15 shows that in terms of the time of the House the second-reading stage is the most costly by far. The only session when the time taken at that stage did not exceed the time taken at all the other stages combined was 1970–72, when Bill C-259, to amend the Income Tax Act, was before the House. (The time taken by Bill C-259 was as follows: second reading stage—33 hours, 14 minutes; in the committee of the whole House—122 hours, 22 minutes; and third-reading stage—19 hours, 19 minutes.) The table shows that the activated report stage has not been very expensive in terms of time.

Table 15 shows also that in every one of these five sessions the

TABLE 15
Time Taken at the
Several Stages of Government Bills in the House
(Appropriation Bills Excluded)

	Number	Second Reading	Committees of the Whole House	Report	Third Reading	Senate Amendments
1969–70						
PASSED						
Whole	11	24:14	30:42		3:56	
Standing	49	135:12		74:55	19:20	1:18
NOT PASSED						
Whole						
Standing	1	2:50		3:40		
Not Committed	4	38:40				
	65	200:56	30:42	78:35	23:16	1:18
1970–72						
PASSED						
Whole	7	76:03	201:10		36:37	
Standing	47★	146:45		96:35	39:42	1:50
NOT PASSED						
Whole						
Standing	2	16:47		22:03		
Not Committed	4	30:42				
	60★	270:17	201:10	118:38	76:19	1:50

★ Bill C-172, to establish the Federal Court, which was reintroduced and advanced to the report stage, is included.

	Number	Second Reading	Committees of the Whole House	Report	Third Reading	Senate Amendments
1972						
PASSED						
Whole	5	7:01	8:47		1:27	
Standing	9★	51:27		16:15	6:51	
NOT PASSED						
Whole						
Standing	2	40:57		11:55	5:38	
Not Committed	4	31:20				
	20★	130:45	8:47	28:10	13:56	

★ Bill C-204, to amend the Wheat Board Act, which was reintroduced and advanced to the report stage, is included.

	Number	Second Reading	Committees of the Whole House	Report	Third Reading	Senate Amendments
1973–74						
PASSED						
Whole	16	38:16	39:47		4:58	
Standing	26	182:06		89:20	35:23	:56
NOT PASSED						
Whole						
Standing	2	21:21		8:44		
Not Committed	2	7:48				
	46	249:31	39:47	98:04	40:21	:56

New Remedies 269

	Number	Second Reading	Committees of the Whole House	Report	Third Reading	Senate Amendments
1974						
PASSED						
Whole	4	11:25	11:36		5:01	
Standing	4*	6:06		8:29	4:31	
NOT PASSED						
Whole						
Standing	1	6:59		2:37		
Not Committed	8	45:08				
	17*	69:38	11:36	11:06	9:32	

* Both Bill C-164, re C.N.R. Financing, and Bill S-4, re the National Parks Act, which were reintroduced and advanced to the report stage, are included.

government invested a considerable amount of time on bills that did not pass at that session; that no bills sent to committees of the whole House did not pass; and that in 1973-74 and 1974, when in a minority, the government showed a strong tendency to have bills sent to committees of the whole House, rather than to the standing committees.

When we analyze the time taken by government bills at the second reading stage we find, as shown by Table 16, that about one quarter of the bills debated at that stage during the five sessions took very little time—well under one-half hour each. At the other extreme, twenty-seven of the 204 bills took about sixteen hours each. Almost half of the total time—433 hours, 45 minutes out of a total of 921 hours, 7 minutes—was given over to those twenty-seven bills. Moreover, twelve of the twenty-seven did not pass at the sessions in which they were first debated. The time expended on those twelve bills at the second-reading stage amounted to 180 hours, 46 minutes, almost one-fifth of the total.

The change made in the legislative process in 1968, so that the the committee stage of most bills now is taken, not in committees of the whole House, but in standing committees, has proven highly successful. It is significant that the main complaint, almost the only complaint attributable to this change heard in the House from 1968 to 1972 was not that bills were not being considered fully, but that the government was unwilling to accept amendments. When the attention given to bills by the standing committees and by the House at the report stage is compared with the consideration formerly given in committees of the whole House, the conclusion that the new procedure is far better is inescapable. The record shows that government bills are examined far more thoroughly.

What is needed now is a re-evaluation of the second-reading stage. It has two defects. First, it is wasteful of the time of the House. Frequently the debate is a preliminary exercise in which those who have an interest

TABLE 16
Time Taken by Government Bills at the Second-reading Stage
(excluding all appropriation bills)

	Number	Total Time	Approximate Average
1969-70			
1 hour or less	24	11:23	:28
2 hours or less (to 1)	10	14:37	1:27
3 hours or less (to 2)	8	19:42	2:28
4 hours or less (to 3)	9	31:21	3:29
More than 4 hours (to 9)	10	57:42	5:46
More than 9 hours	4	66:11	16:33
	65	200:56	
1970-71-72			
1 hour or less	18	5:43	:23
2 hours or less (to 1)	12	16:23	1:22
3 hours or less (to 2)	2	5:00	2:30
4 hours or less (to 3)	5	16:27	3:17
More than 4 hours (to 9)	12	80:25	6:42
More than 9 hours	10	146:19	14:38
	59	270:17	
1972			
1 hour or less	3	:29	:10
2 hours or less (to 1)	1	1:25	1:25
3 hours or less (to 2)	5	13:14	2:39
4 hours or less (to 3)	2	7:11	3:36
More than 4 hours (to 9)	2	15:55	7:58
More than 9 hours	6	92:31	15:25
	19	130:45	
1973-74			
1 hour or less	12	3:27	:17
2 hours or less (to 1)	4	5:45	1:26
3 hours or less (to 2)	5	12.34	2.31
4 hours or less (to 3)	5	20:06	4:01
More than 4 hours (to 9)	14	93:18	6:39
More than 9 hours	6	114:21	19:04
	46	249:31	
1974			
1 hour or less	1	:50	:50
2 hours or less (to 1)	2	3:28	1:44
3 hours or less (to 2)	3	7:16	2:19
4 hours or less (to 3)	2	6:51	3:25
More than 4 hours (to 9)	6	36:50	6:08
More than 9 hours	1	14:23	14:23
	15	69:38	

in a bill, and only those, hear the minister read an explanation of the bill, and then state their own tentative reactions and initial queries. There is no compelling reason why this should be done in the House. Moreover, as we have noted, the government has been bringing forward a fair number of bills which either are not ready for enactment or to which it is not deeply committed. Second, to use the second-reading stage as the first active stage is to inflict unnecessary frustration on the private members. It is true, of course, that by the time a major bill is ready for introduction it has taken on something of the character of a multilateral treaty—a treaty among the interested ministers and departments—so that the minister is reluctant to accept amendments. This is not as true of bills that involve only one or two departments. In either case there is much to be said for having a government bill examined and explained in detail before party positions have been declared and before the members are asked to vote for or against it.

Four remedies are available. They are set forth in order of importance. The first is that the legislative process for government bills be changed so that the first active step need not be taken in the House. The idea behind the legislative process now followed—an idea inherited from the seventeenth and eighteenth centuries, when it was valid—is that much of the work of preparing a bill is done at the committee stage, and that no committee should spend time on a draft bill until the House has ordered it to prepare the bill. Consequently, the second-reading stage is now the first major stage. But three points must be noted. First, nowadays the bills that go forward are government bills, which already are in a high state of preparation when introduced. Second, the second-reading stage is not the decisive test or screen that separates out the bills the House will treat as important. The House has distinguished between government bills and private members' bills in a most emphatic way: it has put most of its time at the disposal of the government, and very little at the disposal of the private members, so that almost the only bills that pass are government bills. And, third, as argued in chapter 4, the second reading ought not to be regarded as an occasion to vote for or against a philosophic principle; consequently, it would not be preposterous for members to examine a government bill before second reading.

The proposal is that provision be made so that immediately after the first reading of a bill a minister may make a motion, which would not be debatable, that the subject-matter of the bill be referred to a specified standing committee (or to a special committee), and that after the committee had presented its report, regardless of the content of the report, an order for the second-reading motion would be added to the list of Government Orders. This new stage, between the first and second readings, should not be a part of the due process; in the case of simple bills and of bills preceded by Green or White Papers, it probably would serve no purpose. The subject matter of bills that go of course to committees of the whole House would not be referred. Formally, the committee should have before it a simple motion, e.g., that the committee recommends that Bill C-000 be read a second time. The committee should not be authorized to adopt or amend the bill, but the minister, before he moved second reading, would be permitted to table any amendments that he wished to have made, and these would be deemed to have been made. The bill could be reprinted when the minister's amendments warranted that step. The balance of the legislative process would be as at present.

One advantage of sending government bills to a committee after first reading would be that in such cases the first major step would not be a debate. The minister and his officials could provide a detailed explanation of their bill—of both the purposes and main provisions—and could be questioned intensively without the opposition having to declare itself one way or the other. The notion that the exploratory or discovery stage of all bills—the familiarization stage—can be conducted efficiently through a series of speeches, many of which must be vague and hypothetical is patently fallacious in an age of complex legislation. A second advantage would be that the second-reading stage, coming after study, not before it, might indeed occasion a debate and might take far less time. A third advantage would be that interested members of the public could be heard on the subject matter of the bill, rather than on the clauses as at present. A fourth advantage would be that the government could use a committee, rather than the House, as the place in which to acquaint the public with adventurous proposals, and in which to gauge reactions. A fifth advantage would be that the private members would have less reason for complaint that their arguments are rejected, not because ministers believe them unsound, but because they find them inconvenient.

There is nothing new about the purpose behind this proposal. At various times in recent years ministers have felt it desirable to consult the members before bringing in what the government regarded as its final legislative scheme. Five methods have been used. White Papers setting forth government policy have been referred to committees with the understanding that the government was prepared to have its mind changed. The Green Paper approach, in which a paper setting forth both basic information on a topic and indicating different legislative possibilities is tabled and referred to a committee without the government having made up its own mind even tentatively, has been used, notably in 1975 with regard to immigration.[4] Each of these methods entails a major addition to the legislative process; consequently, neither can be used frequently without upsetting the legislative program for a session. During the past few years some ministers have consulted extensively with committees of the government caucus; however, this does not serve to familiarize the opposition parties with a proposal, and they are the ones who take up most of the time at the second-reading stage. A fourth method is inconclusive debate at the second-reading stage—either to break ice or to fly kites. This has two disadvantages: (a) it uses the time of the House; and (b) since the House is a debating body, not an exploratory body, misconceptions and unfounded prejudices may be propagated. The fifth method is to amend the second-reading motion so that the House does not order the second reading, but instead refers the subject matter of the bill to a committee. This does enable a committee to explore the bill, but it prevents its enactment at that session. The present proposal would retain the bill in the program of business for the session. Even when a large number of representations from the public were heard—at the new stage instead of at the committee stage as at present—the program should move forward more expeditiously because arrangements to hear representations could be made earlier.

Strong arguments can be made speculatively for this proposal; yet just how satisfactory or unsatisfactory it would prove in practice cannot be known *a priori*. In other words, this is a proposal with which the House might wish to experiment extensively before coming to a conclusion. Clearly, it is a proposal which ministers and mandarins might view with alarm. It would expose government bills to examination before they had been endorsed by the majority at the second-reading stage. Thus it would expose ministers to heavy pressure to agree to amendments. The argument may be made that to get the interest groups, the departments, the individual ministers, and the cabinet committees to agree on the content of a major bill is difficult enough without inviting radical examination of the bill in the House of Commons. Another argument may be that no Canadian government should oblige itself to have the bulk of its bills ready for introduction during the early weeks of a session because the process by which bills are produced is so complex and arduous that even without such an early deadline herculean efforts sometimes are required to keep the parliamentary mill from running empty.

The latter argument has weight. But it is an argument against the close involvement of the entire cabinet in the day-to-day work of the House as in pioneer days when the sessions lasted only two or three months, and against the inflation of the sessions. If the ministers are to do their work well they must be allowed adequate unbroken time in which to do it. The employment of more mandarins and additional draftsmen is not an answer, for they must wait upon the ministers, even if only for formal approval. On the other hand, the first argument may be dismissed. A major government bill does represent a compromise among interest groups, departments, and ministers, but no one can contend that the members of the House of Commons ought not to test the compromise as effectively as possible. An argument that the present process ought to be treated as a sacred rite because it prevents full parliamentary scrutiny will not bear the light of day.

The second remedy relates to the hour of daily adjournment. In 1927 the hour was set at 11:00 p.m. on Monday, Tuesday, Thursday, and Friday. Since that was a period of relatively short sessions no need was felt for a rule enabling the House to decide to sit late without unanimous agreement. In 1952 the hour of adjournment on Friday was set at 6:00 p.m., as on Wednesday after 1906; and for the other three days of the week it was advanced to 10:00 p.m. Then in 1965, as the result of the annoyance caused repeatedly by two or three members, the standing orders were changed so that now, under Standing Order 6(5), the House on any day may decide to sit beyond the regular hour of adjournment if ten or more members do not object. But S.O. 6(5) is effective only against isolated mavericks. Those members who in a particular instance or as a general principle do not wish to cooperate with the government almost always can carry at least nine other members with them. In the long 1970-72 session, for example, the government resorted to S.O. 6(5) eight times, but was successful only once. Indeed, the outcome is so predictable that the rule seldom is used except to demonstrate that cooperation is not forthcoming. Sometimes, especially before a long adjournment, the House will simply ignore the clock for a time or agree to extended hours, but seldom when it is dealing with highly contentious business. As a result the house leaders normally cannot decide that a certain bill, or two specified bills, or three, are to be the work for a day, and that if necessary the House will sit late. The hours of sitting have become a procrustean bed, since 1952 a short procrustean bed. The remedy is the adoption of the British rule that permits the House to decide by a majority vote to sit late. This would enable the house leaders to settle and announce the work for a week or two. Since it is the second-reading debates that consume most time, the rule would be especially useful when the House was dealing with the second reading of bills that take less than five or six hours at that stage; but these, as Table 16 shows, are quite numerous.

The third remedy relates to closure. The record of the sessions since 1968 shows that some of the bills that take a great deal of time at the second-reading stage move forward very rapidly at the report and third-reading stages. This suggests that the extensive use of an exploratory committee stage would reduce sharply the second-reading time in many cases. This would not be true of those other bills where long debate results, not from the need for detailed exploration and familiarization, but from genuine opposition. At most sessions there will be some government bills which will cause one or more of the other parties to dig in. The Special Committee on Procedure (1967–68) commented favourably on the British convention that ordinarily a debate ends on the same sitting at which it starts. As a general rule that convention is highly commendable; yet it cannot be regarded as the solution to very long second-reading debates at Ottawa. One objection is that without the British closure rule—under which any member may move closure at any time, if the speaker does not object—in periods of high political tension the maximum might tend to become the minimum for several bills. As we have seen, in most sessions many bills take far less than an hour or two. Little would have been achieved if, at the very extreme, each such bill came to take an entire sitting. A second objection is that without the British closure rule, the one-sitting debate on controversial bills might extend for two, three, or four days, marred by emotional eruptions as the members became more and more exhausted. A third objection is that a rule or convention which imposed a one-sitting limit on the second-reading stage of contentious bills probably is simply unacceptable in Canada. In short, what is required is a flexible, not a rigid, approach.

The ideal answer would be the introduction of the British closure rule without the one-sitting limit. Under such an arrangement the debate on a highly controversial bill could continue for two or three sittings, perhaps extended sittings, and then could be brought to an end by closure without the opponents of the bill having to surrender. (It is well to recognize that closure provides an honourable deliverance for members who have sworn to fight a measure to the death.) But neither the House nor the public is ready for the British rule, which depends greatly for its acceptability on the status of the speaker. Accordingly, the best available answer is the use of Standing Order 33—modified so that the vote would come at 10:00 p.m.—not merely for crises, but as an ordinary device. Because the House and the public entertain a strong suspicion of closure, the government would have to take great care not to resort to the rule too early and not to cut debate too short. The most telling argument voiced against closure is that the Canadian House of Commons requires a considerable amount of time to come to appreciate the significance of bills and that Canadian public opinion is not readily evocable. This argument would be blunted by an adequate exploratory stage prior to the second-reading debate.

The fourth remedy relates to reasoned amendments to the second-reading motion. As argued in chapter 4, there is no sound reason why the practice of the House should not be changed so that an amendment opposing the advancement of a bill on any relevant ground—and not only an amendment opposed to the principle of a bill—could be moved. This would allow a far wider latitude to the opposition in selecting the field for battle. That in turn should make for better debates. Obviously, this proposal could not be implemented without some kind of effective time limit on the second-reading stage.

REGULAR ADJOURNMENTS

In its fifteenth report the Special Committee on Procedure and Organization (1964-65) recommended that the House should adjourn at regular intervals for two weeks at a time to enable its standing committees to work intensively and to enable the members to spend a week at a time in their constituencies. Between each such adjournment the House would sit for three weeks. The recommendation was intended and was discussed primarily as a way to improve the operation of the committees.

At present the time and energy of members are expended extravagantly. Too much time is spent travelling. This is not a result of an extension of the notorious, old Tuesday-to-Thursday club. What happened was that the rules and practices of the House with regard to hours of sitting, the times of votes, committee meetings, etc. were modified years ago to accommodate those members from central Canada who went home each weekend for a long weekend. Friday and Monday became light days insofar as the accomplishment of government business is concerned. This fact was supplemented after World War II by long sessions, and in the past two decades by the availability of air travel. The result is that it now is possible and therefore politically necessary for many members to make the weekly trip. There are sound reasons why a member should spend time in his constituency during a session over thirty weeks long, but as things now stand too much time is spent shuttling back and forth to Ottawa. Too little time is spent in Ottawa and too little time is spent in the constituency between the trips. The member's parliamentary work suffers; his constituency work suffers; and he himself becomes weary.

The best way to shorten the sessions—in terms of the number of sittings—would be for the House to work full five-day weeks while sitting and to adjourn regularly for a week at a time. Perhaps occasionally the House might wish to adjourn to allow its committees full possession of the parliamentary stage; that is a different question.

The main reason why the recommendation of the Special Committee (1964-65) was not endorsed by the Pearson government was that regular adjournments would be likely to lengthen the time required by items of government business. The members would return to the adjourned debates ready to begin all over again. This was, and is, a good and sufficient reason for rejecting the proposal. However, if it was accepted that the House will complete the business planned for a period by extended sittings and by the occasional use of a reasonable closure rule, the proposal would become feasible. The use of an improved form of closure already has been proposed for other reasons. Here is another reason for renouncing the old hostility to the rule. Alternatively, time allocation—especially under S.O. 75A or S.O. 75B—might be used to assure that debates on bills were completed within an agreed period so that the House could adjourn.

TAXING AND SPENDING

Before 20 December 1968, a budget statement, although not required by any rule, in practice was a prerequisite for any change in the tax laws. The two—the budget statement and debate, on the one hand, and bills to amend the tax laws, on the other—no longer are linked together, as we saw in chapter 5. As a result, it is possible for the minister of finance to employ taxation far more readily as an instrument of economic strategy and tactics. A tax change can be initiated at any time without a budget debate. This new arrangement seems to have been found acceptable by the House. This is not to say that there is no room for improvement.

In contrast, the changes made in 1968 in the procedures by which the business of supply is done subsequently were denounced vehemently by the Progressive Conservatives, with some support from the New Democratic Party, and the Social Credit Party. The main cause of their dissatisfaction was the supply timetable, under which all supply business before the House in the fall, at the end of the fiscal year, and in the late spring is dealt with conclusively by fixed dates—10 December, 26 March, and 30 June. This arrangement has made it impossible for members in opposition to exert pressure on the government by filibustering supply. The complaint made is that the new procedure robs the House of its right to have its grievances satisfied before supply is granted. To paint the picture in lurid colours some members have stated that the estimates have not been examined carefully in the standing committees, while others have implied that billions of dollars are being appropriated without any prior consideration whatsoever.

Whatever the defects of the new procedures, a return to the old would be retrograde. As stated by opposition members repeatedly during the 1950s, the Committee of Supply had become virtually useless. It was a tedious farce. The validity of the claim that the House has a right to refuse supply before its grievances have been met—a claim derived from the constitutional struggles between the Crown and the House during the seventeenth century—is challenged by nobody; but it does not mean that one member or even one party has the right to prevent the House itself from voting whether or not to grant supply. Besides, when we review the instances when supply was held up during the 1960s we must conclude that while in some cases the opposition enjoyed roasting ministers, it derived no discernible political benefit from its exertions; indeed, the truth may be that the opposition's efforts were found offensive by the electorate.

What impedes a radical appraisal of supply procedure is an outdated theory inculcated by British constitutional history in which the cautious, thrifty Commons, the representatives of the landed and monied interests, carefully dole out money to feckless kings prone to loose living and madcap foreign wars. Given the fact that the government may be defeated in the next election, the ministers, especially the minister of finance and the president of the Treasury Board, now are keenly aware of the desirability of avoiding unpopular taxation. On the other hand, now that the Crown spends most of the money, not on palaces, favourites, and adventures, but for the benefit of the country at large, most members feel duty bound to demand larger and larger expenditures in their own constituencies and on behalf of those groups whose cause they champion. A few members ferret out notable, but minor items of ministerial extravagance, together with the salaries of the top public servants at Ottawa, but this is merely exploitation of the prevalent mythology. The House would mislead itself badly if it were to adopt supply procedures that depended for their efficacy on a keen desire by the private members to cut expenditure. The only guards against wasteful grants of supply for which any claim of efficiency can be made outside the departments themselves are the Treasury Board and the minister of finance.

What is more, the retention of the old paradigm has kept the House from seeing its modern duty. While feigning a watch for rabbits, it lets the big game stalk by. The spending estimates are important nowadays, not because of the wharves and runways to be built, or the salaries to be paid, but because of the impact of government spending on the nation's economy. Because of the old assumption that the members are eager to prune them the estimates are examined department by department, and vote by vote. But no provision has been made for the discovery and the evaluation of the government's general economic and social strategy for the current year and for future years; indeed, it may be that while some ministers and mandarins are concerned to formulate such a strategy—witness the adoption of planning, programming, and budgeting techniques—the government as a whole does not feel strongly the need to clarify its long-term goals, and for the most part is content to drive the stretch of road seen immediately ahead.

At this point we must bring in taxation, the other instrument of fiscal policy. The old view that taxing and spending are quite distinct processes, related only by the need to assure that the tax yields will be high enough to cover the expenditures should be abandoned. Both are faces of that Janus-figure, fiscal policy; consequently, they should not be dealt with separately. I submit two points. First, while the budget debate may be a healthy exercise in partisanship—with the minister of finance announcing modestly that it is "a pretty good budget, a realistic budget," while the leader of the opposition invariably is "disappointed," and the third-party leaders are "bitterly disappointed"—and as such should be retained, the budget statement and the annual economic review should be subjected to a far more painstaking examination by the members. Second, the estimates as a whole—the balance among the major programs such as defence and welfare, the long-term projections of costs, and the implications of the proposed expenditures for the economy—should be carefully studied. The approach still followed comes from an era when men relied mainly on "the invisible hand" to create the best possible world. Now that the government of Canada has undertaken to participate extensively in the providence of the future, the House of Commons has a right to know whether or not the governors know what they are up to, and if so, what they are up to.

A major standing committee on economic policy would appear to be the best remedy. The Standing Committee on Finance, Trade and Economic Affairs has done outstanding work, but it has not had a continuing commission from the House to examine the government's economic and social policy. The ministers and their officials have not appeared before the committee to explain the implications of either the budget statement or the estimates. Moreover, it has been overburdened with short-order tasks. Perhaps the easiest way to introduce the new committee would be simply to refer the budget statement, the economic review, and the annual estimates to the Standing Committee on Finance, Trade, and Economic Affairs for the consideration of the policy implicit in them, without prejudice to the right of the House to proceed with the tax changes proposed by the minister of finance and the appropriation of the money sought in the estimates. In this way the committee could carry on its work on a long-term basis without becoming involved in short-term questions. A new committee would be required to deal with much of the work now sent to the Standing Committee on Finance,

Trade and Economic Affairs. There is no reason why the estimates of the several departments should not be referred to standing committees as at present. This procedure affords new members a valuable opportunity to gain an understanding of the work of the departments.

Let us now turn to the treatment of supply business in the House. Under the 1968 rules the opposition has at its disposal five days in the fall, seven days before the end of March, and thirteen days before the end of June. On each of those days it may move any motion that it wants to have debated. On two of the days in each period the debate ends with a vote, i.e., there are opportunities for six no-confidence motions. This arrangement has not been a complete failure. Neither has it been a complete success. Although there have been some very good debates, debates of a kind that rarely occurred under the old rules, most supply debates have sagged badly. Moreover, the opposition, as we have noted, has felt that the ministers have been shielded against effective attack. The first of these shortcomings in large part results from the fact that it is unreasonable to expect the opposition to find twenty-five good topics for debates each year. The second shortcoming is largely the result of the fact that on supply days the members sit, not as a committee of the whole House, but as the House. Undoubtedly, the opposition ought to have opportunities to demonstrate to the public the bungling and arrogance of some departments, and the malfeasance, incompetence, and churlishness of some ministers; and this they cannot do nearly as effectively in the House as in a committee of the whole House. In the House each member may speak only once, so once the member leading an attack has spoken and the minister has replied the tension drops, especially if a third-party spokesman intervenes with a long diverting speech. In a committee of the whole House, the member leading an attack may speak repeatedly, returning to a point again and again, and the minister may rise, or be taunted to rise, again and again to answer questions or to reply.

Under the experimental provisions adopted on 24 March 1975, and continued in the second session of the 30th Parliament by order made on 12 December 1975, the opposition may have items in the estimates withdrawn from the standing committees and send to a committee of the whole House for consideration on supply days. At the end of each supply day used in this way—or at the end of the second or third day if more than one day is given over to a department—the committee votes on any opposition motion to reduce the item (or items) and, if such a motion has been defeated, on the item (or items) itself. Moreover, under the new provisions the six days used for debating opposition motions in the House no longer need be used for no-confidence motions. This means that if the opposition puts down a motion which either with or without amendment is acceptable to the government, the ministers may vote for the motion, as did the Pearson government in 1963. The general result of the new provisions is that the twenty-five supply days are to be used as follows: (a) six days are to be used for debates on opposition motions with the question put; (b) up to nineteen days may be used by the opposition for the consideration of estimates in a committee of the whole House with the government free to decide whether a decision to reduce an item entails no-confidence; and (c) any remaining days are to be used for debates on opposition motions without the question put. This new arrangement seems likely to satisfy all reasonable complaints. It will not please those who yearn for the restoration of unlimited time in the Committee of Supply. The new provision assures that those ministers who are singled out for grilling have reason to take seriously the defence of their estimates. To assure that the ministers are present the notice time for supply days might be extended to forty-eight hours.

PRIVATE MEMBERS' HOUR

Four hours a week—one hour midway through the sitting on Monday, Tuesday, and Thursday, and one hour at the end of the sitting of Friday—are given over to private members' business. However, that business is of only very limited significance. As we have seen, almost all the business formerly dealt with by private bills has been directed into other channels. Private members' bills pass very rarely—only fourteen in the thirty-year period, 1944-74, excluding bills to change constituency names. Private members' motions carry even more rarely. And when the government has a majority the outcome of a vote on a motion for the production of papers is predictable.

It has been argued that the importance of private members' hour ought to be revived.[5] That argument springs largely from the view that the private members are important, not from the view that private members' business is important. Unless private members' business is inherently important it never will serve to enhance the standing of private members, no matter how desirable that may be as a goal. There is no convincing evidence that private members' business is important in the sense that their bills ought to be passed and their motions ought to be carried.

Most of the private members' bills and motions debated in the past ten or fifteen years have been put forward by members of opposition parties, especially the New Democratic Party, but the government party regularly has provided the greatest number of members in attendance. The quorum of the House is nineteen members and the speaker. If when the speaker is asked to count the members he finds fewer than the quorum, he is required by the standing orders to adjourn the House to the next sitting day. For this reason—to prevent the loss of the balance of the sitting—the government whip undertakes to keep a quorum. The result generally is that opposition orators find themselves addressing a captive audience of backbenchers. The way the rule works was exemplified on 17 December 1974. The main business before the House that day was Bill C-44, to increase the indemnity of the members. During the afternoon Mr. Edward Broadbent, the interim parliamentary leader of the New Democratic Party, spoke against the bill. At five o'clock the House turned to private members' bills. At the top of the list was one put forward by Mr. André Fortin, of the Social Credit Party. (The following day Mr. Fortin described his bill as "of paramount importance to my colleagues and myself.")[6] About halfway through the hour, Mr. Arnold Peters, of the New Democratic Party, objected to the continuation of the sitting on the ground that there was no quorum. A count of the House revealed that only the acting speaker and eighteen other members were present: nine Liberals; five Progressive Conservatives; two New Democratic Party members; and two Social Credit Party members. Accordingly, at 5:35 p.m. the House was adjourned to 2:00 the following day.

For a period during the 1960s—from 11 June 1965 until 23 April 1968—the time available for government business was increased by having the private members' hour begin at six instead of five o'clock. However, the government whip soon learned that he and the same small group of Liberals regularly had to keep a House while other members dined, and to do so while opposition members made speeches! That arrangement was not revived at the beginning of the 1968–69 session. (When the private members' hour was put back to five o'clock in 1968 the hour of sitting was advanced from 2:30 to 2:00 p.m.)

The credibility of the private members' hour as a part of the regular business of a sitting has become very difficult to defend: it simply is not sufficiently productive. Over the years the time reserved for the private members has been reduced again and again as the importance of their business has declined. The argument that the hour has outlived its usefulness would be difficult to refute in the court of public opinion, particularly a court now highly sensitive to the high cost of maintaining the House. Yet there are those who hold that the hour permits private members to put proposals and suggestions before the public, and that it provides the private members with opportunities to speak in the House. Moreover, a few bills do pass. The remedy would seem to be to have private members' hour between six and seven o'clock p.m. on Monday, Tuesday, and Thursday, and to change the standing orders so that if the House is found without a quorum during that period the speaker would adjourn the House, not to the beginning of the next sitting day, but to eight o'clock p.m. that day. No change is needed for Friday.

THE STANDING COMMITTEES

The contention that a strong and active committee system is congressional reveals a dangerously erroneous view of our constitution. The British constitution, after which ours was modelled, has both a legal and a political element. One reason why Britain has remained a monarchy is that the real or working constitution has not been allowed to ossify: ways have been found to accommodate new political realities. The view that the government, composed of ministers and mandarins, makes up its mind, while the House simply reacts, like pitcher and batter in baseball, is inaccurate. As argued in chapter 1, the private members, especially the backbenchers, influence the thinking of the government in various ways. If that be conceded, we have only to ask if it would be beneficial to both the government and the House if provision was made for more effective bilateral influence. What would be entailed would not be that the committees would make more decisions—that indeed would be congressional—but that the governors and the members would meet on the issues of the times, and do so before the governors had decided what they, under the full weight of their responsibility, must recommend to the House.

Sometimes the comment—hardly qualifying as an argument—is made that the standing committees must not be emphasized at the expense of the House. This presupposes that there is a quantum of "importance," so that if its committees wax, the House wanes. Much is said, more implied, about the alchemic power of debate, by which error and folly are transmogrified into truth and wisdom. There is something—a good deal—to be said for such claims. But there is another side. Most "debates" are not debates. They simply are series of speeches, often too long, too complex, and too negligent of what others have said. Two or three genuine debates a session are the most that one should count on—the longer the sessions, the longer the droughts. This why many members have come to put their hope in the committees. By the time a bill or a substantive motion reaches the floor of the House the decisions already have been made, and about all that remains to be done is to make a stand publicly and to record the decision. To a large extent what happens in the House, as members admit again and again, is "for the record." But in the committees the members meet both the governors and members of the public. Because questions and answers, not speeches, are the mode of discourse, there is a far better chance that minds will engage. The real work of the committees is not to make decisions, but to prepare the governors to make decisions, and to prepare the House to react to those decisions.

A continuing examination of fiscal policy by a standing committee and the extensive use of a "subject-matter" stage after the first reading of bills have been proposed as major new bridges, supplementing those that now exist, between the government and the House. But there are defects in the committee system that must be corrected before it can be entrusted with an even heavier burden.

THE NUMBER OF COMMITTEES

The present committee system was devised so that the legislature would have a committee parallel to each department or group of departments. No attention was given to the question whether the House had enough members to man such a committee system with active participants. The experience of the period since 1968 has shown that about seventy members do the committee work. The cardinal question is how the time and energy of those members can best be used. The present system sub-divides topics into water-tight compartments; for example, the committees on Regional Development, Transport and Communications, and National Resources and Public Works. What would appear desirable is a small number of key committees dealing with inclusive topics such as general economic policy, regional development, manpower and immigration, justice and legal affairs, health and welfare, and external affairs and defence. These committees might wish to establish small sub-committees; for example, the Committee on Regional Development might wish to have a sub-committee on transportation. That their client groups are served best by having committees on Agriculture, Fisheries and Forestry, Indian Affairs and Northern Development, and Veterans Affairs is questionable. Each group's interests are made known to only a few members who basically already are true believers.

QUORUM

Given the unpredictability of the size of the party contingents in the House, the present rule which sets the size of most standing committees at "not more than 20 Members" seems sound, provided that the implication that smaller committees ought to be named when possible is taken seriously. The same cannot be said for the rule, carried down from 1927, that requires the presence of a majority of the members of a standing committee when a decision is to be made. If the purpose of the rule is to prevent the committees from misusing their powers *vis à vis* the public and public servants, the rule ought to be rendered obsolete by relieving the standing committees of powers thought susceptible of dangerous abuse. If the purpose of the rule is to make members dutiful, it should be admitted that it serves mainly to increase the burdens of the more conscientious members. If twenty members are enough—as most members would agree—to constitute the House itself, a body with over 260 members, it is very hard to see why sixteen members should be required for bodies with no independent powers such as the Standing Committee on Agriculture and the Standing Committee on External Affairs and National Defence. A more defensible figure would be one-quarter of the membership.

There are two arguments against high quorums. First, they give power to the lazy, the uninterested, and the uncooperative. Wittingly or unwittingly, simply by absenting themselves, such persons may be able to prevent work from being done. This point takes on added significance in a political context where there may be strong partisan reasons for wishing to prevent decisions from being made. In the 1974–75 session the standard party proportion on the twenty-member committees was eleven Liberals, seven Progressive Conservatives, one from the New Democratic Party, and one from the Social Credit Party. If the opposition parties were represented by only one or two vigilants almost all the Liberals would have to be present for a meeting to be held.

If committee work is a part of the work of the House, those members who do not participate seriously ought not to be protected by a high quorum requirement, which makes other members take up the slack. One predictable result of a lower quorum would be that quite early in the life of a parliament the members would sort themselves out: some would be willing to do committee work, and others would not be willing. Those in each group soon would become known to the party leaders, the media, and the public. (This is not to say that every private member ought to regard committee work as his highest obligation.)

A lower quorum would not relieve the government party of the need to watch the attendance of its own members. As at present, there would be nothing to prevent opposition members from staying away for days, and then suddenly turning out in full force to win votes. This makes desirable, especially when the government has only a thin majority, either (a) a fixed time for votes or (b) a procedure by which members may be added quickly to the committees. The first alternative would be cumbersome. Accordingly, in 1968, rather than have the major part of the reforms then under consideration stymied, the latter alternative was adopted. As we saw in chapter 7, this led to opposition outcries, which were echoed by Liberal opponents to the reforms, that squads of government members were being shuttled from one committee to another. The government whip's defence was that since he had no way of knowing in advance where the opposition would strike on a particular day, he had to use mobile troops to supplement the basic membership. In 1968 the standing committees were envisioned as highly specialized in membership. This ideal, it may be contended, was ignored by those opposition members who failed to attend the meetings regularly and by the government whip who intruded new members merely to win votes. As those who are hostile to the use of the committees insist, there is no easy solution. If the House decides to return to the method by which committee membership was changed before 1968—a motion in the House—it might wish to consider the desirability of a rule that any member who absented himself from a committee would be deemed to have resigned from that committee, and would not be eligible for renomination at that session.

Two ways stand out to reduce conflicts among committee meetings and between the House and the committees. The first is to move business forward to the committees much earlier in the sessions or to have the sessions begin after Christmas and end in the late fall. The fall months have been slack months in the committees; few important bills have come forward, and the only estimates are the fall supplementaries, so that most of the committees' work is on miscellaneous references, e.g., annual reports and White Papers. In contrast, the months of February, March, April, May, and June have been extremely busy. By February a large number of bills have been committed. In March, April, and May the main estimates are before the committees. June is the month when the committees give most time to miscellaneous references, presumably to clear their slates before the summer. Table 17 shows the activity in the committees by months during the 1969–70 session.[7] As mentioned above, one of the chief advantages of having the exploratory or familiarization stage in the standing committees, rather than in the House, would be that the committees could begin work on the legislative program at the very beginning of the session.

The second way to reduce congestion is to lengthen the committee week. In 1969–70, for example, about 83 percent of the 851 meetings took place on Tuesdays and Thursdays, and about $7\frac{1}{2}$ percent on Mondays and Fridays. There were 38 meetings on Mondays; 376 on Tuesdays; 84 on Wednesdays; 330 on Thursdays; 22 on Fridays; and one on a Saturday. Of the Monday meetings, 23 were held by the Standing Committee on Finance, Trade and Economic Affairs, which

TABLE 17
Standing Committee Meetings Per Month (1969–70)

	Oct.	Nov.	Dec.	Jan.	Feb.	Mar.
Miscellaneous	3	58	31	43	46	$31\frac{1}{2}$
Bills	0	12	4	3	41	27
Estimates	0	7	4	0	3	$40\frac{1}{2}$
(Total)	3	77	39	46	90	99

	Apr.	May	June	July	Aug.	Sept.	Oct.
Miscellaneous	40	49	108	38	6	26	7
Bills	38	$51\frac{1}{2}$	35	0	0	10	4
Estimates	48	$36\frac{1}{2}$	0	0	0	0	0
(Total)	126	137	143	38	6	36	11

was studying the White Paper on Tax Reform. Now that the parliamentary indemnity has been increased so that as of 8 July 1974, members receive the equivalent of an annual salary of $24,000 with escalation, it seems reasonable that the committee week be a three-day week. Some committees could meet on Mondays, but rarely on Fridays; others could meet on Fridays, but rarely on Mondays.

COMMITTEE POWERS

In chapter 7 we saw that some of the procedural problems related to the standing committees derive from the multifunctional nature of the committees. Basically the committees are investigative in character, but various quite different roles have been given to them, one role on top of another. One approach to a solution would be to replace most of the existing committees by three different sets of committees—one for bills, one for estimates, and one for miscellaneous references—and to give each set the powers appropriate to its particular kind of task. The alternative is to continue the present committee system, but to specify the powers of a committee considering a public bill, the powers of a committee examining estimates, and the powers of a committee studying a subject-matter reference. The second of these approaches seems the better. The Canadian House of Commons is far too small to sustain two or three different standing committee systems.

The power to send for persons, papers, and records now is conferred on all the standing committees indiscriminately. That power is the power of what in Britain would be called a "select" committee. It is the power to summon witnesses and to require the production of evidence. It is the power that the House might be expected to confer on a special committee appointed to investigate a serious charge or allegation. Yet because all the committees were lumped together, over the years it was conferred on all the committees, including at times even the Committee on the Restaurant, regardless of their work. The only standing committees to which it is appropriate are the Committee on Privileges and Elections and the Committee on Public Accounts. It should not be conferred on standing committees which, strictly speaking, are not intended to conduct, and which in fact do not conduct, investigations. (The power is not used: ministers attend because of political reasons—because they need the cooperation of the House—not because they are afraid of the committees' power to subpoena them, and public servants attend on the instruction of their ministers.) The practical effect of removing this power would be to make obvious the need to confer other powers on the committees, powers appropriate to the various kinds of work assigned to them. Undoubtedly, the committees would wish to hear explanations and representations from ministers, public servants, and members of the public when studying—studying, as distinct from investigating—annual reports, Green Papers, etc. Presumably, the House would wish to authorize them to continue to hear such persons—"witnesses" is the term appropriate for those testifying before an investigating committee—as make themselves available when invited. The desirability of hearing explanations of the clauses of bills from ministers and public servants is obvious; but the present practice of hearing representations against bills at the committee stage is highly questionable, for only the text of a bill, not its purposes, is committed after second reading. In the case of estimates it would seem desirable to limit the committees to explanations from the government.

REPORTS AND CONCURRENCE

When the House sends a bill to a committee the form of its report is known: it sends back the text of the bill with or without amendments, and without a commentary. Similarly, a committee sends back a set of estimates, with or without having reduced the amounts, with no change in the purposes for which the Crown requested money, and with or without a commentary. But what should be the form of the report submitted by a committee to which a Green Paper, for example, has been referred for study? Standing Order 65 simply empowers the committees to report from time to time. It is not unusual for a committee to prepare and submit a long dissertation, sometimes with and sometimes without specific recommendations. Two questions have arisen in the House. Are minority reports in order? Who should move concurrence in committee reports? The House, as we saw in chapter 2, states its will in the form of orders, and its opinion in the form of resolutions. It is difficult to see what the nature and status of a long descriptive and argumentative report can be after concurrence. The point is not that such reports ought not to be presented—they may be very informative—but that the House ought never to be asked to concur in them. Concurrence in a report should be in order only when a committee, pursuant to an order of the House, has made a report setting forth, without commentary, either a proposed order or a proposed resolution. This would not prevent a committee from providing a commentary in another report, but concurrence in the commentary would not be moved.

At present, since formally each committee is conducting an investigation, its report is its "findings." It is the committee, not the members of the committee severally, who have been given the investigative reference by the House; accordingly, there can be only one finding or set of findings, that of the (majority of the) committee. By expunging from the committees the investigative character now conferred upon them, as proposed above, and by eliminating the possibility that someone will move that the House concur in reports which are not "findings," but instead descriptive or argumentative essays, the problem of minority reports would be eliminated. In drawing up a report a committee well might decide to mention views which had not found favour with the committee.

The view that only its chairman or some other one of its members authorized by a committee ought to move concurrence—when in order—is impossible to defend. A committee is authorized by the House to make up its mind on the matter referred to it and to report to the House. No authority is conferred to move concurrence, which is a House proceeding, not a committee proceeding. There are certain practical reasons why the chairman may be the best person to lead off in a concurrence debate; but the report, once presented, belongs to the House, not to the committee. The present arrangement, under which any member may move concurrence, but the debate may be adjourned, seems the most satisfactory of all the possibilities. The best protection against the danger that too much time will be taken up by debates on concurrence motions is care that committees are not instructed to report proposed orders and proposed resolutions on matters on which the House is not prepared to spend its time.

III

Much of the resilience of a constitution embodying Responsible Government derives from the fact that the relationship between the House and the government is based on confidence. The government has no independent political status of its own: it is not elected separately, and it has no fixed term. It depends for survival, not on its legal rights, but on the support and cooperation of the House. Because the relationship is one of attitude, not counter-balanced rights, the constitution is highly flexible. It can adjust to the work of new times without either formal or judicial amendment. We have seen something of how this has happened in Canada since 1867.

But this does not mean that the House of Commons (or on the other side, the government) automatically changes its forms and procedures to suit changes in the constitutional relationship. The House follows the thrifty practice of handling much of the new wine in old bottles. At times, however, old forms and procedures, devised to accommodate the needs of their day, become obsolete. Instead of facilitating achievement, they misdirect, impede, and waste the efforts of workers. At such times to preserve and revitalize the basic institution its forms and procedures should be appraised and reformed. Although old, they are not sacred. What is of prime importance is the successful performance of the institution's functions.

Over the years Canadian parliamentarians were loath to make an examination of their forms and procedures. They hid indifference, perhaps even laziness, behind a screen of adoration for a British model long after the British themselves, out of concern for the genius of the system, had reformed the model radically. In recent years members in all the parties have shown a new realism, as the changes made since 1963 evince. Yet there still may be a lesson for us in Francis Bacon's admonition against obstinate traditionalism: "He that will not apply new remedies must expect new evils, for Time is the greatest Innovator."

Notes

ONE

1. See Sir Courtenay Ilbert and Sir Cecil Carr, *Parliament: Its History, Constitution, and Practice*; 3rd ed. (London: Oxford University Press, 1948), pp. 11–14.
2. See C. H. McIlwain, *The American Revolution: A Constitutional Interpretation* (Ithaca: Cornell University Press, 1958).
3. Professor Bernard Bailyn has shown that the writings of the English critics of the rise of the prime ministership and the cabinet were received warmly by discontented colonists throughout the two or three generations before 1776 and constituted an important source of the revolutionary ideology. See his *The Ideological Origins of the American Revolution* (Cambridge: Harvard University Press, 1967), pp. 22–54. The term "corruption" was used by the "Country" critics of strong "Court" leadership to denote all the means by which the ministers, especially the "prime" minister, exerted political influence at elections and in the Houses of Parliament. It had a far wider meaning than its twin, "bribery." See J. G. A. Pocock, "Machiavelli, Harrington and English Political Ideologies in the Eighteenth Century" in his *Politics, Language and Time* (London: Methuen & Co. Ltd., 1972), pp. 124–33.
4. The royal assent to a bill has not been refused at Westminster since Queen Anne turned down the Scotch Militia Bill in 1707.
5. Maitland's advice on the term, "the Crown," is worth remembering. "I do not deny that it is a convenient term," he wrote, "and you may have to use it; but I do say that you should never be content with it. If you are told that the crown has this power or that power, do not be content until you know who legally has the power—is it the king, is it one of his secretaries: is this power a prerogative power or is it the outcome of statute?" F. W. Maitland, *The Constitutional History of England* (Cambridge: The University Press, 1955), p. 418.
6. Frequently after an election in which a provincial or national government has been successful in retaining a majority the newsmen refer to the forthcoming formation of a "new government" or a "new cabinet." This presupposes that the old cabinet was a committee of the former House. Actually, in such an instance the pre-election cabinet simply continues in office, perhaps with some changes in its membership. The election of 8 July 1974, was Canada's thirtieth general election, but Canada has had only twenty governments or cabinets since 1867.
7. Professor M. J. C. Vile has examined the history of the terms. As he shows, Locke was only a prominent peak in a long range of discussion in England. See his *Constitutionalism and the Separation of Powers* (Oxford: Clarendon Press, 1967), pp. 53–75.
8. Locke's clearest and longest statement on the need to separate the

legislative branch and the executive branch is to be found in para. 143. Later in para. 159, he takes it as obvious that those two powers are in distinct hands "... in all moderated Monarchies, and well-framed Governments...." *Two Treatises of Government*, ed. Peter Laslett (Cambridge: The University Press, 1967), pp. 382, 392.

9. See *The Spirit of the Laws* (New York: Hafner Publishing Company, 1949), p. 152. See also Vile, *Constitutionalism and the Separation of Powers*, pp. 85-88.

10. Walter Bagehot, writing in the 1860s, was eager to refute "the traditional theory as it exists in all the books, [that] the goodness of our constitution" springs from the separation of the legislative, the executive, and the judicial powers. See *The English Constitution* (London: Oxford University Press, 1949) pp. 2, 9. Yet he himself adopted the analysis of governance on which that theory is based. For example, he describes the cabinet as, "The committee which unites the law-making power to the law-executing power...." p. 12.

11. It is on this basis that Sir Kenneth Wheare justifies the use of the term. "Yet, when all this has been said, it remains justifiable," he writes, "to speak of parliaments and congresses and the like as legislatures. And the justification, shortly stated, is that these bodies are, if not actually, at least potentially superior to other law-making bodies." *Legislatures*; 2nd ed. (London: Oxford University Press, 1968), p. 2.

12. It should be remembered that the governor general of Canada is not simply a lieutenant for the queen of Canada. He does not simply "fill in" in her absence. The two offices are legally distinct. See J. R. Mallory, *The Structure of Canadian Government* (Toronto: Macmillan of Canada, 1971), pp. 35-38.

13. *In re George Edwin Gray* [1918] LVII S.C.C. 150

14. *The Queen* and *Joseph Drybones* [1970] S.C.R. 282

15. The House has just as much reason to be concerned about the activities of the judges, as a cursory review of the history of England during the seventeenth century will reveal. For them the strategy has been to provide internal controls by appeals. If ultimately the law of the judges is unacceptable to Parliament, that law can be changed by statute. In addition, a procedure has been provided by which to deal with individual judges whose conduct is found intolerable: their removal from office can be effected by a joint address of the Senate and the House of Commons.

16. Two misleading usages of the term "Responsible Government" are common. First, the term sometimes is used with a qualitative rather than an institutional meaning. It may be that a government will act responsibly because it is responsible to the House of Commons, but that it will do so invariably is not implied, and ought not to be assumed. Second, the term often is used as if it meant that the government is institutionally responsible to the electorate. Undoubtedly ministers often worry about what the voters are thinking; however, there is no constitutional way in which the voters can precipitate the defeat of a government other than by electing members who will oppose it in the House. My conclusion is that the term, "Responsible Government," should be used with a narrow meaning. In Canada it should

be used to refer to the relationship between the government and the House of Commons.

17. To protect the members from "Court" influence, it is provided in the Senate and House of Commons Act that no person who holds an office of profit under the Crown, no person who has a contract with the Crown, and no sheriff, etc. may be a member of the House. Ministers are exempt from this prohibition, as are parliamentary secretaries up to a certain number. Since 1970 the Canada Elections Act provides that a candidate with the written consent of the leader of a party may have the name of that party printed with his own name on the ballot paper. However, inability to obtain the consent of a party leader does not mean that a person otherwise eligible cannot be a candidate, as was demonstrated by Mr. Leonard Jones in the Moncton constituency in 1974. Moreover, neither that act nor any other imposes a legal obligation on a member to act as a loyal member of the party for which he ran as a candidate.

18. I do not contend that my use of "backbenchers" is the only proper way to use the term; but it is the use that enables me to state my argument most easily. In addition, the reader should notice that I have used the term, "the opposition," to refer to all the members who, unlike the backbenchers, oppose the government, and that I have used the term, "the official opposition," to refer to the leader of the opposition and those who follow his lead for party reasons.

19. One of the reasons why opposition parties are reluctant to agree to time limits on debates is that once a time limit has been set the backbenchers feel free to participate. They then know, first, that they are not delaying the measure, and, second, that the time they use is lost to the opposition.

20. A member's views on the role of the opposition may have a decisive influence on his conduct in the House and on his attitude to procedural changes. At least three notable members gave addresses on the role of the opposition that are relevant to the period discussed in this book: John G. Diefenbaker, "The Role of the Opposition in Parliament" (Empire Club of Canada, Toronto, 27 October 1949); Stanley H. Knowles, "The Role of the Opposition in Parliament" (Empire Club of Canada, Toronto, 31 March 1957); and Lester B. Pearson, "The Role of the Opposition" (Canadian Club, Ottawa, 27 January 1959). The Knowles address was published as a pamphlet by the Ontario Woodsworth Memorial Foundation, Toronto: 1957.

21. No reader interested in the nature of parliamentary legislative activity in the century before 1832 and in the change in the governance of Britain which took place in the nineteenth century should fail to study J. A. G. Griffith's article, "The Place of Parliament in the Legislative Process" in *The Modern Law Review* 14 (1951) 279–96, 425–36, and S. A. Walkland, *The Legislative Process in Great Britain* (London: George Allen and Unwin Ltd., 1968). See also Ilbert and Carr, *Parliament*, pp. 36–37.

22. Quoted by Bailyn, *The Ideological Origins of the American Revolution*, p. 50. The prevalence in the eighteenth century of the myth of an ancient (or Gothic) constitution in which "the legislature" was free from the control of "the executive," so that one balanced the other, has been shown by Pocock

in "Machiavelli, Harrington and English Political Ideologies in the Eighteenth Century." In his book, *The Ancient Constitution and the Feudal Law* (Cambridge: The University Press, 1957) Professor Pocock showed how the myth of the ancient constitution arose during the conflicts of the seventeenth century.

23. Lord Melbourne resigned in 1839 after what he regarded as an unsatisfactory vote in the House of Commons, but when Queen Victoria refused to give up even some of her Whig ladies the Tory leader of the opposition, Sir Robert Peel, refused to take office. Melbourne then returned. In 1841 the Whigs were defeated in a general election. By then the queen's understanding of the constitutional situation had changed, and Peel found her quite willing to agree that the offices of the royal household were not beyond the fortunes of political warfare. With this point established, Peel assumed office. This event, the acceptance by the queen of the need to follow the electorate even in the choice of her household, marked the acceptance of the principles of democratic government according to Sir Ivor Jennings. See his *Cabinet Government* (Cambridge: The University Press, 1947), p. 9. Professor Norman Gash describes the election of 1841 as "... the first modern general election that the country had experienced. For the first time in British history a party in office enjoying a majority in the Commons had been defeated by an opposition previously in a minority." *Sir Robert Peel* (London: Longman, 1972), p. 265.

24. The rule that a member who became a minister lost his seat and could redeem himself only by winning a by-election was adopted in Canada, but only because that was the British rule. In 1926 the rule was the cause of great embarrassment to Arthur Meighen. Subsequently, in 1931, a private member's bill to abolish the old rule became law. The rule had been abolished in the United Kingdom in 1926.

25. *The Report of the Earl of Durham* (London: Methuen & Co., 1902), p. 63.

26. See the detailed analysis of political behaviour during the period in Paul G. Cornell, *The Alignment of Political Groups in Canada, 1841–1867*. (Toronto: University of Toronto Press, 1962).

27. Much of this business was done in the Standing Committee on Banking and Commerce and the Standing Committee on Railways, Canals and Telegraph Lines. No record of the considerations of those committees is available.

28. The Westminster figures are misleading because some of the bills are provided by the government whips to members who have won a top place in the ballot by which priority to introduce private members' bills is determined. According to the minister of housing in Mr. Wilson's government, in 1966 Mr. Duncan Sandys, a Tory who had won first place in the ballot, asked him for "a nice Bill about keeping the countryside clean." On 20 May 1966, the minister was able to tell Mr. Sandys "that the Cabinet Committee had given its consent to the main outlines of his bill." See Richard Crossman, *The Diaries of a Cabinet Minister* (London: Hamish Hamilton and Jonathan Cape, 1975), I, pp. 520–21, 525, 531. But at the very least it can be said that at Westminster deference is paid to the fiction that private members can

initiate changes in the general law. The number of private members' bills enacted at Ottawa in each session since 1867 is shown in Table 10.

29. According to Senator Eugene Forsey nine of the defeats suffered by Sir John A. Macdonald's first ministry cannot be dismissed as trivial. See his "Government Defeats in the Canadian House of Commons, 1867–73" in *Freedom and Order* (Toronto: McClelland and Stewart Limited, 1974), pp. 123–28.

30. Thomas A. Hockin, "Adversary Politics and Some Functions of the Canadian House of Commons," in *The Canadian Political Process*, ed. Orest M. Kruhlak, Richard Schultz, and S. I. Pobihushchy (Toronto: Holt, Rinehart and Winston of Canada, Limited, 1973) pp. 361–64.

31. The terms "party discipline" and "disciplined party" are somewhat deceptive, especially when applied to parties in the Canadian House of Commons. They imply that the private members are prone to rebel, and that party unity is maintained to a large extent by various kinds of rewards and punishments meted out by the whips and the other party managers. At Ottawa the members show much less independence than at Westminster. Most of them understand that they were elected to support their party; as a result, party loyalty tends to be strong. In Britain, where revolts are far more common, rewards and punishments are applied quite systematically; yet even there, as Professor Robert J. Jackson has demonstrated, party loyalty is far more important than discipline. See his *Rebels and Whips* (London: Macmillan and Co., Ltd., 1968).

TWO

1. The British North America Act fixes the quorum of the House, prescribes that questions are to be decided by simple majority votes, prohibits the speaker from voting except in the case of a tie, makes English and French equal languages for all the purposes of the House, and denies to the House the right to vote on any question relating to the appropriation of public money not recommended by the governor general in the current session.

The "privileges, immunities, and powers" of the members, both individually and collectively, according to the British North America Act, s. 18, as amended in 1875, are to be defined by Act of the Canadian Parliament; but those privileges, etc. are not to exceed those of the British House of Commons at the time of the enactment of the Canadian statute conferring those privileges, etc. The relevant Canadian statute—the one based on s. 18 of the British North America Act—is the Senate and House of Commons Act. An argument can be made that the House is the master of its own proceedings only within the limits set by s. 18; but those limits are now very wide, and in any case since 1949 the British North America Act, s. 18, can be changed by an Act of the Parliament of Canada. See W. F. Dawson, *Procedure in the Canadian House of Commons* (Toronto: University of Toronto Press, 1962), p. 32.

2. Before 1910 the House heard petitions from the public. These were brought up and laid on the Table by a member. If upon examination they

were found to be in good order, they were read to the House. In this way the House permitted itself to be instructed, informed, and importuned by "strangers." Many of the petitions were part of "prayer campaigns." In the 1870s, for example, there were scores of petitions "severally praying for the passing of a Prohibitory Liquor Law." In 1905 a prayer campaign was conducted for the enactment of a law to prevent telephone companies from erecting poles along municipal streets and roads without the consent of the local municipal councils. Then in 1910 the House changed its rules so that thereafter although petitions could be tabled by members, ordinarily they would not be read. Thus the House asserted its right to stop intrusions. Afterwards petitions went out of style. From the beginning of World War I until 1975 there have been only four great campaigns to influence the House by petitions: in 1917 and 1919 for prohibition, in 1917 against conscription, and in 1926–27 for the transfer of natural resources to the western provinces. At the thirteen sessions beginning with 1960–61 only twenty-one public petitions were presented: one in 1962; one in 1963; one in 1964–65; three in 1965; two in 1969–70; two in 1970–72; five in 1972; five in 1973–74; and one in 1974. Public petitions now are segregated from petitions for private acts in the *Journals*.

3. On 5 November 1974, Mr. Speaker Jerome ruled that parliamentary secretaries, too, may not ask oral questions. *Debates*, p. 1060.

4. Sir Robert Borden's motion began: "That in the opinion of this House, it is expedient that regulations respecting Military Service shall be made and enacted by the Governor in Council in manner and form and in the words and figures following, that is to say...." The text of the proposed order was then set forth in the motion. *Debates*, 19 April 1918, p. 933.

5. *Debates*, 5 June 1964, p. 4010.

6. *Debates*, 14 December 1964, p. 11138.

7. P. D. G. Thomas, *The House of Commons in the Eighteenth Century* (Oxford: Clarendon Press, 1971), pp. 178–82.

8. The form, "That the question be now put," now is used at Westminster for an entirely different purpose, namely, to bring on closure. At Westminster that motion is not debatable. If it carries the question before the House is put immediately. See Dawson, *Procedure in the Canadian House of Commons*, pp. 119–20.

9. According to Sir Robert Borden, "As was anticipated, Sir Wilfrid became violently enraged and his rage was shared by all his followers who made loud demonstrations." *Robert Laird Borden: His Memoirs* (Toronto: McClelland and Stewart Limited, 1969), I, 196. The following day the Hon. Arthur Meighen explained candidly to the House why the government had moved the previous question. *Debates*, 10 April 1913, c. 7521.

10. Before 20 December 1968, a notice could not be given on a day when the House was not sitting. This meant that if some emergency requiring legislation sprang up during an adjournment, the responsible minister could not give notice of his motion for leave to introduce a bill until the first day the House sat, which, in turn, meant that the House might not even see his bill until the forty-eight hours notice period had elapsed. In 1968 provision

was made by Standing Order 42(2) for a notice to be circulated by the speaker prior to the first sitting of a session or the first sitting after an adjournment. This new rule first was used in 1971 when after the summer adjournment the government wished to put before the House at the earliest moment a bill to counteract the effect on the Canadian economy of President Nixon's surtax on imports. The House met on 7 September 1971. Since notice already had been given, the government was able to introduce its bill at once. Then the House gave leave for the second-reading motion to be moved later that same day. *Debates*, pp. 7545, 7547.

11. The standing orders provide that if all the orders in one category are finished the House is to go on to the next category, and then the next. On Tuesdays for example, Government Orders are first, then Public Bills, then Private Bills, and then Notices of Motions. Although it is logically possible that the House would go through all the items on the various lists at a single sitting, this is most unlikely. For this reason the full Order Paper, showing all the items in all the categories, is printed only once a week, on Monday.

12. Sometimes new members do not understand the significance of the expression, "by leave." For example, on 13 March 1964, Prime Minister Pearson, wishing to gain support by a joint resolution for the dispatch of a Canadian peace-keeping force to Cyprus, without notice said, "By leave, I wish to move,.: 'That it be resolved by the [Senate and] House of Commons: That it is expedient that the Houses of Parliament do approve the participation of Canadian forces in the United Nations international force in Cyprus, and that this house do approve the same.'" After Mr. Pearson had begun to speak one of the Créditiste members raised an objection to the moving of the motion without forty-eight hours notice. However, the deputy speaker ruled that the objection had come too late; it ought to have been voiced at the words, "By leave." *Debates*, 13 March 1964, pp. 910–11.

13. Frequently at Westminster the adjournment is moved by a minister with the agreement of the opposition to enable the House to debate some matter which needs to be aired, but on which it would be difficult to frame a question. The Canadian rules do not provide for such adjournment motions. Aside from "the late show," adjournment motions are not debatable unless moved under S.O. 26. In 1967 the government house leader, the Hon. A. J. MacEachen, made a move towards the British practice. On 20 December 1967, he moved for a special order under which the House would sit between 10:00 a.m. and 1:00 p.m. on Thursday, 21 December at which time "housing" would be debated on a motion, "That the House do now adjourn." The order was made, and the debate took place. Again in 1971 he asked for a special order to permit a debate on an adjournment motion with the condition of the economy as the topic. The debate, on 14 October 1971, lasted from 8:00 p.m. until 2:45 a.m.

14. Occasionally members refer to Standing Order 5, usually to call attention to the absence of a minister; however, according to Mr. Speaker Lamoureux's information the last occasion when the rule was enforced was in 1875. *Debates*, 16 June 1970, p. 8153. See Dawson, *Procedure in the Canadian House of Commons*, pp. 89–90.

15. One member, Mr. Stanley Knowles, regularly introduces a bill—viz. C-257 in the 1974–76 session—to increase the quorum from twenty to fifty. The obvious effect of such a change would be to make the task of the government whip far more difficult without increasing the burden of the opposition parties.

16. The argument has been made that the standing orders of the House ought to be entrenched. On 13 April 1970, Mr. T. S. Barnett, with the rules changes of 1913 and 1969 in mind, moved to provide that, "The Standing Orders shall be amended only by the affirmative votes of at least three quarters of the Members of the House of Commons." His colleague, Mr. Stanley Knowles, felt that the motion did not go far enough. He contended that the standing orders should be amended only by "consensus among the members of all parties in the House." Mr. Barnett's motion did not come to a vote. *Debates*, pp. 5797–806.

17. Lord Campion, *An Introduction to the Procedure of the House of Commons* (London: Macmillan & Co. Ltd., 1958), p. 185. See also *Debates*, 15 April 1920, p. 1265 and 26 March 1928, p. 1681.

18. It often happens that orders for the production of papers will not have been satisfied before the end of the session, but the government treats them as still valid, and returns are made to the office of the clerk even although the House is not in session. Neither the clerk nor the sergeant at arms is appointed by the House, so both can perform inter-sessional duties.

19. For example, during the 1969–70 session the bill to establish the Federal Court of Canada, supplanting the Exchequer Court, had been reported by the Standing Committee on Justice and Legal Affairs before the end of the session. On 21 October 1970, in the next session, the House ordered that the bill was to be deemed "to have been introduced, read a first time, ordered to be printed, read a second time, referred to and reported by a Standing Committee, and that the said bill [together with the amendments of which notice had been given at the previous session] be ordered to stand on the Order Paper for consideration by the House at the report stage on or after October 28, 1970; ... " *Journals*, p. 46.

20. This was done when the Special Joint Committee on the Constitution was appointed in the fall of 1970 to resume the work of its predecessor. *Journals,* 15 October 1970, pp. 23–24.

THREE

1. The House meets at 11:00 a.m. on days when the debate on the motion for an Address in Reply to the Speech from the Throne is in progress. The two notable exceptions to the ordinary hour of daily adjournment are (a) when the closure rule, Standing Order 33, has been invoked, and (b) when a motion to adjourn moved under Standing Order 26 is being debated at length. S.O. 33 provides that after one o'clock a.m. no member is to rise to speak in a debate that is being closed, i.e., the vote takes place as soon as the member who had the floor at one o'clock had finished his speech, which is limited to twenty minutes. S.O. 26 permits the sitting to continue until the

speaker is satisfied that the debate had been concluded. If during a sitting the session is ended by prorogation or if the Parliament is dissolved, there is no adjournment.

2. Originally the rule read: "A motion may be made by unanimous consent of the House, without previous notice." The requirement for an explanation was added in 1927. In its report the Special Committee (1926–27) to revise the rules commented: "The unanimous consent of the House is usually granted with such readiness and so little opposition that in many cases motions are passed before the House has had time to understand them. Members are asked to waive notice and rules are suspended without the members realizing that some questions in which they may be keenly interested are being considered. A satisfactory explanation should be given by the member who wishes to secure the unanimous consent of the House." *Journals*, 22 March 1927, p. 334.

3. See the detailed analysis of the meaning of this principle given by Mr. Speaker Jerome on 14 April 1975. *Debates*, pp. 4762–64.

4. See the debate on 11 October 1968. *Debates*, pp. 1095–1113.

5. The new procedure was explained to the members by Mr. Speaker Jerome on 18 April 1975. *Debates*, pp. 4990–91.

6. Both ministers and private members introduce public bills and give notices of motions. Those public bills initiated by ministers are called "government bills," and the notices of motions given by ministers are called "government notices of motions." This usage leaves the basic terms, "public bills" and "notices of motions" to be used—somewhat deceptively—for private members' public bills and private members' notices of motions.

Ministers never sponsor private bills, so the term "private bill" always refers to a private bill sponsored by a private member. Similarly, since ministers never move for the production of papers, the term "notices of motions for the production of papers" always refers to notices given by private members.

7. Sometimes after the explanation has been heard the motion for leave to introduce a bill is opposed. On 22 February 1932, Mr. J. S. Woodsworth moved for leave to introduce a bill to amend s. 98 of the Criminal Code. Leave was refused. *Debates*, pp. 380–84. On 7 March he tried again with a somewhat different bill; but first reading was refused. *Debates*, pp. 843–46. On 6 April 1964, a motion for leave to introduce a bill to abolish the Senate, moved by Mr. Stanley Knowles, was opposed. The motion carried, 104 Yeas to 54 Nays. On 3 August 1964, Mr. Auguste Choquette sought leave to introduce a bill to replace the name "the Dominion of Canada" with the name "the Federal State of Canada." The speaker was asked to call the Yeas and Nays. The Nays prevailed. On 13 November 1967, Mr. Choquette sought leave to introduce a bill to replace the present oath of allegiance as prescribed by s. 128 of the B.N.A. Act. The oath he proposed was: "I swear to be faithful to the democratic government of my country and to its constitution and to do everything in my power to serve them well and to ensure their progress under law." The Nays prevailed. On 5 December 1967, Mr. Fernand-E. Leblanc sought leave to introduce a bill that would have replaced "the effigy of the Queen which appears on certain Canadian stamps by the stylized

maple leaf which adorns the Canadian flag." The Nays prevailed. On 13 February 1973, Mr. Stuart Leggatt moved for leave to introduce a bill to remove the subject of abortion from the Criminal Code. The House divided on the first-reading motion, which carried 179 Yeas to 56 Nays.

8. This is the regular procedure. It no longer is followed at the beginning of a session when there will be scores of bills to be introduced. On 20 May 1963, the speaker asked the House for permission to assume that all the private members' public bills then waiting had been introduced and read a first time. This method has been followed at the beginning of each session since then, e.g., on 15 January 1973, and on 15 October 1974.

9. *Debates*, pp. 4209–11.

10. A table showing the number of written questions, the number of starred questions, and the number of motions for papers dealt with at each session since 1867 was printed in *Hansard* on 25 September 1968, at pp. 461–62.

11. On 15 March 1973, the government house leader tabled a set of guidelines to be used in dealing with motions for papers. These were referred for study to the Joint Committee on Statutory Instruments; however that committee made no report on them in the 1973–74 session. The same guidelines were tabled again on 19 December 1974, and were again referred to the committee. The guidelines were printed as an appendix to *Hansard* on 15 March 1973, p. 2288.

12. As a result of this change the House may have to come back on a Wednesday evening or to continue late on a Friday. The first time a member was successful under the new S.O. 26—on Wednesday, 22 January 1969—there was some consternation when it was realized that the House would be sitting that evening. *Debates*, pp. 4610–11. The number of times applications have been made and have been successful is shown in Table 13.

13. Special rules of procedure apply to private bills. The House has made standing orders to be followed by those members of the public who wish to have the House pass a private bill. These are published regularly in the *Canada Gazette*. The first step is a petition to the House. If the petition is found sound the petitioner(s) may have a bill presented through the clerk's office. They must find a member to act as "the sponsor" of the bill.

FOUR

1. At Westminster the formula of assent is still the Norman French, "*La reyne le veult.*" The formula for withholding assent—at least when last used, in 1707—is, "*La reyne s'avisera.*"

2. Until it has had the final approval of the House and the Senate the document is only a "proposed bill." If it does not pass the House it never becomes a bill (or request) from the House. However, the distinction between a proposed bill and a bill is awkward to maintain, so the term "bill" almost always is used even when what is referred to is only the very first published draft of a proposed bill.

3. At Ottawa the great reduction in the number of debatable motions took place in 1913. See Borden's comment on the previous situation as quoted

Notes to pages 81–94   301

in chapter 8. Fourteen stages on which debates and divisions are known to have occurred at Westminster during the eighteenth century are listed by P. D. G. Thomas, but he comments that no bill was debated at all the fourteen stages. *The House of Commons in the Eighteenth Century* (Oxford: Clarendon Press, 1971), pp. 63–64.

4.   This chapter deals only with the process used in preparing public bills. Private bills have been dealt with quite differently since the fourteenth century.

5.   *Journals*, 13 March 1968, pp. 763–64.

6.   The rejection of bills duly introduced has gone out of style. May mentions (p. 526) that on one occasion Sir Edward Coke moved successfully that a bill be "torn in the House." On a later occasion a motion to reject a bill carried, whereupon the speaker threw it over the Table, and several members kicked at it. Nowadays offensive bills usually are simply ignored. However, it is worth noting that on 3 December 1970, the House tendered its consent to the president of the Treasury Board to withdraw Bill C-190, respecting the auditor general of Canada, which had turned out to be an embarrassment. Although it had not been sought, the government accepted the consent of the House with some relief. It withdrew Bill C-190, which thereafter no longer was in the possession of the House.

7.   *Beauchesne*, para. 384. This refers to the standard authority on Canadian parliamentary practice. Arthur Beauchesne, *Rules and Forms of the House of Commons of Canada*; 4th ed. (Toronto: The Carswell Company Limited, 1958).

8.   *May*, p. 388. This refers to the standard British authority, Erskine May's *Parliamentary Practice*; 17th ed. (London: Butterworth & Co. (Publishers) Ltd., 1964). All references to *May* are to the 17th edition. A new edition, the 18th, was published, in 1971, and yet another, the 19th, in 1976.

9.   *Beauchesne*, para. 381; also *May*, p. 525.

10.   *May*, p. 571

11.   See the argument made by Mr. Trudeau on 27 February 1968 (*Debates*, p. 7041) and the comments of Mr. MacEachen on 11 March 1968 (*Debates*, p. 7475).

12.   *Debates*, 11 March 1968, p. 7495.

13.   *May*, p. 528.

14.   *Beauchesne*, para. 382.

15.   *Beauchesne*, para. 393.

16.   Over the years relatively few attempts to move reasoned amendments have been successful at Ottawa. The speakers have taken the view—contrary to the explanation given in this chapter—that what is to be decided at the second-reading stage is whether or not the House is for the principle of the bill. Recently the Progressive Conservatives have sought to move a fair number of reasoned amendments, and have contended that they are in order because of an alleged change in the meaning of the second-reading motion brought about by the rules change on 20 December 1968. This is a flimsy foundation, for at that time the House made no change in the meaning of the second-reading motion. See *Debates*, 13 September 1971, pp. 7763–73; and 18 and 19 May 1972, pp. 2412, 2428–34.

The Special Committee on Procedure (1968) presented three main reports, on 6 December 1968. Two of them contained the texts of proposed new standing orders, and were concurred in by the House on 20 December 1968. The third report provided a commentary on the proposed changes. That commentary does suggest that the meaning of the second-reading motion was to be changed; however, the proposed standing orders made no change, and the House never was asked to concur in the commentary. *Journals*, 1968–69, pp. 429–39.

A firmer basis for the amendments offered by the opposition would be an argument that the second-reading motion, because it is an ancillary motion, not a substantive motion, inevitably asks the House more than whether or not it is in favour of the principle of a bill; and that, therefore, a second-reading motion may be opposed for reasons other than opposition to the principle of the bill. The counter-argument then would be that if this view were to prevail even circumstantial considerations, e.g., the lateness of the season, or the weakness of the economy, could be given as a reason in a reasoned amendment, so that the House soon would find itself debating the prevailing political, social, and economic conditions, rather than the purposes of particular bills. But surely those conditions may be very relevant, and ought to be adduceable against a bill. Moreover, the opposition would not be likely to range too far afield in adducing reasons against a bill if the time available for the debate on the second-reading motion were limited as at Westminster.

17. *Beauchesne*, para. 418.

18. The Special Committee on Procedure (1968) seems to have followed the example of a change made in 1958. Previously the motion, "That Bill C-000 be now read a third time," was followed by another motion, "That the Bill do now pass and that the title be. . . ." On the suggestion of Speaker Michener these two motions were combined so that the final ancillary motion now reads, "That Bill C-000 be now read a third time and do pass." See *Journals*, 14 May 1958, p. 26. Since the House for years had treated the decision to read a bill a third time as meaning that the bill was to be allowed to pass, that combination has been entirely satisfactory.

FIVE

1. Formerly the minister of finance tabled a White Paper setting forth data concerning the condition of the economy and the government's finances a few days before he made his budget statement. On 25 April 1972, the minister tabled an "Economic Review." He said that in the future this review would be issued regularly and not necessarily at the time of the budget presentation. *Debates*, 25 April 1972, p. 1596.

2. Both the Progressive Conservatives and the New Democratic Party had given notice of their intention to seek leave to move the adjournment under S.O. 26. However, the government house leader proposed that the minister of finance should initiate a debate on the state of the economy by moving that the House adjourn; and a special order was made to permit him to make that motion as a debatable motion. Normally an adjournment motion, unless

moved under S.O. 26, is not debatable. *Debates*, 14 October 1971, pp. 8659, 8688.
3. *Debates*, 20 March 1972, pp. 963–64.
4. It is interesting to note that in the early years after 1867 the budget statement was made in the Committee of Ways and Means. In 1892 it was made on the motion to go into the Committee of Supply. *Debates*, 22 March 1892, p. 315. The requirement that a tax bill be based on the ways and means resolution restricts the government somewhat. It cannot make changes freely in a tax bill after the bill has been introduced. *Debates*, 18 December 1974, pp. 2380–81; and *Debates*, 14 July 1975, pp. 7549–50.
5. Notice the remarks made by Mr. Robert McCleave on this point on 16 March 1972. *Debates*, pp. 905–907.
6. At Westminster these two kinds of appropriation are referred to as (a) Annual Supply charges and (b) Consolidated Fund charges.
7. For years the Treasury Board has included in supplementary estimates one-dollar votes to authorize the Crown to transfer money from one vote to another, i.e., to use money already granted for one purpose for another approved purpose. In addition, one-dollar votes with a substantive legislative intent frequently were included in main and supplementary estimates, i.e., the House was asked to change the law under the guise of appropriating money. The latter practice attracted much opposition criticism over the years. Since 1968 the speaker regularly has turned back legislative one-dollar items when they have been challenged. See *Debates*, 8 and 10, March 1971, pp. 4022–26, 4125–27; and *Debates*, 10 December 1973, pp. 8605–09. The Senate and House of Commons Act, s. 41, provides for payment of $4,000 to the leader of a party with twelve or more members in the House of Commons. That Act, s. 10, also disqualifies for membership in the House of Commons any person who receives a payment from the Crown. To that disqualification certain exemptions have been made by statute for ministers and parliamentary secretaries. After 1974 the Social Credit Party had only eleven members. Supplementary Estimates "D" for 1974–75 (Bill C-54) contained a vote "to provide, notwithstanding Section 10 of the Senate and House of Commons Act for payment to Réal Caouette of an amount based on an annual rate of $4,000 in respect of that portion of the current fiscal year commencing 8 July 1974, throughout which he is a member of the House of Commons and the Leader of the Social Credit Party of Canada. . . ." No objection was raised in the House.
8. After the 1972 election Prime Minister Trudeau described the stance of the minority Liberal government as follows: ". . . this government is not going to cling to office for the sake of clinging to office, swallowing everything and anything so long as it is still permitted to occupy the treasury benches. But we are not going to give up simply because we are defeated on some motion or bill, or some part of a bill or some amendment unless we feel that that defeat goes to the roots of our policy." When Mr. David Lewis, leader of the N.D.P., arose to reply, he said: "I want to start with something the Prime Minister said in his final words. If I understand them, he said that the government would decide whether or not defeat on a certain piece of legislation was

a matter of no confidence. I want to tell him that as far as we are concerned, it will be parliament that will make that decision. If in our view defeat of a piece of legislation is important to parliament and to this country, but the government does not consider this a motion of no confidence, then we will make certain that this House votes no confidence in the government on a special motion." *Debates*, 8 January 1973, pp. 61–62. The two positions are not contradictory. A government is free to decide that a particular loss makes it impossible for it to continue. On the other hand, if a majority of the House think that a government should not continue, the government can be defeated. But there is no law that requires a government that has lost a no-confidence vote either to resign or to bring on an election. Ultimately what would force a reluctant government to go would be the refusal of the House to renew its supplies of money. However, a no-confidence vote is sufficient evidence to convince a prime minister that the money will be cut off at the first opportunity. It is not to be thought that the defeat of the government on one or more particular supply votes is fatal. For example, on 26 March 1973, a vote in the amount of $19,000 for Information Canada was denied, 138 to 107; yet the Trudeau government did not resign, nor was it forced out. *Journals*, pp. 212–13.

9. *Journals*, 12 November 1963, pp. 546–48. See also *Journals*, 12 June 1951, p. 485, and *Journals*, 6 May 1953, p. 628.

10. *Debates*, 4 May 1970, pp. 6525–27.

11. On 18 June 1970, there were separate decisions by the House on eleven votes (or items). On 16 June 1971, two votes were opposed. On 22 June 1972, members in opposition asked for separate votes on 88 items. On 26 June 1973, there was opposition to eight votes.

12. A defect in the new supply procedure was discovered in June 1972. Opposition motions take precedence over government motions except at the very end of each supply period, but no question is to be put to the House unless the opposition motion is a no-confidence motion. At the very end of the last supply day in each of the three periods the government's motions for concurrence in the votes in the estimates take precedence. This means that there is no convenient way in which a member in opposition can bring on a decision by the House on a motion to reduce the amount of a particular vote. The question put to the House is whether or not the full amount in a vote will be supplied to the Crown. The changes in the standing orders made on 24 March 1975, cover this point. See *Debates*, 22 June 1972, pp. 3415–17, and 10 December 1973, pp. 8568–69, 8600–05.

13. In commenting on the British practice under a similar standing order Sir Ivor Jennings states that their standing order, too, was interpreted as requiring a prior financial resolution. But then he goes on to say that, "If this interpretation were carried out strictly, there could never be a debate on a Bill until a financial resolution had been passed in committee. In fact, however, it has for long been the practice for Bills which authorise expenditure only incidentally to proceed as far as second reading without a financial resolution. Such a resolution cannot effectively be debated until the purpose of the expenditure is known, and this implies at least publication (i.e. first reading)

and perhaps second reading of the Bill. Consequently, the financial clauses are printed in italics (known as 'blanks') and the financial resolution is moved in committee after the second reading debate." *Parliament*; 2nd ed. p. 257. It is interesting to observe that the Canadian practice was in conformity with the strict interpretation of the standing order, and not with the more practical British usage. In 1947 Mr. Speaker Fauteux commented on the cumbersome nature of the "resolution stage." *Journals*, 5 December 1947, pp. 11–13.

14. *Debates*, p. 4231.

15. The old practice of using a recommending message as the text of the proposed resolution has had the effect of making "the message and recommendation of the Governor General" a distinct document, which now under S.O. 62(2) is to be printed. It would seem that no documentary recommendation is required to satisfy s. 54 of the B.N.A. Act. All that is required may be that the governor general recommend the bill. On this point Mr. Speaker Lamoureux commented: "As the honourable Member for Winnipeg North Centre (Mr. Knowles) has very clearly said—and I am very strongly inclined to go along with his reasoning—we appear to be confusing the resolution stage of the bill, which has now been discontinued, and the Recommendation. It may be that before we changed the rules these were two separate matters— the Recommendation made in the terms I have just indicated, and then a resolution which delineated the four corners of the bill which would come before the House but which was not then known to honourable Members and, indeed, not known to His Excellency as his Recommendation was directed to the resolution. It may well be that this is all that should be required to allow honourable Members to proceed with consideration of a measure advanced for study by the Government." *Journals*, 3 November 1970, p. 82.

16. *Debates*, 23 April 1975, pp. 5115–17.

17. The criticisms of the examination of the estimates in the standing committees voiced by the opposition after 1968 are dealt with in chapter 7, and the experimental changes made on 24 March 1975, are described in chapter 10.

SIX

1. At the committee stage of the legislative process the text of a bill is *considered*. Before 20 December 1968, every bill was *committed* to a committee of the whole House to be considered. This practice was followed even when a bill had been *referred* to a standing committee for examination, for the standing committees were not authorized to adopt the clauses of bills. When a public bill that had been referred to a standing committee after second reading had been reported back to the House, the bill had to be committed to a committee of the whole House.

2. The difference between the *appointment* of a committee and the *nomination* of the members who are to serve on the committee should be noticed. At Westminster, for example, the members of a select committee may not be nominated in the motion for the appointment of the committee.

3. For an account of the experimentation see John P. Mackintosh, *The*

Government and Politics of Britain; 3rd ed. (London: Hutchinson University Library, 1974), pp. 147–51.

4. The standing orders do not specify the number of standing committees. There now are seven ordinary standing committees, which are considerably smaller than before World War II. In addition there is the Scottish Standing Committee. This committee is not to be confused with the Scottish Grand Committee, which is composed of all the members representing constituencies in Scotland together with from ten to fifteen other members added to assure that the political balance is somewhat similar to that in the House. A bill that relates exclusively to Scotland may be committed to the Scottish Standing Committee. When this has been done the Selection Committee nominates the committee for the bill. The standing orders prescribe a committee of thirty members from Scotland and not more than twenty other members (either from Scottish constituencies or others) chosen because of their qualifications and the political composition of the House.

5. The practice by which members are added to a committee before it begins its work on a bill often in fact gives the committees a high degree of specialization. It means that some backbenchers, instead of following the minister in charge of the bill, tend to curry favour with either particular interests or with their own constituents. See Sir Ivor Jennings, *Parliament*; 2nd ed. (Cambridge, The University Press, 1957), pp. 270–71. See also S.A. Walkland, *The Legislative Process in Great Britain* (London: George Allen and Unwin Ltd., 1968), p. 75.

6. Since these committees are nominated by the Selection Committee, and not by the House itself, they are not regarded as select committees. *May*, p. 636.

7. *Journals*, 1867–68, p. 5.

8. Although the Committee on Printing was included as a "select standing committee" of the House of Commons, from the beginning it was, and it continues to be a joint committee of the Senate and the House of Commons. In 1875 the committee was made responsible for the preparation and publication of the Official Report of the Debates, but after that one session that task which proved very troublesome over the next ten or fifteen years was given to a small select committee. See *Debates*, 5 February 1875, p. 4. Nor did the Printing Committee have responsibility for Votes and Proceedings. The authority to approve that paper and to have it printed was conferred exclusively on the speaker.

9. *Journals*, 1964–65, p. 84. It is instructive to notice the close similarity between Mr. Pearson's motion and the one used in the Legislative Assembly of the province of Canada at its first session. On 18 June 1841, the assembly approved a motion to appoint certain "standing committees," and then ordered that those committees "... shall have power to report to the House, from time to time, their observations and opinions upon the subjects and matters which shall be referred to them by this House, by bill or otherwise, as belonging to that class of objects for which they are severally appointed, with power to send for persons, papers, and records." *Debates of the Legislative Assembly of United Canada*, ed. Elizabeth Nish (Montreal: Presse de

l'Ecole des Hautes études Commerciales) I, 55.

Prior to the 1907–08 session the same powers were conferred on *all* the standing committees. This was done at the beginning of the 1907–08 session, but later a motion was passed rescinding the general powers in the case of the Committee on the Debates and the Committee on the Library of Parliament. In 1909 and thereafter until 1925 the power "to send for persons, papers and records" was not conferred on those two committees. But in 1925 and thereafter the distinction was not made. Moreover, at times—e.g., the 1928 to 1935 period—the Joint Committee on the Restaurant was included in the list of committees to which the House of Commons gave the power "to send for persons, papers and records." Since 1935 that committee has had to carry on without investigative powers.

10. The work done over the years by the Standing Committee on Public Accounts has been examined by Professor Norman Ward, *The Public Purse* (Toronto: University of Toronto Press, 1964).

11. *Journals*, 1876, pp. 109 and 216. See also *Debates*, 29 March 1876, pp. 909–10. The wording in the *Debates* is slightly different. The original order read: "59. Every Private Bill, when read a First time, is referred to the Committee on Private Bills, if any such shall have been appointed, or to some other Standing Committee of the same character; and all Petitions before The House for or against the Bill are considered as referred to such Committee." *Journals*, 20 December 1867, p. 120. When the House adopted its first standing orders on 20 December 1867, the Hon. Christopher Dunkin explained that the committee that had examined the matter had found the rules of the legislature of the old province of Canada suitable to be carried forward with no important change except in the mode of dealing with private bills. Such bills thereafter were to go to the committees after first reading to move them forward earlier and to prevent unnecessarily long debates on second reading. *Debates*, p. 333.

12. *Journals*, 15 May 1873, p. 351.

13. At least one of the committees acquired a reputation as a graveyard. When, in 1902, the government proposed that a private member's bill relating to cattle-guards along railways be sent to the Committee on Railways, Canals and Telegraph Lines, some members protested. Said Mr. Sproule: "There is one reason why I would object to refer it to the Railway Committee, and that is the history of what has taken place in that Railway Committee. I do not desire to reflect in any way on that committee, yet I cannot refrain from thinking over a large number of important Bills that go to that Railway Committee and are killed there, and never find their way back to this House, Bills that are usually in the public interest. It seems to be the graveyard of very many important Bills that are in the interest of the public." *Debates*, 27 February 1902, c. 457. But notice the contrary view expressed on the same day by the Hon. David Tisdale. *Debates*, c. 466.

14. *Debates*, 1 June 1887, p. 668. D'Alton McCarthy did not state the problem clearly. Following the practice adopted in 1876, the bill had been sent to the committee after second reading. The committee had approached the bill as a public bill, that is, it had turned directly to the clauses. After it

had gone through the clauses, it went back to the opening words. It treated the opening words as if they were comparable to the preamble of a private bill; but the opening words were the enacting formula, and the enacting formula is not preambulatory. By stating its opposition to the enacting words the committee had rejected the decision of the House. Because private bills and private members' bills were read a second time before being referred the second-reading decision of the House could not have been taken as an instruction to the committee to report the bills; otherwise, no bills could have died in committee. Notice the important debate in 1927 on a private bill respecting the Montreal, Ottawa and Georgian Bay Company. *Debates*, 14 March 1927, pp. 1199–1200.

15. Ward, *The Public Purse*, pp. 85–96.

16. The committee appears to have been used by the Department of Agriculture to further its missionary activity among the rural population. See J. E. Hodgetts, *Pioneer Public Service* (Toronto: University of Toronto Press, 1955) pp. 227–29.

17. *Journals*, 4 May 1894, p. 124.

18. *Journals*, 14 May 1895, p. 72.

19. *Debates*, 15 April 1902, c. 2817.

20. See *Debates*, 1 February 1909, cc. 355–73, and 8 February 1909, c. 688. See *Debates*, 19 February 1909, cc. 1319–20. See *Debates*, 27 March 1924, p.729. See *Debates*, 12 September 1945, pp. 109–110, and 18 September 1945, p. 244.

21. See *Debates*, 22 January 1908, cc. 1691–1731, and 3 February 1909, cc. 483–521. See *Debates*, 19 February 1909, cc. 1319–20. Also *Debates*, 30 May 1958, pp. 681–82.

22. Note the debate on 11 March 1925, on a private member's motion proposing a reduction in the size of the standing committees. *Debates*, p. 1034–41.

23. See *Debates*, 26 January 1911, cc. 2429–33; also *Debates*, 15 February 1911, cc. 3599–3605.

24. It should be noted, however, that in 1946 the leader of the opposition, John Bracken, recommended that the House deal with only the principles of public bills, and that the consideration of the details be undertaken outside the Chamber. *Debates*, 18 March 1946, p. 36.

25. Although appointed annually from 1924 until 1965 the committee never was added permanently to the list of standing committees. At each session the standing order in which the standing committees were listed was amended for the duration of that session by adding a committee on "Railways and Shipping Lines owned, operated and controlled by the Government." Accordingly, we may say that the committee was a sessional, select standing committee!

26. See statements by Gordon Graydon, *Debates*, 29 January 1943 (pp. 8–9); 2 April 1943 (p. 1784); 24 July 1943 (pp. 5386–87); 26 October 1949 (pp. 1157–58); 12 June 1951 (p. 3969); and 7 April 1952 (pp. 1184–86).

See a statement by John Bracken on 18 March 1946, *Debates*, p. 36.

See statements by Donald Fleming, *Debates*, 29 September 1949 (pp. 347–48); 26 October 1949 (pp. 1156–57); 22 February 1950 (pp. 139–40);

Notes to pages 151–160   309

and 8 June 1951 (p. 3853).
  See a statement by George Drew, *Debates*, 26 October 1949 (pp. 1164–66).
27. *Journals*, 5 December 1947 (pp. 13–17).
28. See statements by George Drew, *Debates*, 13 September 1950 (p. 683) and 12 June 1951 (p. 3965).
29. Note the comments of J. L. Ilsley, *Debates*, 24 July 1943 (pp. 5385–86) and of Douglas Abbott, *Debates*, 26 October 1949 (pp. 1159–61).
30. *Debates*, 8 February 1955 (pp. 937–57, 963–76).
31. *Debates*, 28–29 February 1956 (1639–55, 1668–91) and 26 February 1957 (pp. 1654–87).
32. *Debates*, 30 May 1958 (p. 696). It is worth noting that in 1955 Mr. Green's future colleague and his successor as government house leader, Mr. Gordon Churchill, voiced deep scepticism about the usefulness of attempting to study estimates in any kind of small committee on the ground that the real purpose of supply business is not to consider and pass estimates, but to criticize departmental administration, a purpose best achieved in the Chamber. He did not share the general attitude of approval of the use of the External Affairs Committee to study the estimates of that department. *Debates*, 8 February 1955 (pp. 965–68).
33. *Debates*, 4 August 1958 (p. 3060). Mr. Diefenbaker is quoted as having said, "cast out;" but it may be assumed that he said, "cast doubt."
34. The activities of the Public Accounts Committee in the 1946–60 period are discussed by Norman Ward, *The Public Purse*, pp. 201–23.
35. *Debates*, 26 February 1957 (p. 1655).
36. *Debates*, 30 May 1958 (p. 681).

SEVEN

1. When moving for the appointment of the Special Committee on 18 October 1963, Prime Minister Pearson described as "one of the most serious problems of parliament" the need to make changes to provide for "the more effective discharge of work through committees in a way that will give the committees authority and power to make decisions" so that when "the decisions are referred to the House of Commons we will not have to go through the same debate over and over again that has taken place in the committees." It should be noted that Mr. Pearson did not suggest that the committees should be non-partisan; rather, his point was that a decision made by a standing committee should not have to be made over again by a committee of the whole House. *Debates*, p. 3752.
2. *Journals*, pp. 985–96.
3. *Debates*, 18 March 1965, p. 12512.
4. *Debates*, 18 March 1965, p. 12544.
5. *Debates*, 23 October 1963, p. 3926.
6. *Debates*, 19 March 1965, p. 12582.
7. *Debates*, 19 March 1965, p. 12593.
8. *Journals*, 14 December 1964, p. 989.
9. *Debates*, 2 April 1965, pp. 13183–84.

10. The Special Committee in 1963 had time to make only a careful preliminary analysis of the work to be done. Its successor in 1964–65, which was composed almost entirely of the same members, followed up with a long series of studies and reports on various aspects of procedure and organization.

11. It is important to notice that none of Mr. Diefenbaker's staunchest supporters served on the committee. *Journals*, 20 March 1964, p. 112. This fact may help to explain both the nature of the committee's recommendations and the adverse reaction of Mr. Diefenbaker and Mr. Churchill.

12. The fifteenth report was presented on 14 December 1964. Concurrence was moved and an explanatory statement was made by Mr. H. A. Olson on 18 December 1964. The rest of the debate took place on 18–19 March 1965. The eighteenth and nineteenth reports were presented on 26 March 1965 (*Journals*, pp. 1173–76, 1176–77). The 1964–65 session was prorogued on 2 April 1965, and the 1965 session began on 5 April. The Pearson government put its own plan for procedural reforms—known as "the McIlraith Reforms," after the government house leader at the time—before the House on 12 May 1965. *Journals*, pp. 97–103. Debate began on 19 May.

The government house leaders since April 1963, have been as follows:

Twenty-sixth Parliament (1963–65)
   1st session (May 1963 – December 1963)   the Hon. J. W. Pickersgill
   2nd session (February 1964 – April 1965)   the Hon. Guy Favreau
      (after October 1964)   the Hon. G. J. McIlraith
   3rd session (April 1965 – June 1965)   the Hon. G. J. McIlraith

Twenty-seventh Parliament (1965–1968)
   1st session (January 1966 – May 1967)   the Hon. G. J. McIlraith
   2nd session (May 1967 – April 1968)   the Hon. A. J. MacEachen

Twenty-eighth Parliament (1968–1972)
   1st session (September 1968 – October 1969)   the Hon. D. S. Macdonald
   2nd session (October 1969 – October 1970)   the Hon. D. S. Macdonald
   3rd session (October 1970 – February 1972)   the Hon. A. J. MacEachen
   4th session (February 1972 – September 1972)   the Hon. A. J. MacEachen

Twenty-ninth Parliament (1972–1974)
   1st session (January 1973 – February 1974)   the Hon. A. J. MacEachen
   2nd session (February 1974 – May 1974)   the Hon. A. J. MacEachen

Thirtieth Parliament (1974 –
   1st session (September 1974 –   the Hon. Mitchell Sharp

13. The 1966–67 and 1967–68 committees consisted of almost the same group of members. *Journals*, 24 February 1967, p. 1443; and 8 May 1967, p. 12.

14. The other house leaders who participated in this decision were: for the Progressive Conservatives, Mr. G. W. Baldwin; for the New Democratic Party, Mr. Stanley Knowles; and for the Ralliement des Créditistes, Mr. Gilbert Rondeau.

15. The maximum size of the committees was specified, rather than the exact size, so that if after future elections the parties could be represented

satisfactorily on smaller committees the Striking Committee could propose smaller committees without an order from the House. On 8 October 1968, the Striking Committee had recommended, and the House had named, a Committee on Miscellaneous Private Bills and Standing Orders consisting of only twelve members. On 18 January 1973, after the 1972 election, all the committees that previously had had twenty members were reduced to nineteen. The two with thirty and the two with twelve were not changed. The Liberals, with 109 members, had eight on each nineteen-member committee; the Progressive Conservatives, with 107, had eight; the N.D.P., with thirty-one had two; and the Social Credit Party, with seventeen, had one. It is to be noted that after the 1974 election, which paved the way for smaller committees, the Striking Committee increased all the nineteen-member committees to twenty, with the exception of the Committee on Privileges and Elections. At the same time the committee recommended that the ceiling on the Committee on Procedure and Organization be suspended to permit the nomination of sixteen members. The House concurred in both these recommendations.

16. On 28 May 1970, a complaint was made that the records of the recent proceedings of the Committee on Agriculture had not been produced. In commenting on the complaint Mr. Speaker Lamoureux gave a detailed description of the difficulties confronting the staff of the House. *Debates*, 10 June 1970, pp. 7941-42.

17. It has been suggested that in February and March 1968, when Canadian participation in NATO was being reappraised by the government, the secretary of state for external affairs and the minister of national defence were eager to have the Committee on External Affairs and National Defence travel to NATO bases in Europe so that the committee would appreciate fully the importance of Canadian military participation and produce a report that would moderate the views of those ministers, including Prime Minister Trudeau, who favoured a reduction in participation.

Professor Norman Ward has drawn attention to the testimony of the minister of northern affairs and natural resources and of the deputy minister of mines and technical surveys before the Committee on Mines, Forests and Waters in 1958. Both were soliciting the support of the committee for the important work of their departments, which was not adequately appreciated by Treasury Board. Norman Ward, *The Public Purse* (Toronto: University of Toronto Press, 1964), p. 270.

18. See the comment by Mr. S. J. Korchinski to this effect on 17 June 1970. *Debates*, p. 8213.

19. Lord Campion, *An Introduction to the House of Commons*; 3rd ed. (London: Macmillan & Co. Ltd., 1958), p. 50. The same point has been referred to by C. E. S. Franks in his discussion of the difficulties experienced after 1968 in attempting to use strong committees in a government system based on the Westminster model. See his "The Dilemma of the Standing Committees of the Canadian House of Commons," *Canadian Journal of Political Science* 4 (December 1971), 461-76. See also Alex MacLeod "The Reform of the Standing Committees of the Quebec National Assembly: A

Preliminary Assessment," *Canadian Journal of Political Science* 8 (March 1975), 23–39.

20. *Debates*, pp. 428–29; 3 November 1969, p. 460.

21. The only general debate on the operation of the standing committees during those years was brought on by a private member's motion moved by Mr. Douglas Rowland of the N.D.P. See *Debates*. 19 November and 17 December 1971, pp. 9738–45 and 10592–97. On 7 March 1973, the government house leader made a motion to authorize the Standing Committee on Procedure and Organization to examine the procedures of the House. The success of the committee system was treated fairly extensively in the ensuing debate. *Debates*, 7, 8 March 1973, pp. 1995–2013, 2069–78.

The question of travel by committees was discussed when the re-appointment of the Special Joint Committee on the Constitution was moved. *Debates*, 15 October 1970, pp. 147–60. On 30 October 1970, a motion to refer the Public Accounts for 1968–69 to the standing committee was debated. During that debate many points concerning the committees were mentioned briefly, e.g., the need of the Committee on Public Accounts for a strong staff, the costs of the committee system, and the need for neutral chairmen. *Debates*, pp. 750–62.

In addition, the role of the standing committees was discussed at some length on seven occasions in relation to the Progressive Conservative claim that the Trudeau government had reduced, and was reducing the power of the House of Commons *vis à vis* the government. Those debates, all on supply days, took place on 5 March 1970; 21 April 1970; 18 June 1970; 7 March 1972; 26 May 1972; 14 June 1972; and 25 May 1973.

22. *Journals*, 13 February 1969, pp. 695–96. See also *Debates*, 14 February 1969, pp. 5533–42.

23. *Debates*, 31 March and 1 April 1969, pp. 7301–12, and 7371–412.

24. The influence of the Committee on External Affairs and National Defence on the decision made by the government are treated by Bruce Thordarson, *Trudeau and Foreign Policy* (Toronto: Oxford University Press, 1972) pp. 127–63.

25. *Journals*, 16 December 1969, pp. 207–10.

26. *Debates*, 19, 20 and 22 January 1970, pp. 2513–23, 2575–76, 2681–727.

27. See the clear explanation of the situation given by the chairman of the committee, Mr. Ian Watson, on 22 January 1970. *Debates*, p. 2720.

28. *Debates*, p. 5695.

29. Other examples are the comments of Mr. Melvin McQuaid on 13 May 1969, *Debates*, pp. 8647–48; of Mr. Eric Nielsen on 19 June 1970, *Debates*, pp. 8365–66; and of Mr. S. J. Korchinski on 10 June 1971, *Debates*, pp. 6564–65.

30. *Debates*, pp. 11069–70.

31. *Debates*, 4 June 1970, pp. 7727–28.

32. *Debates*, 22 October 1968, pp. 1660–61.

33. In the fall of 1974 Mr. Diefenbaker was to comment: "When the so-called reform of the rules of parliament began under Mr. Pearson and was continued under the present Prime Minister, I stood against most of the

changes and was virtually alone. Many of my colleagues fell for the argument that parliament must be made more efficient. That is always the Machiavellian argument used when parliament is about to be emasculated." *Debates*, 3 October 1974, p. 79.

34. Note especially the speeches given during the rules change debate by the Hon. R. L. Stanfield on 10 December 1968, *Debates*, pp. 3761–62; by the Hon. Marcel Lambert on 11 December 1968, *Debates*, p. 3826; and by Mr. E. M. Woolliams on 12 December 1968, *Debates*, p. 3860.

35. *Debates*, pp. 8309–10.

36. *Debates*, p. 126.

37. *Debates*, p. 4966. See also his similar statement on 26 May 1972, p. 2605.

38. The motions on 5 March 1970, 21 April 1970, and 7 March 1972, were no-confidence motions.

39. *Debates*, p. 4418.

40. See the debates on 21 April 1970, *Debates*, pp. 6109–50, and on 26 May 1972, pp. 2593–619.

41. *Debates*, p. 594.

42. *Debates*, pp. 595–96.

43. *Debates*, p. 2003.

44. *Debates*, p. 4104.

45. *Debates*, 15 October 1970, p. 150. See also his comment on 30 October 1970, pp. 758–59.

46. *Debates*, p. 599.

47. *Debates*, 19 November 1971, p. 9743. See also his remarks to the same effect on 5 March 1970, p. 4442.

48. *Debates*, p. 622.

49. *Debates*, pp. 3148–49. See his comment regarding committee attendance on 5 March 1970, *Debates*, p. 4454.

50. *Debates*, p. 1685.

51. *Debates*, p. 1998.

52. *Debates*, 27 February 1973, p. 1685.

53. *Debates*, 7 March 1973, pp. 1999–2000.

54. Before 20 December 1968, an order of the House was required to make a change in the membership of a committee. These motions were made on behalf of all the parties by the chief government whip or his assistant. Now, under S.O. 65(4)(b), a change may be made by having the chief government whip notify the clerk of the House of the name of the member coming off a committee and the name of the member taking his place. Notice the incident mentioned by Mr. J. A. McGrath on 28 May 1971, and the speaker's comment. *Debates*, pp. 6165, 6171–72.

55. The contention that many Progressive Conservatives did not attend committee meetings regularly is supported by figures given by Dorothy Byrne for the 1969–70 session. "Some Attendance Patterns Exhibited by Members of Parliament during the 28th Parliament," *Canadian Journal of Political Science* 5 (March, 1972), 135–41. Her figures show that fifty-seven Liberals (or 46.8% of the 122 available) attended more than fifty meetings, that eighteen Progressive Conservatives (or 25% of the 72 available) attended

more than fifty meetings, that eleven New Democrats (or 52.4% of the 21 available) attended more than fifty meetings, and that none of the Créditistes attended more than fifty meetings.

56. *Debates*, p. 1620. Probably Mr. Watson said: "Nine times out of ten questions are asked to embarrass, for the answer is already known."

57. At the beginning of the 1973–74 session, when the Liberals were in a minority, Mr. J. M. Reid, the parliamentary secretary to the government house leader, proposed that some of the chairmen be selected from among the parties in opposition. Mr. Douglas Rowland made a favourable response on behalf of the N.D.P. However, the Progressive Conservatives did not take up the offer, so nothing came of it at that session. *Debates*, 11 January 1973, p. 178, and 15 January 1973, p. 313.

58. The need for leadership on the ministerial side was clearly demonstrated in 1968–69 in the Standing Committee on Transport and Communications. The Progressive Conservatives were well led and very aggressive. On the other hand, the chairman tended to take a neutral role, while the minister, the Hon. Paul Hellyer, was busy elsewhere because of his membership on the Task Force on Housing. There was no parliamentary secretary. As a result the committee was a source of trouble to the government for months.

59. See for example the statement of Mr. David Lewis on 21 April 1969, *Debates*, p. 7729, and by Mr. Douglas Rowland on 19 November 1971, *Debates*, p. 9739. But see also the remarks made by Mr. Diefenbaker, favouring research facilities, on 23 October 1963, p. 3926.

60. *Debates*, 19 December 1969, pp. 2197–98.

61. Samuel C. Patterson, "Congressional Committee Professional Staffing: Capabilities and Constraints," in *Legislatures in Developmental Perspective*, ed. Allan Kornberg and L. D. Musolf (Durham: Duke University Press, 1970), pp. 391–428.

62. Italics added.

63. *Debates*, 12 January 1971, p. 2307.

64. *Debates*, 26 March 1971, p. 4643.

65. *Debates*, 31 May 1972, p. 2736.

66. In 1969–70 the Miscellaneous Estimates Committee undertook to rewrite a vote. The speaker ruled their report a nullity. *Journals*, 24 March 1970, p. 636–37.

67. *Journals*, 18 June 1973, pp. 419–20, and 6 December 1973, pp. 725–26.

68. *Debates*, 10 April 1973, p. 3143.

69. *Debates*, 19 November 1971, p. 9738.

EIGHT

1. The committee named to recommend standing orders for the new House consisted of Sir John A. Macdonald (Kingston), George Etienne Cartier (Montreal East), John Sandfield Macdonald (Cornwall), Stewart Campbell (Guysborough), Christopher Dunkin (Brome), A. A. Dorion (Hochelaga), and John H. Gray (Saint John). In presenting the new standing orders, Mr. Dunkin commented that "almost the only change made in the rules of the old

Legislature of Canada, at any rate the only important change, related to the mode of dealing with private Bills." *Debates*, p. 333.

2. According to the standing orders adopted on 20 December 1867, three of the five days of the week—Monday, Wednesday, and Thursday—were assigned to the private members, but private members' public bills were given a low place in the order of priority on those days. On each they came after notices of motions. The best day for public bills was Thursday, when they had priority after dinner, and Wednesday, when private bills had the first hour after dinner, and the remainder of the evening was available for public bills.

3. Fractions have been dropped. Before 1906 the length of the sessions is an adequate index of the demands made by the House on a member's time. Only two sessions, those of 1867–68 and 1880–81, overlapped two years, and in only two years—1873 and 1896—was there more than one session. But after 1906, and especially after 1941, the actual number of sittings in each calendar year is more revealing than the length of the sessions. See Table 9.

4. See Borden's comments on how the Conservatives in the House became "a well-directed and effective fighting force." *Robert Laird Borden: His Memoirs* (Toronto, McClelland and Stewart Limited, 1969), I, 72.

5. At every session prior to 1877, other than 1871, and the second session of 1873, which dealt with the Canadian Pacific scandal, at a certain point the House gave the remaining Thursdays to the government. In 1867–68, when there was a great deal of government business because of the creation of new departments and the extension of certain laws uniformly throughout the Dominion, the House gave the remaining Thursdays to the government at the tenth sitting; in 1869 at the twenty-third sitting; and in 1870, at the fourteenth sitting. In 1871 it gave the remaining Wednesdays to the government at the seventeenth sitting, and the remaining Thursday evenings at the twenty-third sitting. In 1872 it gave the government the remaining Thursdays at the thirty-second sitting, and in 1873 the remaining Thursdays at the twenty-fourth sitting.

6. *Journals*, 6 March 1876, pp. 108–109.

7. In 1877 Thursday afternoons were given to the government at the nineteenth sitting, and Wednesdays at the forty-seventh sitting. In 1887 Thursday afternoons were given to the government at the twenty-fifth sitting, and Wednesdays at the forty-first sitting. The final Monday of that session also was placed at the disposal of the government. And, in 1887 Thursday afternoons and Wednesdays were given to the government at the twenty-eight sitting, and Mondays at the forty-first sitting.

8. *Debates*, c. 821. Later, on 29 March 1905, at the fifty-third sitting, the House gave precedence to government business on Mondays also.

9. *Debates*, 9 July 1906. c. 7476. Note the brief comment of Sir Wilfrid Laurier to the same effect on 31 May 1904. *Debates*, cc. 3846–47.

10. *Debates*, p. 1054.

11. Sometimes by special order the government was given one or more Mondays or Wednesdays very early in a session, and always the Address debate took precedence over private members' business; consequently, as shown above, there is little relationship between the number of the sitting at

which all remaining Mondays or Wednesdays were given up and the number of days that had been available for the private members.

12. The basic provision for private members' business now is one hour a day on four days each week: between 5:00 and 6:00 p.m. on Monday, Tuesday, and Thursday, and between 4:00 and 5:00 p.m. on Friday. This is modified in two ways. First, when the business before the House relates to the Address in Reply, to the budget, or to supply there is no private members' hour. This modification, it will be noted, does not increase the time available to the government for its bills; rather, it extends general debates. Second, no more than a total of forty hours on Mondays and Tuesdays are to be taken for private members' business in a session. In other words, during the early part of a session four hours a week must be deducted for private members' business, but in the final weeks of a long session only two hours a week must be deducted.

13. *Debates*, c. 3017.

14. The election of 1891 took place on 5 March, and the House met on 29 April. The first Appropriation Act—which included supplementary supply for 1890–91 and an advance for 1891–92—was enacted on 10 July 1891. A second interim supply was provided on 28 August 1891. The balance of the main estimates for 1891–92 was provided in the third Act, on 30 September 1891.

15. *Debates*, cc. 6638–39. Mr. Boyd reiterated his views with even greater vigour on 3 August 1904, and evoked responses from both the prime minister and Mr. Borden. *Debates*, cc. 8261–65.

16. In 1873 the sessional indemnity was raised from $600 to $1,000. In 1901 it was increased to $1,500 and in 1905 to $2,500. In 1906, speaking on a private member's bill to repeal the increase, the leader of the opposition, Mr. Borden, defended the increases by making an analysis of the increasing length of the sessions. *Debates*, 9 May 1906, cc. 3033–34.

17. The Hon. G. E. Foster forecast the failure of the reform, not on the ground that the House moved too slowly, but on the ground that governments are incorrigibly tardy in preparing their legislative business. *Debates*, 12 June 1906, cc. 5098–99.

18. The changes are set forth in the *Journals*, 29 April 1910. pp. 535–37.

19. *Journals*, 23 April 1913, pp. 507–8.

20. A detailed account of how "closure by consent" was achieved was given to the House on 26 April 1904. *Debates*, cc. 2002–8.

21. *Debates*, 9 April 1913, cc. 7389–90.

22. The standing order made in 1913 remained in effect without modification until 1955. It read: "On Thursdays and Fridays when the Order of the Day is called for the House to go into Committee of Supply, or of Ways and Means, Mr. Speaker shall leave the Chair without putting any question, provided that, except by the consent of the House, the Estimates of each Department shall be first taken up on a day other than Thursday or Friday."

23. On 11 January 1911, for example, one member, Mr. W. F. MacLean, informed the House that he had seven amendments to move on days when the government sought to have the members sit as the Committee of Supply.

Prime Minister Laurier regarded this as "a pretty large programme." *Debates*, cc. 1502–03. On Friday, 13 January 1911, before the committee sat the government had to deal with a request for a wharf at Brighton, Ontario; a complaint that the secretary of state (for external affairs) had not gone to Washington to conduct the reciprocity negotiations; a query about a report on technical education; and a demand for a mail car to run north of Englehart, Ontario. *Debates*, cc. 1655–64.

24. The Progressives advocated various changes, but not persistently. See *Debates*, 23 February 1925, pp. 412–29.

25. The question of time limits on speeches is related to time limits on debates, for when the available time for a debate is restricted, the shorter a member's speech the happier will be those who are hoping to be able to participate. From the viewpoint of a government, however, time limits on speeches are now of no great importance except as they make time limits on debates more acceptable to the members, for in committees of the whole House a member may speak repeatedly, and in the House itself a little ingenuity with amendments generally will suffice to permit everybody to speak again and again. Prior to 1927 there was no time limit whatsoever on speeches. In that year a forty-minute limit was set for most members in both the House and committees of the whole House. In 1955 the limit in committees of the whole House was reduced to thirty minutes. Under the 1968 standing orders the general limit on ordinary members is forty minutes; but it is thirty minutes during the Address debate and the budget debate, twenty minutes on a supply day, in committees of the whole House, and during private members' hour.

26. See Mr. King's comments in favour of a fixed hour. *Debates*, 29 June 1920, pp. 4432–33. The hours of sitting are one procedural matter on which many members have definite views. From 1867 to 1906 the basic rule was for the speaker to take the Chair at 3:00 p.m. each day of the five-day week; and the sitting continued, after a dinner recess between 6:00 and 7:30 p.m., on all five days until an adjournment motion was moved and carried. In 1906 the standing orders were changed so that thereafter the House met at 2:00 p.m. on Wednesday, and did not sit after 6:00 p.m. that day. At the same time the dinner recess on the other four days was extended to 8:00 p.m. In 1927, when the hour of daily adjournment on days other than Wednesday was set at 11:00 p.m., the hour of meeting on Wednesday was put back to 3:00 p.m. Then, in 1952 the hour of sitting was advanced to 2:30 p.m. for all five days, and the hour of adjournment, other than for Wednesday, was advanced to 10:00 p.m. The next change came in 1955 when evening sittings on Friday were eliminated, and the hour of sitting on that day was advanced to 11:00 a.m., with a recess between 1:00 and 2:30 p.m. In 1968 the hour of sitting on Monday, Tuesday, Wednesday, and Thursday was advanced to 2:00 p.m., the recess on Friday was shortened to one hour, and the hour of adjournment on Friday was advanced from 6:00 to 5:00 p.m.

In the 1960s the practice of the British House of having no dinner recess was tried, but the problem of maintaining a quorum proved too great. The same small group of members, drawn chiefly from among the backbenchers, attended regularly, but eventually their patience, and that of the government chief whip, was exhausted.

27. See especially the speeches by Claxton (*Debates*, 9 February 1943, pp. 291–97), by Bracken (18 March 1946, pp. 35–37), by Graydon (25 June 1947), pp. 4617–19), and by Drew (12 June 1951, pp. 3962–71). See also the speeches by Cleaver, Graydon, Knowles, Churchill, Fulton, etc. on 7 April 1952, *Debates*, pp. 1178–1218.

28. *Journals*, 5 December 1947, pp. 7–32.

29. On 12 June 1951, the leader of the opposition, Mr. G. Drew, moved that a supply motion be amended to read: "That this house is of the opinion that appropriate steps should be taken for the appointment of a select committee to consider with Mr. Speaker the procedure of this house for the purpose of making recommendations designed to assure the more expeditious dispatch of public business and to suggest any changes that may be desirable." The government took the unusual step of agreeing to the amendment. In commenting on Mr. Drew's amendment, Mr. Claxton, a persistent advocate of reform, said: "... we are all of one mind in wishing to do something about the present conditions. Certainly the public would like to see us do something about it. The difficulty, however, is a genuine one, in that we would be changing things which have been in existence for a long time, and which, however badly they worked, still worked; and which, if we changed them, would almost certainly run counter to the views or interests, as they see them, of one group or another, or of individuals." *Debates*, p. 3970.

30. From 1867 to 1954 the indemnity was sessional. In 1867 the indemnity was fixed at $600 for a session of thirty days or more. In 1873 it was increased to $1,000; in 1901 to $1,500; in 1905 to $2,500; and in 1921 to $4,000. In 1923 the total duration of a session—not the number of sittings—for which an indemnity would be paid was raised to sixty-five days or more, and provision was made to pay members a daily allowance for shorter sessions. In 1945 an expense allowance of $2,000 a year was introduced. In 1951 the members qualified for two sessional indemnities. In 1954 the indemnity was increased to $8,000, but on an annual, not a sessional, basis. In 1963 the annual indemnity was increased to $12,000 and the allowance to $6,000. In 1971 the indemnity went to $18,000 and the allowance to $8,000. In 1975 the indemnity went to a basic figure of $24,000 and the basic allowance to $10,300. The three-way relationship of (a) the demands of the House on the time of members, (b) the amount of the indemnity, and (c) interest in procedural reform was fully demonstrated during the early 1950s. On 4 June 1951, Prime Minister St. Laurent announced to the House that he planned to have a second session that fall. At that time (*Debates*, p. 3666–67) and on 8 June 1951, the leader of the opposition, Mr. Drew, objected to the plan. He contended that the main purpose of the proposal, at least as interpreted by newsmen, was to give members two sessional indemnities in 1951. Against him Mr. Clarence Gillis of the C.C.F. insisted that those who objected to the second session simply wanted time off to make money outside—in their law offices—and that the time had come to admit that membership was a full-time occupation. (*Debates*, p. 3849). The decision to increase the indemnity to $8,000 and to have it paid annually satisfied fairly well both those who wanted an indemnity commen-

surate with full-time work and those who did not want to be required to attend two sessions each year. See the speech by Mr. St. Laurent on 26 January 1954. *Debates*, pp. 1451–54.

31. *Debates*, 9 May 1906, c. 3011.

32. A remnant of the old pattern survived. The new standing order provided that the questions on the sub-amendment and the amendment were to be put to the House successively at 8:15 on Tuesday evening. Generally the divisions were completed before nine o'clock. For the remainder of the sitting the main motion was before the House. This meant that for about one hour individual members—as distinct from the parties—had upwards of an hour in which to raise grievances.

33. Sir Robert Borden commented on this plan in his *Memoirs*. "The session of 1907," he wrote, "began on November 22, 1906. This early date was in pursuance of a proposal much favoured by Mr. Fielding. It was hoped that if the session began in November it would be possible to prorogue in April, or in May at the latest. Eventually the experiment proved completely unsuccessful. It was particularly disliked by members from a distance, especially by those from the four Western Provinces. Very little progress was made before the Christmas holidays and the session virtually began in January instead of November. The members residing at a distance were faced with the necessity of a long journey to their homes or with the alternative of spending Christmas in Ottawa." *Robert Laird Borden: His Memoirs*, I, 72.

34. The dates of the main appropriation act in each fiscal year during the period from 1 April 1955 to 31 March 1976 are shown below. For 1957–58 and 1962–63 parliamentary approval of appropriations made by Governor General's Warrants was given *ex post facto* on 6 September 1958, and 22 July 1963, respectively.

1955–56 28 July 1955	1965–66 9 March 1966
1956–57 14 August 1956	1966–67 30 November 1966
1957–58 (not enacted)	1967–68 6 November 1967
1958–59 6 September 1958	1968–69 19 December 1968
1959–60 18 July 1959	1969–70 27 June 1969
1960–61 10 August 1960	1970–71 26 June 1970
1961–62 29 September 1961	1971–72 23 June 1971
1962–63 (not enacted)	1972–73 30 June 1972
1963–64 21 December 1963	1973–74 28 June 1973
1964–65 2 December 1964	1974–75 30 October 1974 (Election 8 July)
	1975–76 26 June 1975

35. See Mr. St Laurent's statement of 8 June 1956, and the tentative replies of Mr. Drew and Mr. Knowles. *Debates*, pp. 4843–44. See also the speeches by Mr. Drew and Mr. Knowles on 11 June 1956, on the minister of finance's motion that an interim supply for June be granted. *Debates*, pp. 4892–97. The C.C.F. attitude was summed up by Mr. Knowles as follows: "Mr. Chairman, it is not possible for a free parliament to have done to it what we have suffered here in the last few weeks and then for it to go on in the normal

way. In our view the civil service and others should not be made to suffer, but in our view the government has no moral authority to make the request that it now lays before this house." William Kilbourn takes us behind the scene: "On Friday afternoon, June 8, Stanley Knowles and Davie Fulton parted on the assumption that both their parties would oppose, by delay, the government's request for interim supply. But George Drew was in Toronto that weekend and he apparently had sober second thoughts about mounting a second filibuster and facing an election after the exhaustion of the pipeline debate. Some Ontario Tories were reluctant to raise funds and fight a campaign over an issue that has brought Howe much sympathy from the business community and had divided federal and provincial leaders of their own party." *Pipeline* (Toronto: Clarke, Irwin & Company Limited, 1970), p. 136.

36. *Debates*, pp. 3007–12

37. After the demise of Robert Thompson's Social Credit Party, the *Ralliement des Créditistes* took up the name, the Social Credit Party.

38. *Debates*, 3 October 1963, p. 3197.

39. *Journals*, 14 December 1964, p. 990.

40. *Debates*, 18–19 March 1965, pp. 12509–27; 12535–53; 12562–65; 12576–98.

41. *Journals*, 26 March 1965, p. 1176–77. See *Debates*, 2 April 1965, pp. 13182–84.

42. This order was proposed by the government. The Special Committee on Procedure and Organization (1964–65) was presided over by the speaker, so that unanimity in the committee was required before a report could be made to the House. By proposing its own motion the government was able to go much further than would have been possible in the committee. On 19 May 1965, Mr. Pearson moved for sessional orders relating to (a) the business of supply and (b) the allotment of time to bills. On 27 May the government amended its motion. On 8 June 1965, on the suggestion of Mr. Diefenbaker, the motion was divided into two parts. The first part, dealing with the business of supply, was adopted by the House. The second part, which contained a draft time-allotment rule, S.O. 15-A, was referred to a special committee. That committee reported, but not unanimously, on 11 June 1965. Its report, which contained S.O. 15-A, was concurred in by the House that day, 103 Yeas to 33 Nays. All those voting against S.O. 15-A were Progressive Conservatives. *Journals*, pp. 219–223.

43. In the case of ten departments there was no difficulty because the money for those departments had been appropriated early. Certain other departments had balances from earlier interim supplies sufficient to meet their requirements. However, nine departments or agencies did not have enough money in their own votes to meet their mid-November obligations. The Treasury Board covered their requirements by transferring money from Vote 15 (contingencies) of the Department of Finance. *Debates*, 14 November 1966, pp. 9858–60 and 9893–94.

44. *Journals*, 20 March 1968, pp. 791–92.

45. Neither of the Procedure Committees (1967–68; 1968) was presided

over by the speaker. This meant that the committees were not limited to such recommendations as could achieve unanimous support. The reports of the 1967–68 committees were unanimous, but those of the 1968 committee were not.

46. The idea of adjourning for the summer commends itself to both ministers and private members. The ministers are favourable because if there is an emergency requiring parliamentary action during the summer, e.g., a postal or railway strike, the members can be called back to Ottawa and confronted immediately with the government's proposal without the formality of beginning a new session. The idea appeals to the private members because some of the perquisites that they need for their constituency work are not available when Parliament is not in session. Another argument for summer adjournments is that some of the committees may wish to meet during the late summer.

47. On Tuesday, 20 October 1970, for example, the House by special order adjourned from 1:00 p.m. until 8:00 p.m. to enable members to attend the funeral services in Montreal or the special service in Ottawa for Pierre Laporte. The House had met at 11:00 a.m., as is normal during the Address debate.

NINE

1. Sir Wilfrid Laurier saw no need for a radical change. Quite aside from his opposition to the naval aid bill, he took the position that when the government and the opposition were in complete disagreement on an important question there should be an election. Experience had demonstrated, he argued, that such disagreements would be very rare. See his historical review of obstruction in the House. *Debates*, 9 April 1913, cc. 7435–37.

2. The naval aid bill had been in committee of the whole House at five sitting—28 February, 3 March, 10 March, 7 April, and 8 April—but each of the two sittings in March had lasted six days. On 9 April, the prime minister moved that the House adopt three new standing orders, one of which was a closure procedure. His motion was carried on 23 April 1913. Subsequently, on 6, 7, 8, and 9 May the bill was considered again in committee. At the sitting on 9 May the committee stage was terminated by the use of closure. The third-reading debate took only one day, Thursday, 15 May 1913. The bill then went to the Senate, where it was rejected by the Liberal majority on 29 May 1913.

3. *Debates*, 10 April 1913, cc. 7524–25.

4. Prime Minister King was not in the House of Commons when closure was moved by Ernest Lapointe on 2 March 1926. Mr. King had been elected in the Prince Albert by-election on 15 February 1926, after his defeat in North York in the general election of 5 October 1925, but he did not take his seat until 15 March 1926. He was not opposed in principle to closure. His complaint in 1932 was that the Bennett government had misused the rule.

The motion that the speaker leave the Chair for the House to go into committee on the resolution preceding the Unemployment and Farm Relief

Continuance Bill was brought to a vote by closure on 29 March 1932, the eleventh day of debate. The committee considered the resolution and reported it later that day. The following day the second-reading motion carried, on division, and the House went into committee on the bill. Late the next day, 31 March, with the committee still on clause 1, Mr. Bennett gave notice of closure on that clause and the remaining two clauses. On 1 April 1932, after the closure motion had carried, the opposition let the committee stage come to an end after about one hour. At about 9:00 p.m. that day the third-reading debate came to a conclusion. Mr. King proposed that the motion be allowed to carry. "On division"; however, Mr. Bennett asked for a recorded vote. The House spent the remainder of the sitting on other business. Clearly, this was no battle to the death.

Mr. King's complaint was based on two grounds. First, in view of the Liberals' conduct in the second-reading debate, when they had put up only one spokesman (and one reasoned amendment), Prime Minister Bennett was displaying irresponsible impatience in cutting off the consideration of the bill in committee. Mr. King said: "It is perfectly apparent, Mr. Chairman, that the introduction of closure in this manner at this time is not for the purpose of expediting the enactment of any measure with respect to relief, but clearly for the purpose of shutting off all discussion on the subject." *Debates*, 1 April 1932, p. 1610. A few minutes later he commented: "As you yourself have said, Mr. Chairman, section one of the bill is the only section that has been discussed, yet by the most coercive and arbitrary act of which a government is capable, we are being prevented from discussing sections two and three of the measure and discussing at any further length the first section." *Debates*, pp. 1610–11. Mr. King's second ground was that the measure being extended was virtually unconstitutional because it delegated to the governor in council the power to spend unspecified sums of money. On 9 May 1932, speaking on the second reading of another bill, the Relief Act, 1932, he stated: "Closure has a proper place with respect to measures which may be brought before parliament, namely, to see that a measure that is appropriately and properly before the house is not unduly obstructed. But the closure cannot properly be used to prevent a house of commons from seeing that the constitution itself is not being undermined by any measure that may be under consideration." *Debates*, 9 May 1932, p. 2719.

5. It would have been surprising if the pipeline debate had had no influence on the views of members on the procedural questions discussed during the 1960s. On the one hand there were few Liberals who did not feel that the St. Laurent government had misused S.O. 33 inexcusably. Although the Hon. C. D. Howe had been right in wishing to enable Trans-Canada Pipe Lines to begin construction in 1956, which meant that the pipeline bill had to be passed by 7 June 1956, and although the lurid suggestions of improprieties voiced by opposition members were invalid, the government had precipitated the confrontation by resorting to closure on the very first day of the debate. This mistake meant that the government never was able to put its arguments for the bill to the House in an effective way, and that it was committed to the use of closure to terminate the second-reading debate, the committee stage,

and the third-reading debate. The government had lost sight of the constitutional role of the House of Commons. Moreover, from a partisan viewpoint it was guilty of having acted imprudently in not allowing the debate to proceed normally until the opposition had demonstrated that it was bent on obstructing the bill. On the other hand, the incessant use of obstructive ploys, which made for unseemly clashes with the speaker, and which eventually produced a formal attack on the speaker, however excused, inevitably left painful memories. It is notable that the Liberals used S.O. 33 with great reluctance in 1964 and 1969, and that the proposal to eliminate appeals from the speaker's rulings—provisionally from 11 June 1965, and permanently from 20 December 1968—was accepted without controversy. Indeed, it may be that some of those who opposed S.O. 75C in 1969 did so after calculating that if the House had had S.O. 75C as one of its rules in 1956 the pipeline bill could have been carried through the House well within Mr. Howe's timetable, that is, between 14 May, when he moved for the speaker to leave the Chair, and 7 June, the announced deadline. On the pipeline debate see E. A. Forsey, "Constitutional Aspects of the Canadian Pipe Line Debate" in *Freedom and Order* (Toronto: McClelland and Stewart Limited, 1974), pp. 129–48. See also W. F. Dawson, *Procedure in the Canadian House of Commons* (Toronto: University of Toronto Press, 1962), pp. 125–31. The whole story of the pipeline project is recounted by William Kilbourn in *Pipeline* (Toronto: Clarke, Irwin & Company Limited, 1970). An insider's view of the pipeline debate has been given by J. W. Pickersgill, one of the three ministers who decided the government's tactics, in *My Years With Louis St. Laurent* (Toronto: University of Toronto Press, 1975), pp. 269–99.

6. *Journals*, 11 June 1965, pp. 222–23.

7. *Debates*, 20 April 1967, pp. 15119–49, 15157–72.

8. It would be a mistake to conclude that all the Progressive Conservative members were equally opposed to S.O. 15-A or some variation of it. The Diefenbaker faction was staunchly opposed; and this left the less intransigent members with little choice unless the party was to be split openly. Moreover, the issue was one which provided an opportunity to demonstrate unity under its new leader, the Hon. R. L. Stanfield.

9. The text appears at *Journals*, 6 December 1968, pp. 439–40. The Liberals took great delight in reminding both the Progressive Conservatives and the New Democrats that the proposed standing order had been drawn with close attention to British practice and experience. See especially the Hon. A. J. MacEachen, *Debates*, 19 December 1968, pp. 4166–73. The basic procedure for the allotment of time at Westminster entails a government motion specifying the days to be allotted to the several stages of a bill. That motion is debatable for one day. Once the proposed general timetable has been adopted, the "Business Committee" recommends to the House how the time available at the committee stage and at the report stage should be apportioned among the clauses and amendments. The Business Committee consists of the Chairmen's Panel and not more than five other members nominated by the speaker. The bills and other business to which this procedure has been applied over the years are listed in *May*, p. 488. See also Sir Ivor Jennings, *Parliament*; 2nd ed.

(Cambridge: The University Press, 1957), pp. 241–46. According to the report of the (British) Special Committee on Procedure (July, 1967), there were two complaints against this procedure: (a) the day-long debates were a waste of time because the arguments for and against guillotine motions had become stock arguments, and (b) the procedure did not foster discussion with the opposition to ascertain if an agreement could be reached. Late in 1967 the British House sought to overcome these shortcomings by adopting a new rule, S.O. 43-A, under which if no general agreement has been reached for the allotment of time at the committee stage or on report, a minister may move that the committee on the bill shall report the bill on or before a specified day and that the Business Committee shall make recommendations to the House as to the number of days or portions of days to be allotted to the parts of the bill in committee and at the report stage and as to the time for the third reading. The minister's motion is debatable for no more than two hours. This new procedure did not supplant the basic guillotine rule. If it prefers to do so, the government can propose its own timetable.

10. *Debates*, 20 December 1968, p. 4231.
11. *Debates*, 10 December 1968, p. 3763.
12. *Debates*, 8 July 1969, p. 10965. See also the statement by Mr. Knowles on 10 December 1968, (*Debates*, p. 3778), in which he proposed that the government might have not just one, but two members on a five-member committee. See also Mr. Macdonald's reply, 11 December 1968, pp. 3819–20.
13. *Debates*, 8 July 1969, p. 10977. See also p. 10982.
14. This interpretation was given by Mr. Knowles on 8 July 1969 (*Debates*, p. 10965) and on 1 December 1971 (*Debates*, p. 10048). But on 8 July 1969, he argued, as we have noted, that the inclusion of S.O. 75C in the package completely nullified the possibility of the kind of bargaining for which he had devised S.O. 75A and S.O. 75B. The third proposed standing order was so much part of the package recommended by the committee that its inclusion made the whole package unacceptable.
15. *Journals*, 2 July 1969, pp. 1283–84. Mr. Macdonald's motion would have clarified S.O. 75C also by inserting the words "at that sitting," so that the order would have read, "...and has given notice at that sitting of his intention so to do...".
16. That there still were members who as a matter of principle were opposed to closure was shown by the votes on 14 December 1964. Eleven members who voted for concurrence in the sixth report of the Special Committee on a Canadian Flag earlier that day had voted against closure. Eight were N.D.P. members—Messrs. Douglas, Howard, Howe, Knowles, Martin, Mather, Peters, and Scott—and three—Messrs. Grafftey, Ouellet, and Ricard—were Progressive Conservatives. Some of the seventy-four others who voted against the closure motion may have done so primarily as a matter of principle, but since they voted against concurrence in the sixth report they cannot be identified.
17. *Journals*, pp. 951–52.
18. *Journals*, p. 975.
19. *Journals*, p. 1014.

20. *Debates*, 30 December 1971, pp. 10846–47.
21. It must be noted that the attitude of the House to closure and time allotment may have undergone something of a change recently. Just before the summer adjournment in 1975 the House agreed readily to the use of S.O. 75A. to prescribe a time allotment for the final two stages of two bills. On 13 June 1975, two days were allotted to the report and the third-reading stages of Bill C-8, to establish a national petroleum company; and on 25 July 1975, two days were allotted to the report and the third-reading stages of Bill C-2, to encourage competition in business. What is more important is that during the same session, 1974–76, the government house leader had resort to S.O. 75C three times, all at the second-reading stage. On 13 November 1975, the standing order was used to allot five additional hours for the conclusion of the second-reading debate on Bill C-58, the *Time* and *Reader's Digest* bill. On 10 March 1976, it was used to allot five additional hours for the conclusion of the second-reading debate on Bill C-68, to amend the Medical Care Act. On 1 April 1976, it was used to allot four more days for the conclusion of the second-reading debate on Bill C-83, related to the better protection of Canadian society from crime. In the first two instances, those of 13 November 1975, and 10 March 1976, the time allotment was tantamount to closure; yet the reaction of the House was relatively mild, and there was hardly any public reaction. Perhaps emboldened by this experience and certainly keenly aware of the desirability of terminating this longest-ever session immediately after the 1976 summer adjournment, the house leader, Mr. Sharp, felt free to use S.O. 75C on Bill C-83 as a time-planning rule.

TEN

1. Norman Ward in 1951 showed that 33.1 percent of the members elected in the 1930 election were lawyers although lawyers constituted only .2 percent of the gainfully occupied population. *The Canadian House of Commons: Representation* (Toronto: University of Toronto Press, 1950), pp. 134–35. The same point has been borne out by Roman March's studies. See *The Myth of Parliament* (Toronto: Prentice-Hall of Canada, Ltd., 1974), p. 43.
2. Professor Ward showed that in every House since 1867 "... approximately three-quarters of the members have had either no previous experience in the Commons whatever, or but a single term of four or five years." *The Canadian House of Commons: Representation*, p. 137. Professor March shows that 59 percent of the members elected in 1935 were freshmen, and that the average number of new members after each election since then has been about 40 percent of the whole House. Moreover, 50 percent of the freshmen members are not back after the next election.
3. Recent changes in the relationships among "the governors" have been described and evaluated by G. Bruce Doern in two essays, "The Development of Policy Organizations in the Executive Arena" and "The Budgetary Process and the Policy Role of the Federal Bureaucracy," in *The Structures of Policy-Making in Canada*, ed. G. Bruce Doern and Peter Aucoin (Toronto: Macmillan of Canada, 1971). Robert J. Jackson and Michael M. Atkinson

discuss the inner circle of policy makers, especially as it is involved in the process by which government bills are prepared, in *The Canadian Legislative Process* (Toronto: Macmillan of Canada, 1974), pp. 51–73.

4. White Papers have been used at Ottawa since 1939, and were especially common during the Pearson years. The difference between White Papers and Green Papers is difficult to state because in Canada, unlike Britain, White Papers always have been somewhat tentative. See A. D. Doerr, "The Role of White Papers," in *The Structures of Policy-Making in Canada*, pp. 179–203.

5. See the debate on private members' bills which took place on 2 November 1970. *Debates*, pp. 797–804.

6. *Debates*, p. 2345.

7. The 1969–70 session is a very good model session. The 1970–72 session was prolonged by Bill C-259, to amend the Income Tax Act, and an effort was made in the fall of 1971 to have very few standing committees meet in conflict with the committee of the whole House to which Bill C-259 had been committed. The 1972 session started late, as did the minority sessions of 1973–74 and 1974.

A Note on Books and Articles

The working of their parliamentary institutions has not attracted much of the attention of Canadian writers. First, there is the Todd, Bourinot, and Beauchesne series, three books which successively served as guides for Canadian parliamentarians. Second, there are two books, both old, on particular topics, Gemmill on parliamentary divorce, and Todd on private bill legislation. Third, there are two books intended for a more general audience, Dawson's *Procedure in the Canadian House of Commons*, and Norman Ward's *The Public Purse*.

The reader will find both Dawson's book and Ward's book highly valuable. The former gives a survey of all aspects of procedure—the role of the speaker, privilege, the rules of debate, etc.—and shows how they have developed over the years since 1867. Ward, in contrast, takes one strand, control by the House of the money granted to the Crown, and follows it from pre-confederation days to the Diefenbaker era, with a strong emphasis on the constitutional importance of parliamentary procedure in the area of financial control. New editions of both are eminently desirable.

The general books by Todd and Bourinot will be of interest to those who wish to recover some of the feel of the nineteenth century House. Bourinot is still useful as a source of explanations. Beauchesne, as the title implies, is primarily a technical handbook, a convenient quiver in which to rummage for points-of-order arrows. It is not a book to be studied by a beginner, either in a university or the House of Commons; moreover, it is very badly outdated.

The House is dealt with, but not from a strictly procedural viewpoint, in two recent books. Robert J. Jackson and Michael M. Atkinson, in *The Canadian Legislative System*, discuss the House (and its committees) as an important part of the larger "legislative system;" and they recommend reforms. Roman R. March, in *The Myth of Parliament*, argues emphatically that parliamentary government has become an illusion in Canada.

Canadians have been keen imitators. We began by taking over Responsible Government. Then Canadian academics received and taught the doctrines of "the Westminster model" with little or no regard for what actually went on in Ottawa. And now that British writers—following R. H. S. Crossman's introduction to the 1964 edition of Bagehot—have shown that the Westminster model does not describe the modern British constitution, that it ignores the role of the parties and the great power of party leaders, which in the case of a prime minister tends to become "presidential," we too have made a similar discovery in Canada. The strong influence of Britain on our thinking was demonstrated in 1968 and 1975 by the House itself. In those years the House authorized visits by the procedure committee to Westminster for consultation with British parliamentarians and experts, and that consultation contributed greatly to the reforms made subsequently at Ottawa. It follows that a reader who wishes to examine the Canadian reforms and controversies should not study them apart from what has been happening at Westminster.

The most famous British book on modern procedure, Erskine May's *Parliamentary Practice*, first published in 1844, and kept contemporary by one learned clerk after another, is an empire of information; but like *Beauchesne* it is a compendium for a working parliamentarian.

I. PRIMARY SOURCES

The standing orders are to the conventions of the House of Commons what statute law is to common law. This means that to understand the practice and procedures of the House one must study both what is done in particular instances and the written standing orders. Moreover, since the speakers, like Supreme Court judges, interpret both the conventions and the standing orders, one must examine their rulings.

A complete account of the business done by the House, and not just the members' speeches, now is to be found in the *House of Commons Debates* (or *Hansard*), but the *Journals* is the official record of all rulings, votes, and proceedings. The analytic index to the *Journals* is the first place to which to turn for specific information, e.g., when a particular bill was given second reading, how many times applications under S.O. 26 were successful at a session, and the dates of supply debates. The daily papers, Votes and Proceedings, are of only ephemeral importance. Once the *Journals* for a session has been published Votes and Proceedings cease to be useful. (Readers will notice that the style of the *Journals* differs considerably from that of the *Debates*.) The Order Paper, which shows all the work awaiting the attention of the House at any particular sitting, loses its importance once the sitting is over; however, recently a running summary of the items dealt with under the various heads is included in the full (or Monday) Order Paper, and the final summary for each session is of permanent value. The text of bills is not to be found in any of these publications. Each bill is printed separately after its first reading in the House of Commons, and may be reprinted if major changes are made at either the committee or the report stage. All these materials are available from Information Canada.

House of Commons Debates	for each sitting and each session
Votes and Proceedings	for each sitting
Journals of the House of Commons	for each session
Order Paper and Notices	for each sitting
Standing Orders of the House of Commons	(October 1969)
Provisional Standing Orders of the House of Commons	(24 March 1975)

II. CANADIAN BOOKS

Arthur Beauchesne, *Rules and Forms of the House of Commons of Canada*; 4th ed. (Toronto: The Carswell Company Limited, 1958).

J. G. Bourinot, *Parliamentary Procedure and Practice in the Dominion of Canada*; 4th ed. (Toronto: Canada Law Book Company, 1916).

W. F. Dawson, *Procedure in the Canadian House of Commons* (Toronto:

University of Toronto Press, 1962).
J. A. Gemmill, *The Practice of the Parliament of Canada upon Bills of Divorce* (Toronto: Carswell & Co., 1889).
Robert J. Jackson and Michael M. Atkinson, *The Canadian Legislative System* (Toronto: Macmillan of Canada, 1974).
Roman R. March, *The Myth of Parliament* (Scarborough: Prentice-Hall of Canada, Ltd., 1974).
Alfred Todd, *Private Bills in the Parliament of Canada*, 3rd ed. (Ottawa: Hunter Rose & Co., 1869).
Alpheus Todd, *The Practice and Privileges of the Two Houses of Parliament* (Toronto: Rogers and Thompson, 1840).
Norman Ward, *The Public Purse* (Toronto: University of Toronto Press, 1964).

III. ARTICLES ON THE CANADIAN HOUSE

James H. Aitchison, "The Speakership of the Canadian House of Commons," in *Canadian Issues*, ed. Robert M. Clark (Toronto: University of Toronto Press, 1961), pp. 23–56.
Edwin R. Black, "Opposition research: some theories and practice," *Canadian Public Administration* 15 (1972) 24–41.
Ronald Blair, "What Happens to Parliament?" in *Agenda 1970*, ed. Trevor Lloyd and Jack MacLeod (Toronto: University of Toronto Press, 1968), pp. 217–40.
R. B. Byers, "Perceptions of Parliamentary Surveillance of the Executive: The Case of Canadian Defence Policy," *Canadian Journal of Political Science* 5 (1972) 234–50.
R. H. S. Crossman, "Canadian Issues as seen from Outside," in *Order and Good Government*, ed. Gordon Hawkins (Toronto: Canadian Institute of Public Affairs, 1965), pp. 139–43.
C. E. S. Franks, "The Committee Clerks of the Canadian House of Commons," *The Parliamentarian* 50 (1969) 159–60.
C. E. S. Franks, "The Dilemma of the Standing Committees of the Canadian House of Commons," *Canadian Journal of Political Science* 4 (1971) 451–76.
C. E. S. Franks, "The Reform of Parliament," *Queen's Quarterly* 74 (1969) 113–17.
E. Davie Fulton, "Getting Things Done in Parliament," in *Order and Good Government*, ed. Gordon Hawkins (Toronto: Canadian Institute of Public Affairs, 1965), pp. 43–50.
Thomas A. Hockin, "Adversary Politics and Some Functions of Canada's House of Commons," in *The Canadian Political Process*; rev'd. ed., ed. Orest M. Kruhlak, Richard Schultz, and Sidney I. Pobihushchy (Toronto: Holt, Rinehart and Winston of Canada, Limited, 1973), pp. 361–81.
Pauline Jewett, "The Reform of Parliament," *Journal of Canadian Studies* 1 (1966) 11–16.
Allan Kornberg, "Parliament in Canadian Society" in *Legislatures in Developmental Perspective*, ed. Allan Kornberg and Lloyd D. Musolf (Durham: Duke University Press, 1970), pp. 55–128.

Philip Laundy, "Canada's Speakership Attains Independence," *The Parliamentarian* 50 (1969) 12–15.

Philip Laundy, "The Current State of Procedure in the Canadian House of Common," *The Table* 39 (1970) 37–47.

Philip Laundy, "The Future of the Canadian Speakership," *The Parliamentarian* 53 (1972) 113–117.

Philip Laundy, "Procedural Reform in the Canadian House of Commons," *The Parliamentarian* 50 (1969) 155–57.

Trevor Lloyd, "The Reform of Parliamentary Proceedings" in *The Prospect of Change: Proposals for Canada's Future*, ed. Abraham Rotstein (Toronto: McGraw-Hill, 1965), pp. 23–39.

J. A. A. Lovink, "Parliamentary reform and governmental effectiveness in Canada," *Canadian Public Administration* 16 (1973) 35–54.

J. A. A. Lovink, "Who Wants Parliamentary Reform?" *Queen's Quarterly* 79 (1972) 502–13.

Donald S. Macdonald, "Change in the House of Commons—New Rules," *Canadian Public Administration* 13 (1970) 30–39.

J. R. Mallory and B. A. Smith, "The Legislative Role of Parliamentary Committees in Canada: the Case of the Joint Committee on the Public Service Bills," *Canadian Public Administration* 15 (1972) 1–23.

J. R. Mallory, "Parliamentary Scrutiny of Delegated Legislation in Canada: A Large Step Forward and a Small Step Back," *Public Law* 1972, pp. 30–42.

J. R. Mallory, "The Uses of Legislative Committees," *Canadian Public Administration* 4 (1963) 1–14.

Donald Page, "Streamlining the Procedures of the Canadian House of Commons, 1963–1966," *Canadian Journal of Economics and Political Science* 33 (1967) 27–49.

Michael Rush, "The Development of the Committee System in the Canadian House of Commons—Diagnosis and Revitalization," *The Parliamentarian* 55 (1974) 86–94.

Michael Rush, "The Development of the Committee System in the Canadian House of Commons—Reassessment and Reform," *The Parliamentarian* 55 (1974) 149–158.

Denis Smith, "President and Parliament: The Transformation of Parliamentary Government in Canada" in *Apex of Power*, ed. Thomas A. Hockin (Scarborough: Prentice-Hall of Canada, Ltd., 1971), pp. 224–41.

Denis Smith, "The Speakership of the Canadian House of Commons: Some Proposals" in *Contemporary Issues in Canadian Politics*, ed. Frederick Vaughan, Patrick Kyba, and O. P. Dwivedi (Scarborough: Prentice-Hall of Canada, Ltd., 1970), pp. 177–92.

Norman Ward, "The Committee on Estimates," *Canadian Public Administration* 6 (1963) 35–42.

IV. SOME BRITISH BOOKS

Bernard Crick, *The Reform of Parliament*; 2nd ed. (London: Weidenfeld and Nicholson, 1968).

A. H. Hanson and Bernard Crick, eds. *The Commons in Transition* (London: Fontana, 1970).
Eric Taylor, *The House of Commons at Work* (Harmsworth: Penguin Books, 1951).
S. A. Walkland, *The Legislative Process in Great Britain* (London: George Allen and Unwin Ltd., 1968).
D.W.S. Lidderdale, ed. *Erskine May's Treatise on the Law, Privileges, Proceedings, and Usages of Parliament*; 19th ed. (London: Butterworth & Co. Publishers Ltd., 1976). [Generally called *May* or May's *Parliamentary Practice*]

V. SOME BRITISH ARTICLES

C. J. Boulton, "Recent Developments in House of Commons Procedure," *Parliamentary Affairs* 23 (1969–70) 61–71.
Bernard Crick, "Parliament in the British Political System," in *Legislatures in Developmental Perspective*, ed. Alan Kronberg and L. D. Musolf (Durham: Duke University, 1970), pp. 33–54.
Henry D'Avigdor-Goldsmid, "The House of Commons Expenditure Committee," *The Parliamentarian* 54 (1973) 205–208.
Edward Fellowes, "Control of Expenditure by the Commons," *Parliamentary Affairs* 21 (1967–68) 16–18.
John P. Mackintosh, "Reform of the House of Commons: The Case for Specialization," in *Modern Parliaments: Change or Decline?* ed. Gerhard Loewenberg (Chicago: Aldine-Atherton, 1971), pp. 33–63.
John Palmer, "Allocation of Time: The Guillotine and Voluntary Timetabling," *Parliamentary Affairs* 23 (1969–70) 232–47.
Michael Partington, "Parliamentary Committees: Recent Developments," *Parliamentary Affairs* 23 (1969–70) 366–79.
Donald R. Shell, "Specialist Select Committees," *Parliamentary Affairs* 23 (1969–70) 380–404.
Robin H. Turton, "Reform of Parliamentary Procedure," *The Parliamentarian* 53 (1972) 69–74.
H. V. Wiseman, "Supply and Ways and Means: Procedural Change in 1966," *Parliamentary Affairs* 21 (1967–68) 10–15.

Index

Address debates, 217–18, 219
Adjournment motions
　dilatory, 38
　emergency debates (S.O. 26), 43, 53, 67–69, 208–9, 231–32
　late show, 54, 75–78
　special order debates, 43, 302n2
　summer adjournments, 231
　adjournments, a remedy, 186–87, 276–77
Aiken, G. H., 173, 174–75
Allotment of time. *See* Time allotment
Allotted days, 120–23
Ancient constitution, myth, 293n22
Announcement of business, 73
Announcements, 57–58
Annual economic review, 279, 302n1
Appeals from speaker, 322n5
Appropriation acts. *See also* Supply
　when enacted, 115, 209, 222, 229, 230
　not enacted, 226
Armed forces unification bill, 223, 229, 247
Atkinson, M. M., 325n3
Attendance (S.O. 5), 44–45
Auditor General, 109, 152, 177, 180

Backbenchers, 17–18, 168
Bagehot, Walter, 292n10
Bailyn, Bernard, 291n3
Baldwin, G. W., xi, 157, 169, 173, 175, 177–79, 184, 188
Barnett, T. S., 298n16
Barrette, J. A., 95
Bedchamber crisis, 294n23
Bennett, R. B., 321n4
Bill C-193 (1967–68), 92–93
Bills. *See also* Legislative Process
　types, 299n6

private bills, 27, 201, 300n13, 326n5
public bills: introduction, 60–62; numbering, 62; Senate public bills, 62; private members' bills, 27, 62, 75, 201–2, 281
Blue Book, 112
Bolingbroke, 24
Borden, R. L., 39, 95, 96, 206, 212, 220, 300n3, 315n4
Blouin, Gustave, 172
Bourassa, Henri, 217
Boyd, N. K., 210
Bracken, John, 308nn24,26
Broadbent, Edward, 58, 282
Budget debate. *See* Ways and Means
Budget debates limited, 101–2, 216, 219
Business Committee (S.O. 15–A), 246–48
Byrne, Dorothy, 313n55

Campion, Lord, 46, 167
Caouette, Réal, 227, 303n7
Cardin, Lucine, 43
Choquette, Auguste, 299n7
Churchill, Gordon, xi, 44, 158, 160 309n32, 318n27
Clarke, Joe, 75
Claxton, Brooke, 318nn27,29
Closure
　Previous question, 38–39
　Westminster, 108, 241–42, 323n9
　S.O. 33: origins, 242–43; defects, 243–44, 249; use, 244–45, 246, 253; King's views, 321n4; pipeline debate, 223, 225, 241, 245; proposed abolition, 246, 256
　fixed adjournment hour, 215, 245, 274, 298n1

334 *Index*

a remedy, 276–77
Committee reports
  presentation, 58–59
  concurrence, 59, 63
Committee of Supply. *See* Supply
Committee of Ways and Means. *See* Ways and Means
Committees Branch, 166
Committees of the whole House, 86–90
Congressionalism, 1–4, 169
Consolidated Fund (U.K.), 99
Consolidated Revenue Fund, 9, 10, 100, 101, 108–9, 124
Coyne, James, 63, 225

Deachman, Grant, 181
Defence production bill (1955), 223
Diefenbaker, J. G., 60, 117–18, 151–52, 158, 160, 219, 225, 226, 228, 246, 256, 293n20, 310n11, 312n33, 314n59, 320n42
Dinsdale, Walter, 175
Division bells, 47
Douglas, T. C., 90, 260, 324n16
Drew, George, 225, 318nn27,29,30
Drury, C. M., 181
Drybones' case, 8–9
Durham, Lord, 26

Fauteux. *See* Speaker Fauteux
Favreau, Guy, 60, 310n12
Fielding, W. S., 213, 319n33
Filibusters, 211, 213, 227, 239–40, 245, 321n1
Financial Administration Act, 111
Financial resolutions, 127, 128–29, 231
Fiscal year, 114–15, 209, 210–11
Flag debate, 36, 64, 223, 246
Forsey, Eugene, 295n29
Fortin, André, 282
Foster, G. E., 316n17
Franks, C. E. S., 311n19
Fulton, E. D., 225

Gash, Norman, 294n23
Gillis, Clarence, 318n30
Government notices of motions, 62
Governor-General's Warrants, 111–12, 226, 229, 319n34
Government activity, 214–15, 233–34, 238–39, 260–61, 279

Gray's case, 8
Green, Howard, 151–52
Grégoire, Gilles, 227
Griffith, J. A. G., 293n21

Harkness, Douglas, 43, 44
Hazen, J. D., 39
Hellyer, Paul, 314n58
Horner, Jack, 192
House of Commons
  functions, 13–14, 16, 30–31, 263
  standings of members, 11–12
  roles of members, 17–19, 27–28
  characteristics, 260–62
Howe, C. D., 322n5

Indemnities, 215, 221, 287, 316n16
Interim supply, 112–13. *See also* Supply

Jackson, R. J., 295n31, 325n3
Jennings, I. W., 294n23, 304n13
Jerome, James, 181, 182. *See also* Speaker Jerome
Jones, Leonard, 12, 61, 293n17
Judges, control, 292n15

Kilbourn, William, 319n35, 322n5
King, W. L. M., 206–7, 213–14, 217, 321n4
Knowles, Stanley, xi, 44, 180–81, 225, 252–53, 256, 293n20, 298nn15,16, 299n7, 318n27, 324nn14,16

Lambert, Marcel, 106, 125, 176, 313n34
Lamoureux, Lucien. *See* Speaker Lamoureux
Lapointe, Ernest, 321n4
Late show, 54, 74–78
Laurier, Wilfrid, 39, 95, 206, 208, 316n23, 321n1
Leblanc, F.-E., 299n7
Leggatt, Stuart, 299n7
Legislative Process
  basic stages, 80–82
  debatable motions, 211–12
  first reading, 82
  second reading, 82, 83–85, 267–71
  committee stage, 82, 85, 86–87
  report, 85–86, 90
  third reading, 90
  amendments: hoist, 90–92; reasoned, 93–95, 275–76 recommittal, 96

Index 335

ancillary motions combined, 96
bills rejected or withdrawn, 39, 81,
  91, 93, 301n6
Legislature, 4–10, 23, 237–38
Lewis, David, 44, 125, 303n8
Locke, 4–5, 291n7

McCarty, D'Alton, 141–42
Macdonald, D. S., xi, 164, 173, 253,
  254–55, 310n12, 324n12
Macdonald, John A., 27–28, 137, 142,
  202, 209
MacEachen, A. J., xi, 92, 126, 137,
  182–83, 184, 191–92, 256–57,
  297n13, 310n12, 323n9
McGrath, J. A., 172, 176, 313n54
McGuigan, Mark, 170
McIlraith, G. J., xi, 310n12
McIlraith Reforms, 310n12
MacInnis, Grace, 193
Mackenzie, Alexander, 28
MacLean, W. F., 316n23
Macnaughton, A. A. *See* Speaker
  Macnaughton
Maitland, F. W., 291n5
Majority rule, 44, 298n16
March, Roman, 325nn1,2
Martin, Paul, 63
Matte, René, 92
Meighen, Arthur, 243, 294n24, 296n9
Michener, D. R. *See* Speaker Michener
Military service bill (1918), 8, 36, 95–96
Ministerial statements, 59–60
Miscellaneous Estimates Committee,
  129, 161, 192–93
Monk, F. D., 205
Monteith, Waldo, 95
Montesquieu, 5, 7–8
Motions
  types, 37–38
  routine, 62–64
  without notice (S.O. 43), 54–55
Munsinger incident, 43–44

Naval aid bill (1913), 211, 243
Nesbitt, W. B., 173–74
Nielsen, Eric, 44
Northrup, W. B., 39
Notice Paper, 41, 297n11
Notices
  requirement, 40, 42–43
  government notices, 62

motions by leave, 42
Notices of Motions (Papers), 66–67,
  74, 211, 300n10
Notices of Ways and Means motions,
  103–4, 303n4
Nowlan, George, 117

Olson, H. A., 310n12
One-dollar votes, 193, 303n7
Opposition, 17, 18, 19, 20, 168–69,
  293n18
Opposition days, 40, 120–23
Orders, 36–37
Orders-of-the-day proceedings, 52–53,
  69–72
  government business, 72–73
  private members' business: private
    bills, 74; motions, 74–75; motions
    for papers, 74; public bills, 75, 281
Otto, Steven, 173, 191

Parliamentary papers, 40–41
Participatory democracy, 163, 170,
  171, 173
Parties
  caucuses, 18–19
  discipline, 22–30
  importance, 12–13, 14
Party rivalry, 202, 203, 211, 221, 223,
  261–62
Party views on reform, 85, 120, 151,
  153, 160, 175, 219–20, 247, 248, 249,
  251, 277–78, 317n24, 318n27, 324n16
Pearson, L. B., 60, 93, 117, 137,
  157–58, 260, 293n20, 297n12, 309n1,
  320n42
Pepin, J.-L., 192
Peters, Arnold, 92, 282, 324n16
Petitions, 211, 295n2
Pickersgill, J. W., 256, 260, 310n12,
  322n5
Pipeline debate, 223, 225, 241, 245
Pocock, J. G. A., 291n3, 293n22
Prayers, 54
Presidentialization, 264
Previous question, 38–39
Private members' time
  days, 205–7, 315n2
  hours, 73–75, 281–82, 316n12,
Privilege, 57–58, 295n1

Questions

oral, 53–54, 55–57, 231–33
Order Paper, 53, 64–66, 211
starred, 53, 65–66, 300n10
made orders for returns, 65
Quorum, 44–45, 282–83

Reid, J. M., 58, 182, 314n57
Resolutions, 36–37, 289
Responsible Government, 11–12, 13, 21, 26–27, 28, 29, 168, 170, 259, 263–64
Roster, 57
Routine proceedings, 52–53, 55–66
Royal assent, 127, 291n4, 300n1
Rowland, Douglas, 195, 312n21, 314nn57,59

St. Laurent, L. S., 215, 225
Sessional committees
  Estimates, 151, 152
  Railways and Shipping Lines, 142, 150
  Railways, Air Lines and Shipping, 150, 153
Sessions
  length, 30–32, 197, 203, 209, 210–11, 220, 221, 265–66
  ends business, 48–49
Sharp, Mitchell, 310n12, 325n21
Sittings, length, 51, 54, 213–14, 245, 274
Speaker
  tie-breaker, 46
  head of procedure committee, 215, 216, 320nn42,45
Speaker Fauteux, 151, 215, 304n13
Speaker Jerome, 129, 296n3, 299nn3,5
Speaker Lamoureux, 55, 93, 106, 126, 173, 175, 191, 193–94, 305n15, 311n16, 314n66
Speaker Macnaughton, 160
Speaker Michener, 63, 96, 302n18
Special committees on procedure
  (1940–54), 215
  (1963), 157, 310n10
  (1964): fifteenth report, 157, 158–59, 160, 228, 310n12; eighteenth report, 159, 160, 228, 310n12; nineteenth report, 159, 310n12
  (1966–67), 164
  (1967–68), 83, 84, 85, 119, 164, 229, 230
  (1968), 85, 86, 102–4, 119, 128, 164, 185–89 passim, 218, 230, 249–50
Speeches, time limits, 208, 213
Sproule, T. S., 307n13
Standing Committee on Finance, Trade and Economic Affairs, 279
Standing Committee on Procedure and Organization, 250
Standing committee system
  Westminster, 132–35, 164, 306nn4,5
  (Pre-1965): origin, 135–37; list, 138; powers, 137; work, 137–45; procedure, 141–42, 307n11; size and quorum, 145–47; estimates, 153; characteristics, 153–54; Agriculture and Colonization, 136, 139, 143–44, 148; Banking and Commerce, 136, 139, 140, 142–43, 148, 150; Contingencies, 136, 137, 139; Estimates, 137, 139, 152–53; External Affairs, 137, 139, 149, 150, 151, 153; Expiring Laws, 136, 136–37, 139; Forests, Waterways and Waterpower, 145; Industrial Relations, 137, 139, 149, 153; Industrial and International Relations, 145, 150; Immigration and Colonization, 136, 143; Library of Parliament, 137, 306n9; Marine and Fisheries, 137, 139, 145, 153; Mines, Forests and Waters, 137, 139, 145, 149, 153; Mines and Minerals, 145; Miscellaneous Private Bills, 136, 139, 140, 144–45; Printing, 136, 137, 139; Privileges and Elections, 136; Public Accounts, 136, 137, 139, 142, 152; Railways, Canals and Telegraph Lines, 136, 139, 140–41, 142, 148, 153; Report of the Debates, 137; Restaurant, 306n9; Standing Orders, 136, 139; Veterans Affairs, 137, 139, 145, 153;
  (1965 and 1968 changes): lists, 161–62, 165; powers, 162–63, 165; new work, 85, 120, 163; size and quorum, 165–66; implications, 167–69; early problems, 172–73, 311n17; criticisms, 171, 175–81, 184; further changes: proposals, 178, 179,

180–81; response, 181–83, 280–81, 314n57
continuing difficulties: attendance, 184–87, 284–85; leadership, 187; staff, 188–89; status of House, 185; public servants as witnesses, 189; procedure, 189–92; reports and concurrence, 192–95, 288–89; remedies, 283–89
Standing Orders changes: (1873), 140; (1876), 205; (1906), 53, 67, 114–15, 135, 208–11; (1910), 211; (1913), 115–16, 211–13; (1927), 147, 213–14; (1952), 215, 317; (1955), 101, 116–17, 216–18, 222; (1962), 219; (1965), 161–63, 228; (1968), 54, 59, 68, 85–86, 96, 101, 120, 165, 230; (1969), 253–54, 255; (1975), x–xi, 52, 55, 59, 59–60, 63, 65, 165, 280–81, 305n17
Standing Order 15-A, 161, 171, 246–47, 320n42
Standing Order 16-A, 119, 171, 175
Standing Orders (1867), 197, 202, 205
Stanfield, R. L., 92, 169, 177, 252, 313n34, 323n8
Statutory expenditures, 110–11, 127
Supply
  relation to Ways and Means, 98, 99
  Crown initiative, 98, 100, 109, 124, 127, 128, 129, 175, 193–94, 305n15
  importance, 113
  annual program, 112–15
  desiderata, 114
  old (pre-1968) process: supply motions, 115–16; no debate on Thursdays and Fridays, 116 212–13; number limited, 116–17, 216, 219, 228; criticisms, 118–19, 149; eliminated, 119
  Committee of Supply: criticisms, 99, 118–19, 149, 151, 152, 155; time used, 222–23, 225; time limited, 227–30; eliminated, 119, 228, 230–31; revival proposed, 176, 178, 180
  Interim supply, 112–13, 119–20, 222–27, 229
  new (1968) process: adopted, 119; goals, 119–20; supply days, 120–23; no-confidence motions, 123; a government order, 123, 125; opposed items, 123–24; urgency, 125–26
  1975 changes, 280–81

Tabling of documents, 59
Taxation. See Ways and Means
Thomas, P. D. G., 300n3
Thordarson, Bruce, 312n24
Thompson, Robert, 117, 320n37
Time allotment
  Westminster, 241–42, 255, 323n9
  S.O. 15-A, 161, 246, 247, 248, 320n42
  S.O. 16-A, 119, 171, 175, 250
  S.Os. 75A, 75B, 75C, 250, 252–53, 254, 255–58
Time of House, 73, 205–8, 315n2
Trudeau, P. E., 12, 58, 117, 303n8
Turner, J. N., 107, 125

Vile, M. J. C., 291n7
Voting, 45–48

Walkland, S. A., 293n21
Walpole and "corruption," 24
Ward, Norman, 307n10, 309n34, 311n17, 325nn1,2
Watson, Ian, 185–86, 312n27
Ways and Means
  old (pre-1968) process: origin, 101–2, 124; Committee of Ways and Means, 99, 103, 124; defects, 102–3
  new (1968) process: notices of Ways and Means motions, 103–4; budget debates, 104, 105–6; initial experience, 104–5; corporate tax bill (1973), 107; remedies, 279
  provisional collection of taxes, 107–8
Wheare, Kenneth, 292n11
White papers, 272
Woodsworth, J. S., 299n7
Woolliams, E. M., 313n34

Yewchuck, Paul, 173, 193